FUTURE
SMART

Managing the Game-Changing

Trends That Will

Transform Your World

JAMES
CANTON

DA CAPO PRESS
A Member of the Perseus Books Group

Designed by Pauline Brown

Set in 11 point Adobe Caslon Pro by the Perseus Books Group

Library of Congress Cataloging-in-Publication Data

Canton, James, author.

  Future smart: managing the game-changing trends that will transform your world / James Canton.

    pages cm

  Includes bibliographical references and index.

  ISBN 978-0-306-82286-5 (hardback) — ISBN 978-0-306-82287-2 (e-book) 1. Strategic planning. 2. Technological forecasting. 3. Economic forecasting. 4. Social change—Forecasting. 5. Technological innovations—Social aspects. 6. Twenty-first century—Forecasts. I. Title.

  HD30.28.C358 2015

  650.1—dc23

                            2014035366

First Da Capo Press edition 2015

Published by Da Capo Press
A Member of the Perseus Books Group
www.dacapopress.com

Da Capo Press books are available at special discounts for bulk purchases in the U.S. by corporations, institutions, and other organizations. For more information, please contact the Special Markets Department at the Perseus Books Group, 2300 Chestnut Street, Suite 200, Philadelphia, PA, 19103, or call (800) 810-4145, ext. 5000, or e-mail special.markets @perseusbooks.com.

10 9 8 7 6 5 4 3 2 1

For Gayle, Mariah, Sofia, and Trevor,
who make my journey miraculous

CONTENTS

INTRODUCTION
What Is Future Smart?

Imagine for a moment you have a unique smartphone, a type of portal, an innovative fantastic device with which you could look into the future to 2030. This would be your personal YouTube of the future. You might see strange new lifestyles, marvelous inventions, radical technologies, entirely new jobs, dynamic businesses, and even new societies on this device. This YouTube of the future would give you a new awareness of risks, opportunities, and challenges that would change your thinking about today in fundamental ways.

The images and streaming videos of future events, people's lives, and innovations would give you valuable insights into today. You might change your present business strategy, start a new career, or even consider a new life mission based on the insights learned from this experience of looking forward in time.

This glimpse of the future, what life would be like in 2030, might give you answers to important questions that would be invaluable today, such as: What if you could predict how climate change would create a huge new marketplace? How might the emergence of new innovations in technology transform society? Which alternative energy types will radically change the future of transportation? How could you make a huge difference on the planet? When is a good time to start that new space venture or the organ bioengineering farm that millions of customers will need? What will the future hold for emerging markets in Africa?

Are you ready to become a Game Changer of the Future?

Now imagine for a minute how you could benefit from this ahead of time, well before the general population or the media, if you gain this essential knowledge. Consider if you were able to answer just one of these questions and the awareness that might come from building a new career, business, or organization around this insight into tomorrow.

Perhaps you can.

Welcome to *Future Smart*.

This book will give you insight into how the future may unfold. *Future Smart* may enable you to compete in your business or career smarter and faster. This book may also disrupt your thinking and catalyze your actions so you might have an advantage in becoming aware of not just specific trends that will shape the future but also how to see emerging signals, change drivers, and early warnings that come *before* trends emerge. You could become Future Smart: be able to see the changes and signals that will create a trend or alter the future before that future emerges.

I can promise you that the trends in this book may give you an inside track, an insight that may transform your life, work, and, of course, transform your future for the better. Reading *Future Smart* will grow your awareness to consider new possibilities for you and our world. Getting an early warning of what's coming next in markets, innovation, workforces, health care, climate, or energy might be invaluable to you.

Now, not every forecast here will pan out. In fact, these forecasts may be too tame, and some may be wrong. Reading this book is an experiment in learning and speculation about what may come tomorrow. But I can promise you that an early warning of trends will better prepare you for the challenges of an accelerating future that is coming now. Future Smart could make you a Game Changer of the Future.

PAST FORECASTS THAT MISSED

- Computers would be of little use.
- Airplanes will never be a mode of transportation.
- People don't want to know about their DNA.
- Consumers will not watch much television.
- There is no value in the Internet.

Running Futures

This is not the usual type of book. *Future Smart* is designed to disrupt your thinking to create new ideas that are actionable and may actually change how you think—it may inspire you to be predictive, to challenge you to think and look ahead. I forecast that some readers will take this seriously, this challenge I am suggesting about learning to Run Futures and look for and embrace trends, paying attention to the early warning signals of change and exploiting these opportunities to make their future and the planet's future a better future.

This type of thinking may lead to breakthrough ideas for business, innovation, community, and social change. New jobs, careers, and organizations may be created around an emerging trend that is found in this book. I can promise that.

But, of course, you need to do the work to apply this information. You have to consciously Shift Your Worldview to look ahead, to cultivate a long view about what's coming in the future. Most of us are living in the Now and miss out on anticipating the future—this is a conceptual shift in thinking. It's very much up to you, the reader, to take the actions that make manifest that new career, innovation, business, or social contribution.

I have discovered that the unifying concept that enables highly successful people to be successful is that they have the capacity, the courage, and the particular Future Smart Worldview to forecast, to look ahead into the future.

In this book I am pointing to possible futures, what may come in the near and far future as well as *a way of thinking about* what may come in the future. *Future Smart* requires paying attention to emergent signals, early warnings, news, or consumer behaviors that precede and later shape trends. This may include an innovation or discovery that could change the fundamental nature of an entire industry, global lifestyle, or economy.

Predicting Health

I was speaking with a noted neurosurgeon about his breakthrough surgical procedure to operate on patients while they are having strokes, surgically opening up the arteries in the brain to prevent a stroke from seriously damaging or killing patients. His perspective on the future of medicine is to get to more patients who are having strokes in that first hour—the golden hour—and this would save more lives. Now this is an objective I share: getting to more patients while they are first experiencing a stroke makes sense. I got to thinking, maybe we can do more, like prevent illness from even occurring. Now, that would be a shift in the Worldview for medicine—we could prevent illness from showing up. Why not direct more medical research toward prediction and prevention?

For the next one hundred years, if we can diagnose stroke victims and treat them earlier, this will save millions. Although this innovation in itself will not alter the future of cardiovascular medicine, I asserted to my surgeon friend, we must make a quantum leap to the next level of medicine that I believe is coming in the near future.

There is great potential for the future of medicine based on the same idea that lies at the foundation of being Future Smart: prediction. Prediction about health before people get ill is smart. We shall someday soon have the genomic data that is personalized for populations and be able to prevent strokes or at least know who is at risk before they have strokes and then prevent them. Being able to predict people's health status will save people's lives, the economy billions, and increase the general health of the public. That is Future Smart.

This will change medicine in radical ways from being disease care, reactive to being authentic health care, to being predictive. Now, that would be Game Changing. Today medicine is reactive, and yet evolving to be able to comprehensively predict people's health will completely transform medicine—it will become Future Smart. Someday this will change, and the change drivers of the future are evident today: population health, data science, synthetic biology, and consumer genomics are just emerging and will transform medicine well before 2030.

The large number of health-oriented apps available on smartphones and the high download rates of consumers interested in using these apps to gain insight into their future health make this point: people want to more accurately predict, manage, and prevent illness as well as promote their health. This is Future Smart, taking responsibility for your health.

This trend points to a future that is emerging and will become a planetary trend of immense market value: Consumer Self-Care. Consumer use of knowledge and tools to take more responsibility for their health and a desire to know, through diagnostics of their DNA and current health status, about what their future health may be, whether it be one minute to twenty years in the future, will transform medicine. This trend will redefine health, helping consumers take control over the information about their personalized health.

Consumer demand—people's intent to know about their personal health futures—as a trend is creating a new industry of global health prediction that will be transformative. Digital health smartphone apps are sensing, watching, monitoring, and analyzing our personal health status and will eventually becoming predictive, able to forecast our health, with accuracy. These will create a new form of health care with more impact than any new drug, device, or procedure. Get ready for the Self-Care Trend. Future signals point to the possibility of prediction as the key change driver of better health, not just smarter medicine. Numerous new jobs, new careers, and businesses will emerge to enable this future of medicine—a more predictive medicine.

Designing the Future

Future Smart is about understanding and exploring the possible scenarios of the future so you will be able to better prepare for it today. Also—and here comes the disruptive idea . . . wait for it—you might actually be able to design your future based on your goals. You might want to shape the future of your career, industry, or a social cause. You may want to alter the direction of an entire marketplace, field, or industry for the better. You may become a Game Changer of the Future from reading this book. Game Changers design their own future. It is possible to become the impact you want and to change the future through your actions.

Predicting the future, better preparing for the future, taking actions to apply this knowledge to create the future—these are the three strategic objectives of *Future Smart*. This book is a strategic guide for what may come and how it will transform society, business, culture, and, most important, your life.

The Business of Predicting

In my career as a global futurist who runs a leading think tank that advises companies and governments on the trends that will shape the future, I have also put into action the advice I suggest to you. I have helped create or consulted with organizations that invent the future in biotech, education, technology, medicine, and finance. This experiment has been an exciting way to reality-test, to put into action my own forecasts about trends. There have been misses as well as hits.

Overall the business of predicting has taught me that understanding the Game-Changing Trends that are fast shaping our world and then applying the lessons learned from deciphering these trends can lead to great benefit, competitive advantage, and survival as a business, nation, or individual. Running Futures, the strategic application of making and analyzing forecasts and using this insight to advise companies such as IBM, Phillips, GE, FedEx, Tata, and many others has been rewarding.

In addition, helping to build new enterprises and working with entrepreneurs has been a great learning experience. Maybe the experience related in this book will inspire you to shape your future, not just share ideas about the future.

Having this strategic knowledge about the key trends that will shape our future might enable you to achieve success and maybe make a difference in the world—innovate, create, discover, or fix something that would touch millions. This would almost be an unfair advantage to have this early warning of these key trends. If you gained an awareness of the game-changing future trends to the point that you would be able to compete better, be more aware sooner, and benefit ahead of time, this would be quite valuable. That's what *Future Smart* is about.

Now, I am not saying every trend reported here will deliver the same value or be a guarantee of success—that's for you to determine and explore and work toward if you so desire. What I am saying is that the global trends predicted in this book will change markets, economies, cultures, and business in fundamental ways. How you decide to take advantage of these trends may change your personal destiny and, perhaps, the destiny of the world. You may take my challenge seriously and become a Game Changer of the Future. That will require a shift in your worldview, a change in what you think is possible for yourself.

Looking Forward

The most important idea I want to convey in this book—and I will repeat it often—is that becoming *Future Smart* is not just about becoming aware of the trends that may shape the future but also how you can use these trends to shape that future. This is the big idea that I advise my clients about and I present to you, the reader.

Knowledge of possible trends is essential to being prepared to manage risk and opportunity in the future. But a deeper understanding of the future, the trends that will shape the future, is 50 percent of what being *Future Smart* is about. The other crucial 50 percent is about taking actions, designing innovations, formulating plans, and crafting strategies, tactics, and collaborations to shape the future you desire. This is true on a personal, organizational, national, and global level.

So what kind of future do you think is possible? What do you want to create? What do you want to change? What do you want to make happen in your life, your business, or on your planet? This is the exploration I want to have with you in this book: What do you want to change, solve, create, or invent? That is the territory I explore here.

Becoming Future Smart is an evolutionary shift in how we think about our world from being reactive and passive, in which the future just happens, to being proactive and catalysts, true architects of change. You have to own the change you want to create, the future you think is possible.

This is a strategic choice—to become an architect of change, a designer of futures—to become a Game Changer of the Future. That is what's possible.

We will get the future we create. What kind of future do you want? Maybe *Future Smart* will help you figure out what's possible or enable you to expand your Global View and potential to Think and Act Big.

Future Smart is a map to guide you through what's coming next. *Future Smart* informs you of what trends are coming. It suggests *what to do* to profit from them, how to manage the key trends to better your life as well as perhaps make your mark on the world. What is the Grand Challenge you want to take on in your life? Maybe there is a Game-Changing idea here that will become your future. Are you open to that possibility? I forecast that if you are to embrace the Idea Alchemy this book delivers, if you are paying attention and are ready to shift your Worldview, something different could happen to you in your life.

You might start thinking differently—looking ahead, developing a predictive awareness of future possibilities. You could not just Run Futures, become predictive, but also become a force to shape the future—a provocative idea, indeed, but I assert it is possible.

You're either managing the future or the future is managing you. *Future Smart* describes the essential strategies every person, leader, entrepreneur,

executive, or student needs to know NOW to manage the accelerated changes that are coming. If you are interested in shifting your Worldview and creating new possibilities for yourself, if you have a vision or mission to accomplish or you want to discover one, then becoming a Game Changer of the Future by reading this book could help launch you. That's my promise to you.

Chapter 1

From Future Ready to Future Smart

Most people living normal lives are unaware of what's coming, how extreme changes and trends may disrupt every aspect of our world and lives. Most people are not prepared for the drastic changes on the horizon that will change work, business, health, or population. They have not run the scenarios, evaluated the risks, thought about the possibilities, or fully understood the drivers of change. They are not Future Ready.

Many of these changes will be productive and helpful, but many others, such as the future of work or climate change, will require new learning, adaptation, and global solutions. Understanding what the change drivers that underlie the future are is one of the insights you may take away from reading this book. The opposite of being Future Ready is being disrupted or at risk from unawareness. This is what you want to avoid.

Are you Future Smart? Are you ready for the future? Do you have a clear idea of what is coming and how to prepare?

Only through understanding these dynamic and kinetic forces can one prepare and strategize about how to best navigate the future—your future. I am sure some folks who live in the moment may not care, but for the rest of us, prediction will make a difference. This book engages with you, the reader, in this discovery about the possible futures that may emerge faster and stranger than, anyone can imagine. Becoming Future Ready is preparing, adapting, and learning for the future, and this leads to becoming Future Smart, the end state of readiness.

We are all living in an era best characterized by radical, complex, and accelerated change. It is the central driver of the future. We live in a time of explosive, dynamic, and quickening change that creates Strategic Surprise—an unanticipated abrupt change that blindsides you, that is totally unexpected and strikes

1

with a force that is large, disruptive, and can be disturbing. In every aspect of our lives, from work to leisure, business to entertainment, energy to climate to health, radical change is the mantra of the day. The sheer velocity of change offers a mixed bag of risk and opportunity. The future is coming faster, and it threatens more disruptions almost daily. We have to learn how to anticipate faster and manage complexity smarter.

No one likes change. We don't like change because it upsets what's known—the rules, practices, and norms we have gotten comfortable and familiar with. In addition, we are in control when events are the same. When work is comprised of the same rules, practices, and processes we know how to achieve our goals and be effective. But what happens when work changes in fundamental ways that require new skills and new capabilities and the actual jobs we are good at are not just changed but eliminated because of trends in industry, commerce, innovation, or business? Change is all around us, and we often feel like a victim of it.

If there is one question my clients from around the world ask, it is about how to manage the speed and comprehensive nature of change, or what I call the Fast Future: How do I deal with accelerated change? How do I cope? Clearly they are asking about this because they are concerned about accelerated change, and they see this as a burden that does not appear to be slowing down—in fact, it is speeding up.

FUTURE SMART SKILLS

- Paying attention to emerging innovations
- Attracting collaborations
- Redesigning work processes
- Rethinking purpose of organizations
- Collaborating globally
- Deciphering customer desire
- Predicting future trends
- Having courage to create

Becoming Future Smart

The central theme of *Future Smart* is that most of us are not fully prepared for the complex challenges of the future. We are not ready to manage the fast and radical future trends that are coming. We are not *Future Smart*. That's what this book seeks to convey to the reader. To get us ready for the future. To grow our awareness. Tell us about strategies and opportunities and how to manage the future. We don't have the time or expertise to consider the future of one, let alone ten years from today.

The sheer complexity and velocity of change going on around us is often bewildering. All around us change is emerging in small signals, embryonic telltale changes—the future is coming. By becoming more aware of the trends that lie in our future we can learn to better adapt and navigate that future with success.

Though his task about knowing the future and preparing for it appears daunting, even unknowable by most, my argument is that we are facing radical changes that will shape our future, so we must become more predictive of that future. Becoming Future Smart is a learning process. Becoming Future Smart is part becoming aware of trends and part taking action to best navigate through the future and, perhaps, to shape our own future. We too can become Future Smart—predictive and adaptive for the future—if we prepare now. This book does not defend every forecast as 100 percent accurate but rather suggests forecasts as potential outcomes that are reasonable, fact based, and may even be revolutionary.

My second argument is that only by attempting to predict the future, to grapple with understanding trends, embracing scenarios, designing the forecasts can we learn to actually shape the future, to navigate the ups and downs, steering clear of risk and exploiting opportunity and innovation. Those who are ill prepared for the future complexity, change, and disruptions will have a rough ride—they will be buffeted by the surprising changes coming.

Future Smart is about the radical acceleration of Game-Changing Trends that will alter civilization over the next thirty years:

Humans will change—becoming smarter and healthier and living longer.
Business will change—becoming predictive, agile, moral, innovative.
Technology will change—becoming connected, faster, intuitive.
New business models. New innovations. New global risks. New competitors. New markets. New powers.

Are you ready for the fast and radical changes that will transform the next thirty years?

The World of 2030

Fundamental changes in technology, population, business, energy, climate, globalization, and work are emerging. We are living in an entirely new era, a new conversation, a dynamic time of provocative and kinetic change. Accelerating and complex changes are transforming our world, but which ones are important? How will these changes emerge, and why?

Future Smart gets you ready.

Future Smart is about the key driving changes, forces, power shifts, and a shifting landscape that every person, business, and government must understand in order to thrive over the next thirty years. This is your briefing on how to survive and thrive in the New Future. The old rules, old systems, old strategies are dead. There is a new global narrative emerging that will create massive opportunity for wealth, power, and positive change on the planet. As well as new risks, threats, and hazards, as we shall see.

Future Smart is a new understanding about the intersections of global power, real-time business, globalized markets, disruptive innovation, social change, population dynamics, massive prosperity, and deep collaboration. It is an appreciation of where we are going and how civilization, not just nations or individuals, will evolve. The changes that will drive this future are already emerging. The signposts are everywhere. My job is to read them and then offer an analysis. *Future Smart* identifies and defines these signposts.

Those who are ill informed about change will be at risk for a rough future. *Future Smart* informs, challenges, and offers scenarios and stories about likely futures that will affect everyone throughout the world, in every nation, in every city for the next hundred years.

Complexity. Velocity. Convergence. Sustainability. Connectivity.

These are the themes that will define the future. Fundamental changes in technology, lifestyle, markets, population, business, energy, climate, globalization, and work are emerging. We are living in an entirely new era, a new conversation, a dynamic set of forces of provocative change that will upend and transform markets, society, and the economy.

Accelerating and complex trends will transform our world. Which trends are the most important? How will these trends change your work, life, and future?

Future Smart charts a new global narrative that will create massive opportunity for wealth, power, peace, prosperity, and positive change on the planet. If you want to know what's coming next, read this book.

BECOMING FUTURE SMART

- Adapt smart
- Be a fast learner
- Boldly discover
- Collaborate deeper
- Embrace radical innovation
- Catalyze change
- Experiment daily

Trends: The Hidden Forces of the Future

Trends are the hidden forces that shape the future. Trends are how change manifests and transforms our lives, work, entertainment, competition, and health. Trends emerge often invisible as change drivers and reality shapers. But before you know it, everyone has a robot in the home, 3D printers are big, smart drugs are the rage, and wearable smartphones are popular. Trends are born of forces converging to create a new market, product, lifestyle, or culture. Trends shape new expressions of reality that provide risk and opportunity.

By understanding trends ahead of the crowd, an individual might take an effective action—create a company, design a new product, plan a new service, change a career, learn new skills, or invest in a new marketplace. Individuals who understand and can predict trends can start revolutions. Trends can be opportunities or risk factors that, if known, can be used to craft a new strategy that may propel a career, competitively give an advantage to an organization, or chart a new direction for an entire nation or even the planet.

FUTURE SMART FORECASTS

What will be the realistic impact of climate change?
Which trends will shape the next breakthroughs in health care?
Which trends will make you highly marketable to employers?
How will trends affect your financial future?
How might connectivity create prosperity?
What is the breakthrough technology you want to make?
What global problem do you want to solve?
What is the secret career you desire?
What is your highest future vision for yourself?
What is the grand future challenge you want to address?

If any of these trends are of interest, this book is for you. Trends are the change forces and drivers, often indiscernible in their early stages, that will transform business, markets, society, culture, and our lives in the future. That future can be next week or ten years from now. Trends are all around us, often emerging as weak or hidden signals well before they become a dominant force everyone recognizes.

Examples include the progressive warming of the climate in parts of Europe and the Southwestern United States, the rise of mobile electronic commerce, domestic robots for elder care, DNA testing to look for disease susceptibility, commercial space missions, and the increase in wealth transfer to cities, to name a few.

We all know and marvel at who got the trend right and who did not. Of course, this is often after the fact. Getting in early on a trend means you may avoid a problem, manage a risk, or benefit or perhaps even profit from a trend, all before others do.

This book is about the trends that are emerging and have yet to be obvious or create value, not the ones you missed. But those examples of both individuals and companies that missed the trends and those that got it right are good lessons in smarter forecasting. That is one of the objectives of this book: to make you more aware of the trends that are coming.

Why Read This Book?

Though sounding simplistic, the idea of looking ahead, of developing a purposeful future-oriented strategy, requires some skills that are not easy to acquire. But the mindset, the approach, is logical: the more aware we are of trends that may shape our future, the more capable we may be in managing the challenges, risks, and opportunities that we will face in this future. If you want to be ready for the future, *Future Smart* can get you there. This is your briefing on what's coming next.

The reason to read this book is that you might learn how to both better prepare and thrive in the future—your future that is beginning about ten minutes from now. Trends, both emerging and in future three to twenty years away, will shape your future. The more you know, the more prepared you will be. Gaining Predictive Awareness about what's coming next is more than reasonable; it is smart—Future Smart. Most people are focused on the present and don't have the time to study or research the future. They are busy with the now that dominates their time and energy.

Collapsing Time, Predicting Tomorrow

I predict trends. I advise business and governments on how to strategize about the future. I help entrepreneurs and enterprises capitalize on the future to create a more prosperous future. This is my job. The future of technology, business, society, energy, capital, demographics, and climate has fascinated me for over thirty years, and I built a career around forecasting. I have a decent track record on the top trends that have shaped the world. In this book I intend to increase your awareness of the future trends that will completely shape every aspect of your future life, work, society, health, family, and our planet.

I have made a career out of forecasting the future and helping my clients become Future Smart. This may entail getting them ready to invest, change strategy, develop a new product or service, or prepare for the challenges of the future. From governments to over one hundred corporations and associations

that have been my clients, I have learned much from their challenges and perspectives on the future. Here I have distilled the forecasts and trends I have learned while working with them.

My job is to raise your awareness about the future. That's what I do. I am a futurist, and organizations and governments hire my company to advise them about what risks, challenges, innovations, threats, disruptions, crises, and opportunities are looming over the horizon. I am writing this book to share with you what I share with my clients: let's get ready, let's look ahead and understand the risks and opportunities, what's likely coming. Let's be smart about dealing with all of this change and prepare for the future—let's become Future Smart.

In fact, this book is a compendium of select research and analysis that my organization, the Institute for Global Futures (http://globalfuturist.com) has conducted over the past few minutes, days, months, and years. I have distilled it down from the voluminous reports and client briefings that we do into a concise guide to the future. This is your briefing about what the future may bring.

Another reason to read this book is that you might actually reinvent yourself, your business, or your organization, or you may start an enterprise that capitalizes on some of the trends I am going to reveal to you in this book. In fact, that may be the most important reason to read this book. If you can identify a way to benefit by preparing smarter for a trend, building a business around one of these trends, or even shaping your career based on the future, you may thrive in that future. Preparing is the first step. You want to know what's coming.

TOP TEN BIG FUTURE SMART GLOBAL FORECASTS BY 2030

1. Africa becomes the next China.
2. Computers become as smart as humans.
3. Managing climate change becomes a new industry.
4. Space mining revenues exceed $125 billion a year.
5. Robots are a $500 billion industry.
6. Smart drugs enhance 60 percent of the population.
7. Digital entrepreneurs make up over 70 percent of the global economy.
8. Regenerative medicine extends life and health.
9. Mobile commerce transforms economies.
10. Global prosperity decreases terrorism.

Friendly Warning: Dangerous Ideas Here

There are clearly dangerous ideas here that may shake your world or, at least, change your perception of reality. Change alters reality. Your mind will be disrupted—in a productive way—by reading this book. You may see things

with a new awareness; you might even think differently. Your agility in taking advantage may accelerate. Your capacity to innovate may become attuned to new opportunities.

You may see new possibilities, identify emerging trends, or start to profit from the dangerous ideas about changing the world, running futures, or building a new life or business for yourself. You might change in productive and positive ways. You might learn to become predictive and alter a future scenario.

Now, some of these trends may offer fantastic opportunities and risks—it all depends how you see it, how you perceive the future. I am going to disrupt your thinking here by offering a glimpse of a possible future. Most risks are hidden opportunities to profit, get ahead, or benefit. This thinking requires risk and can be dangerous thinking that requires courage and perseverance. Not everyone will thrive with this new awareness.

Are You Ready for This Radical Future?

Some of these trends will seem strange and bizarre, such as your car talking back to you, actually arguing that you're driving in the wrong direction. Or you might be offered a job not from a living person but an AI, an artificial intelligence—would you consider working for a nonhuman?

Most of us are not ready for the extreme future that's coming. Join the crowd. Fast-changing climate, costly energy, disruptive technology, rising populations, shifting wealth centers, megacities, even space travel will change our beliefs and frustrate the traditions we are used to. All of these factors in the future will affect you. Are you curious? Don't you want to know what's next? *Future Smart* will enable you to prepare for and thrive—not just survive—in the future that is coming very quickly.

It Is Possible to Predict the Future—Just Not All Accurately All the Time

There you have it—the heresy exposed. Everyone is so busy denying the possibility to foresee the future that they don't even consider the possibility that we can seen it emerging, hinted at, signaled, and even, yes, predicted. Let's dispense with where the flying cars are.

This book presents a simple yet powerful idea: those who can predict the future will benefit from that insight in unique ways. Smarter investments, risk management, entrepreneurial actions, new inventions, hyperinnovation, new job creation, profit, and maybe even survival itself. Prediction is the New Competitive Advantage of individuals, organizations, and nations. The power of prediction is the currency of the future. Better prediction will enable leaders,

entrepreneurs, executives, and the soccer moms and dads of the world to be equipped to face the challenges of the future.

Better prediction will enable us to address the Grand Challenges of our time, from job creation, to reducing carbon, to cures for disease, to ending poverty, and developing sources of clean energy. Understanding trends better may also just help people find a career and job they like.

Those who predict faster and with more accuracy will be the winners in the future. They will be better equipped to succeed and thrive in the future. Those who act on those predictions—to invest, change, innovate, invent, learn, and adapt—will profit and do amazing things. Those who don't will be playing catch up. This is being Future Smart.

Future Smart is a strategy for everyone to become aware and to encourage action. This global competition to be prepared for the future will be fiercer than battling over natural resources, advanced technology, talent, or energy. Future Smart is about having the right strategy to predict with accuracy and courage and then to take effective actions to capitalize on those predictions.

FUTURE SMART SOCIAL IMPACT

Food crops such as corn catalyze Latin American food riots.
Shrinking polar ice caps start a multination race for Arctic petro-resources.
Tropical diseases affect Europe.
North American energy discovery produces more jobs than talent available.
DNA prediction will outpace corrective medicine.
New energy discoveries will realign global power.

The Truth Forecast

You want to get this right. Here's the truth. Too many jobs are going away and not coming back. Too many organizations that did not adapt fast enough are now gone. Too many industries, careers, and markets are finished. They are not coming back. Governments know this and cannot fix things.

Only committed individuals empowered with information and courage to act can make a difference in their life and the lives of others. We are living through a massive number of transformations in medicine, manufacturing, finance, security, business, climate, and energy that are ALL fundamentally changing the future we encounter every day. The next ten years will be mind-blowing, and no one is ready. My job is to get you ready. That's why I wrote this book.

Future Smart is about empowering you to adapt, learn, become aware, and understand the trends that will shape your future. This is the future of your

business, lifestyle, and society. If you can get one Big Idea here that can enable you to adapt and get ready for the future, well, then I did my job. Your job is to read the book.

That future could be ten years or ten minutes from now. This is survival of the Future Smart. The key skill is how well you can predict the future faster and more accurately than others. This is the new competitive advantage, the new work ethic, and the new way to navigate your life and career on the planet.

In this book I will brief you on what's coming next, just as I do my clients for my think tank, the Institute for Global Futures. When you're reading this book you are my client. My job is to prepare you to understand what's coming and how to prepare. My job is to convince you that the reason to prepare is that the future is coming faster, with more impact, more destructive and constructive force, and if you are not ready, you will be swept aside. These trends will alter the world deeply, and there is a choice you, the reader, will face when you read this book.

If you are going to become Future Smart, you will want to learn about what scenarios and trends may emerge to change your future. Or you could make the choice and realize that, given these massive shifts in business, markets, climate, technology, and society, to name a few, you have to change your actions in fundamental ways if you want to thrive or even survive in the future. Go profit from these trends—that may be the simplest and most direct reason to read this book. Start a new career, invent a new product, solve a big problem, transform your organization . . . make the world a better place.

FUTURE SMART STRATEGIES: START FORECASTING YOUR LIFE

- Learn a new skill completely different from your education or career (programming, alternative energy, big data, etc.).
- Attend a trade show that is unfamiliar to you in gaming, health care, mobile technology, education—anything new that might be of interest.
- Talk to ten people you don't know who are very excited about their careers and find out why.
- Consider two trends in this book and decide how you could create a new technology, organization, venture, conversation, or way to make a difference.
- Start forecasting your life: Where do you want to be in your life, career, relationships, location, or education in five years?

In order to change in fundamental ways, given these massive shifts, you need to take new actions with this knowledge. So to become Future Smart as an entrepreneur, individual, or an organization, you need to put this knowledge

to work, to adapt, to innovate, or to invent something new to capitalize on the emerging trends explored here.

FUTURE SMART STRATEGIES

- Create a Game-Changing new idea, product, or organization.
- Invent or harness an entirely new innovation.
- Solve a pressing global or local conflict.
- Start an organization that is meaningful to you.
- Go become an expert at something.
- Be a source of knowledge about something others value.
- Discover a solution to a big global problem.
- Design an innovative product or service that is needed.
- Streamline a new way to connect or collaborate with others.
- Build a company around how data creates new value.
- Pick one trend you read here and start an organization around it.

The Fast Future of Jakarta

I am sitting in Jakarta, the capital of Indonesia, a bustling nation of 240 million people, where there is an explosion of commerce, trade, and growth, with over 8 percent GDP. Just leaving my hotel and traveling five miles to the other side of town can take forty-five minutes, as the traffic is jammed up and the highways were not designed for the progress that is now Indonesia.

I am taking meetings in the hotel except for one important meeting at the National Palace. As I enter the meeting room, the president and cabinet are already there, waiting for us, sitting at the largest circular meeting table I have ever seen, over forty feet around. This circular hardwood table is symbolic of the huge topic of conversation: the fast future is coming. These leaders have many questions: How do we, as a nation, adapt and plan for this future? Will climate change eliminate 10 percent of our seventeen thousand islands? What can we do now to prepare for future trends that will shape Indonesia's future?

In many ways Indonesia is the future, today. Indonesia is a modern democratic state that promotes diversity, openness, and, especially, innovation. They are emerging as a new democracy in a region of dynamic change, surrounded by India, Vietnam, Singapore, Malaysia, China, Korea, and Japan. These are the Association of Southeast Asian Nations (ASEAN). Modeled like NATO and the EU, ASEAN composes this region in Southeast Asia.

They also take a keen interest in business and finding out where the next markets are, where the future consumers will emerge. Businesses that understand how the future is unfolding here in ASEAN are the ones that will thrive.

They will be a part of the cities, markets, and industries that shall play a leading role in the future, when skilled knowledge workers, on-demand manufacturing, and agile supply chains will be the way the world competes.

The Indonesians are also deeply concerned about the future of their nation, given that climate change may deluge their island nation. That is why I am here: to advise and exchange ideas about the future. There are those who are preparing for the future and those who are not. Some of the key ideas for *Future Smart* have come from my interactions with my clients worldwide who are dealing with real-world global challenges that the future will bring.

I am struck that Indonesia ranks fourth in the world in computer software programmers. This is an amazing metric that signals to me that Indonesia is on its way to becoming Future Smart. Though they, as a nation, face tremendous challenges in education, health care, trade, and business, they are leap-frogging other nations in encouraging their young people, their talent pool, to learn skills that will enable them to compete globally in the new knowledge economy.

Computer software programming is one of the most valuable Future Smart skills for the fast future emerging. Software programmers will program the future—of medicine, finance, energy, the stock market, logistics, and transportation as well as create intellectual property and patents that will change the world.

Every company and government possesses at the core of their industries the need to code, program, and create new software applications to better serve customers. At the heart of every business there will need to be data scientists who understand how to program the business for success. Indonesia is on the path to compete in a global marketplace.

Indonesia prepared for being Future Smart by educating, nurturing, and enabling its citizens with a social culture that encouraged people to pursue software programming. It didn't just happen overnight; instead, the president and his administration have engaged in an effort to prepare the nation for the future.

With enlightened leadership, they are preparing for the future of jobs and work by creating a knowledge society that can compete in the global marketplace for the most valuable commodity that will shape the future—the Knowledge Economy. If you want to compete smarter on the global stage, building a nation highly skilled in computer programming is adaptive, agile, and forward-thinking. This is an important example of being Future Smart.

The Future Smart Mindset

There are two types of mindsets, attitudes, or worldviews about the future. The familiar mindset says things are unpredictable and unknowable, that events just happen, that I am at the effect of these changes and I will never and can never know what is going to happen next. Moreover, the future is an event way out

there, an abstract thing that is separate from me. I am passive about the future. Others in power decide my fate; my future is uncontrollable by me. I can have little if no impact on my future and the future of others in my life, work, community, or world. I call this being Future Challenged. This is the resistance to attempting to become Future Smart, to have the courage to become more aware of the emerging trends, adapt to change, manage complexity, or attempt to develop new models of understanding the future. Some people or organizations think it is just not possible to predict what's coming next. It is mentally impossible, they think. The future is unknowable—see all of the stupid forecasts that were off? Where are those flying cars, anyway? And for them, this is true; this is their reality on which they hold dearly because this is the easy way out—things are too complicated to forecast. Mindsets rule. Ironically, they are right. Wherever you look, you will find what you're looking for. You can validate almost anything based on your worldview, your mindset of what is possible. That does not mean that it is true. But this mindset is limited, and the resistance to forecasting the future could be dangerous to your survival.

Over the last few decades too many leaders, companies, and governments have not embraced forecasting or even bothered to develop a future vision. Missed opportunities to push ahead on life science innovations in stem cells delayed discoveries by many years. Renewable energy innovations are still underfunded given the lack of future vision of tomorrow's climate change realities. Many nations, including the United States, don't even have a renewable energy or any energy long-range plan for the future. And few seem to care, even though this is illogical. These examples are actions made by people— individuals' mindsets that can lead and shape the future of new possibilities or hold back the future.

You would think that the idea of looking ahead and using forecasting tools to conduct strategic planning would be an important part of every business, government, or organization. But this is not the case. Partly this is due to how forecasting is conducted, but mostly it is because it is believed that disruptive changes are impossible to predict.

Mindsets that resist the value of forecasting influence many organizations. They are stuck in the now and cannot see ahead in developing a strategic vision of what may come. Organizations are not skilled in forecasting or, frankly, just not interested in exploring the scenarios that may influence their future. Organizations often suffer from resisting making predictions of the future regardless of how illogical and misguided this may seem. Entire industries have been dominated by mindsets of denial that resist attempts to look ahead, to attempt to forecast changes that will alter markets, industries, and society. The US auto industry missed the hybrid car trend, many big companies did not take the Internet seriously as a shaper of the future of business, mobile commerce was ignored at first, and climate change data about rising seas, storms, and warming

was not viewed as a risk factor affecting financial assets or public health or human safety. In fact, even when it comes to the most repugnant threat facing humanity, terrorism and war, it has been consistently a battle between Mindsets of Prediction.

The Future Smart mindset is one that embraces change, looks to the future not with dread but with a positive opportunistic mindset and considers the impact of emerging trends. The Future Smart mindset recognizes that changes in the future can be disruptive, but it can be more disruptive not to prepare, to resist prediction and miss an opportunity or even not to survive. This mindset says: I am a Game Changer of the Future—I can have impact. I am an active catalyst of the future a change agent, not just reactive but proactive. I matter and can shape outcomes.

Individuals have the power to change the future or alter the future outcome of events. I can make change, not just be buffeted by change. I can influence and shape the future of my life, relationships, work, and society. I can be an architect of my future.

These are the possibilities that lie at the core ideology of being Future Smart. This book is not just about the trends and cool technologies or global risks that will influence our future; it is also about the ideas that empowered individuals around the world can explore to shift their thinking, to embrace a new mindset of opportunity that will not just transform their life, work, or career but also act as a catalyst to transform organizations, industries, governments, and even our civilization.

If we are only using, as some scientists say, less than 10 percent of our brains' capacity, how different would our world be or how different would you be if you were using 50 or 100 percent? Imagine the future you could create by developing your existing brain's potential? Now, what if I told you that you could do this by Thinking Differently? What if I told you the Power of Ideas to disrupt your normal ways of thinking, your mindsets, might be possible, that not just information about emerging trends but also a new way of thinking about those trends could transform your life, work, health, and even possibly transform the world is possible.

Are you ready to choose new mindsets? If you read this book in this way, you may find some interesting new ideas that will open up your mind to new actions, new possibilities, even new lifestyles, all masquerading here in these pages. This is your future, after all. How do you want to make this future?

The stakes are greater today and shall be greater still in the future, given the high velocity of change that is coming. Knowing the future may be difficult, but it is possible. Learning, exploring, and, perhaps, discovering what's next is a valued competency. Though no one can precisely forecast the future, we can try, and often we may be right or learn what is possible, even how we can shape that future—that is being Future Smart.

Companies and individuals that embrace the challenge of looking ahead, of having the courage to discover and the willingness and openness to understand the trends that may shape the future are usually rewarded with market share, competitive advantage, prosperity, market leadership, and a talented workforce. These are the Game Changers of the Future. They are not just surviving; they are also thriving amid change, even chaos. They are leaders who not only look ahead but also take actions to adapt, learn, and innovate for the future of their customers, partners, shareholders/owners, and employees. They are Future Smart.

Which are you? Are you open to change? Ready to innovate? Ready to Run Futures—embrace the future trends that may shape tomorrow? Are you ready to become a Game Changer of the Future and take these trends and do something with them—start a company, transform an industry, or even transform yourself? That's the challenge of this book: Are you willing to consider the future as predictive opportunities? *Future Smart* will open up new opportunities for how you think about and deal with your future and the future of our planet. These trends may inspire you to become more predictive and actually shape the future, a better future for us all.

Chapter 2

The Connected Planet

The world is moving rapidly toward ubiquitous connectivity that will accelerate how people collaborate, share, learn, gather, do business, and exchange knowledge. The most important impact on the world of the Connected Planet Trend will be universal access to all human knowledge by everyone on the planet. Connecting and enabling new innovations, discoveries, solving world challenges, creating new products, solutions, generating economic prosperity—that is what the possibilities are of the Connected Planet in the near future. The massive empowerment of individuals and societies through the power of global connectivity captures the essence of this trend. The Connected Planet will empower individuals with the tools of the mobile web, digital money, linked online markets, and, above all, fuel a market for innovative new ideas.

The next new pharmaceuticals, computers, energy, and climate change fixes will come from connected minds—the innovators, inventors, entrepreneurs of the Connected Planet. We are altering, accelerating, and enabling human minds with access to the world's knowledge in ways we could not have dreamed about even five years ago. The Hyperconnectivity of connected minds over the Internet with each other and connected things, data devices, products, even the coming Smart Machines as our allies, will revolutionize every aspect of human endeavor. Eight billion minds will define the future of the Connected Planet—across borders, cultures, markets, and networks. No words can properly characterize the accelerated prosperity and opportunity this trend will offer. The Connected Planet will be a singular transformational event in our civilization's history—a leap in collective consciousness from the connections of billions of people to the knowledge and tools of the Internet, social media, mobile media, and other information technologies. Based on the collective knowledge, access to tools, and radical new ideas, over the next one hundred years we will be building an entirely new civilization. The very idea of this, a Connected Planet, will pose a challenge of immense scale.

16

Most people do not think of their connectivity to the planet. They think about their connections to their family, friends, work, or community. Maybe they feel a connection to an ideology or religion or a nation or sports team. But the idea that we are all part of a Connected Planet—this is a mindset that opens new possibilities for understanding cultures, doing business, embracing technologies, and, most of all, perhaps gives us a global perspective about ourselves that we are all connected on one planet.

There are many trends in this book that I think are vital to your career, business, and future, but one big trend above all that you want to embrace is the Connected Planet. Your capacity to grasp and navigate the changes that are coming—to become Future Smart—depends on your understanding of the scope of global connectivity that is coming. Smarter, faster, deeper connectivity will transform our world, enabling open communications, dynamic commerce, cultural understanding, and access to a more prosperous world.

Connectivity will define the next hundred years. Connectivity is and will be the superglue that binds all transactions, technologies, relationships, and businesses. It will define how you will interact with your world, your career, and your destiny, and it will define how you interact with people, nations, markets, business, and, most of all, entrepreneurs. Connected networks of people, capital, data, and smart products—Always Aware and Always Online—will create a new Global Digital Culture that will expand global prosperity well beyond what we have seen today. The Connected Planet has the potential to deliver even greater benefits to society in the future, with the potential of connecting almost anything and anyone, which will offer new insights. The world of 2025 will offer a range of essential services powered by a vibrant mobile web ecosystem that connects the physical and digital worlds to markets, entrepreneurs, companies, and supply chains.

Your Connected Future: 2025

As you get into your car, your Always-Aware Car connects to your Private Cloud Network over the Internet, and even before you got into the car, your car knew you were coming. It sensed you and got a communication, a signal from the house AI that you were on your way. The door knob auto-connected over the Internet with your car's cognitive computer brain and downloaded your calendar of where you needed to be by 12 P.M. today.

Your House AI read your e-mail and reminded you via Quick-Link to your Wearable Glasses that lit up yellow that you should not forget to grab your computer tablet. Your Car AI, Gayle, already has the route dialed in and checked for traffic by the time you turn the ignition. You have the option to Auto-Drive or Go Manual. Each device, surface, habitat, and vehicle senses,

communicates, and enables you. This is the Internet of Things—Always On, Always Aware, and Always Connected.

The Connected Planet trend—propelled by the mobile Internet, fused with business, and enabled by the availability of all human knowledge—will define the future of global business, trade, economics, and our civilization's future. Connecting the unconnected—the things, products, networks, services, and, most important, minds—will bring forth a unique transformation in new business models, industries, and products that could not have existed before.

The connected globalization of markets, assets, technologies, knowledge, talent, and industries is creating something new we have not seen before. It could not have even been conceptualized without the convergence of the mobile and smart networks that will become the backbone of a new marketplace: exponentially larger, by many exabytes of data, with billions of connected people and trillions of connected devices. The awareness and leveraging of this new Connected Planet Trend will open doors to education, commerce, health care, and business in entirely new ways as we learn to predict smarter.

Whether we pass or fail, learn to collaborate or compete, end up at war or at peace, it will all be shaped by how smart we are about understanding our connectivity, how well we understand our connections, and, most of all, how we connect with each other to solve problems, innovate for the future, create prosperity, and conduct business. You want to understand the architecture of connectivity. Connectivity as a business model, as a way of building entirely new ways of interaction between humans, markets, and cultures will bring the world into a more dynamic and transparent network of ideas, commerce, and opportunity. Connectivity could bring a world of ample resources, smarter solutions, and new economic value.

The logic of connectivity is the existential collaboration of billions across nations and diverse cultures, and yet it is a recognition that we live on one Connected Planet. Profound discoveries, unlimited imaginations, data insights, and dynamic new engines of innovation and productivity will come.

Connectivity is a fundamental shift in the way we think about the future. If all systems of knowledge, business, technology, communications, and commerce are connected, then the convergence of these systems will shape the future— and perhaps it will be a better future, with increased innovation, prosperity, and peace. Greater connectivity will open markets and empower entrepreneurial companies and individuals from around a world who are not connected today. More productivity, more transparency, and more knowledge will be accessible to more people than ever before.

The Connected Planet Trend is an interlinking of systems that will create a dynamic and innovative trade, technology, and communications marketplace that shall inspire creativity, imagination, and solutions to the largest challenges

facing our world. The global connectivity of these systems will become essential to our world, as it will define economic prosperity, commerce, multicultural exchange, and wealth creation. The fusion of connected knowledge, individuals, technology, and markets will shape the destiny of our planet.

- Connected transportation will be safe.
- Connected networks will find patterns and solutions to problems.
- Connected Innovation Ecosystems—convergence of talent, technology, collaboration, and markets—will create competitive advantage.
- Connected enterprises will reach new customers.
- Connected governments will operate with transparent effectiveness.
- Connected technologies will enable new products and services.
- Connected supply chains will speed production and raise quality.
- Connected entrepreneurs will harness innovation.
- Connected health care will enable more effective care.
- Connected education will enable smarter learning.
- Connected products, Always Aware and online, will enable security.

How Future Smart we are about the connectivity of the mobile online global economy will shape our civilization's prosperity and progress for the next hundred years. The convergence of connected systems will help us understand our world and ourselves, from better predicting population health, to broadcasting education, to opening new markets, to connecting buyers and sellers who have never been connected before.

Smarter connectivity will also shape the challenges we will face. How well we meet the challenges of the next ten years will shape the next hundred. There is much at stake when discussing how we need to think completely differently, as one connected planet, in order to even conceptualize the globalized challenges that face our future world: extreme climate change, global conflict, food and water stress, economic instability, opening markets, terrorism, rogue technology, global crime, and increasing population. Our connectivity may be the source of how effectively we meet the Grand Challenges of our future.

As an individual, if you want to become Future Smart—adaptive, agile, and predictive—to thrive in the future, you want to understand the Connected Planet. There will be more opportunities for wealth creation, jobs, and prosperity for individuals in the Connected Planet than ever before. As all systems become connected, the unleashing of ideas and harnessing of innovation will create massive entrepreneurial opportunities to deliver new business value. Accelerated awareness of customers' needs and market demands through this connectivity will build more intimacy with and understanding of organizations.

The Connectivity Dividend

No nation, business, or individual can detach itself from the vitality of the rest of the planet. No climate change policy can focus only on one separate region, nation, or city alone. No employee-seeking corporation can attract talent by focusing on locality rather than globalization. No organization can expect the interlinked Connected Planet Trend to be anything other than the largest influence on their markets, customers, industry, or competition.

You can no longer afford to limit your future in developing resources, capital, talent, markets, technology, or customers. The planet is your marketplace, factory, talent pool, research lab, customer base, and Innovation Ecosystem. Innovation Ecosystems will become an essential part of the how commerce is conducted in the future, bringing together four key elements: (1) digital commerce, (2) mobile connectivity, (3) entrepreneurial business culture, and (4) Smart Machines. Innovation Ecosystems will spawn online collaborative networks of interactive markets, resources, expertise, suppliers, enablers—humans and Smart Machines (various new forms of AI, software bots, machine intelligence, and social intelligence systems), mobile devices, and Internet connected things that come together to harness innovation to produce commerce. Innovation Ecosystems are the future of business that will monetize global connectivity, Big Data, analytics, and knowledge processes over the Web.

Mobile will become an accelerator of the Connected Planet that is coming. Mobile is already a proven enabler of economic opportunities on the planet. The mobile industry contributed around 4 percent of global gross domestic product (GDP) in 2013, equivalent to over US$2.7 trillion. This will increase to 7.1 percent of global GDP by 2025. The mobile industry, as an enabler of the Connected Planet trend, will shape the future global economy as an innovation platform to catalyze commerce, provide services, and connect buyers and sellers across borders over electronic network markets.

Mobile networks will provide unique opportunities to reach new customers, open new markets, and to market products and services in ways that were impossible in the past. The deep collaboration of people, technology, and services, all online connected by commerce, will be a primary global growth accelerator.

The industry has spawned a number of early stage Innovation Ecosystems that have emerged across the world. These mobile innovation ecosystems contribute to the empowerment of individuals, businesses, and societies not only through the opportunities they create but also through the solutions and services they deliver, which will increase productivity, quality of life, and prosperity. In the future this will become dominant as Innovation Ecosystems spread throughout the world propelled by the spread of mobile web access. Innovation Ecosystems will become the backbone of the Connected Planet. Some of the

Innovation Ecosystem deliverables may be based on education, health care, and business-to-business commerce, to name a few.

Innovation Ecosystems of the future will be built on the global mobile architecture of the Internet. The mobile web will be the chief accelerator of the Connected Planet, shaping the future of every nation, business, and society for the better. Greater efficiency, cost effectiveness, and productivity will be the outcome of connected resources, capital, work processes, and talent that are combined over the mobile web.

This convergence of people, technology, and mobile business processes will unleash a new dimension of services that improve the quality of consumers' lives and the productivity of enterprises. The benefits of mobility will spread far beyond communications to provide dramatic efficiency improvements in sectors such as energy, logistics, banking, finance, security, and manufacturing.

Welcome to the new reality of the Connected Planet. The Connectivity Dividend is the economic, business, and social value that shall be gained from connecting people, markets, products, supply chains, and, perhaps most interesting, minds.

The huge innovation breakthroughs from connecting innovative ideas from the connected minds of 8 billion people cannot be measured in any currency. The Connectivity Dividend for humanity may be in healing disease, accelerating global wealth creation, stimulating new inventions in energy, managing climate, or ending war. The infinite power of connected minds may be the most underutilized and most obvious natural resource on the planet.

As more markets become digitally connected and more products become connected to each other and to people, a new understanding of real-time value will emerge: What is the power of a billion connected minds? It is the power to create new solutions, innovations, and a New Productive Future for humanity. Once every hospital is online and all of the equipment, devices, staff, doctors, and patients are all connected, when every drug, cell phone, and device is connected and able to speak to every doctor, system, and patient, then we will have a Connected Health Care System that is self-aware and self-healing and can operate with a level of effectiveness, safety, and awareness that is not possible today.

Then our Smart Hospital will know how to prevent illness, predict our future health, and heal. The convergence of connected people, systems, networks, and devices will create new value—this is the Connectivity Dividend. New value creation from the connected minds, devices, and systems of our world will transform medicine.

Pharmaceuticals will be Always Aware and "know" what types of patients they are most effective for based on personalized Big Data. Patients' real-time digital health records will "talk" to the doctor, patient, and the Smart Machine Medical Management systems to improve diagnostics and better health care. This is a 2025 scenario, when Smart Machines and automated medical decision

support systems evolve, learn, and develop a predictive capability to diagnose, prevent, and treat illness. When a Big Data analysis of millions of research trials, discovered by an online computer doctor—not a human but a Smart Machine—finds the ideal procedure for your cancer condition and then advises your doctor, then you will know the Connected Planet has arrived.

The Connected Planet Trend also reflects a recognition that you need to play the game of business differently. Thinking about how you might fit into an Innovation Ecosystem will give you competitive value. How might you grow your business in the future by thinking about collaboration and partnering? What global markets or customers that you don't have now would you want in order to grow your business and expand your markets? How could you use connectivity to create a competitive advantage?

Global Hyperconnectivity by 2025

- Every minute over two hundred hours of video is uploaded to YouTube.
- There will be over 100 billion connected devices on the planet.
- There will be 1 trillion connected chips, sensors, and machines.
- 300 million wearable devices will be connected online.
- Mobile devices will generate over fifty exabytes of traffic per month.
- Mobile devices will exceed the world's population.
- Over 7 billion people will be connected over the mobile Internet.
- Smart Machine and M2M networks will traverse the globe, enabling entrepreneurs and businesses to collaborate, innovate, transact, and conduct business.
- Digital applications and mobile digital services will transform work processes and enterprises.
- Deep Collaboration between global entrepreneurs over mobile networks will create a New Vibrant Global Marketplace.
- Cognitive computing will transform the Internet of Things, IoT, embedding intelligence in every Thing.
- Global Innovation Ecosystems will develop, manufacture, analyze, market, and distribute 70 percent of all products and services.
- Enterprise intelligence systems will predict what customers want before they do and give it to them.

Our Connected Future

Let's imagine what 2025 may look like . . .

A California rancher, Phil, gets a text from his Avatar Trixie, a digital agent with artificial intelligence (AI) that sold his cattle herd to a China customer just before global beef prices went up by 25 percent—as she predicted.

Jomo Mobasa, in Kenya's Personal Cloud Computer, a Class-5 Asimov model in Singapore, is selling over 1 million virtual reality games such as Crazy Birds, downloaded every minute into 120 million mobile wearable computers.

Five hundred million entrepreneurs across Africa, the European Union, North America, and Asia buy and sell renewable energy credits (RECs), over Baidu-Google's mobile e-commerce network, an innovation ecosystem, generating millions in sales per second across 180 nations.

The Connected Enterprise

Welcome to the Connected Planet, where the dynamic, kinetic, and high-velocity connectivity of networks of people, sensors, computers, virtual agents, mobile devices, and Smart Machines will all create prosperity across markets, ecosystems, and nations. The sheer volume of connected millions of supply chains, organizations, and individuals that are looking to create, buy, or sell, as well as the millions of niche markets and producers for products and services that are predictive to market demands, will stream across virtual reality worlds of commerce, education, health care, and culture, creating the core of the Connected Planet. More connections means more vital markets and a velocity of commerce, capital, and communications.

Connectivity will also be the competitive advantage of business invention. Connected enterprises will be able to deploy resources faster and more efficiently in order to empower customers, to enable their success and well-being. Connected nations will compete for talent and productivity. The smarter and more efficient the connectivity, the better the nation at retaining and attracting talent. Connectivity as a competitive advantage of nations will support this same equation—the high-performance connectivity of nations will attract business and talent.

This Connected Planet Trend is an emerging fusion of innovation, business, technologies, economics, and entrepreneurs. This trend will drive commerce, especially for the bottom of the global population, who need a stable, secure, and transparent digital marketplace to conduct business. This is being invented now by a series of forces that are converging, moving us into the future.

We will look back in ten years and marvel at how primitive, unconnected, and unproductive our world was. Unconnected no more, we will build a Connected Planet that, between 2020 and 2030, will transform our civilization for the better, allowing more individuals to participate in wealth creation, prosperity, and innovation. The Connected Planet Trend will do more to enable entrepreneurs than any government has or can. Organizations and entrepreneurs should get ready for 1,000 percent more growth, opportunities, and jobs as the global markets get connected.

The Five Forces Driving the Connected Planet

The Mobile Internet: The spread of the mobile Internet will enhance global connectivity fostering more collaboration, new business creation, and innovation. This will be a more integrated and transparent world of shared ideas, values, and worldviews that together will build a planetary culture in the future. The mobile Internet will evolve into a network of connected markets made up of dynamic human and synthetic intelligences—always on, always aware, always open for business, 24/7.

This global market will fuel over US$1 trillion in sales by 2025. This will be accelerated by connected digital mobile systems reaching 90 percent of humanity, connecting them to supply chains, producers, distributors, Smart Connected Machines, logistics, makers, buyers, and sellers. This market fused with technology—such as high-speed computers, digital assistants, digital cash, and Smart Virtual Machines—will dominate commerce.

This will be good news for entrepreneurs and companies who will need to adapt to the real-time access of data these connected technologies find. More connectivity will bring global collaborations, learning, smarter health care, access to education, and, most of all, Innovative Ideas—ideas that create value. The Connected Planet will be the network of Innovative Ideas—the currency of learning, trade, media, and communications. Organizations that understand this evolutionary shift will prosper. The Connected Planet will crowdsource ideas, networks, and markets faster than ever before. Innovative Ideas that create wealth, opportunity, and invention, that transform our world, are what's coming.

On the Connected Planet of 2025 the real-time visibility of Innovative Ideas shared in one part of the world—say, Kenya—can be instantly picked up in Hong Kong, London, and Paris. We see this real-time sharing of ideas today in the instant connectivity of social media like Twitter and Facebook postings, which instantly show up and then get picked up and shared around the world.

There will be a deeper collaboration with a speedier Internet, as 5G networks stream at nanosecond speed hundreds of exabytes of video, data, voice, images, and text around the block and around the world. Those entrepreneurial companies and individuals who can access this hyperconnected network will have a competitive advantage.

This is the Connected Planet at work—engaging, enabling, and empowering individuals to use network connectivity as a model for every aspect of human endeavor. We will be smarter with connected enterprises. We will be more productive in connected organizations. We will be more efficient in connected supply chains. We will have more entertainment value in connected media.

This will enable local, regional, and global communications—connecting buyers and sellers, people, enterprises, and machines. Accurate data about supply and demand that affects real-time pricing, customization, and resource sourcing

will be available all through your smart phone. The mobile web will become the connected nervous system of our civilization in the future—smart, open, aware, secure, and connecting billions of individuals and companies.

The Future Smart Entrepreneurs: They will be agile, adaptive, global, predictive, and innovation-savvy. Future Smart Entrepreneurs are a different type of entrepreneur. They will operate with a different mindset—one of connected minds, mobile technologies, systems, and markets. They will use the Connected Planet to create new business value and work processes. Future Smart entrepreneurs will shape the future of the global economy with innovation-fueled new ideas for business that could not exist without global connectivity to markets, talent, and networks.

The Innovation Economy: This is born out of the recognition that tech innovations are the key driver of economic growth and value, resulting in jobs, prosperity, productivity, growth, and free societies. The Innovation Economy thrives where there are free markets, free enterprise, and free societies, where individuals can thrive best. Advanced technologies of today—bio, nano, neuro, robo, and others—will be the foundation of higher advanced technologies of tomorrow, far beyond the imagination of what is possible today. Advanced technologies—always on, always aware, and always connected—will be the backbone of the electronic marketplace of tomorrow.

This Connected Planet will be dominated by mobile, wearable, and embedded computing that will be linked together in the Internet of Things (IoT). The Internet of Things is the emerging technology wave of wirelessly connecting products, systems, computer chips, and devices to each other so they may sense, understand, analyze, predict, and exchange information, such as location awareness, and communicate with each other and us over the web.

THE INTERNET OF THINGS: IOT IN 2025

- Connected transportation systems—automated cars, buses, highways
- Connected cities—managing power, water, security
- Connected health care—creating safer and better care
- Connected agriculture—creating more efficient yields
- Connected manufacturing—managing higher productivity
- Connected homes—enabling energy, media, communications
- Connected enterprise—enabling big data, analytics, cloud services

This will enable individuals and companies to harness artificial intelligence (AI)–enhanced cloud computing for business, entertainment, social services, and idea harvesting. Those who can envision and shape this emerging future will prosper.

The Connected Society: The Connected Planet Trend has as much to do with connecting individuals to each other for social issues and causes as it is about connecting entrepreneurs and business. In 2011 Twitter played a key role in the Arab Spring in the Middle East, galvanizing thousands across the world who were connected and could mobilize for events supporting each other's actions in real-time. This was unprecedented. The role of connected social media enables, motivates, and drives support for social change. In the future connected technology will drive more uprisings and increased citizen awareness.

In 2009 more than two hundred cities around the world held a Twestival, bringing together the Twitter community for an evening of focusing on resource scarcity and raising money and awareness for an important global issue—water. Over social networks they organized an event globally by using Twitter as a connected network, with additional information on videos and Facebook pages. The event resulted in providing clean water for over seventeen thousand people. The Twestival's success was experimental in its method to change the world in an impactful way on one single night. This will be a model for the future.

The social challenges humanity faces are beyond borders and nations. Today governments are not prepared to create a Connected Society to deal with public health, education, water and food scarcity, climate change, and other social challenges. By 2025 they must to manage the future of their nations, or else sovereign power will decline.

The Quest for a Better Future: There is a Global Values Shift coming that will change people's worldview. Individuals will see themselves as a part of the connected planet, not just as individuals from one nation. There are many serious challenges and problems that face our world, such as climate change, resource scarcity, job creation, poverty, peace, and security. There is a Global Values Shift coming that will redefine the purpose of the enterprise and the individual so as to create a better future through connectivity.

Being connected on the planet with the shared values of making this a better world gives new meaning to connectivity. We share these Planetary Challenges together across cultures, economies, and as one civilization—this is what is coming. If making the world better is increasingly shaping your worldview, then your decisions about your work, lifestyle, employer, and government will change to embrace this New Worldview. This is a fundamental driver of the Connected Planet Trend—the idea that the individual's purpose is to align with others on the planet in order to bring about a better future, a more prosperous, secure, and productive future. Future Smart companies that understand this trend will have a competitive advantage.

The business of the future will be about the Connected Planet. Working toward leveraging connectivity as a deliverable when running your business is a good start.

My bet is that innovative technology will be the strategic accelerator for the Connected Planet. More connected supply chains, buyers, sellers, markets, and social media–enabled mobile platforms—even the Smart Machines doing our bidding (for now) will connect us. This is what you want to build. Embracing the Connected Planet in your career, inventing the connections that will bring innovation to your business or profession would be Future Smart.

Chapter 3

The New Future of Business: Predictive, Smart, and Mobile

The year is 2025. A vibrant global hyperconnected Innovation Ecosystem has emerged, generating millions of jobs and businesses. Innovation Ecosystems are high-performance collaborative global web networks that are predictive, real time, and mobile. Innovation Ecosystems will be highly agile and enable innovative entrepreneurs to create new global digital markets. They bring together talent, innovation, supply chains, markets, makers, capital, and experts—both humans and technology—to produce commerce. Most jobs are entrepreneurial and project based, working across borders and engaging deep, collaborative networks of people, companies, and technology. Digital Tribes, specialized networks of people, companies, and Smart Machines, collaborate and compete across the many Innovation Ecosystems.

There is an explosion of innovation that is shaping opportunities and electrifying buyers, sellers, makers, and producers across 150 nations that fuel global trade in yottabytes (1 YB = 1000^8bytes = 10^{24}bytes = 1,000,000,000,000,000, 000,000,000 bytes = 1,000 zettabytes = 1 trillion terabytes) and in nanoseconds by the speed-of-light web networks. Business by the speed of photons fuels a dynamic global Innovation Economy.

Products and services are designed and sourced in real time across Innovation Ecosystems that bring together talent, supply chains, digital markets, and projects on demand, serving billions of customers every minute of every day. These Innovation Ecosystems are agile, predictive, postindustrial networks in which products, services, and ideas which serve a global marketplace

of customers. Moving from new idea to product can take seconds in the New Future of Business. Automated intelligence plus humans will make markets, create innovations, and monetize ideas instantly. Smart Prediction will be a new competitive advantage.

Multiple Innovation Ecosystems with domain-specific expertise in materials, electronics, and customer service interact with freelance experts from specific industries, such as security, health, real estate, finance, and media. Knowledge-Value Specialists interact with Smart Machines, distribution, and robots.

Drones, flyables, digital personalities, avatars, and Smart Machines are integrated into the global business culture. Individuals have digital clones that serve customers and conduct commerce while their Authentic Personas—actual humans—create, play, travel, or work on other projects. Entirely new digital business models create Super Gigs—freelance projects for hire in alternative energy, health enhancement, consumer genomics, adaptive finance, predictive simulation, Big Data, and immersive entertainment, all of which didn't even exist five years, or even five minutes, before.

In this New Future a fundamental global shift in the way business functions has emerged. Smart Prediction, the evolution on the convergence of Big Data, Analytics, and Cognitive Computing, has transformed business. Customers are producers. Competitors are collaborators. Crowdsourcing drives marketing.

This is business reinvented at the speed of light.

Producers make things and sell things, but *what* is made and the *how* it's made is different. On-demand virtual foundries and connected supply chains from off-world factories in space drive a vibrant marketplace of 3D Makers to simulators as digital currencies electrify new choices for commerce. Product designs are simulated and uploaded to 3D Maker factories that produce and distribute across this planet as well as other off-world orbiting cities.

Companies predict customers' desire and market those Big Data Desires to Knowledge-Smart businesses offering health enhancement, deep learning, gaming, entertainment, and finance.

The emergence of the Global Innovation Ecosystem—a convergence of mobile, TV, auto, habitat, computer, sensor, and wearable platforms—is the largest global marketplace in history, linking up 8 billion people who are not only both consumers and producers but also who share knowledge and talent in dynamic ways. It is a constantly evolving, morphable digital platform that adapts based on who you are, where you are, and what you're searching for. This Innovation Ecosystem links networks, smart devices, people, smart machines, and markets. This is where talent, projects, trade, and innovation converge—the Makers World.

3D nano-manufacturing has transformed health care, consumer products, industrial products, and entertainment. Most homes and businesses have 3D

Maker-Bots at their location so they can make on-demand personalized pharmaceuticals, food, tools, clothing, and even complex devices. Everyone is a 3D
Maker—the self-sufficiency of the population has altered business. 3D Makers
are linked up to cloud networks, where they can download programs, power,
and tools when they need it to be functional. Knowledge as a product is the
most demanded product offered in the world, enabling finance, health care,
manufacturing, trade, media, and entertainment to reach new heights of personalized commerce.

Entirely new business value is spawned, hive networked, crowdsourced,
exchanged, and traded across dynamic real-time markets, channels, and virtual
pop-up e-commerce universes. Everyone is a creator, maker, producer, and, at
the same time, a customer. Business in the future is a fast-evolving network of
people and Collaborative Smart Machines—cognitive cloud computers networked to deliver value to customers and companies.

The collision of advanced mobile web networks and free enterprise is
the chief enablement of the future of business. Free markets, free trade, and
free enterprises operating over mobile web-based Global Innovation Ecosystems accelerate growth, entrepreneurship, and global commerce. Most
individuals and companies will prosper in this fast-paced, kinetic New Future of business.

Billions of individuals who did not have access to global markets to buy and
sell, produce and trade, build and distribute are now connected together. New
ideas are floated in the Innovation Ecosystems: Smart Machines and Transmedia Tribes compete for Maker Rights to turn ideas into products for the
commercial markets. InstaMarkets, emerge quickly, connecting a global mix of
buyers and sellers, makers and developers, investors and digital Banker-Bots—
then dissolve away. Different InstaMarkets emerge and dissolve away every day,
1 million times a day, generating over $1.5 trillion a week. You need to have a
Future Smart organization to be able to manage the Game-Changing business
opportunities in this future.

The global market of 9 billion customers are online NOW. Will you be
ready to go?

Free enterprise over the Global Innovation Ecosystem of makers, producers,
agents, sellers, and buyers will do more to transform the world's economy—
creating wealth and reducing poverty—than what any government could hope
to do to improve the future of their citizens or economy. Governments will need
to support this or get out of the way. The Global Innovation Ecosystem will
transform the global economy, where the fusion of free enterprise, individuals,
and digital technology, lifts up economies and society.

It's a New Future in which the rules have changed, the opportunities are
global, and only the Future Smart will thrive.

THE TOP GAME-CHANGING TRENDS THAT WILL SHAPE THE FUTURE OF BUSINESS

1. Innovation is the chief competitive advantage: embrace it and thrive; resist it and perish.
2. Every enterprise must embrace socially responsible business practices.
3. Predictive Knowledge-Value business models will change every enterprise and career.
4. Disrupt and reinvent your business model, products, work processes, talent, strategy, and values—before you create your competition.
5. The Mobile Web Marketplace will connect over 7 billion people by 2025.
6. Automated bots, computer algorithms, and Smart Machines will transform every business—learn to leverage this revolution.
7. The Global Innovation Ecosystem will create collaborative and connected networks of markets, companies, entrepreneurs, and commerce.
8. Predictive analytics, the cloud, Big Data, social media, and mobile are the top trends that will transform business in this century.
9. A new kind of customer, the Click-Streamer, points to a new digital global culture.
10. The Start-Up Culture will change every business, making every enterprise more entrepreneurial.

Digital Money: The Future of Transactions

Your cell phone is your new bank. Person-to-Person (P2P) transactions can use a variety of digital currencies in the future to conduct business. Every day new digital banks will manage billions in global digital currency markets, such as M-Pesa, P2P Money, DigiCash, MyBucks, Bitcoin, and Mobil$. Digital money—or what was first called *crypto currency*—is now an accepted form of money for all transactions.

In real time people can create digital currency based on virtual or hard assets such as commodities and then use them for conducting business. People even trade the algos—the formulas for creating digital cash. You will be able to design online your own digital cash and use it to conduct business. Even today you can customize your own digital money based on the Bitcoin platform and use it for transactions—assuming you can find someone or some business to accept your digital cash. This opens the door for a new era of customized digital currency—on demand and personalized for the moment or the business. The

implications for a world where you can customize digital currency will create new opportunities for commerce, especially over mobile networks.

There are over 100 million people on the planet that have access to mobile digital money. From Africa to Asia, to the poorest to the richest nations on the planet, mobile digital cash—money on your mobile—is the not just the future; it is the Now Market and growing fast, every second. By 2025 there will be over 1 billion people who use digital mobile money as their primary transaction platform.

MK Ultra: 2022

The hacker group MK Ultra's specialty is cyber-hacking—or "liberating," as they say—crypto currencies. By 2022 there are numerous crypto-currencies, or digital cash, as they are known. Led by an early experiment by Bitcoin, digital cash models were developed in the early part of the twenty-first century as an alternative to sovereign-issued currencies like US dollars, Euros, and Chinese Yuan.

Today the digital cash that MK Ultra is looking for is called DigiTrade, and it is used for energy trading by major energy companies in an attempt to manage currency risk. One program, hacked wirelessly via the Google Glass worn by a careless risk manager in London, gave MK Ultra the codes they needed to steal more than $150 million.

In order to adapt to this new economic reality, businesses developed new ways to secure transactions, so customers and suppliers who prefer to use digital funds can interact with them. A Digital Central Bank monitors all digital currencies larger than US$1 billion. Person-to-person (P2P) digital currencies number in the millions as individuals develop new ways to exchange value and commerce outside of the traditional currency marketplace. This disrupts traditional monetary controls but will persist, as the central banks will learn to adapt to this New Future of money.

The Freelancer Market: 2025

Global digital businesses that crowdsource talent with few full-time employees drive a Freelancer Marketplace that is responsible for over 70 percent of all new jobs. Though this seemed hard to believe in 2015, by 2020 this trend exploded. Every organization will need to adapt to this New Future. Freelancers have become a valuable talent asset, as they are mobile, virtual, and have innovation skills that many organizations rely on for projects.

The result is flatter network-based organizations that maintain freelancer networks of talented people who may work their entire life on projects for many companies on demand. These projects might last minutes, days, and, sometimes,

years. Freelancers with specialized talents in specific industries have become valuable resources for most organizations.

Freelancers bring a much-needed entrepreneurial culture shift to business, in which compensation is based on the project performance, thus creating new business value and the return on *innovation* (ROI). This trend has changed how people work with organizations, introducing a new agile era of high-performance innovation. These are Future Smart companies that are emerging.

Genomic Analytics: The Future of Marketing

DNA sequencing combined with neuromarketing and Big Data is used to predict customer needs, design products, understand workforce compatibility, redesign work, and formulate careers. As DNA tests got cheaper and the science of genomics was developed for understanding how people, companies, and even products might interact, a new industry was born.

Genomic Analytics is now used throughout the world, offering new insights into marketing, employment, and digital services. Specialists called Genomers provide customized forecasts of the Genomic market profiles so businesses can better identify new opportunities.

Neuro-Ads

Adaptive Personalized Advertising connects billions of consumers and businesses with a massive predictive real-time capability, identifying what you desire. Sound intrusive? It can be. Neuro-Ads can enable, interpret, and predict what you need and then even provide it. The massive global automated advertising system uses neuroscience with cloud networks to generate billions of personalized ads customized for your desires, needs, and problems.

These ads don't just sell but also empower people with information that is highly relevant for what business predicts individuals will desire. People are paid with digital credits for the use of their time and attention by choosing to interact with the advertising. They may also Ad-Produce customize advertising, with themes for their interests such as the Pepsi Treasure Hunt, Taco Bell Auto Racing, and the Great Race Travels to the Future.

Digital Maker Networks

Digital Maker Networks that specialize in different industries will emerge. If you're a struggling media maker, an entrepreneur such as the Transmedia Smart Machines from the Bangkok Network can generate that new online game show you have developed and are now shopping around for a paying audience. Real-time tests show that a remote part of China is hungry for this

type of entertainment and will prepay in Bitcoins 40 percent of the production cost.

The rest of the costs will be offset by a loan from the Bangkok Bank Network to you, secured by 50 percent of your orders, or you can borrow against those carbon Bitcoin credit contracts you have—that's if they can produce and sell the special effects to a corporate sponsor and get the digital marketing rights to Southeast Asia, of which they will prepay. Each week millions of media productions are made this way. Now you are ready to go.

Big Data Revolution

Every business will be transformed by Big Data. It is also important to understand our world by analyzing and unlocking the data that defines our world. Big Data is used to better predict which drugs work best, what services and brands deliver superior quality, and what innovations will produce the highest customer value.

Big Data is about extracting meaning from the data that captures how employees work, and this enables them to succeed as well as mine the customer data generated by sales. Big Data is a way to visualize, conceptualize, and operationalize how to create entirely new lines of business as well as enhance the business opportunities you have now. Big Data is a weapon for competitive advantage if you understand the data science that unlocks the mysteries of information.

Big Data will also reveal what customers will need in order to predict with accuracy what will enable, empower, and deliver value to citizens from government and to customers from business.

Headlines from the Future: 2025
Personalized Adaptive Advertising
Anticipates Your Secret Desires

Brain-Streaming:
Future Marketing Trend 2025

Direct-to-Brain (D2B) broadcasts games and entertainment, and this will generate over $200 billion a year in sales. D2B, also known as Brain-Streaming, has become a huge global industry, generating millions of jobs and spawning new services almost daily. D2B is highly immersive and engaging as it stimulates the brain.

Entertainment media that analyzes consumer interests and then auto-generates gaming and media personalized for billions of individual profiles is now both a feature on WebTV and a standalone media service. Though illegal in some nations, D2B has also become a powerful tool for education and learning, used by both online schools as well as businesses to train people.

The Human Performance Enhancement Market: 2025

The Human Performance Market (HPE) focuses on augmenting intelligence, regenerating organs, and enhancing cybernetic human mobility. Creating healthy aging now dominates over 45 percent of consumer digital wallet share. With over five hundred new business sectors and over 100 million jobs, HPE is a growing global industry. The augmentation of intelligence has become a highly in-demand service for business and individuals, and 40 percent of all jobs require an enhancement certification.

Managing age-related diseases has become the number-one challenge facing our world. As the next generation ages, Generation X reaches middle age at sixty-five, and with depopulation threatening lower productivity throughout the world, HPE has become the largest industry on the planet. Government and corporate subsidies as well as insurance support large-scale HPE for the population.

The Autonomous Economy

Fully automated buildings, homes, autos, and devices buy and sell energy over an online global energy microgrid network. Automated factories in space build customized pharmaceuticals, autos, agriculture, and computing devices. Smart Machines, both autonomous and human managed, will shape the Autonomous Economy, as they will be running the factories, Innovation Ecosystems, Maker Networks, and global businesses that will dominate economic growth in the future. By 2025 the Autonomous Economy will be well defined—in fact, it is emerging now.

The Autonomous Economy developed out of the convergence of automated machines that run factories based on computing, geo-intelligence, and the Internet of Things (IoT) to create Smart Machines based on what we used to call AI, or artificial intelligence. The New AI is based on cognitive computing, neuroscience, genomics, and nanotechnology and is used to create a new era of Smart Machines that perform all types of industrial and Knowledge-Value work. They also upgrade themselves and operate entire global enterprises independent of humans.

3D Cloud Printing Marketplace

Cloud computing delivers, on demand, 70 percent of all products direct to the consumer, including the local molecular manufacturing of products. 3D printers generate most products, even complex devices and machines. As nano-assemblers became inexpensive and almost given away by governments and companies like microwave ovens had been decades before, every person came to have access to 3D printers linked to cloud networks for the personal production of certain goods.

Microgrid Marketplace

The development of distributed energy networks, known as microgrids, has transformed the energy marketplace, increasing efficiency and eliminating waste. The combination of rising energy costs and the concern for better managing our global energy resources and dealing with climate change has led to this innovation.

Microgrids are networks of smart, efficient collaborations of traditional and renewable sources connecting energy resources, producers, and consumers. Microgrid development has merged with the Autonomous Economy to better manage cost-effective energy usage for businesses and consumers.

The Sustainable Planet

The risk factors facing the planet due to climate change, pollution, and the demands of a rising population on natural resources such as water, food, and energy has led to a new global agenda on sustainability. The failure of governments to take decisive action to address the challenges pressed the business sector to take a leadership role in tackling these issues.

Consumers have made businesses accountable for making sustainable choices and embracing an era of social accountability. Consumers vote with their wallet, supporting businesses that embrace a sustainable planet and rejecting those that don't. Business leaders are now influencing politicians to support more sustainable policies that over 90 percent of consumers demand—climate change management.

What the Marketplace Teaches

The future of business is emerging now. The power of digital Knowledge-Value goods is accelerating more so than labor-intensive goods. In the future, by 2025, Knowledge-Value goods will dominate the marketplace. There are millions of entrepreneurs who have companies that sell online, every day around the world.

These companies may sell products or services, but the most profitable are those that enable others to succeed. These digital entrepreneurs have found the ability to connect with customers over the mobile web to be the basis of a radical new business model. These digital entrepreneurs enable other entrepreneurs to succeed. They help them sell more, get found by customers, digitally market over social networks, and get their businesses noticed over the Internet. Their work processes and services are digitally enhanced to optimize productivity and profitability.

The fusion of online marketing, analytics, and computer science has created success where there was no business model prior. The key has been to create an Innovation Ecosystem to serve customers and automate the sales of digital Knowledge Products that others find of great value. This is a vastly different marketplace from what the universities are teaching and how most people were taught as well as how most businesses operate today. But this is what the future will bring.

Are you ready to play in this game? Becoming Future Smart will require you to think and operate completely differently from how you do today. Sustainability, social accountability, social media, exponential technologies, Always Aware Web, mobile commerce, connectivity, the innovators mindset—this thinking should change how you lead, invent, predict, and understand reality: markets, cultures, business, and organizations.

The New Future is altering what a business does and challenges the very idea of what a business is. To see this future, consider what companies like Facebook make billions at—monetizing relationships. Twitter enables global publishing and communications. Google enables search and commerce over markets that connect people. Baidu has transformed China by connecting a billion people and creating a vibrant market of entrepreneurs that were not connected before. Bitcoin offers a new mobile currency that is agile, digital, and used for trade.

Uber is disrupting every business. That future is coming fast. Unrelenting change from new markets, new technology, new competition, and new innovative business models is unfolding.

You cannot use yesterday's tools, ideas, business models, or tech to deal with the changes coming in business. You need an entirely new mindset, tool set, organization structure, and supply chain. We, as a civilization, are inventing a New Future that business can thrive in. The New Future is a radical morphing of the economy, society, and culture that will electrify business. The New Future is the state of tomorrow—kinetic and explosive change. Best to prepare for the storm that's coming.

Every aspect of business is changing. What a market is, how to sell, where to connect with customers, what customers want and expect, how to attract employees or freelancers, and even what the products and services will be will

change. The entire idea of what a business is, does, and how it acts to create value is changing. You have to change with these trends to survive.

Innovation is the only competitive advantage. Innovating work processes in business—increased collaboration and connectivity, blending Smart Machines with human operators, harnessing Big Data, leveraging the cloud, building in predictive analytics—is the application of leading-edge innovations that make the difference. It's doing what others cannot see, what they are not doing or missing that you could embrace—a new distinction in business. Understanding this will build your future success and empower your workforce, customers, and competition. Innovate fast and often and build innovation cultures that embrace the radical ideas, talent, and work processes before your competition does.

Social media is how customers influence customers who then adopt or reject your brand. The power shift to the customer who is more social media savvy than business is a challenge.

Simulation and games are new, emerging ways to simulate, with computers and games, real-life and real-market challenges. Using sims and games to better understand the changing business or customer landscape may reveal new opportunities that were missed before.

Digital marketing is the chief interaction with your brand and the market. Traditional marketing is dead. The mobile web will be the dominant marketplace—prepare for this now. Stop moving atoms—move bits.

Analytics is what you can learn about the market, the customer, or your competition that can help you compete and grow. Create analytics teams of Big Data wizards to figure out how customers are changing and how to interpret their changing needs.

Embed Knowledge Value into every product and service: What is the Knowledge Value that can be added to excite, enable, inform, or empower the customer? If you have not figured that out, then STOP everything and do so.

The Predictive Enterprise, at its core, leverages data, ecosystems, digital tools, and markets. If you understand how prediction will transform competition and your industry, have another hard look around you. Change is endemic. Competition is growing. Customers are looking for change agents to help enable them. You're either predicting your future or someone else is.

Seven Business Trends

The very idea of what a business is, what it does, and who it does it for is changing. How a business creates value for customers will change as well. From new business models and new innovations to new customers and new markets—there is a New Future emerging. This New Future requires a different perspective on decision making in organizations, with fewer hierarchies and more distributed power networks.

Business that leverages Knowledge Value is creating a new enterprise distinction, a new way to think about what a business is. Innovation that creates new opportunities to collaborate and solve problems will be key to navigating this New Future. The New Future is an era of business defined by speed, accelerating digital innovations, Knowledge Value, and globalization.

The customer is driving change in this New Future. Customers discovered the Internet, put computers to work, told companies how they wanted to shop online, made smartphones the next computers, and will make wearable computers the next marketplace. The customer lives in the New Future, and your job is to catch up, to predict faster, to give them value before someone else does.

The New Future is a dynamic global marketplace of new ideas, innovations, and trade and talent collaboration. The New Future is also an expression of a new complex and sophisticated way that humans and machines work to produce value.

THE NEW FUTURE WILL BE DEFINED BY

- Accelerated change
- Fast innovation
- Smart technology
- Predictive systems
- Connected markets
- Digital everything
- Mobile commerce

Of all the business services produced in all of human history, over 80 percent were created in the past decade. The global innovation economy is in its infancy. Computers, smartphones, and the Internet have accelerated business productivity, creating entirely new industries, new markets, and millions of new jobs. Global trade is in its infancy.

Developing nations are growing faster than those in the developed world. Innovation continues to have a positive impact on GDP. We still don't have half the people on the planet on the Internet, and this will be the largest marketplace in the future. The prospects for the future of business could never be better.

Overall quality of life on the planet is improving. Global prosperity is rising. Since 1980 over 1 billion people have come out of poverty. Since 2000 over fifty developing nations have seen their GDP grow, on average, about 5 percent per year. Despite the tumultuous events of the last few years, global prosperity is increasing.

Big technological advancements drives this growth, as more and more people gain access to the tools and knowledge vital for business and entrepreneurship to thrive. Also driving global prosperity are huge advancements in global health and a reduction in war. Life expectancy is rising, especially in Asia and

Africa, where there are emerging huge markets that will be game-changing opportunities for growth.

There are also great challenges that will face business and the economy in the future, such as unemployment, social stability, available talent, crime, uncertain financial markets, slow growth, and sustainability. These challenges and others are part of the evolution of our civilization toward a better world, where quality of life, prosperity, peace, and freedom are the long-term endgame. My forecasts of this future are, overall, positive, but they are not without the risk factors that could derail this forecast. I forecast more upside opportunity than downside risk. I believe the private sector is uniquely qualified to manage risk, yet every person needs to manage his or her risk own as well.

Four Future-Smart Domains

To grow an existing company or grow a new business there are four Future-Smart Domains that need to be integrated all together, like parts of a high-performance race car that are finely tuned for performance. These are: people, process, product, and technology. It's not enough to be adaptive, predictive, and to embrace innovation as well as other factors; you must also achieve a values balance with people, processes, products, and technology to be successful, to become Future Smart. Get it right today, and thrive in the future.

1. People
   - What values should you embrace to attract the right people to grow the future of the business?
   - What kinds of people do you need to work with who could make a big difference in the business?
   - How do people in your organization create a culture that is innovative, adaptive, and open to change?

2. Process
   - How should you rethink your business processes to accelerate innovation, customer service, productivity, or competitive advantage?
   - What work processes must change for us to be more effective at delivering customer Knowledge Value?
   - How is your business changing, and how can you better predict and adapt to these changes?

3. Products
   - What are the innovations you could integrate into products or build into services to enlighten, delight, or serve?

- What are the most amazing products that deliver the most customer value?

4. Technology
   - What type of technologies are emerging that could create an entirely new competitive advantage in your business?
   - What technologies might be game changers for your customers or marketplace?
   - What business innovations require an investigation into technology?

Disrupt Yourself First

Are you ready to disrupt yourself before your competition disrupts you? If you don't swiftly adapt and innovate with courage, this is what will happen: you will crash your organization. It happens often.

People crash organizations by not adapting to change fast enough to embrace the future. Narrow-minded, change-resistant thinking is a common challenge in business today. This myopia will be tolerated less in the future, when the speed of prediction and adaptation will be furious and the very survival of business will be at stake. Only the Future Smart will survive.

Leaders who don't understand this, who think the future will be identical to the past, who resist change will be left behind. Or, unfortunately, this form of Dysfunctional Leadership that breeds Dysfunctional Organizations will become the norm in some industries where change is slow and governments unknowingly subsidize this dysfunctional type of business. This is the opposite of Future Smart and is unsustainable over the long term.

Actual statements I've overheard:

"Innovation is something those other folks do, not us."
"Why would a customer trust another customer's review more than us?"
"Social media, that Facebook and Twitter, is for kids with too much time."
"We don't need to adopt a social agenda."
"I see no reason to change how we operate just because customers want us to."

How could you crash your organization, you might ask? Of course, not on purpose, but there are those leaders who will not innovate or who resist deep change and are looking to the past to know what will happen in the future. This is dysfunctional thinking—the opposite of being Future Smart. Not surprisingly, this type of thinking, which is not sustainable, is the enemy of business growth.

THE TOP TEN WAYS TO RESIST THE FUTURE

1. Ignore investing in new technologies and innovation such as mobile, social media, or cloud computing.
2. Stop listening to customers' needs and complaints.
3. Ignore the redesign of your business processes.
4. Limit your future vision to the next quarter.
5. Don't hire talent that wants to change, innovate, or grow.
6. Think that your competition is slower or less innovative.
7. Believe that customers are not interested in innovation.
8. Build a culture that resists innovation daily.
9. Think that the future will look just like the past.
10. Don't build a learning, collaborating, connected organization.

Now the point is that no one would purposely set out to resist the future, ignore change, or crash their organization, would they? Of course not—that sounds absurd. Yet everyday most organizations, big or small, expend energy on working hard to accomplish one or more of the Ten Top Ways to Crash Your Organization. I see it every day. Many organizations just don't get it, and that is great for companies such as mine, which advise companies that are stuck and struggling with dysfunctional business behaviors and want to change.

Many more organizations just continue to resist the changes that have come and are coming, and they think that the head-in-the-sand strategy is sustainable, but it is not. This lack of insight into the Predictive Awareness that being Future Smart is about has held back entire industries.

I often hear from leaders of teams and organizations who could change if they understood the impact but don't choose to change. They resist the future. They will let the next guy take care of that. But there will not be another leader to always step in and save the day. Leaders who avoid dealing with the hard realities of the future marketplace or disruptive forces of change, such as technology, do a great disservice to their organizations by not looking forward.

By avoiding decisions that could help make the organization more Future Smart—ready for the future challenges that are coming by investing and growing talent and innovation today—these leaders doom their companies to the trash heap of history. It does not need to be like this. Organizations need to develop and educate their people to become Future Smart—agile and ready for what's coming. This is a shift in mindset, culture, and behavior, not just some words on the computer screen.

The Annual Future Smart Awards:
Who Got It Right

There are leaders and companies that demonstrate the ideals of being Future Smart today. The common elements are an attention to innovation, bold new visions of the future, and a focus on creating new ideas that form new markets not envisioned before. Some of these are:

- Elon Musk from Tesla and Space X, who invented the electric car and private-space industry by not following everyone else but instead creating agile new innovation projects.
- Virgin Galactic, who decided that the space tourism market was real and invested early to create the first consumer space industry.
- Craig Venter, who mapped the human genome and went on to invent an artificial cell that is destined to transform health care.
- Ratan Tata, who bought and redesigned the classic Jaguar car and built a global empire of innovation industries based on cool designs.
- Apple Computer, for never compromising on future design and innovations that lead the market in music, phones, and computing.
- Alibaba, which developed a combination of Amazon and eBay all rolled into one in a huge China-focused company that offers probably the largest Innovation Ecosystem in the world.
- Amazon, the largest book and media seller in the world that redefined the online retail experience.
- Netflix, which broke the movie business distribution paradigm by offering direct downloads first, producing direct-to-consumer shows, and captured the market.
- Google, which transformed the advertising industry by creating a digital juggernaut based on giving away software services online and watching, analyzing, and predicting what consumers want.
- Salesforce.com, which realized that sales had shifted to the cloud and thus empowered tools to reinvigorate the virtual business offered.

TEN GAME-CHANGING POWER SHIFTS EVERY BUSINESS MUST PREPARE FOR TODAY

1. Social media impact on the enterprise
2. The coming Data Tsunami
3. Cyber Risks and industrial espionage
4. Purpose before profit business strategies
5. Geo-intelligence as a business enabler

6. Wearables, drones, and flyables as new business models
7. Attracting and keeping Future Smart talent
8. Building and using Innovation Ecosystems
9. Mobile and the Internet of Things as markets
10. Impact of customer's Big Data on the enterprise

How to Create Your Competition

This is an easy forecast because the logic is impeccable and easily proven. I have seen this dozens of times: The company that refused to create a customer portal or offer computerized online billing. Ignoring customers' demands for new services to help streamline productivity. Being irresponsive to customers' value shifts, such as sustainability, cultural diversity, or social accountability.

Most companies create their own competition because they are not being Future Smart. They are not working on adapting for the future; they resist change, avoid innovation, or don't plan for what's coming. They miss how the market is changing. They don't really listen to customers' needs and how they're changing. They avoid the front-line employee feedback about what new services are needed. They avoid having to change, and in so doing, they create their own competition.

No one has a death wish, but most companies who are conducting "business as usual" will not make the final cut when it comes to competing in the New Future. Too much resistance to change is deadly. Denial is not a management competency that helps you look to the future. Innovations like mobile commerce, cloud networks, predictive analytics, and Big Data are not cool innovations—they are how business is conducted in the New Future of one minute from now.

This is not the standard of excellence but rather Business 101. If you are reading this in 2015 and this makes no sense, then I humbly suggest you do a lot of thinking. Read the rest of the book first, then go invent your future.

Lessons from the Start-Up Economy

I have enjoyed my work over many years with both start-up companies and big organizations that wanted to learn how to become more like start-up companies. Having an unfair advantage to have grown up in Silicon Valley, first working at Apple Computer in the early days and then with numerous start-up companies, I have come to realize that big companies will not be sustainable unless they become more entrepreneurial, especially as we move into the New Future. Being sustainable, adaptive, and predictive is at the core of what this book is about.

Forecast: The Future Smart Enterprise must embrace the Start-Up Economy and change their work cultures and business models, or they will not survive. The cultures of a start-up company—to learn, experiment, have passion for innovation—are values every company should embrace.

We see this radical game-changing shift starting, but as we move into the future of five to ten years from today, it will be unfortunate if organizations don't change quickly enough. I don't think leaders understand how fundamentally important this transformation is, and I don't think business leaders understand how to get there, how important it is to embrace the Start-up Economy now.

Most of the failures and problems I have seen in business, with large corporations, is that they develop an entrenched and hardened culture that too often resists innovation, cannot attract or retain the top talent, and loses its way when it comes to dealing with accelerated change initiated by consumer, marketplace, or technological factors. They cannot seem to get out of their own way.

TEN LESSONS FOR BUILDING A FUTURE-SMART ORGANIZATION

1. Be curious—be persistent in embracing innovations.
2. Innovate or die—spawn a culture of consistent innovation.
3. Fail fast and frequently—failures are part of learning.
4. Embrace leading-edge tech—before your competition does.
5. Pay attention—to how and why customers are changing.
6. Get the talent-to-job fit right.
7. Find out what do customers and employees need to better prepare for the future.
8. Investigate how your industry is trending—looking to the future.
9. Create brief strategic plan to map your new business strategy.
10. Consider how leaders, teams, and culture could be Future Smart—ready to adapt to future changes.

Twitter had failed in their first business model and, as a backup, had this idea about texting short messages over a network. It was not the first big idea, and they were on their way out of business because the first idea failed to catch on with consumers and investors. Now they are the social media platform for collaborating with short communications.

Google didn't even have their own search engine when they started the company. This evolved later. Now they own the search market.

Apple's Lisa Computer was too expensive and failed to catch on with consumers, almost leading the company into bankruptcy. Macintosh was born out of that experimentation, as was iTunes and the iPhone.

GE, an industrial giant in energy, reinvented itself as an innovative leader in addressing the global ecological challenges that had been a risk factor for them in the past.

IBM got out of the declining PC business to focus on business services and innovative new technologies such as cognitive computing, cloud computing, and Audi, which was once known for quality issues but now makes some of the highest-quality and well-designed autos in the world.

Seeing the Invisible

Experimentation. Persistence. The ability to see the invisible. That is what Future Smart companies do, but the most important thing they do is that they Shape the Future through a strategy, business model, product, or service. They Shape the Future of what is possible by creating value that the customer embraces. The action that validates the value is more than sales revenues; it is a Customer Engagement Experience that rewards the company and the customer. It is a collaborative culture of exchange, well beyond the traditional supply and demand, of "we make a product and you buy it."

Google does this by constantly tweaking their programming to offer more personalized and relevant information when you search for something. Amazon, working invisibly in the background, watches what you like—in books or products—and then instantly crowdsources with a recommendation software agent that matches people with likes: people who bought this book about magic also bought this magic wand.

Companies' ability to leverage the invisible to better engage, predict, and present offers or information that are personalized just for you is an essential strategy. Most people who use Google or Amazon don't see it; it's not obvious what these companies are doing to create Knowledge Value.

In the future, organizations that understand that the rules are changing and know how to be attentive to and understand these New Rules will grow their organizations, be they large or small, into successful Future Smart companies.

Future Smart Leadership

The central challenge facing organizations is how to lead in an era of accelerating change, radical exponential technologies, and innovative business models that offer both risk and opportunity. You cannot look to history and think leadership of the past will be the same in the future. This type of reactionary thinking will doom leaders to lead poorly or even to collapse organizations.

There are many examples of leaders who attempted to lead by following the old rules and were out of step with the current reality or were not prepared for the future. Not being prepared for the future is the most common and lethal

strategic error that leaders can make. Unfortunately, this strategic error is too common and results in an organization's decline. Organizations' decline is due exclusively to their inability to see what's coming next, to envision the future, and to being capable of acting on making that future vision a reality.

The Future-Smart Leader thinks differently. His or her mindset is about being ready for innovation, being hungry for change, being willing to learn, being ready to adapt, and even being competent at shaping a preferred future for the organization or even the entire industry. Leaders lead others into unknown waters where, inevitably, they need to change in order to transform the organization into something better, bigger, and more successful for the future. Future-Smart Leaders have a future plan. They recognize that it takes a plan to get from today to tomorrow. It's amazing how few leaders have a plan for the future. Their time frame for adapting and planning for the future is the next few months. This is short sighted.

Future-Smart Leaders are bold in marshaling their troops to go after a big objective that may stir the soul or seem impossible or even chock-full of hubris. That's what sets great leaders apart from the common fare. Future-Smart Leaders have a vision for the future that they enroll others to embrace, collaborate on, and contribute to making a reality.

They inspire greatness in others and evangelize the future vision. They embrace new talent and change the organization's culture, structure, and work processes to attract and retain talent. This is a different way of leading from what we see today. Most leaders mold the employee to the company culture; in the future this will be reversed.

Future-Smart Leaders are unafraid of the future; they embrace the changes that are coming. They shape the future. They are inventors of tomorrow, pioneers of the future. They are the Bransons who dreamt of a different type of airline, The Elon Musks who invented an entirely new electric car. Space X that took us to space. The Steve Jobs who saw the future of music and built the iTunes store. All around us there are examples of Future-Smart Leaders who are creating the future—a better future for their customers and the world.

Future-Smart Leaders must forge a bold vision of the future they wish to create. This is different from the dominant paradigm of leadership today. Future-Smart Leaders will have evolved a new set of values that embraces purpose, sustainability, and innovation, and most of all, these leaders will have a compelling vision of the future.

GAME-CHANGING BUSINESS TRENDS

- Managing Knowledge-Value will be the growth engine for business.
- High-level talent, the people who will be required to manage the complex organizations of the future, must be developed.

- Smart Machines will design, manage, and service 40 percent of all global businesses by 2025—utilities, commerce, finance, and manufacturing.
- Smart Machines that enable humans and provide value will be a competitive advantage in the global economy—right up until they take your job. Maybe.
- Managing the Future Data Tsunami from the collection of health, media, web, financial, social, and geospatial sources will be a competitive advantage for every enterprise.
- Organizations must become learning networks, constantly upgrading and enhancing the collective intelligence of their work cultures.
- Companies that embrace Big Data, analytics, and the cloud will be prepared for the future explosion of customer demand.

You're either managing your future or someone else is because they are moving faster and smarter or innovating in ways you're not. Becoming a Future-Smart Enterprise is a change process and a learning strategy to get from where you are to not just being ready for the future but also actively designing your future. The choice is yours.

Chapter 4

The Social Enterprise of the Future

Meeting Grand Challenges

Taking on the Grand Challenges of our world—global poverty, violence and national conflicts, climate change, pollution, health care, social injustice—is going to be more prominent as a trend in the future than it is even today. Every business must become a social enterprise and embrace a higher purpose in order to conduct business, compete, and relate to the changing customer.

Customers are driving change. Most customers will expect, if not demand, that every business has a social purpose—to make our world a better and more just world. Understand this and thrive; go against this, and you threaten the very core of how customers will evaluate a business.

If in the future every product and service is a commodity due to technology and production efficiencies, then the social issues of purpose that a company embraces may be the only ways a company can competitively distinguish itself in the minds of the Empowered Customer—the majority of customers on the planet by 2020.

Where governments may fail to address climate change or slavery, consumers will expect business to take the lead and make a difference. You really don't want to get this wrong. This will be a reaction to most governments that drop the ball and do not lead in either cleaning up, protecting, or preventing issues, such as climate change and poverty, or supporting issues, such as alternative energy, economic equality, and other pressing social agendas. Consumers will demand that if they buy your products and services, *you need to care about what they care about.*

Companies that care about what their customers care about will have a competitive advantage in the marketplace. The trick is to find out what social issues and concerns your customers share. Every business must learn to listen, adopt, and care about what their customers care about, or they are doomed.

Business leaders that put profit before social purpose will find a tough battle in retaining and attracting talent as well as in surviving as a business if their customers' expectations are ignored. This trend has already emerged but is not as comprehensively accepted across the world as yet. In the future—five to ten years forward—only the businesses that change their practices and embrace the values of the Social Enterprise will be able to compete effectively.

Headlines from the Future: 2025
Know Your Future Customers!
Prediction Industry Now Dominates 80% of Business

Business with a Higher Purpose

Every business in the future must embrace a Higher Purpose or else they will not be able to compete given customers' changing attitudes and values. The marketplace and customers are changing, and business must keep up. A Future Smart organization takes on improvements in human, social, and environmental sustainability rather than only maximizing profits for shareholders. They enable Social Capital, which uplifts societies, individuals, and communities.

Social Capital is a values-based asset that is as important as human capital or money. Future Smart companies have a higher purpose beyond just making money as the sole endgame. Making a difference, not for show but instead as the core business value of an organization, is how this business framework sets itself apart.

In fact, it is not hard to predict that Future Smart enterprises that follow this Purpose-Before-Profit strategy and embrace a Higher Purpose will actually be highly profitable and successful because they will be in sync with the changing needs of the marketplace and customers will prefer them. Customers will reward companies that signal that they care about the social accountability agenda and are doing something about it. This is a path to monetize a Higher Purpose.

The company Zappos understands this already. Zappos built a business culture based on purpose over money and has become wildly successful, with over $1 billion in sales. Part of this is due to its social commitment to core values, which attracts both customers and employees. The founder, Tony Hsieh, left an earlier company because they had not built a culture based on a purpose beyond money. This is a fundamental ingredient of what the future of every business should embrace: giving back, a Higher Purpose, may, in the future, be more important than innovation, profits, and success, as it says something about your organization's values.

I advise every enterprise to consider that this trend, these Future Smart enterprise values, will drastically alter the competitive landscape of business. Companies that embrace this model will thrive and survive the changes in the global economy ahead. They will better weather the storms of change and disruption in the markets. Those that don't will have a disadvantage at some point or miss an opportunity.

Our research and forecasts have revealed that there is a social and ethical shift in the marketplace happening. This research started with studies conducted for IBM on trends in the marketplace, and it found that customers expect organizations to do the right thing, the ethically appropriate thing. After the 2008 global economic crisis a massive consumer rethinking occurred; new values emerged.

There was a sense, still unresolved, that opportunity that was once clearly available because of a more level playing field for all individuals was no longer available. Consumers' trust of all institutions, both government and corporate, has eroded, and the use of social media, by which consumers trust consumers more, has fueled this distrust. This power shift is part of a restructuring of trust that is playing out with this rising trend.

Social Purpose First

The era of profit without Higher Purpose may be over for many customer-facing organizations hoping to attract customers' loyalty and wallet share. This is a trend that cannot be ignored. The demands of the marketplace, of both employees and customers, will shape the destiny of every business. With over 90 percent of the customers today embracing values of people and purpose over profit, it is certain that in the future every business must be aware of this social agenda.

Organizations that are committed to making the world a better place, who understand that the role of business is to be socially accountable, will be the Future Smart leaders in the future. In fact, the defining risk factor for businesses is to come to understand, predict, and adapt to the demands of employees and customers to embrace social accountability as a business competency, one that is not outside but rather inside the enterprise. How well an organization "owns" this Sustainable Planet Trend may define their own destiny as a business. If they consider how sustainability affects their supply chain, their workers, their materials, and their social commitments to giving back to society, this will all affect their identity as a responsible or irresponsible company. Companies that pay lip service to this trend may do so at their own peril—the customer has awoken to this social value and expects companies to be Game Changers of the Future. This is the new standard for business that is emerging now and will shape the future of every company.

What this means is that every organization must be a steward for the future of the planet—a nonpolluter, a nonexploiter of people, and a contributor to a sustainable planet. This is Future Smart. Business in the future must have a chief innovation competency that is focused on making a social and environmental difference that is acceptable to both customers and employees.

Without this awareness and action plan every business will be operating at a risk that is simply illogical given the rising demands and change in social values on the planet. Business can and must be the leader of the social agenda in which social accountability for everything that is produced, bought, or sold has a fair, equitable, ethical, and sustainable component. If this sounds to you like a tall order—to balance profit and sustainability—welcome to the reality of the New Future. Embrace it and thrive. Reject it, and you will suffer the consequences. Companies such as BP, after the US Gulf oil spill disaster, learned this lesson quickly. You want to be on the right side of this trend.

Get this right, and you will remove a Big Risk Factor. Get it wrong, and it's clean-up time—if your business can even recover from making such a huge error. Heads will roll, and they should. Any business that is not planning to seriously transform into a socially relevant business with a purpose is not going to adapt and survive in the future. Sure, there will be plenty of backwater locations where avoiding social responsibility will enable you to survive, but not for long and not in an increasingly competitive global economy.

What every business must consider: by 2015 there will be little argument that climate change is real, fossil fuel energy is polluting the planet, and environmental factors that affect our and the planet's health are on the rise. It is clear that social accountability and issues such as valuing diversity at work are of paramount importance to employees, partners, and customers. Every organization lives in a social media window through which billions can see in. Transparency is in real time and unforgiving. You want to get this right.

The only questions that remain are what we are going to do about it. What actions will businesses take to assume responsibility for change? How will we apply innovation in order to solve the Grand Challenges of our time? How will customers in every market reward that brand they buy from with loyalty or reject it based on the company's actions?

Like it or not, this trend tips the scale for business in the New Future. You could be the fastest innovator with great new products that are cool and cost effective, but if you are not a business with a Higher Purpose, you are history. The Future Smart Enterprise works with a purpose and everyone knows it. Companies that reject striking a balance between profit and purpose, who do not embrace efforts to address poverty, inequality, disease, and other global challenges risk being run aground by customers, media, and, most important, employees who will increasingly share their wallets, attention, and talents only with businesses with a social purpose.

The Millennium Goals

The role of business in changing the future and in crafting a better world cannot be overestimated. The problem is that too few companies are doing enough today. Tomorrow this will be the norm or you will go out of business. I would maintain it is the private sector that can and should lead the way to business with a purpose to address authentic social change. More private-sector organizations are endorsing a new global mandate set by leaders of both the private and the public sector at the United Nations. It is a bold plan for every business to follow and make efforts to include these goals into their business strategy and actions.

The Millennium Goals are a set of eight goals that world leaders at the UN Millennium Summit in 2000 embraced with the aim of addressing major global issues such as poverty, sustainability, and education. Leaders agreed on set targets to be met for each priority as early as 2015. The eight Millennium Development Goals (MDGs) form a blueprint to which all of the world's leaders have agreed. (See "Millennium Development Goals," United Nations, www .un.org/millenniumgoals.)

These goals have increased awareness and supported efforts not only to meet the needs of the world's poorest but also to align leaders in the private and public sectors to think and act differently so as to build a better, more equitable future. There is still much work to be done.

THE EIGHT MILLENNIUM GOALS ARE:

1. Eradicate extreme poverty and hunger.
2. Achieve universal primary education.
3. Promote gender equality and empower women.
4. Reduce child mortality.
5. Improve maternal health.
6. Combat HIV/AIDS, malaria, and other diseases.
7. Ensure environmental sustainability.
8. Global partnership for development.

The Empowered Customer

An additional framework through which to examine the future customer is the Empowered Customer. This customer should be an important element for every business in the New Future to pay attention to. You will want to understand the Empowered Customer if you are to succeed in the future of business. I noticed the values shift emerging in the marketplace, in the attitudes first of

Generation X and then the Millennials as it became clear that there was an important shift in social values emerging.

Keep in mind that if you are reading this book in 2015 to 2020, there is still a large share of the workforce who are Baby Boomers, though they are retiring quickly. Behind them is Generation X, but it is the Millennials who are most inclined to be the Empowered Customer, and they will make up 70 percent of the workforce in the United States, the EU, and, eventually, Asia.

THE EMPOWERED CUSTOMER IS DISTINGUISHED BY THE FOLLOWING VALUES THAT THEY EXPECT OF BUSINESSES THEY SUPPORT

- The company must care about my concerns for social issues and the environment.
- The company must be working to make the world a better place through committed social actions.
- The company must believe as I do that business should lead in making the world a better place.
- The company must care about what I care about—the environment, social issues, equality, diversity, and so forth.
- The company must be fair and equitable about their people practices.

The key takeaway we can glean from the Empowered Customer is that they will expect businesses that they buy from to adopt a social agenda with a purpose, to make a positive socially relevant difference in the world. This customer segment will be global and, for the most part, Millennial.

They will make up the majority of both the workforce and the marketplace in the New Future. You must consider the implications of listening to both your future customers and your future employees or outsourced freelancers. Future Smart enterprises must listen in order to hone their prediction strategies, as this will be a central competitive advantage in the New Future.

A New Business Mindset

Future Smart leaders today are setting a new mindset and model for business. They are influencing what the future of the enterprise may look like in five to ten years. Though it is early in this evolution to a new corporate model, many organizations have established leadership. Companies such as GE, which made dramatic changes so as to lead sustainability; Apple, which made changes to its supply chain to increase fairness and accountability; and J.P. Morgan, which

directs certain investments for social endeavors; as well as many other big companies do make a social difference every day.

I forecast that Future Smart leaders will influence all enterprises in the future as traditional business will embrace this model—giving back, making a difference, and using this social commitment to attract customers and employees. Today there is a growing group of enterprises, mostly nonprofits, that demonstrates a hybrid model that will morph and change traditional business.

Be Accountable, Be Future Smart

The Social Enterprise trend will change the corporate model. You want to get in front of this trend. This is relevant today, as many companies are rethinking their social accountability, environmental sustainability policies: Is it enough? Is it right as a strategy? As companies also rethink their products and service impact on their community and the world, new types of business models, such as Social Enterprises, may influence their planning for the future.

Companies such as Starbucks, Disney, Coke, J.P. Morgan, and Tata have made major shifts toward becoming more Social Enterprise oriented. In the future we will see more Future Smart Enterprises that will give back and make a difference as well as make a profit—do good and do well.

The Future Smart Enterprise

A new type of business entity is being created that looks to the future, that predicts, adapts, learns, and is fueled by entrepreneurs who leverage innovation and leading-edge technologies to create outstanding value for customers. This new paradigm of business, the Future Smart Enterprise, is based on leveraging technology and digital tools, moving with agility and velocity, embracing change, attracting innovation, and developing a capacity to predict and invent the future.

Here are some of the other differences in how Future Smart Enterprises differ from traditional organizations:

POWER SHIFTS FROM THE TRADITIONAL TO THE FUTURE SMART ORGANIZATION

Top-down power to Distributed power
Profit only to Higher Purpose
Work performance to Innovation and Knowledge Value
Hierarchical organization to Network organization

Reactive to change to Predictive of change
Compliance culture to Innovation culture
Customer service to Customer engagement
Innovation resistant to Leading innovation
Employee mindset to Entrepreneur mindset
Controlled information to Open information
Silos of operation to Integrated operations

The Future Smart Enterprise: Empower Me

The Empower Me trend will redefine the fundamental relationship between employees and customers. You're either Empowering Me, your customer or employee, to be effective and successful and to thrive, and address my social agenda to make my world better, or you are not. Every organization that understands this fundamental shift in the relationship between business and the customer can then move to develop a powerful business strategy to answer this question—how can you Empower Me?

Customers' and employees' values will shape the future of business more so than even technology in the near and far future. Customer and employee shifts in values predict what they want from the businesses they buy from or work for, and they want to know what these businesses believe in. The key transformation of business will be that businesses will be expected to have a Higher Purpose: they must be sustainable, preparing everyone for the future, socially responsible. The key difference is that the Future Smart enterprise is taking a stand on empowering its customers and employees to be ready for the future, to enable social empowerment to make productive changes to better the world.

There may be some organizations in failed states or backwaters that truly don't give a damn about anything more than profits, but the shifting values of the marketplace, especially that of Generation X and the Millennial, will demand that every business be a Social Enterprise.

What this means is that consumers will expect businesses to lead and shape the future of a Sustainable Planet. This is not about words in a mission statement that 90 percent of businesses have today; rather, this is about committed actions by businesses to do what governments have not done and what customers expect—leadership for the future. In the future people will want to see businesses lead the way toward a more purposeful world.

Business leaders who understand that they must embrace how the market is changing, what Generation X and Millennials believe, will create the future of the marketplace. This will require Future Smart organizations to take specific and measurable actions to make this a better world. Only then will they speak the language of the future workforce.

Keep in mind that customers are watching for this values shift. Make money AND make a difference in the world that has nothing to do with money. Customers are looking for businesses to restore their trust in the basic relationships customers have with organizations. The trajectory from mistrust to trust, for brands and companies to understand their customers, may well define your future.

Chapter 5

The New Future of the Economy

Modern economics needs an upgrade. We need a New Future of Economics to enable us to better predict and prevent economic crises, stimulate growth, create more jobs, and, especially, incorporate innovation into economic thinking. There is one big question I don't think economists are well equipped to answer: What is the role of knowledge, innovation, and technology in creating economic value for the future?

You can't get ten economists to agree with each other about the state of the economy—good luck getting economists to forecast the future of the economy. Economics makes most folks feel bewildered because there is so much complexity and so little clarity.

Economics doesn't address many of the key change drivers that are shaping our world or will prepare us for the future. Some of my best friends are economists, and in their defense, they don't completely disagree with me; it is just that what we need economics to do, it cannot: forecast what's coming and how to deal with it in order to prosper.

Now, before I charge on here, you might well ask: Why do I care? Our economic system will shape much of what will affect our future. Economics is about distributing goods, labor, money, markets, and industries. Economics should also be about how to run the economy better—stimulate growth, enable jobs, support business, and avoid risk. If you want to become Future Smart, then you need to prepare for the future by understanding how economics will enable you to better predict the changes that are coming.

Economists struggle with this forecasting business because their capacity to predict with precision is, frankly, limited. They can explain the economy, but they have a spotty record on prediction. The last global crisis in 2008 was an example of heroic after-the-collapse fixing of a dangerous global event that

could have created a massive financial meltdown (which it did, but not to the extent it could have).

You might ask now: Why didn't our economists—any economists—predict this? Or, to be even bolder, why did they not *prevent* this crisis? The simple answer is that they would have if they could have. This is the point of this book.

Being predictive about the future may well protect and preserve that future. The answer is that economics is not equipped to deal with the massive and complex modern social and technological scenarios that create economic change that shape the data on capital, jobs, currency, trade, commodities, and stock markets, to name a few factors. Bubbles about to burst—such as what occurred during the 2008 financial crisis—the dot-com blowout, or the inflated housing market usually are recognized after they all dive, not well before the crisis emerges. This has historically been a problem for economists.

We need to make economics Future Smart—able to predict and prevent risk factors that might take down national or global economies. Also, if we could create this Predictive Economics, we might be able to figure out with accuracy how to generate jobs and revitalize an economy. I cannot think of anyone who could argue against that desire for upgrading economics. And the likelihood is that another global financial crisis is brewing, but how would we really know? The only logical challenge is to understand how we can upgrade economics and make it predictive by incorporating key trends like innovation industries that are creating new capital, productivity, jobs, and wealth.

Let's consider what is *not* well integrated into economics, what they don't consider, what is outside of their awareness but that they should look at. Technology, networks, connectivity, innovation, energy, supercomputers, big data, and globalization are not well considered—in fact, they are left out of economic analyses. Economics is, for the most part, a hodgepodge of market, capitalist, or socialist theories based on who you are and where you are in the world. Though the basic relevant elements, such as the nature of labor, wealth, and supply and demand, are similar, the very nature of what makes up an economy has changed fundamentally over the past few decades.

Technology industries have changed wealth creation and jobs growth. Globalization and capital flows among nations have altered markets and productivity. An alternative energy economy will emerge in the future, and economic analyses should recognize that nontraditional drivers of what constitutes an economy are important to understand. And different economic models, with various blending of social welfare and market economies, persist around the planet.

Economists have not kept up, and even the postindustrial nod to technology (i.e., after the Industrial Revolution) is not enough to help prepare us for the future. How we know economics needs an upgrade is that the advanced economies of the world, chiefly now in North America, Europe, and

Asia (though tomorrow in perhaps Africa and Southeast Asia)—the catalysts of the global economy—are facing uncertainty, higher unemployment, low productivity, and slower growth, and there is little that current economic theory can do to predict what may come and what we should do now.

These economies face problems such as chronic unemployment, resistance to growth, attacks on free enterprise, tight capital markets, asset-value erosion, and an overreliance on government stimulus, or not enough stimulus. If these economies continue to fail to recognize that the world has changed so we had best alter our economic theories to embrace these changes, then there is trouble ahead—not just the proverbial head winds that economists like to talk about, but serious social challenges. The test for the validity of economics is how well it prepares us for the future, how well it helps us avoid and prevent economic crises, and how well we can address current problems effectively.

High Finance Meet High Technology

The credit that economists should get on the actions taken once crises have emerged is notable but inferior to being able to predict and prevent crises. Ironically the very things that economists fail to understand—technology's role in the economy, jobs, and prosperity—is what may save modern economics. Advanced supercomputers that can simulate Big Data to model economies and create multiple network-based scenarios to then predict outcomes and prevent risks would be the very tool set that modern economists should embrace.

High finance has not met high technology, and it should. We need a mash-up—the convergence of computer science, networking, and economics—like a climate-changed planet needs a global air conditioner on hot day in Dallas. Data science needs to enable economists to build Predictive Economic Models to better forecast risk by understanding the massive data complexity of factors that make up the economy. Supercomputers that model the extreme complexity of astrophysics and nuclear war can certainly also focus on creating the New Future of the Global Economy.

Beyond predicting risk as well as the next global crisis, this would be useful in order to better understand how to design a more productive, employment-rich, innovation-driven, purposeful economy based on Uber-Prosperity. There is no possibility of designing a New Future for the economy unless we use Big Data, cloud computing, data science, computer science, the Internet, and computer simulations to create a Predictive Global Economic Model.

We cannot model all of the complexity, huge data sets, machine intelligence, infinite scenarios, job info, trade, economic, social, and financial information to simulate the future without building an entirely new way to model economics. And we need to add in all of the factors that economists leave out of their models that they don't use today, including technology, networks, knowledge

innovations, new digital business models, mobile, and connected systems. You get the idea. We need to disrupt economies to make it relevant for creating the future economy we desire.

Some steps in the right direction demonstrate the viability of this strategy: Google Trends data was useful in predicting daily price moves in the Dow Jones industrial average, which consists of thirty stocks. Research has found identifying trends by looking at the effects of media information on price changes in stock exchange markets as a predictor of the economic performance of markets.

My own organization's use of news, social media, big data, and web sources to forecast global risk, business, social sentiment, and behavior trends—a system called Trend Trakker—has further explored how forecasting select trends is possible from large data sets. But no one as yet has modeled the complexity of Big Data in the global economy as I am suggesting with a comprehensive, predictive, real-time, Big Data simulation that we could all benefit from in order to manage risk, predict how economies will behave, or prevent the next crisis as a consistent deliverable.

Companies that crunch big data, such as Bottlenose (http://bottlenose.com), focus on examining the social media and media universe. They show the potential for expanding our understanding of complex trends and prediction. The Sonar product from Bottlenose also examines global risk factors that have become useful for brands and companies to consider what is going on where, by who, and what it may mean. Large firehouse analytics that are focused on the now make Bottlenose a valuable resource to gain actionable insight into the global mind via what topics are trending. This is a step up substantially from what Twitter, Google, and Facebook provide.

Blab (http://blabpredicts.com), a company in the social media prediction market, also mines multiple terabytes of data but focuses on prediction for brands. Blab predicts over the next seventy-two hours what will occur or what the conversation will be like, again over social media. This claim for identifying what will be trending is an interesting new take on the Big Data industry, and as with all deep learning systems, it evolves. There is potential for applying these global online social media tools to create predictive economics.

The emergence of Smart Machines—networked computer intelligences— may enable us to model larger data sets, such as the Global Economy Model I suggest. Once directed, Smart Machines will be able to crunch exabytes of data in order to analyze multiple complex scenarios and identify patterns that today defy human perception. Black boxes, a code word for the special-purpose computers that analyze opportunities that humans do not find, could be better used by economists, not just their brothers-in-arms who use these tools for high-speed trading at the local hedge fund. I suspect they will begin to use this technology, especially as the increased sophistication of the financial markets challenges economists to look forward rather than backward.

Our ability to stimulate markets and resolve these problems is failing in great part because we don't fully understand how the global economy has changed, especially in the advanced nations, which have been the largest contributors of global GDP. But perhaps this won't be so in the future when developing economies surge. It's like when older doctors resist noninvasive robotic surgery and other technological innovations that would lead to healthier patients and billions of dollars saved because these advances required skills they did not have or understand the value of.

It's tough to convey how economics needs to change when you're looking in the rearview mirror of what worked just fine and your power and expertise are based on a set of ideas and mindsets that most believe in—even if they're wrong. Adam Smith is turning over in his grave.

In an era of fast change, when innovations disrupt every traditional rule and mindset, the disaster may be that we wait too long to adopt a new mindset and that we are unfit to adapt, learn, and predict. We don't see or imagine what is possible because we refuse to see it. This is what is happening in economics. Time to hack economics?

Economic theories that involve the redistribution of wealth through taxation may be politically popular in Europe but have little to do with driving new investment, producing jobs, stimulating authentic productivity, attracting capital, and—the largest factor inventing the future—transforming economies by investing in building technology-rich economies and Innovation Ecosystems that create value that generates wealth, jobs, and new business formation. Somebody just has to tell the truth here.

Sorry to tell my European friends who have been preaching the dystopian end of capitalism for ten years, but if there were a better way to grow an economy, lift up the fortunes of citizens, increase jobs and productivity, I don't see it yet. And in all fairness, the US model of capitalism needs a refresh as well if it is to shape a prosperous New Future of Economics.

The elephant in the room—and the driving change in business—is technology. Social media, nanotech, cognitive computing, genetics, networks—technological innovations have been and shall be the chief shapers of the economy. This is where we will find the jobs, the start-up companies, the new markets, and the new customers. There are few mainstream economists who have integrated this essential shaper of the economy into economics. This is, of course, amazing, as the trillions of dollars and Euros of new wealth creation attributed to technology businesses is clear, yet economists have not rallied to embrace a new economic model that integrates technology as a creator of new value, wealth, and business.

Yet our economic theories have not really been altered so that we can both recognize and integrate technology and innovation into new economic theories. And if there is a smarter way to create more equality, which is such a rage, other

than stimulating growth, educating people, and investing in tech innovation–based industries, I have not seen it.

The idea of taxing the successful to achieve equality rather than investing in job training, education, and innovation R&D seems illogical. We need a million Silicon Valleys if we are to transform the world to give equality a chance, to create a level playing field of education and quality of life by growing a billion new jobs, industries, or entrepreneurs. Government investments with the private sector to create the next high tech powerhouses that will generate jobs should be the focus of government—or just get out of the way and allow the private sector, the unfettered market, and free enterprise do what it does best—create widespread prosperity, innovation, and wealth.

Some evidence: the relationships of innovation to jobs, capital, and labor are not well understood. In fact, after all of the trillions of wealth creation and new enterprises, digital markets, and e-commerce that we have all observed (Apple is the largest company in the world in value), economists are still refusing to upgrade their dismal science to embrace the obvious. Technology has had an *immense* economic impact and shall continue to affect jobs, growth, markets, productivity, asset values—all of the stuff that makes up an economy. Technology as a contributor of the economy is a value driver and a wealth and job creator that should be altering the very fundamentals of economics.

I hashed this out with a friend, a former Harvard professor and White House economic head. I railed on about why economics doesn't integrate technology and innovations into economic theory. Though he was sympathetic, I was not making any progress with him, as logical as I thought I was being. The point is that we need new economic thinking to get ready for the future. And we need leaders who understand this to do some critical new thinking about stimulating economies, jobs, and prosperity—before the next war takes this off our minds, which has been the case every few decades, like clockwork.

Neuro-economics and behavioral economics are also not factored into modern economics. The authentic ROI, return on innovation, cannot be measured if economists are not looking at it as a metric; instead, they are looking at the traditional paradigm about economics, but that era is over. Even the newest ideas about factoring in innovation's impact on markets have not been well received or are used inconsistently.

We need fresh thinking about a New Economics for the New Future we are creating through the rapid explosion of innovations on the near horizon. The Nano-Economy—a microeconomy with an underlying value driver of the larger economy—is one example.

The nanotech microeconomy is the global market value of the over $1 trillion worth of jobs, markets, and products that design matter at the atomic scale, using nano-materials. The Microeconomies of the Future may be a more accurate perception of the economic drivers of business, wealth creation, jobs, and

capital. Microeconomies are global and have the distinction of having some primary technology at the core of the economy that will generate new opportunities for job, enterprise, and wealth creation.

Microeconomies may be more important to understand as Capital Attractors that shape opportunity so public policy makers, venture investors, job seekers, and entrepreneurs can invest in these fast-growth Microeconomies. By investing in resources to stimulate jobs, education, and new ventures around the Microeconomies of the Future, this will stimulate jobs and global competitiveness and steer education in the right direction. Here is a sampling of the Microeconomies of the Future that I forecast will generate the most revenues, innovations, new organizations, and jobs.

They represent in global value (revenues, jobs, investment, research) over $7 trillion in US dollars today, increasing to over $10 trillion by 2025. Here is a global forecast of where to invest, what to start that new business in, or what next career or job might be Future Smart to pursue.

THE GLOBAL MICROECONOMIES OF THE FUTURE

- The Nanotech Economy
- The Mobile Economy
- The Neuro-Economy
- The Drone Economy
- The Cloud Computing Economy
- The Renewable Energy Economy
- The Smart Machine Economy
- The Connected Economy
- The Big Data Analytics Economy
- The Health Enhancement Economy
- The Knowledge Engineering Economy

Together these Microeconomies are the shapers of the future Global Innovation Economy. Microeconomies are smaller representations of the total economy. They act as economic drivers of change and are often not well understood or are not viewed as valuable in traditional economic thinking. Perhaps if we understood these Microeconomies as shapers of future change, we would be more Future Smart about stimulating future opportunities around these emerging Microeconomies. We need new thinking for a new era. But we owe this most to the public. Each of these Microeconomies is often shaped by dynamic innovations, new competitive advantages, and disruptive change. For example, if you add up the collective businesses value and revenues of the list of Microeconomies of the Future listed above and then look at the relative

growth, capital investments, and job creation value, you will get a deeper understanding of what economists are missing today and should be forecasting tomorrow.

We owe the world an upgrade to economics to generate some Future Ready thinking so they can find new jobs, get educated for sustainable work, and live in economies that are growing and innovating beyond the limitations of today. Shifting our thinking to understand these Microeconomies of the Future is a good start.

These Microeconomies may get us to think differently about the economy. This is even critically more important as we look into the future, as I forecast there will be a tenfold impact of new technologies that will disrupt, change, and create new risks and opportunities over the next thirty years. So let's look at updating economics to get us ready for 2020 and beyond.

THE NEW FUTURE OF THE INNOVATION ECONOMY

Do you know how Facebook makes its money from relationships?
Do you understand how algorithms shape business strategy?
Can you predict how Alibaba will create new online markets?
Do you realize how Royal Dutch Shell decides to invest in new energy?
Do you know how Google predicts what you're going to search for?
How does Apple create business value?

The combination of free enterprises connected across borders, distributed knowledge, emerging technology, and innovation's disruption of markets all lay at the center of our global economy. The attunement of these factors, their interplay, makes for a robust economy. If you know this, you can stimulate more productive growth by investing in those economic drivers. If you don't know this, then your ability as a leader, businessperson, consumer, teacher, inventor, or politician is going to be limited, or it may fail.

There are two economic ideas that are the predecessors of the Innovation Economy trend, which will transform business. The first is Schumpeter's Gale named for Joseph Schumpeter, which says capitalism can only be understood as an evolutionary process of continuous innovation and creative destruction. This applies to all business, but it is especially relevant for entrepreneurship, which is continually dealing with the rapid process of invention, technology, and disruption. Entrepreneurship is the key force affecting all size of businesses and no longer refers to just start-up companies. Every business is being transformed by the culture of entrepreneurs, which creates value from innovation and change. Capital is being attracted by innovation-based companies that are undergoing extreme change.

The second idea is Evolutionary Economics, inspired by evolutionary biology, which deals with the study of processes that transform commerce for enterprises, industries, employment, production, trade, and growth. Evolutionary economics credits an up-trend in economic growth coming from a process of technological innovation. It is fair to say that these two influencing theories have not transformed modern economics as they should have so we could have a deeper insight into the future of our civilization, but maybe you should have a look at them, as they will help make clear the New Future of Economics.

Innovation Economics identified innovation as the chief influencer of productivity. This idea transforms economics by recognizing the valuable role that innovation plays in an economy. More innovation in an economy results in more productivity in the economy—a more robust economy. The observation in the value creation of new biotech drugs, Internet companies, and mobile commerce demonstrates innovation as the key driver of productivity—new jobs, wealth, and contribution to GDP.

Innovation Economics focuses on a theory of economic creativity that affects the organization, jobs, and labor itself by recognizing the type of work that generates innovation value. It also incorporates new ideas of information, computing, and communication technology into the global economy as productivity drivers.

Innovation Economics is based on a fundamental idea that separates it from traditional economics: the central goal of economic policy should be to stimulate higher productivity through greater innovation. More innovation-stimulus investing in research and development, education, entrepreneurship, venture capital, and training creates more productivity. This is in contrast to the two other conventional economic doctrines, neoclassical economics and Keynesian economics.

I forecast that Innovation Economics may just offer a new way to not only view but also understand economies—how we grow, change, or stimulate an economy. Future Smart strategies that focus on the new ROI—the Return On Innovation from investments in science, tech, education, and building a nation of entrepreneurs, of enlightened individuals—Game Changers of the Future—will transform the future economy. Innovation will lead the way.

If you want to get Future Ready, you want to understand this New Future of Economics.

By 2030 innovation industries will contribute to over 70 percent of the growth in the world economy. The future of the global economy is innovation. Innovation that creates value that can be monetized, resulting in new technologies, new jobs, new companies, new industries, and, ultimately, a new civilization. Innovation will drive productivity, labor, markets, and growth. Innovation creates new value that electrifies markets and job growth. Innovation drives foreign and domestic investment. Innovation drives security and defense.

Innovation will shape the future of all economies, the creation of economic wealth. Innovation is what makes workers globally competitive, attracts foreign investment, makes corporations want to hire smart talent, educates and prepares the future workforce, drives wealth creation, and increases prosperity. Innovation is also the fundamental DNA that will make products and services competitive.

As new cloud computing becomes the dominant model for all products and services, an era of Continuous Innovation will emerge. Cloud computing will enable every connected product or service to get updated, upgraded, and enhanced with new functionalities 24/7, forever.

All leaders must focus on enhancing the Innovation Economy within their nations so as to stimulate jobs, innovation, global trade, and research and development. Growth is not sustainable by fiat from government subsidies, social welfare, or cheap funny-money loans that create bubble economies. Innovation comes from investments in education, job training, and research and development of new ideas.

The Innovation Economy: Exponential Change

Innovation Capital and the Power of Ideas are creating a New Innovation Economy. The Innovation Economy is the next evolution of economics. At its core is exponential technology change. It is the turbo-charged global economy that is fueled by the Power of Innovative Ideas. Exponential Technology is transforming our civilization—Internet, mobility, genetics, nano, neuro, quantum, innovation ecosystems, and the free markets, all driven by entrepreneurial companies and individuals that are creating the next economy.

The Innovation Economy is also about the fundamental connectivity of economies. The world's largest economies today and tomorrow—China, the United States, India, Germany, Japan, and Brazil—have a foundation of cross-border sovereign investments that create global and economic prosperity. China holds over a trillion Euros and European sovereign bonds as well as another trillion-plus in US dollars and US sovereign bonds. The global trade flows between the United States and China alone are in the trillions.

The global trade flows between North America, the Eurozone, and Asia dominate the global economy and, at the same time, secure it. China needs the North American market to produce for, and North America needs cheap goods that China makes. China subsidizes the US and Eurozone economies by buying sovereign debt and currencies so as to play their role in protecting their market interests. The EU, Asian, and North American trade is the core of the global economy.

To illustrate this, during the 2008 financial crisis the Russians floated the idea of crashing the US economy by trying to convince the Chinese to dump their US bonds on the market. The Chinese leadership quickly rejected that

idea, demonstrating the end of this kind of Cold War thinking. We are too connected now, and that connectivity is a chief driver of the Innovation Economy
that is emerging and will dominate the future of the planet, creating prosperity
and a higher quality of life.

For half a century the United States has occupied the center of the global
economic system, and capitalism has been a rational model for growing economies, opening markets, and increasing GDP. The world has benefited, not just
the United States. In the future the center of gravity may shift. Prosperity based
on free enterprise propelled by technological innovation is the central focus of
the Innovation Economy. If embraced as an economic model, the openness
of markets, the rise of the new middle class, and poverty reduction all are positive signs that capitalism can be a source of global and sustained productivity.

Competition breeds opportunity and innovation. A new form of global
capitalism—not just Western capitalism—is emerging, as both the Chinese and
the Europeans will compete against each other as well as the United States
in the future. Europe, as a productive social welfare model, and China, as a cen-
trist capitalist model, will compete against the United States (North America),
which is what I would call the Innovation Economic model. Technological innovations will lie at the center of the future of the US economy.

The advanced economies that, in 2000, consumed 75 percent of the world's
output will, by 2050, consume just 35 percent. And innovation will be at the
core of the transformation of the emerging economies of the future.

One measure of Innovation Capital and the value of technology is the number of patents filed. With the United States and China in the lead, you can see
where the future may take us. Patents lead to new innovations and companies
that create jobs, opportunity, and wealth. Innovation, evidenced by up-trends
in patent filings, is an excellent measure of innovation's potential on a society.

Still, a vibrant and significant entrepreneurial class with patents but without venture capital to invest in the future makes little sense. There is not nearly
the venture capital liquidity in the European Union that we find in the United
States. Tomorrow's innovations may come from Asia, Africa, and Turkey if
those economies keep investing in innovation as they are today.

At some point all nations will realize that growth and productivity, security and stability come from investing in people, infrastructure, and education,
thereby sparking investment and innovation to prepare them for the future.

A key unique shaper of the Innovation Economy model is also venture capital and the innovation culture that creates new patents, new digital business
models, explosive innovation, knowledge jobs, products, and start-up companies.
There is a dynamic Innovation Ecosystem of entrepreneurs, venture capitalists,
banks, angel investors, suppliers, coders, producers, designers, factories, shops,
and component makers emerging on the planet. What was once unique, the
Silicon Valley phenomena, is now happening around the world.

The Innovation Economy—the increasing exponential economic and social value delivered from technological innovations—will grow as a force around the world in the future. This Innovation Ecosystem is supported by the ethos and culture of innovation, which is shaped by advocates like Steve Jobs, Sergy Brin, Elon Musk, Bill Gates, and Craig Venter, all of whom have a history of inventing the next big thing—from computers to biotech to electric cars.

By 2030 the Innovation Economy model that has emerged in the United States will become a model for the world economy, with some important changes. Innovation Economics will drive wealth creation, jobs, new industries, and cross-border trade. Innovation such as technologies—nano, bio, neuro, Internet—are the drivers of new businesses, jobs, products, and services that together shape an economy's result: GDP. This model has innovation, free enterprise, and capitalism as the center of what drives growth in economies.

These changes are a balance of a purposeful social agenda, with investment and changes in education, and venture investment in new R&D. In addition, a more sustainable and social-enterprise business model with a purpose, one that embraces innovation but has a soul, will become the new Future Smart business model. If there were any hope about creating more equality, social mobility, affluence, and productivity, it will come from the Innovation Economy. This is a Future Smart economic model.

High-tech innovation—nano, bio, IT, neuro, and quantum—are more than tech innovations; they are economic forces that create jobs, industries, growth, and trade. The future of health care, the future of prosperity, the uplifting of cultures will all comprise the Innovation Economy for the future.

India and the majority of Asia will embrace this future and enjoy GDP growth in their economies. The European Union will have to resolve the rapid aging of their societies and the declining productivity by stimulating innovation and capitalism while balancing social investment, educating their large immigrant populations rather than investing in social welfare as a long-term strategy.

The future of the European Union depends on catalyzing authentic innovation-based growth like that of the Innovation Economy more so than what social welfare models can deliver. It is possible to build a socially responsible society with the engine of growth that is Techno-Capitalism.

Future Smart leaders who understand this will create a New Era of Enlightenment, a new era of invention and innovation. Across the pond the US challenge will be to integrate more social well-being into the Techno-Capitalism model. A fusion of social welfare economics and techno-capitalism will likely be the blend that will endure by 2035.

Future Smart nations invest in the future of their citizens by investing in research and development in innovation and everything that supports that investment, from improving education and job training to essential services such as education and health care. Furthermore they remove all barriers to

entrepreneurship and business, as these are where the jobs come from, where the productivity comes from—not government.

I have advised my European clients of this strategy: it is not sustainable to provide the size and scale of rich social entitlements and also hope to stimulate economic growth and productivity. We all would like to have it all, but there is a price. It will buy votes, but it is a Band-Aid at most. Kicking down the road the pain to effectively deal with structural reform, technology investments, higher education, and jobs training until the next generation can deal with the inability to modernize your technology, education, and jobs is a recipe for long-term disaster.

At the same time, the United States cannot create a sustainable future with the increased drag on the future economy of social entitlements of an aging society any more than the Europeans can. Consistent, organic growth and productivity that comes from revitalizing education and the business sector with innovation in every industry is the only long-term strategy for making sustainable economies that survive.

The aging US and EU economies face long-term challenges to economic sustainability that require a rethinking of what type of future we want and what the cost of that future will be. This is the fundamental existential challenge that all societies will face given slower economic growth and higher demands for social welfare from aging populations.

How well we navigate this future will determine the future security and economic state of the planet, not just a nation or region. In the future aging—as a phenomenon, more than a trend—will bankrupt nations that did not plan for this future. The drag on economic growth and vitality will be the aging of society unless significant resources are planned decades ahead of the 100 to 500 million aging citizens across Europe, North America, Japan, and Asia, particularly China, by 2040. No one is prepared for this future.

The United States may be neck-and-neck with China for the future engines of growth, as two of the leading and most connected economies on the planet. The Eurozone will be third, as a grouping of economies after North America. After Germany at fourth comes a cluster of countries with less than a trillion dollars of GDP separating them today, but they might break out of the Eurozone and become the dominant economies in Europe by 2030. France and Britain are in the top grouping. Brazil, Russia, Japan are all major economic forces today, but all of this might change by 2030 or before.

Malaysia, Mexico, Turkey, Thailand, India, and Indonesia are quickly growing economies and could soon pass Italy, Brazil, and France. Russia's future could change for the better with the Arctic oil rush or crash if a new energy source is found. This might offset Russia's decline in life expectancy due to the inadequate health care system.

Indonesia, Turkey, and Malaysia (due to oil) could be the new leading growth economies, especially if they can bring their populations into the global markets by increasing the quality of their manufacturing sectors and upgrading their innovations and tech infrastructure to compete with India and China.

Singapore, though small in size, is an innovation global leader and will be successful due to social stability, business-friendly climate, and visionary leadership about innovation that keeps it on the forefront of high technology. If most nations just followed Singapore's polices and strategies, they would thrive by 2025 or before. I see Singapore moving into the future. Even with few natural resources and under 5 million people, they are Future Smart.

It is likely that Europe, especially France, Spain, and Italy, may well drop in leading rankings due to drags on their economies by social welfare, taxation, and aging populations. The lack of replacement workers and low investment in next-generation research and development could spell danger ahead. The Eurozone must stimulate and encourage the next generation of entrepreneurs or else their job creation capacity will not keep pace with the growth demands of the economy.

The United States faces similar serious issues, as, in the future, low-tech jobs and even knowledge jobs are not going to be plentiful, and this will create a drag on the US economy. Many of the industries in climate change and strategic exponential technologies of nano, neuro, computing, Internet, and biotech will transform the markets of the near future and drive new economic value—jobs and GDP.

China's Future

China is rising to take over the top economic spot by 2040 or sooner unless the "China Fails to Get Rich Before China Gets Old" scenario happens. What could derail China's future would be the crushing impact and economic drag of China's aging society in the future, when there is not enough growth and new workers to offset the older generations' social needs and reduced contribution to GDP. In this scenario China would not become a leading economy unless worker replacement and economic prosperity is addressed.

There might be an argument for China as well as Japan and other Elder Societies being sustained by huge investments to replace lost labor due to aging populations with Smart Machines, which would accelerate GDP. Smart Machines are high performing, can work more hours, are more competitive than humans, and cost less to operate. I think this likely scenario, the Smart Machine Microeconomy, is coming by 2030.

Robo Future

Italy and Japan are examples of nations that are depopulating and not replacing a retiring workforce or attracting skilled immigrants to keep GDP strong for the future, which puts the future at risk. Without massive Smart Machines such as robots to offset lower labor pools and dropping productivity, these fast-depopulating societies will decline economically. Japan understands this trend and has enacted policies to offset it; Europe is slow to embrace their inevitable robot future, so they are experimenting with creating a more culturally diverse population.

Bring on the robots! This will actually enable the European social welfare model in which Smart Machines will generate the highest productive growth of the economy. I forecast the Smart Machine Microeconomy will provide for humanity a future of less work, more progress, and at a higher quality of life. The challenge will be how to deal with the Human–Smart Machine Jobs Gap and the social decline of quality if we don't invest in tech innovations quickly or deeply enough that will integrate Smart Machines into our societies to pick up the productivity slack.

There will be an almost ten- to fifteen-year gap between having the large scalable and affordable Smart Machines required to make a significant economic and productivity impact as we make the transition into the Smart Machine Economy in Europe. The United States and Asia will lead this Smart Machine Economy. Africa, China, and India will resist, but eventually, to balance out global trade and to be competitive, they all will embrace the economic logic of the Smart Machines,

Robots to offset aging societies are coming and will be viable alternatives even to immigration. Robots have no political affiliations and don't join labor unions. We can see this future emerging now, as Foxcomm ordered thousands of robots to replace human workers after worker protests disrupted their ability to produce Apple's iPhones. Until governments step in, look for tech investments over labor in the future. The battle between the Smart Economy, based on Knowledge Values versus labor, and capital-based economies will emerge by 2025.

There is an intimate economic connectivity between China and the United States, as China invests in US treasuries and the United States is China's largest customer. Even with local domestic markets picking up, I see a stable future for the global economy as well as that for China and the United States. Each of these respective Superpowers, certainly the two largest economies in the future of 2020 and beyond, have enough internal growth factors to weather crises and increase productive growth for generations.

China and Europe have a similar interlinking of economic interests, with holdings of billions of Euros/dollars of sovereign debt that has created a new

fundamental Economic Global Intimacy that is unique in history. This investment is also a stabilizing force for the future of China as well as the world economy. China's robust economy and investments in the US dollar and treasuries as well as the Euro and sovereign assets will go far in stabilizing China as well as the world economy. China is the New World Superpower, and given its access to capital and strong GDP, it has every interest in being a stable economic force on the planet for the foreseeable future.

The intimate connectivity of the three economic zones—North America, Europe, and China—will help stabilize a decline in the United States or the European Union and other more fragile parts of the world economy. This is in the interests of all parties who will shape the New Future.

The population of the United States will grow to 500 million with a grand opening of immigrations by 2020 or before, and this will be highly productive for increasing jobs and offsetting depopulation and an aging society. By 2025 or, likely, before, huge tech-infrastructure investments, research, and development in science and tech as well as energy independence will set up the United States and North America as a region that will dominate the global economy on par with or beyond China.

A smaller, leaner, smarter Eurozone is possible if it handles its immigration, jobs, and social welfare policies and offsets the entitlements with tech investments and education to bring the next generation of immigrants and knowledge entrepreneurs to the market. Without this huge incentive-based transition from an entitlement to an Entrepreneur Society, the Eurozone, minus Germany, the UK, and possibly the oil-rich Scandinavian nations of Norway, will decline in economic importance by 2025. Germany's rise, though, will help the Eurozone unless they bail out the European Union. I bet they stay and dominate the Eurozone in the future, as they do today.

Germany and the United Kingdom are the productivity leaders in the European Union—always have been. If the rest of the European Union was to model their education and trade schools, industrial sectors, and productivity strategies based on Germany, the European Union would be able to boast of their increased growth. I don't see this happening in the future, but it could. The EU nations transforming their economies based on the German model would indeed be Future Smart.

Rising Stars

Turkey, though not part of the Eurozone, will play an important role in collaborating with European markets and will rise in economic and political power to rival most of the EU states. The trade and energy alliance of Germany and Turkey could be an interesting stability pillar for the future. Old ideologies will need to play a lesser role as economic access to markets and the Connected

Planet trend provides growth and commerce. Turkey, as a model of a moderate economic Islamic society where innovation has a positive role in shaping a more productive society, is important for the future of the planet.

Another pillar that will shape the future of Europe is, of course, a resurgence of an Aggressive Russia. Emboldened with energy assets and a nostalgic thirst for expansion, Russia's interactions with Europe and Turkey, the rising economic star of a greater Europe, will shape the future of Europe—if the EU allows it. Innovation, especially around alternative energy, could be a corrective balance of power to counter a resurgent Russia. I don't think the Europeans as a whole relish being Russia's energy vassals. Innovation in energy and new technologies could be a Future Smart investment for the future well beyond their embrace of nuclear. Radical energy innovation is needed to turn this risk into an asset.

Game-Changing Societies for the Future

The Middle East, especially the small, oil-rich nations, will have stagnant growth but numerous and complicated risks. The quality of life in some of these nations is not sustainable unless there are investments beyond oil that stimulate modernity. These states are vulnerable to other states and nonstate actors who in the future could seek to take over these oil-rich and powerful small nations by offering that which the current rulers do not—an alternative future of governance. The rise of the Islamic State is one example. Be it democracy or theocracy, a liberal society or a religious one, it is likely that change is coming to the Middle East, where the most powerful attraction resides, energy.

If the Arab Spring could be transformed into a Silicon Valley and the Arab states were to embrace the Innovation Economy model, the increased productivity, security, and prosperity would be a game changer in our lifetimes. Peace and security for the entire Middle East; jobs and prosperity would lead to peace. This could come from a new global synthesis of leaders, both inside and out of the region, who have the courage to look to the future of the region—what the children of 2015 want for 2040. So many conflicts on the planet would benefit from all parties looking to a plan for the future. The Innovation Economy could be a model for a just, peaceful, and productive society with respect for traditional values. Rather than bombing each other, imagine building Innovation Ecosystems for trade, commerce, and prosperity. Imagine building a Game-Changing Society for the Future in the Middle East. What would that would say to the world?

The game changer in the Middle East is Israel, a robust and dynamically high-tech growing economy that could surpass Turkey, Indonesia, and even China. What would enable Israel's growth in the future—or curtail it—is war. A Middle East peace would be an accelerator of the region's economic growth.

Imagine what Israel could teach its Arab neighbors about innovation and commerce. Imagine no more conflicts but instead collaboration to build productive societies, Game-Changing Societies for the Future.

Peace could add 10 percent to Israel's GDP and direct that entire R&D from military into commercial economic value—swords into plowshares, so to speak. Israel's Innovation Economy is one of the largest and most high tech, which, ironically, has been honed to a high degree of sophistication and performance by the threat of war since its founding. Eliminating this Threat Future as the predominant driver of innovation may be challenging, but a more peaceful Middle East would be a long-term sustainability driver of Israel's future.

Of course, energy sustainability and figuring out immigration to drive proper jobs can be a driver of productivity but not without a larger plan that includes attracting and building an entrepreneur society. As the ideology of entrepreneurs is freedom, innovation, and experimentation, these goals face a big challenge, because this is the antithesis of the bureaucracies and socialized swelling governments of today. Changing this to embrace a leaner government that is accountable for innovation, job creation, and high-tech investments that make a difference could happen, but it is not likely without enlightened leadership that embraces enterprise over social welfare. In France this may not be possible.

Governments do a poor job at creating wealth and employment. The current political ideology across the pond in the United States as in Europe has the same outcome. Social welfare states that don't plan for the future of jobs, innovation, energy, climate change, and education will not have a sustainable and prosperous future. There is little mystery here.

The most sustainable economies now have a more sophisticated understanding that what drives innovation, investment, jobs, productivity, and growth is lower taxes, free markets, and low regulation. What's changed in economics is that most economists are living in theory of the nineteenth or twentieth centuries, before technological innovations had the size of economic impact on the economy they have today and shall have tomorrow. This is what has changed. This Game-Changing Trend, the impact of advanced technology on the economy, is the core difference that will define tomorrow's economy.

Africa, the Next Superpower

The region I think holds the most new promise is Africa. Once known as the Dark Continent, it has been the fastest-growing regional economy after those in Asia. Governance is becoming better as modern societies start to take over from the tribal systems. Investments in resources, technology, manufacturing, and communications have made a difference. Though corruption is still a problem, Africans are becoming smarter and asserting their political clout at the

polls. Democracy and productivity has spread—the real marker of change. Per capita income, what people earn per year, is on the up-trend.

Africa will not be far behind South America by or before 2025 and may go well beyond it achieving Superpower scale. South America just fifteen years ago was dominated by powerful elites exclusively, now a middle class has emerged. Africa's long-term growth will increasingly reflect interrelated social and demographic changes creating new domestic engines of growth. Key among these will be urbanization, an expanding labor force, and the rise of the middle-class African consumer.

In 1980 just 28 percent of Africans lived in cities. Today 40 percent of the continent's 1 billion people are urban dwellers—a proportion roughly comparable to China's and larger than India's. By 2025 that share could rise to 50 percent, and Africa's top twenty cities will have a combined spending power of over $1.8 trillion.

In March 2013 Africa was identified as the world's poorest continent, where poverty is extreme. The history of Africa as a European postcolonial carve-out did not help to make matters better. Most often Africans themselves did not divide the African states, so ancient tribal lands and traditional borders were abandoned and new borders were drawn. This has contributed to the conflicts that have marred the continent. Few visionary leaders have emerged.

We are used to hearing about how conflict ridden and poor Africa is. Now most of Africa is characterized in this way, and although it is true, it's changing fast—faster than you think. And the economic data is getting better, as is the quality of life, pointing to a New Africa awareness perhaps. The rate of return on foreign investment is higher in Africa than it is in any other continent. So something important is shifting in Africa—key trends in investment, infrastructure, growth, resource extraction, and education—and this is leading to a New Africa that may be in line for becoming a new Superpower.

The World Bank expects that by 2025 most African countries will reach middle-class status, which in Africa is about $1,000 per capita, or per person, a year, if current growth rates continue. Africa was the world's fastest-growing continent, at 5.6 percent a year, and GDP is expected to rise by an average of over 6 percent a year through 2023. Growth has been consistently on the up-trend, with over 75 percent of African countries pushing 4 to 6 percent or higher growth rates. This is impressive growth for a continent known more for refugees, conflict diamonds, war, and corruption. What if there were a power shift here that might further accelerate a New Africa?

From Tigers to Lions

Over the past decade the Lion Economies of Africa have grown faster than the East Asian Tigers. Six of the ten currently fastest-growing countries in the

world are in Africa. Africa's telecommunications, construction, banking, and retailing are booming. Private-investment inflows were over $100 billion over the past twenty years. I forecast we could be looking at over $500 billion by 2030.

Most of Africa's economies face serious challenges, including poverty, disease, and high infant mortality. Yet Africa's collective GDP, at $1.6 trillion, is now roughly equal to Brazil's or Russia's, and the continent is among the world's most rapidly growing economic regions. For Africa to get to $3 to 5 trillion by 2025 is not hard to forecast. This acceleration is a sign of dogged progress and potential that may surprise the world.

According to the UN, as a continent, Africa has more than 12 percent of the world's oil reserves, 40 percent of its gold, and 80 to 90 percent of its chromium and platinum. Africa is also home to 60 percent of the world's underutilized arable land and has vast timber resources.

The idea that these abundant natural resources can be the driver for a united African innovation revolution is on the mind of many leaders. This will require visionary Future Smart thinking from the continent's business and political leaders to overcome the silo thinking that continues to hold back the building of a successful Africa as a Superpower rather than a collection of nations—small, disconnected, and vulnerable.

Africa has a chance to take a great leap forward into embracing innovation and modernity, learning from all of the other nations in creating peace, security, and prosperity. The strategic opportunity is there. Will Africa emerge in our future and realize its potential for greatness?

Africa Resource Exchange: 2025

By 2025 a new generation of enlightened, educated, and visionary Future Smart leaders of African nations will form a regional Resource Exchange, where they offer a stock exchange based exclusively on Africa's natural resources. The aim is for the African nations to better manage Africa's resources, not unlike what the oil-rich nations did when they formed the Organization of the Petroleum Exporting Countries (OPEC). Forming OPEC centralized pricing and made individual petro-states a geopolitical power to be recognized.

This organization of states around a resource, oil, held by developing nations was in modern times a global paradigm shift. This was the first time developing nations were able to organize a trading bloc to deal with much more powerful and developed nations, global multinationals, and the Western oil companies.

This example will lead Africa to become the new Superpower. Africa will then join the other Superpowers in the world in leading a new global economy based on Future Smart resource management and innovation. This order brought by the Exchange will eliminate corruption and streamline revenues direct from the market to the nation with transparency and accountability.

There are many reasons why this scenario may not happen, including a lack of Future Smart leaders, the inability of the African nations to find common ground, the lack of governance and continual corruption, and the absence of a vision of the future. If that is the case, then this scenario will not emerge. But I forecast that there is a strong possibility that with the global demands on Africa's resources in a world of resource scarcity, Africa may just emerge as a Superpower. Stay tuned.

The Connected Planet is coming in a future when old alliances, traditional economic models, and new innovations drive change. It is likely that how we earn our livelihood, work, and jobs will change in fundamental ways. The economics of yesterday will not hold up in a world of digital products, cloud computer services, renewable credit trading, and the fantastic new digital Innovation business models that have not even been conceived of yet. Some of what is imagined in these forecasts will create vast wealth—weather machines, nano-bio devices, renewable smart grids, and next-gen computers.

The future innovation ecosystems of collaboration, driven by mobile commerce, crowdsourced business models, and more will invigorate new global trade. There will still be winners and losers in the global economy—fast adapters, predictors, and laggards who resist the future—perhaps with good reason. There will still be buyers and sellers, supply and demand, and customers looking for that next good deal. Entrepreneurs will come out on top here. Regardless of the innovation, the market, the location, there will always be an entrepreneur who can see a need, identify a problem, and provide a solution—for the right price.

And as long as there are customers for his or her service or product, there will always be a market, be it over the smartphone between villages in India or across the world in London or San Francisco. But the future of the global economy will be based on Future Smart individuals who learn to leverage the innovation tools to reach new customers, build new products, create new ventures, forge new industries, and predict what the New Future may bring.

The Geopolitics of the Future

Geopolitics is about the interests, conflicts, alliances, differences, and policies that nations have with other nations. Geopolitics is also about the impact of politics and government on individuals. Ideas shape geopolitics: How does capitalism and free enterprise jive with social welfare, theocratic, dictatorships, or communistic states? How can we increase more equality and fairness? It's the differences and similarities as well as the dance of how we relate as cultures—the good, the bad, and sometimes ugly that defines peace, order, trade, and stability on the global stage. In the future certain key trends will influence geopolitics, from conflict to collaboration between nations, nonstate actors, and, increasingly, organizations:

- Competition for resources (water, food, metals)
- Demographics (shifting values, population mobility, impact on cities)
- Energy access (oil and gas, renewables)
- Tech innovations (knowledge industries)
- Colliding worldviews (capitalism, social welfare, communism, Islam, transhumanist, liberal, conservative, protectionist, mercantilist)
- Religion and modern society
- Individual freedoms
- Rise of Smart Machines

The geopolitics of the future will likely be messy, as each of these strategic drivers of change—energy, tech, worldviews, climate, and resources—will exasperate, complicate, and stress relations among nations.

Arctic Race

Take the Arctic melt, a once-in-a-millennia change as the ice retreats, opening up trade routes across the top of the world for the first time in the history of the planet. The larger Arctic Race is for the natural resources—probably one of the largest oil reserves in the world as well as other resources yet to be discovered. At least five nations, including the United States, Canada, and Russia, are laying claims. One Russian adventurer placed a Russian flag on the seabed to claim the land for Russia. That must have been a very cold dive.

The point is that the competition for energy resources that will emerge between nations over a new resource-rich area could be substantial. It will not be a conflict-free future, but perhaps order will be embraced. Change is never a factor that nations do well, and geopolitics, the clash of ideas, and different agendas do often become hot exchanges.

There are over ten microwars raging on the planet today in Asia, Africa, the Middle East, and South America. I expect the future of these conflicts over energy, ideology, territory, and power to expand in the future. Many of these conflicts masquerade as religious differences but, nonetheless, remain strategic conflicts over global and regional power, territory and resources, and sovereignty.

Flash Zones

There are ten Flash Zones where conflict and clashes over culture and resources may breakout in the future. Most of these are due to other change consequences such as climate, technology, energy, or even prosperity and progress, such as in Africa.

THE TEN FLASH ZONES OF THE FUTURE

1. Arctic Race (fossil fuel resources race)
2. India-Pakistan Clash (traditional competitors)
3. Resurgent Russia (flexing its muscles)
4. Africa Rising (China exploits rebuffed by leaders)
5. Expansionist Islam (chief target: Middle East oil kingdoms, pan-Euro-Islam, radical versus moderate)
6. Cyberspace (new concepts of virtual sovereignty, virtual geopolitics in a virtual world, cyber hacking, competition among nations and corporations)
7. Asian Ocean conflicts
8. Dark Networks (criminal and terrorist groups)
9. Deep-Space Commerce (off-world commerce, asteroids, planets, terraforming new worlds, space mining)
10. Innovation Ecosystems (e-commerce, mobile, markets)

Nation-states must prepare for these challenges and threats. The changes in climate, declining energy, resource scarcity, and rogue technology were not issues twenty years ago. Non-state actors and dark networks—global networks of criminal and terrorists—were not a factor to the extent that they will be in the future. We are facing converging changes, and in the future the complications between nations as well as cultures within nations will challenge global peace and security.

FUTURE FLASH ZONE SCENARIOS

- China seeks to protect its interests in Africa by direct engagement.
- Fully autonomous drones and robots fight wars.
- Super Intelligence, AI, wakes up and becomes self-aware.
- New energy technologies and resources upset jobs and the economy.
- Criminal, terrorist, and nonstate actors hack the Internet to extort nations and corporations.
- Japan invests in a satellite-based missile defense system.
- A new era of Smart Machines, networked computer intelligences, alters the global balance of power.
- Climate change will shape global political alliances.
- The modern Islamic state will rise, countering religious fundamentalists.
- China's space program leads to a Mars colony.
- A resurgent Russia uses energy to shape political power in the EU.
- Digital currency upends monetary order.

- The United States will disengage from global conflicts.
- A new Space Race becomes a competition among nations.
- The oceans become energy and food resources.
- Large multinational corporations challenge sovereign authority.
- Failed states become havens for global crime and terrorism.
- Climate change will destabilize supply chains, law, and global governance.

The geopolitics of the future will, on one hand, be about trade, innovation, and progressive globalization, which are all positive developments, and this shall be a force for peace, commerce, and prosperity. On the other hand, new threats such as cyber-hacking, robo-wars and the proliferation of advanced technologies such as nano, neuro, bio, and quantum will catalyze terrorism, and rogue actors will also be part of our future. Conflict will shape the future as it has in the past. Even disruptive technologies such as digital currency will provide nuanced threats to established power and global order.

The Battle for the Future: Individual Rights

There is a one primary ideological conflict that will define the future. This dominates all conflict on the planet today, and so it shall in the future. This is the Battle for the Future of Individual Rights. Who shall determine the rights of individuals in the future? There are two parties in this conflict.

First, there are governments, organizations, and religious and nonstate actors who believe that their authority should control individuals. Through sovereign law, religion, ideology, surveillance, edict, and the control of information technologies, they reinforce their mandate.

Second, there are societies, organizations, and individuals themselves, all of whom uphold the individual's rights to freedoms, choice, and liberty.

The balance and conflict between these two global ideologies—one that upholds the democratic rights of the individual and one that seeks to control, manipulate, and coerce individuals—will define global conflict in the future. In the end it is simply whose values do you embrace for your future? No individual has ever asked for less freedom, nor shall they in the future. The tensions of the state versus the individual, especially in an era of the Internet and Twitter, when the control of information and influence is "in the wild," will make for a New Future that favors the power of the individual. The rights of the individual, upheld by the state, is the only sustainable endgame that comes without social conflict and disruption in the near and far future. Religious, fundamentalist, and government autocrats take notice. Individual rights and essentially a New Future of distributed political power enabled by networks, beyond borders or ideologies, will define our future. This New Future when politics, technology,

and the rights of the individual meet will result in more freedom and opportunity spread throughout the world.

There is a great possibility that the increased Innovation Economy, the connectivity of markets, and the intimacy that brings the world together with commonly shared interests will offset future conflict scenarios. I believe we are moving closer to this future.

Chapter 6
Globalization 2.0

———

The next evolution of globalization—Globalization 2.0—has as a foundation of common interests, including increased global prosperity, open markets, and accelerated trade, that most people on the planet share. Globalization 2.0 will be a vast acceleration of economic prosperity driven by ubiquitous Internet connectivity, access to digital markets, and business collaborations resulting in Innovation Ecosystems, all contributing to a robust $100 trillion global market by 2030. Globalization 2.0 will also be shaped by the dominance of Knowledge-Value goods that will come to rival labor-intensive goods production.

Globalization 2.0 will redefine the global economy and deliver higher levels of prosperity and quality of life to make equality a more realistic objective for our civilization's future. Prosperity and equality will become achievable and pillars of what the next chapter of globalization shall bring. Though not a panacea, globalization holds great promise in stimulating global trade and commerce, lifting up societies, and actually driving new jobs and economic growth. Trends such as sustainable energy, Smart Machines, mobile commerce, and health enhancement all can be stimulants for creating productivity across the globe. The very idea of globalization is based on opening markets, stimulating trade, and collaborating across borders, of which the next ten years will be Game Changing for the planet.

At the heart of this shift from Globalization 1.0 to 2.0 will be a massive increase in technological innovation, especially the pervasiveness of mobile Internet connectivity. Though the Connected Planet is a larger, more profound culture change, Globalization 2.0 maps the specific global economic integration of data, markets, business, and people. This will be a central driver of the future global economy.

Globalization 1.0 was the beginning of the process of integration and economic connectivity across the planet based on the exchange of worldviews,

products, ideas, capital, technology, and markets. In its formative stages over the past twenty years Globalization 1.0 has improved the way of life of many nations and increased economic growth. Globalization, though emerging in the seventeenth, eighteenth, and nineteenth centuries, was limited by distance, transportation, capital, trade routes, and markets. The Internet era has introduced digital markets, products, and networks of connectivity that have created an entirely new global, cross-border marketplace that transcends the limitations of time, space, and place.

Many nations in Africa and Asia that are now gaining access to global markets for the first time have seen progress. Mexico, Malaysia, Indonesia, and Turkey have been winners in this progress. Global GDP by 2030 should be over 7 percent due to the Globalization 2.0, assuming there is no global pandemic or war.

Although Globalization 1.0 has brought increased benefits to many sectors, the largest benefits of increased prosperity driven by global entrepreneurs is still yet to come. That is when the Connected Planet, Globalization 2.0 comes in. Increased prosperity, the opening of markets, the empowerment of business and individuals, the access to the Internet, and payment transaction platforms have not happened yet.

This is partly why Globalization 1.0 has not paid off as rapidly in increasing the prosperity of more nations and individuals. Although the connectivity of supply chains, markets, and trade alliances has moved ahead, Globalization 1.0 is in the formative stages. The hyperconnectivity of the mobile web has not clicked in at levels that would reach the global population as it shall in the near future.

The growing intelligence of the Internet as the backbone of the Connected Planet, delivering tomorrow's knowledge, education, health care, and business, is the most empowering force that will change the future for the better. Accelerated communications, when 8 billion people are connected on the planet and have a simple and effective way to trade, learn, transact, sell, buy, and become aware of each other—this is the power to change the world that the Connected Planet will offer.

Technology proliferation, not just the Internet, but with Innovation Ecosystems and other innovations, will be a driver of globalization. This will shape the future economy and wealth of nations. There is a recognition that a new understanding is emerging in which connectivity as a source of enterprise and innovation is creating new opportunities for spreading ideas and business models, opening markets, fueling collaboration, and empowering individuals—not just businesses to achieve success.

All around the world entrepreneurs are benefiting from this wave of new connections that are propelling business and spreading prosperity. This trend will greatly expand as the tech innovations—bio, nano, networks—become integrated into all aspects of society.

Indonesia, Malaysia, and India are the back offices for American companies, providing information technology services. Business analytics is being conducted in Mumbai for Toyota, where thousands are crunching credit and leasing programs. IBM has turned on locations in Ireland, and Israel is doing research for Apple. Even labs and businesses in Africa and China are now connecting with markets in Europe and South America.

I have been to these locations around the world. I see the emergence of Globalization 2.0 at work, where millions are collaborating in real time across borders and time zones, and all are able to access markets and talent over the mobile Internet. This is a revolution of commerce that is kinetically charged and all linked. Globalization 2.0 is enabled by collaborative technologies today and as we step into the future of cloud computing, where every supply chain, talent network, and business is moving to a new era of agility. This will dramatically enhance commerce—more access to markets, entrepreneurs, and business.

This should be the ultimate endgame of globalization—increasing the prosperity of individuals by using technology to accelerate commerce by creating new business value. This alone will not solve the entire challenge to spur on Globalization 2.0. Social innovations, such as improved education, high-speed Internet, improved employment outlook, job training, and better health care, can only improve the society. Access to venture capital and a robust technology sector supported by the private and public sectors would greatly support Globalization 2.0.

Digital Cash Connects the Planet

Money is bits, but we love our atoms. In the future our banks will be our phones and every transaction will use digital cash. Digital currencies will play a vital role in making the Globalization 2.0 more productive. I forecast that digital cash, also known as crypto-currencies, such as Bitcoin and others, have the potential to transform the global payment systems. These virtual currencies will provide easier and more cost-effective solutions for trade.

Of course, these new digital currencies will upend the traditional currency systems that governments and banks control. This will support the global financial velocity of the Connected Planet. Not right away and not everywhere, but by 2020 to 2025 we will see digital currencies transform the global payment infrastructure, bringing financial access to millions, maybe billions of entrepreneurs around the Connected Planet.

Digital currencies have been shown to increase efficiency, reducing the cost of transferring money from one place to another. The currency is also safer to transport, less bulky, and cheaper to save and spend than actual cash. Digital cash, such as Bitcoin has also attracted criminals who see the confidential opportunities, as do entrepreneurs, to operate worldwide. The combination of

pervasive connected mobile devices and digital currency presents a tremendous opportunity to radically expand access to financial services on a worldwide basis, especially for entrepreneurs who can benefit from the direct P2P commerce, free from institutions.

Even today the awkwardness and incompatibility of credit cards and currencies, with banks and borders in the way, frustrate commerce. Digital currencies have the potential to streamline transactions and create new efficiencies in world where everything is digital or can be represented in a digital way. Digital cash will lower transaction costs for businesses, decrease fraud risk, drive more trade across borders, and increase privacy and protection.

Less fraud will be a boon for every business, as digital cash can be protected more effectively than our current analog system of transactions. If you consider that in the future the 3 billion people who will be online and connected who are not connected today, this will be a vibrant marketplace of 8 billion, and digital cash will enable businesses and consumers to join to this marketplace and expand the market for consumer financial products on a global basis.

The point is that in the near future Globalization 2.0 will require a frictionless and easy-to-use transaction system that digital currency can provide. This is an important barrier to globalization that needs to get transformed so business-to-business and P2P transactions over the mobile Internet can be easy and secure. This will accelerate commerce.

Africa's Digital Cash

M-Pesa is the revolutionary approach to banking that is changing economies across Africa and is a model for the future of the Connected Planet. The service allows customers and businesses to pay for anything without needing cash, a bank account, or even a permanent address.

This digital cash enables different entrepreneurs to do business across borders and currencies that have traditionally been a barrier to commerce—and now it is accelerating. The phone is the transaction device—a marketplace to conduct business, to bring together buyers and sellers, to communicate opportunities, price, and products.

In order for the Connected Planet as a force to be a Game-Changing Trend—decreasing poverty, creating wealth, reducing barriers to global trade, opening global markets—ideally there should be free enterprise and a reduction in government regulations. Entrepreneurs need a way to do direct business among each other that is mobile and fast. Traditional banking is cumbersome and, frankly, for many around the world, not possible at all to us. Digital cash holds the possibility of an entirely new supply chain for business.

As with all of the other digital revolutions, such as everything moving to a web platform, the essential future of digital currency will be an accelerator for

doing business in the Connected Planet. Developed and developing nations must do more in the future to stimulate the entrepreneurs in their respective nations and eliminate regulation that hinders free enterprise, open markets, and stimulates innovation investments. Without this support for the Connected Planet productivity and jobs will not increase in value or numbers.

Greece is a beautiful and culturally rich nation, from which so much has been given to the world, such as philosophy, politics, science, and culture. But at some point Greece did not modernize; they did not evolve to the next generation of the global economy or culture shaped by knowledge, technology, and the reinvention of business. They were not Future Smart.

Turkey, however, has one of the fastest and largest growth stories in terms of GDP in the world. At around 8 percent growth in 2013, even with some political issues, Turkey's secret is no surprise. I was the guest of my client Siemens, the global engineering firm, and was presenting to them in Istanbul about the use of the Internet to shape the future of business, learning, training, and e-commerce. The Turkish customers understand that the key to enabling their future business is to use the mobile Internet to collaborate and connect with local, regional, and world markets. This is the reality of Globalization 2.0—technology that can empower the innovative use of networks to find and serve customers no matter where they are.

Our event was packed. These small and large businesses were hungry for the future and knew that a connected global economy was the ticket to their business success and a better, more productive future. You could feel the excitement in the room as the ideas where flowing and innovation was being born in front of us. Turkey has caught up and, in some ways, surpassed the rest of Europe in the rate of GDP, which is more robust there than it is in the European Union.

Other nations that are using the Connected Planet to drive commerce and collaboration across borders to expand their markets are Indonesia, Thailand, Chile, and, especially, Mexico. Mexico has the benefit of the United States to trade with but is expanding beyond the United States with a GDP that will rival Turkey's growth. Technology access, education, mobile Internet, and digital payment systems are driving business growth.

I have had the exact same experience now in packed conference rooms in over twenty nations over the years. What has stuck out for me after meetings with small and large groups, leaders in government and industry, entrepreneurs and students is that the thirst to invent a better future through innovation is universally shared across cultures. Creating a better future through business and innovation is apolitical and nonideological.

The Arabs, Israelis, Iranians, Pakistanis, Indians; from the Middle East to Asia to Europe and to Africa—they are all are beginning to understand the Connected Planet. This is a shared understanding that could shape a better

world if we could find the ways to collaborate smarter. Commerce lifts up and increases economic prosperity, but it also gives people hope of having a future. Prosperity breeds hope for a better future. Prosperity can lead to peace.

This is one reason I wrote this book. I see a way for Globalization 2.0, if given a chance with the emerging new innovations I discuss here, to create a vibrant open free market of free enterprises across all cultures and nations regardless of differences in ideology, power, or historical conflict. Technology, if used properly, can lift up nations, even those in conflict, even reduce conflict. Where prosperity flourishes, conflict decreases. Improvements in the economy lead to people looking forward, not backward. Prosperity leads to a New Future of new possibilities.

The key is to get more collaboration into the game of connecting people to each other, connecting people to innovations, and connecting people to markets in which transparency of opportunity over trade and enterprise may be stimulated. The Internet is the universal connectivity network for accelerating globalization—getting people access to this technology—and high-speed access will stimulate every economy and every entrepreneur. If you want to accelerate the productivity of nations, give free high-speed access to every citizen, every business, every government agency.

I have been a global advocate for the future of technology and entrepreneurs over the decades since I left Apple. I have been lucky to have been sponsored by my telecom, computer, engineering, and tech companies from around the world, working with Cisco, FedEx, Novartis, IBM, Apple, and numerous governments who are Future Smart, including the United States, Singapore, India, China, Germany, Thailand, Malaysia, and Indonesia.

I have spoken to entrepreneurs hungry to invent the future and companies and many governments who understand how to support them. Globalization 2.0 is coming, and many of these folks are leading the charge.

Stimulating Innovation

You must stimulate the sectors that generate jobs—high-quality knowledge jobs driven by advanced technologies—or you will drive business to more attractive locations. France has lost significant business to England, Germany, and the United States. There are some European nations where there is more government regulation than there are entrepreneurs. Do you know where the best and worst locations are for doing business?

Globalization 2.0, if supported, will create a new transparency value by opening up the free trade of goods, products, and services among nations over mobile commerce networks that are beyond borders. Markets can be created to find buyers and sellers where there were no ways to connect buyers and sellers before. A globally connected planet, where buyers and sellers can source,

communicate, transact, and trade, is the panacea for global growth and wealth creation for the next hundred years. Over the Internet entrepreneurs in one village in Peru can find buyers in the United States and conduct trade with electronic money like PayPal or Bitcoin.

This explosion of tech-driven markets that will enable buyers and sellers to connect is what's coming—a vibrant marketplace of real-time electronic commerce in which customization, personalized products, and even new innovations like 3D manufacturing will increase global and regional wealth. The individual will be the ultimate winner in the Connected Planet.

So much of what will happen next to bring together this hyperconnectivity will be to empower the individual with tools, innovations, and opportunity. The ultimate connectivity dynamic will be more global prosperity and free enterprise. Connected economies, markets, and companies that are able to operate free enterprises will reshape civilization.

Megacities Rising

You and about 9 billion people will want to live in a city that provides jobs, education, security, health care, and an excellent quality of life. It is likely that you will find yourself drawn to the megacities of the future for many reasons, mostly because the quality of life and economic opportunity will be attractive.

Now, not all megacities—cities of at least 10 million people each—will be as attractive as others, and many will be crowded and will not have the resources and ideal conditions that others may have. That is because of the onslaught of social and economic conditions that will lag when the rise in population comes into the megacities.

Not all nations will plan ahead, be Future Ready, or know how to manage the influx of people all looking for a better way of life. Not all dreams of the ideal existence for everyone will pan out at the same time. That is also the future of megacities. The varying quality of lifestyles due to the social and economic conditions of where your megacity is located will affect your future.

Even today the lifestyles, opportunities, and risk factors vary greatly between Tokyo's lifestyle and Delhi's, for example. This gap between the more affluent and poorer megacities of the future will persist in the New Future. The good news is that those megacities that struggle today, impoverished and troubled, will emerge as more stable centers of opportunity tomorrow. The Smart Megacities of the future are coming.

A global migration to megacities is already in progress. The bulk of the world's jobs, wealth, talent, resources, energy, goods, and services produced will either be located in or close to megacities. Megacities will become the new city-states of the future. They will, if planned and managed properly, generate their own clean energy; attract business to create jobs; build out their infrastructure

of essential services such as health, water, and education; and address climate change. Attention to security will be most essential.

All cities must become Future Smart—predictive, agile, innovative, and adaptive.

- Trade energy with other megacities
- Manage climate change with controlled environments
- Maintain their own security forces
- Transform and distribute health care cloud networks
- Grow their own food and be fully independent
- Enable Innovation Ecosystems to spur commerce and entrepreneurs
- Invest in their own robot and 3D manufacturing ecosystem
- Enable IoT, Internet of things, integrated into everything
- Be autonomously connected via the web to other megacities
- Have a distributed microgrid energy network and be self-sustaining
- Generate renewable and clean energy

The New Future of megacities is coming fast, and no one is fully prepared to deal with the influx of people and demands on the megacity for essential services. Megacities must become more like city-states—autonomous, self-governing, self-organizing, and self-supporting in terms of economics, commerce, and social services. Neither city governments nor the private sector has considered the acceleration of this trend and how it will shape their cities in the near future. Most of the world's population, especially in the developing world, will, by 2040, be living in megacities. Over 1 billion Chinese will be living in megacities.

The largest cities in the developing world, in India, Pakistan, China, Indonesia, Brazil, and Malaysia, will be megacities. Try to travel ten miles in Beijing or Djakarta in rush hour. I have, and the paralysis of traffic is a reminder of the rising productivity, increased quality of life, soaring GDP, and the congestion that too many cities face today. The megacity of the near future must plan ahead for a massive influx of people, especially as the megacity becomes the place where jobs, education, commerce, and a higher quality of life can be pursued faster than anywhere else.

The largest concentration of wealth and resources, not just talent, will be in megacities. The avalanche of urbanism brought by megacities is a future fast approaching that presents both immense risks and opportunities for our civilization. Megacities will challenge leaders' ability to govern effectively and citizens' capacity to get the services they need for a good quality of life.

There are a variety of scenarios and possible future outcomes that I will explore.

It is also likely that more than one typical megacity will emerge, meaning that many different megacity scenarios will simultaneously coexist at the same time in different locations on the planet. A diversity of power, culture, resources, and governments will vary megacities' survival success rate. Too much population with too many demands on infrastructure will place undue stress on the megacity of the future.

Shaping the Future Smart Megacity

Globalization 2.0 will shape the future of cities. Globalization influences new collaboration across geographies and capital flows, combining trade, law, commerce, finance, and diplomacy. Globalization will have a major impact on accelerating megacities' formation, given the mobility of talent, the rise of innovative technologies, and the population density in cities. The global flattening of markets and economies and, to some extent, even the creation a global culture of frictionless trade has helped to accelerate globalization.

Headlines from the Future: 2025
Cities Trade Carbon Credits Over Cloud Online Exchanges

In addition, the interconnection of economies, of producer and buyer, market and maker, buyer and seller has laid the foundation of abundance that shall shape the future of cities. Finally, the mass consumerism and the pervasive nature of technology, such as mobile telecom and the Internet, are a dramatic accelerator of economic value, touching and linking every city on the planet.

A million people a day are walking into China's cities.

There are over nineteen megacities on the planet today. By 2025 there will be almost twice that amount. By 2050 Asia and Latin America will be where the largest megacities will be found. Most of these megacities will be in the developing world. The collision of cultures, the aging developed world, and the youthful developing world will sharpen the tension over the next decades. In fact, as the global population explodes, the megacities of Asia and Latin America will dominate the global-needs agenda. Prosperity is—or the hope of it is—what will bring the megacity.

A tectonic power shift is coming, as the population and affluence meter shifts from developed to developing cities—not nations. Here are some key megacity trends to watch for:

- Over six hundred cities by 2030 will together host 7 billion people.
- These six hundred cities will generate over 60 percent of global GDP, or $64 trillion.
- They will be home to over 735 million homes in 2025.
- By 2030 megacities will be the dominant consumer of energy on the planet.
- By 2035 China will host the most number of megacities.
- Growing affluence, the rise of the middle class, security, and health care are driving the growth of megacities.
- The majority of megacities around the world must learn to manage climate change.
- The developing world's megacities will dominate the global population.
- By 2030 China will have over two hundred megacities.
- More than 400 million people—more than the population of the United States today—will live in China's megacities by 2025.
- By 2035 over 1 billion people will be living in China's cities.

Chapter 7

Innovation Ecosystems: From Click-Streamers to Knowledge Value

---

If you want to know what's going to happen next in business, these trends will be predictive of a dynamic marketplace of which entirely new industries, technologies, jobs, and markets will be invented every month for one hundred years just to keep pace with the demands of innovation that are coming. Just getting your head around all of this should be exciting and daunting. Only the brave will thrive.

A future of abundance and opportunity will emerge shaped by innovation. Preparing today to meet the challenges of the New Future will require individuals to go on a fast learning curve. You have to get in sync with where business is going and growing, not where it has been. The future belongs to those who can envision it. Here we go. Here's what's coming. Envision this:

- The Internet of Things (IoT) Marketplace will emerge—online connected products, devices, computers, chips, sensors, streets, materials, streets, highways, bots, drones, all linked to the Internet. By 2020 there will be over 100 billion mobile connected devices on the planet—maybe even a trillion connected things.
- Connected minds tied to the Innovation Ecosystems will drive global business, education, health, and finance.
- The Always-On Marketplace: by 2020 mobile commerce will be the leading platform for conducting all types of business.
- The Renewable Energy Market: by 2030 carbon-credit trading will be a 100-billion Bitcoin business.
- By 2030 alternative energy management generates over 25 percent of all jobs.

- By 2030 alternative energy and Climate Engineering will be the largest markets after health care.
- The Talent Marketplace: by 2030 90 percent of new business formation will be created by women entrepreneurs.
- By 2025 Gen Y will have transformed business by changing the corporate culture, nature of work, and values.
- The Next Middle Class: by 2030 there will be over 5 billion people in the middle class, representing over two-thirds of the global population, with the largest numbers in Asia and Africa.
- By 2050 the United States will have over 500 million citizens.
- The Smart Machine Marketplace: by 2030 mobile devices will sense, transact, collaborate, and conduct business—most without human interaction or awareness.
- 3D manufacturing and nanotechnology will transform production and supply chains, enabling real-time personalized products (organs, electronics, bikes, computers, homes, food) to be downloaded direct to homes and business—teleportation devices will be everywhere to accept virtual designs and 3D self-assembly in real-time.
- By 2025 80 percent of the growth of the new global economy will be in the Start-Up marketplace—Start-Ups will be born, evolve, merge, and die in the same day. Day Start-Ups will be the rage.
- By 2030 the Health Enhancement Market will be the largest global market.
- By 2025 the wearable device market will outpace all other device platforms.
- Global Trade: by 2025 over one-third of economic value contributed to world GDP will come from companies that build their business around technological innovation.
- By 2025 over 80 percent of global products and services will be produced in cities.
- By 2020 the Global Connected Home Market will be worth more than $15 billion.
- By 2025 over 75 percent of the planet's population will have a smartphone, creating the largest marketplace in the history of commerce.

The Innovation Ecosystem: The Next Evolution of Business

The decentralization and democratization of science and technology Power Tools is creating innovation—new enterprises, new social and business models. The central drivers of these Innovation Ecosystems are the mobile web, the

connectivity of aware things, geo-intelligence, and the convergence of buyers, cloud computing networks, sellers, and customers streaming into a convergence of commerce and trade.

The proliferation of these Power Tools—bio, info, neuro, robo, quantum, and nano—will create a revolution in jobs, business, and markets. New forms of kinetic and dynamic collaboration across borders and markets will emerge that serve a growing global customer base. These Power Tools empower innovation, prosperity, and commerce in ways that are extremely efficient and transparent—and create new knowledge value.

Future Smart business opportunities will be found by rethinking the basic relationships, transactions, Knowledge-Value exchange, and networks that link makers, producers, marketers, suppliers, and customers all together. An Innovation Ecosystem is a convergence of talent, technology, collaboration, and markets. The collaborating and connectivity of networks of relationships that share the common thread of innovation will define an entirely new type of Future Smart organization.

Key Drivers of the Innovation Ecosystem

- global collaboration among makers, brokers, buyers, and sellers
- specialized talent to manage the ecosystems and the supply chain
- cloud computing applications
- automated mobile-bot farms
- digital currency
- predictive analytics
- immersive media
- digital banks
- on-demand nanofactories
- innovation cultures
- connected supply chains
- customized Smart Machines
- virtual e-commerce
- kinetic marketplace
- global distribution services

Innovation Ecosystems will become the dominant way business is conducted. Innovation Ecosystems will bring together, on demand, real-time virtual and physical resources, capital, technology, assets, supply chains, and talent into a high-performance platform.

Headlines from the Future: 2025
Knowledge Engineering Industry Surpasses $5 Billion

The Innovation Ecosystem will be a unique collaborative network of parties and key stakeholders that uses the best-in-class of innovations. This will connect buyers and sellers across a superfast online mobile marketplace in which real-time Instant Commerce is conducted in exabytes. Innovation Ecosystem, will establish a competitive advantage that is the right fit for the customer and is even designed and built with the customer and for the customer. Crowdsourcing, think tanking, asset trading, rapid prototyping, trend mining, virtual avatars, Smart Machines, digital distribution, 3D printing, simulations, modeling, algorithm bots—all of these are radical new ways to conduct business in the Innovation Ecosystems of the future. Innovation Ecosystems will be the endgame of the fusion of Big Data, predictive analytics, cloud computing, and digital commerce—an entirely new form of online high-performance global marketplace.

Innovation Ecosystems will spring up as agile networks of transactional players and dynamic markets based on short- or long-term projects to create, for example, a new treatment drug, city, device, or service that can help fuel a nation. It will be focused on the collection of talent deployed like a rapid reaction team to address a need and build it, using or inventing the Right Tech for the Right Job. Innovation Ecosystems will form highly innovative, cost-effective, and agile networks to work in a high-velocity marketplace that will replace a large part of traditional organizations' structure.

We see the emergence of Innovation Ecosystems today, but this will become the trend in businesses that are leaner, smaller, and more entrepreneurial. The role of many businesses will be to design, formulate, and manage these Innovation Ecosystems. Customers in the future will greatly value the agility, flexibility, and innovation products and services that emerge from this future marketplace.

Innovation Ecosystems are the evolution of markets and organizations as they embrace a more agile, dynamic, and entrepreneurial network connectivity. Business, both large and small, must understand that these new Innovation Ecosystems are shaped by the Internet, where high-speed collaboration and digital tools are the driver of a new vibrant economy.

If you want to compete in your business or career, you will want to engage or build an Innovation Ecosystem. Examples of Innovation Ecosystems that are emerging and evolving today toward this model include the following businesses.

Alibaba.com (www.alibaba.com) is a global trade business-to-business portal to connect Chinese manufacturers with overseas buyers. It is the largest Innovation Ecosystem on the planet. When it becomes predictive it will be the largest predictive ecosystem. Alibaba includes Taobao, a consumer auction market; Tmall, an Internet retail portal; eTao, a price comparison website; Alibaba Cloud Computing platform; Laiwang, an instant messaging platform; and Ali-Pay, a PayPal-style online payments system. This collection of digital assets gives them a world-class position. They are bigger than Amazon and eBay combined.

Amazon (www.amazon.com), the global marketplace, is a megastore that mostly sells to consumers but increasingly is focusing on businesses, and not just books and media. Amazon is experimenting with prediction by mining their customers' behaviors to determine where products might be needed and setting up distribution centers to Mine Future Desire. Almost every business and consumer product can now be found through Amazon. They are evolving into an Innovation Ecosystem by enabling entrepreneurs and making unique products to sell—books, films, and consumer goods for their marketplace.

Quirky (www.quirky.com/shop) is an innovation platform that brings together inventors to present ideas and sell directly to customers for health, home, travel, and business products. You can join the community as an inventor or a shopper.

Kickstarter (www.kickstarter.com) is an innovation community that uses crowdfunding to bring to life creative projects that bring makers and funders together—part angel investor, part enabler of entrepreneurs.

Elance (www.elance.com) is an online talent marketplace for marketing freelancers to potential clients, cutting out the middle man.

oDesk (www.odesk.com) is another talent marketplace that caters to connecting people to businesses.

Intellectual Ventures (www.intellectualventures.com) sponsors an invention marketplace where patents, investors, and companies can exchange or invest, creating a private market for innovators.

Innovation Nations

Here is the list of Innovation Nations that will attract the most innovators, where Innovation Ecosystems will thrive. This is where ideas, talent innovation, R&D, productivity, patents, entrepreneurs, and businesses converge to bring forth new products and services more so than anywhere else in the world. These Innovation Nations are friendly to innovation, business, investment, and entrepreneurs.

Canada	Germany	Singapore
China	India	South Korea
Czech Republic	Ireland	United Kingdom
Finland	Israel	United States

Emerging Innovation Nations

Here is the list of the next Innovation Nations that will propel the world's economies by creating innovation, prosperity, and business.

Brazil	Malaysia	Argentina
Indonesia	Romania	South Africa

The Innovator's Mindset

The key to business is to understand how to think like an innovator. How do innovators think? They are open. They explore. They envision the future, have long-term forecasts, are not afraid of breaking rules, and are, above all else, they are courageous, even in the face of failure, criticism, and disaster. They have the capacity to change Fast, fail Fast, and succeed Fast. They are always looking for opportunity to embrace emerging innovations to create value.

Innovators embrace change. They see change as an opportunity to create solutions and profit. They are willing to learn new things to gain an advantage.

The Four Mindsets that can be found in every organization, culture, and nation are the Traditionalist, the Maintainer, the Adapter, and the Trailblazer. Conflicts in organizations often result from a clash of mindsets—different ways to accept and be open to change, embrace innovation, and strategize for the future. Often mindsets are incompatible and create inertia, frustrating an organizations' ability to be agile, responsive, and innovative.

The Traditionalist is an overt resister of change and innovation. They will give you many reasons why things should stay the same and not change, with no reason to innovate.

The Maintainer is the covert resister of change and innovation. They say Yes but mean No. They are the least likely to be honest about their resistance. They sabotage innovation on a regular basis. They remain fearful of change, so their resistance to innovation is understandable.

The Adapter is ready for change. Adapters are willing to learn new things. They do not especially like innovation or change but recognize that they must change to thrive or even survive. They are reluctant change agents, ready to embrace innovation if it will provide value and solutions.

The Trailblazer leads change and is Future Smart. Innovators are the Trailblazers; they lead change efforts and are open to change, recognizing its value to transform. Innovators embrace innovation, the new ideas that electrify the enterprise, and are often reactive to changes in the marketplace. They are the first to get attacked by the culture of Traditionalists or Maintainers. Still, the Trailblazer has the potential to lead organizations to success. They are more in sync with the needs of their customers. They are more relevant

and solution oriented. They have the Innovator's Mindset. They are the Game Changers of the Future.

Organizations are networks of minds that operate predominantly with one mindset. This mindset can either kill or lead the organization into the future. It can either become relevant or a part of history. Mindsets rule organizations. The Innovators Mindset is the most powerful to make and lead change. This is what all organizations should strive to create. This is how to prepare for the future. This is Future Smart.

If you think about these trends, it quickly become clear that we are entering a New Future of business that is unlike the past. The speed of change and the complexity of the changes will force a reinvention of business thinking. You can see the changes emerging even now:

The companies with the most assets make Knowledge Products, companies such as Facebook, IBM, Apple, Google, and Twitter. The combined market capital of the world's Top 100 companies has experienced a change of more than $10 trillion after the financial bubble burst in 2008. The Fortune 100 leaders have changed over the past twenty years. New industries are growing up around us, such as drones, robots, gamification, geo-intelligence, and mobile commerce, that are so new that few are leaders in these emerging markets as yet.

Right about now you should consider building or altering a business plan to exploit these market trends—mobile commerce, data, robotics, connected homes, social media, and the list goes on. Ignoring these trends and thinking that life will not change much is dysfunctional thinking. You can do better than that as you envision your future.

Likely the forecasts indicated here are off in one way, at least. The time where these trends will show up will be sooner than later, I forecast. If you subtract two to five years from each forecast, that is a more accurate timeline for when these trends will play out in reality. Why?, you might ask.

Exponential Technologies
Create Exponential Business

Every technology is doubling in processing power, storage, and capability every twelve months. It is a guiding concept, as is the hyperconnectivity of people, devices, systems, markets, and technology. This exponential change is speeding up the time-to-market for innovations to emerge—faster and faster. Exponential change refers to an acceleration in the rate of change—the velocity. Exponential change may see a 2 to 100 times rate of fast change in a brief period of time, defying known metrics.More innovation and more disruption demands faster adaptation—that's where the idea of being Future Smart comes from: learning to predict and adapt faster to keep up with the changes in the New Future.

This means that the industries that rely on computing power—which, of course, is every industry: telecom, banking, finance, medicine, energy, and defense, to name a few—are facing exponential change, a doubling of processing and analytic power compounded 3 to 1000 times each year. Tech innovations that are the key drivers of change in business and society are vastly doubling in power and capability year after year, which means that change is accelerating at a pace unknown in our modern era. There is more technology in that smartphone you carry than existed in the entire world in 1975. But the Game Changing that will drive business, the exponential changes, have yet to come. Let's get ready fast.

Houses with intelligence. All data in the cloud. Robots that clean our houses. Mobile apps transforming enterprise. DNA used to make decisions about marketing and relationships. Real-time supply chains making anything on demand. Digital libraries of endless media entertainment engaging you, the audience in the show. Big Data agriculture feeding 8 billion. These are not just technological innovations; these are Game-Changing business innovations that will shape the future of the economy and create more prosperous growth and innovation to manage the planet.

The new businesses that will come from these exponential innovations will transform every industry, including health care, transportation, media, finance, and manufacturing, to name a few. Here are some of the key trends that exponential innovations will create in all industries:

Connecting Minds to Devices to smart machines to create more efficiency, and creativity will help us understand how to manage everything more intelligently.

Embedding Knowledge into every product or service, with the ability to embed knowledge and upgrade wirelessly and continuously to function and value.

Discovering New Opportunity in exponential innovations that will help us discover new solutions to common problems of use, effectiveness, safety, and productivity.

The New Middle Class

Are you interested in doing business with or selling to the next 2 billion new customers? Global population has risen sharply, and it continues to increase, having doubled over the past forty-five years. At 7 billion today, going to 8 billion by 2040, perhaps 9 billion by 2050, this creates both a challenge and an opportunity. Two billion new customers entering the New Middle Class means a large, vibrant, new marketplace for global business.

They are global, connected, educated, and want to accelerate their wealth status to gain a higher quality of life. There will be increased new wealth from

Asia, Africa, Eastern Europe, and Latin America, whose purchasing power will define business in the twenty-first century. This poverty-to-progress population trend is very positive for business that continues to require what every business needs to become successful—2 billion more customers.

This is the catalyst of the global future economy and the future of business—vast new customer groups who want to catch up with the rest of the developed nations. New entrants into the marketplace will accelerate growth and global business. Their demands for a middle-class lifestyle will transform every business, marketplace, and industry, creating massive growth opportunities and putting resource stress on the world at the same time.

Most of the New Middle Class will live in cities by 2025. There is and will continue to be a human migration to cities on a scale we have never before seen on the planet. The rise of the Connected Cities of the Future will shape energy, trade, and innovation in entirely new ways. The New Middle Class, from Asia, Africa, and Latin America, will transform cities and enable new productivity and growth on a scale we have not seen in the twenty-first century.

There will also be massive challenges such as the sustainability of cities. How will we make sustainable cities of 10 to 20 million? These are the megacities of the future. We will need to invent smart cities to manage the challenges coming. Business will lead the future of managing tomorrow's cities. There is a vast new global marketplace to mine for talent, to produce and sell to, creating numerous new business opportunities in the near future that will come from the concentration of people and capital in cities.

Click-Streamers

By 2020 about 70 percent of the global marketplace will be made up of Click-Streamers—always online, digitally savvy, connected, and mobile. These are the customers who use their wearable computers to conduct business, play videogames in their driverless car, navigate the web on their phone, collaborate with drones and flyables, buy from Innovation Ecosystems, and use digital technology to market and manage around the world over networked markets.

Click-Streamers are always connected by the cloud, mobile, social media, and Big Data. They live, work, and play in the digital universe of hyperconnectivity, augmented reality, and mobile everything. They are beyond geography, age, or demography; they have adapted to the click-stream lifestyle.

Corporations and business leaders are facing some of the most disruptive changes of a generation. Digitally savvy consumers and advances in technology are at the forefront of a paradigm shift that will affect every business on the planet. There are emerging customer expectations that are obvious now, expectations that point to this new market of customers around the world—more so in developing nations than in the West. The emergence of a new generation

of digitally savvy customers called Click-Streamers is reshaping the expectations of the end-customer. This is who business is going to serve in the near and far future.

The Click-Streamers are your new customers. Complex changes in culture, especially technology and the marketplace, require new ways to better understand customers and how they are changing. The traditional ways to identify customers—to separate them by age, location, or interest—often misses key insights in their relationships with digital technology as a lifestyle and culture. The aging Baby Boomers, Generation X, the Millennials—these are some of the traditional categories that marketers have assigned to customer segments that, given the onslaught of new technologies such as mobile, social media, and wearable computing technologies, do not tell the whole story about who customers are.

A new way to characterize customers is by their common, collaborative, and predictive click-stream lifestyle. This approach brings together a diversity of people that would not be normally associated unless they shared a common set of attributes beyond age, culture, or location. In fact, customers who are linked in new ways will present new marketing opportunities for business. Click-Streamers have certain consistent behaviors and sentiments that distinguish them:

- Click-Streamers will live and work online.
- After 2020 over 5 billion people will be connected online.
- They will spend over 100 hours a week on the web—working, playing, or entertaining.
- They will be game players, YouTubers, and innovation junkies.
- They will live on their mobile connection 24/7.
- They will click to get work, play, relationships, games, and love.
- They will be enabled by mobile, Big Data, and cloud.
- They will each have a social agenda that defines their identity.
- Brands that care about what they care about will thrive.

One of the key attributes that has emerged and will only become more pervasive is this category of customers who use the same Digital Transmedia (for media, finance, news, commerce, health) and similar Digital Platforms such as computers, autos, phones, and tablets.

These customers transact, produce, entertain, inform, buy, and sell over the Click-Stream of digital networks that are enveloping our world. The key behavior that connects these customers is that they click to know, buy, sell, and communicate, and they do this over the Click-Stream—the Internet, cloud computers, private networks, media, and cellular networks.

Enter the Click-Streamers—the customers of the future.

Click-Streamers are customers who live and work in the Click-Stream of digital information. They are global, cross-border, and connected, and they use a combination of digital tech to stay connected. They travel through the Click-Stream of mobile, web, apps, and information platforms that connect autos, markets, homes, health, gaming, media, and entertainment. They buy, sell, search, share, and collaborate with others via the Click-Stream.

They are globally connected to networks of affiliated interests. They crowd-source funds, collaborate across borders, download apps, upload pictures, share videos, play games, and invent programs. They live in the Click-Stream—it is a new global marketplace.

Click-Streamers in the near future will be the largest global customer segment on the planet because they will spend the most online, will be location independent, will be always online, will be mobile, spend the majority of their purchases online, and conduct their business, relationships, and commerce online. Click-Streamers will define the future of the marketplace for business.

Click-Streamers' customer behavior—from telecomputing, telemedicine, game playing, media watching, and media producing, to entertainment, e-commerce, and web shopping—will be defined by the amount of time they spend online and their behaviors conducted there. In an Always-On world, the mobile web will always be aware, always communicating, watching, and engaging us, the humans in the room.

Click-Streamers will comprise over 6 billion people across 120 nations who will spend or control over $50 trillion in spending by 2025.

Click-Streamers will drive e-commerce, from autos, flyables, wearables, or mobile. They will shape the future of brands and companies. Their user behaviors, today mobile, tomorrow augmented and virtual reality, will cause entirely new markets and industries to open up. Every organization must learn to understand the Click-Streamers and engage them as customers, freelancers, or employees.

Managing High-Velocity Change

Are you ready for managing high-velocity change in the New Future? Are you ready to build a business based on innovations that you invent? Are you ready to manage a team or a company that transforms how your customers use social media networks or virtual worlds? To be able to answer these questions, a radical new approach to doing business will be required. We need new thinking that looks forward, not backward, where we have come from.

The explosion of fast trends that will drive the New Future of business will create more opportunity and personal wealth creation than at any other time in the history of civilization. Fortunes will be made overnight. New industry sectors will emerge and disappear. Hypercompetition will challenge everyone

to reach higher, do more, and use technological innovations to shape a new future. This massive transformation of business will create a new generation of jobs, markets, and industries, most of which have not been invented yet. I explore this future and how to prepare for the changes that are coming at an accelerated pace.

The only caveat is that the individual leader, manager, or entrepreneur will need to change his or her self to be able to take advantage of these changes. In order to become Future Smart, you must become adaptive, embrace learning new things, be innovative, and, above all, look to the future—and this will require courage. We don't like change, and the problem is that the central challenge facing our world is that for the next fifty years extreme change will be what defines life and business. So we had best accept this reality and learn to manage the future.

That's the point. The inevitability of radical change, such as economic instability, changing demographics, disruptive technologies, to name a few, is not the challenge to predict; rather, the challenge is how to prepare oneself to thrive in this new complex and fast-changing world that is emerging. My job is to prepare you by mapping out the blueprint of change, to increase your Predictive Awareness so that you can thrive in this New Future.

Most of the products and services that will be sold by 2030 have not been invented yet. These will be products that have embedded intelligence, are tied to the cloud, are mobile, and have knowledge-rich features that will bring outstanding value and meaning to customers. These are the types of changes that are coming fast. Getting ready for this future—to shape this future—will require new thinking. This is not your daddy's economy. There are new rules emerging. Anticipating this future of radical and accelerating change will offer amazing new opportunities.

The future of business will not look like anything you have seen before. Many of the power players, the usual suspects and leaders of today, will not make the cut into the future. No, the past will not look like the future. The organization of the future will need to be agile, predictive, fast, and kinetic. This will require an entirely different mindset to manage. Innovation will not be an unusual risk factor but, instead, the lifeblood of the organization. Real-time innovation, constant reinvention, and experimentation will define the winners and the losers in the future. Talent will be an enabler of this fast future.

Innovate or Die

Most organizations are not Future Ready. Over 25 percent of all business will not change quickly enough and will either be merged, sold, or acquired out of

existence. This process of elimination—who understands this and who doesn't—is starting now. The handwriting is on the wall. Accelerated changes coming in technology, markets, economics, and global competition will forever change what a business does and why. New work processes and business models will be required. The actual authentic value that a company provides will change. The very paradigm of business, the purpose and behavior of business, will be forever altered.

I view all of this coming change as the natural evolution of business that is moving from one state of activity, structure, power, and operations to a more dynamic, kinetic, and high-velocity type of business—the Future Smart Enterprise. Leaders who understand this massive social change—not just in business but also global in scope—will be ahead of the wave. This doesn't mean that anyone has complete certainty of the changes that are coming, but one main catalyst will be advanced technological innovations.

Given my work with both start-up companies and large multinationals, I can say that radical technologies' impact on altering the DNA of business is comprehensive and, in the early stages, where new markets may emerge overnight, not within years. The speed of change is unforgiving for those who are sleeping on the job, so to speak. *Innovate or die* is the mantra you want to live for.

Business on Fire

If you have ever seen a fast-moving fire, it defies a rational explanation. It is explosive. A part-time job as a firefighter in college gave me a quick lesson in this. Wind can affect the direction, weather and the fuel the fire is consuming will shape the fire. Fire can jump, roll, snap, climb, and explode.

This is the impact of radical new technologies that offer almost amazing commercial applications such as the manipulation of matter in nanotechnology, autonomous devices such as drones and robotics, mobile commerce, neuroscience, and biotechnology. The Exponential Future of technology will bring the future faster, and this will be more disruptive.

The point is that advanced technology to create products, offer services, and produce solutions will enable as much as 75 percent of all businesses. The Future Smart organization is one that embraces smarter technology that can deliver better value for customers. Emerging technology will continue to be the driver of the future of business, regardless of industry.

Smarter, faster, smaller, and more cost-effective technology will enable employees and customers to engage the business. The Future Smart business leverages advanced technology to compete and provide value, to enable people to do amazing things.

The Ten New Rules of Business: Shape Your Future

The New Rules of Business are guideposts for big and small businesses that may enable them to navigate change and prepare to compete smarter. Whether it is the big enterprise that needs to become more agile and innovative or the start-up company that is looking to create a big success, the New Rules apply to every business that wants to become Future Smart.

If you are going to own your future and manage opportunity to your advantage and your customers or employees, you need to get this right to be in sync with the future. Miss the New Rules and you may miss the future opportunity to grow, invent, or transform your business.

1. Move fast, be agile.
2. Predict what's next and fulfill it.
3. Delight your customers.
4. Embrace bold ideas that challenge tradition.
5. Develop new Knowledge-Value products.
6. Attract smart talent now.
7. Create an Always-Learning culture.
8. Enable a culture that embraces change and innovation.
9. Deep collaboration wins.
10. Shape the future of your industry before the competition does.

Creating Knowledge Value: Decode Data

In the future the nature of work will fundamentally change. People and companies will still make and sell products and services, the stuff that drives economies, but the high-value work will be the engineering of knowledge. Knowledge-Value Engineering is the process of idea creation that creates products and services that use science and technology to innovate and form new business and lifestyle value. Knowledge-Value work will come to dominate the global economy over labor-intensive work. This will require a huge shift in retraining workers and education and will ultimately take generations to work out.

Knowledge Value envisioned by people to create value will be delivered by data science, unique algorithms designed to solve problems that will dominate business. Businesses will use data to predict what type of products and services people will buy, and when and where they will buy them. Solutions that go beyond consumerism to managing energy and climate, enabling innovation, reinventing education, and delivering social solutions will be in demand.

This capability, Knowledge-Value Engineering, will enhance the enterprise's ability to compete faster, understand customers, create products, and provide

service. Knowledge-Value Engineering, though not a recognized occupation yet, in the future will be an attractive career that will support individuals to specialize as a Knowledge Engineer in medicine, security, education, energy, and other vertical industries.

This expertise will drive jobs, projects, and new companies that do not exist today. Knowledge Value may also change the business model in new ways that others don't fully understand as yet. You can see this starting to happening today.

Companies that are leveraging Knowledge Value often defy the media and the public's understanding of what a business is. Few understand that Google's core technology is not their search business but rather the data science and Smart Machine intelligence that analyzes billions of people's data—the video, texts, e-mails, and search that are going on every second of every day. Amazon uses predictive analytics to create Knowledge Value about what customers will want and then recommend, based on data science, products that that they will likely want to buy.

Data Science Drives the Future

Knowledge-Value Engineering, what we today call data science, embeds products and services with specialized algorithms called Knowledge Value. This Knowledge Value is what brings intelligent functionality to products, services, and even networks. It is an entirely new paradigm of business that is coming.

For example, Bitcoins, the popular digital currency, are produced by specialized computers that have to solve complex computer science problems in order to mine the Bitcoins. This process of creating Bitcoins is called mining. The algorithm that lies at the heart of the dating site Match.com is what enables an automated system to connect people to meet and explore relationships. Now consider that every industry will be using data science for competitive advantage to predict, adapt, and win.

At the heart of more innovations there will be Knowledge Value, engineered data science that provides a unique value by providing features or capabilities that are unique to that product or service. Robots built with specialized Knowledge Value will provide the optimal experience someday. Intel's What's Inside campaign will remind us where the value is—inside the brain.

The creation of Knowledge Value will in itself become a new business innovation. Knowledge as a deliverable, what-we-think, prefer, desire, and then produce and sell is even now on the rise, but in the future the engineering of knowledge will be a global industry worth billions. Companies will compete for who has the smartest Knowledge-Value Platforms, services, and products. Knowledge that is empowering—drives new insights into customers, unlocks meaning from data, empowers customers, leads to innovative new products, enables you to find, transact, produce, or create—is Knowledge Value: information

that enables you to extract value that can be monetized. Knowledge Value will shape all online commerce.

If you're scratching your head while you're reading this narrative about Knowledge Value and think this is hard to understand, in many ways it is today. This is the New Future emerging, but it is not quite here yet. The world of making stuff is not going away. We are just increasing the marketplace for ideas and making new stuff that is more digital and virtual and enables a solution or process that was not possible before.

Knowledge-Engineering Companies

Companies who are Knowledge-Engineering enterprises sell their Knowledge Value to other companies as a business. Blab is such a company on the leading edge, analyzing over 100 million conversations per minute. Blab makes 1 million predictions per minute and analyzes fifty thousand social, news, and blog sources.

Blab (www.blabpredicts.com) predicts what people will be talking about over the next four days by analyzing many terabytes of conversations from social media. They predict what tomorrow's conversations are going to be. They are pioneering predictive social intelligence for companies that want to leverage what the customers are talking about so they can better serve and understand them.

The insights Blab sees are Knowledge Value at work. Their customers then align their marketing and strategy to use this Knowledge Value to compete and serve customers better and faster because of these insights. This is the power of Knowledge Value.

Compete as a data scientist for fortune, fame, or fun, as Kaggle states on its website to the world. Anyone can play and win—maybe if you're smart enough. They are an example of an organization that enables Knowledge Engineers who don't work for Kaggle but are freelancers that Kaggle challenges with cash and contests.

Kaggle is a platform for predictive modeling and analytics competitions on which companies and researchers post their data, and statisticians and data miners from all over the world compete to produce the best solutions (www .kaggle.com). Companies such as Merck, MasterCard, and GE employ Kaggle to crowdsource problems for which they want to use the wisdom of the global Internet—the crowd—to solve. Even NASA uses Kaggle. So Kaggle hosts contests sponsored by companies to solve huge Big Data problems and then pays anyone who can deliver the Knowledge-Value solution.

Here are some competitions from Kaggle that you can join:

- Acquire-Valued Shoppers Challenge: predict which shoppers will become repeat buyers.
- Risky Business: predict the risk of customer credit default.

- Decoding the Brain: predict visual stimuli from recordings of the human brain.
- Sentiment Analysis on Movie Reviews: classify the sentiment of sentences from a leading review site for movies.
- Learning Social Circles in Networks: model friend memberships to multiple circles.
- Random Acts of Pizza: predicting altruism through free pizza.

To give you an idea of how it works, NASA posted a competition to solve a problem that puzzled them for over a decade: measuring the dark energy in the universe. Dark energy is invisible and makes up the larger part of the cosmos. The physical cosmos—that's the seen universe of stars, suns, planets, and us—is thought to be the smallest part of the cosmos.

A glaciologist, who studies glaciers, won the competition when he applied his glacialology models to measuring dark energy. Now the big idea here is that NASA was able to solve a huge problem by harnessing minds, Knowledge Engineers, who used tools of Big Data analysis from an entirely different area, and it worked.

Knowledge Value is basically an invention process that leverages technology to make a new product or service. Knowledge Value is the algorithm, the program that makes a medical device, a videogame, or a financial investment. It is the next evolution of work. Knowledge Value creates products that are knowledge rich and enable capabilities and commerce that did not exist before.

Knowledge-Value Engineering, forged by a coevolution of technology and human brains, will take our civilization into the future and shape the what's coming in the global economy for the next hundred years.

Knowledge-Value Products

Knowledge-Value Products, developed with digital and social media tools, embedded knowledge, with dynamic algorithms and data science, will propel many industries and provide many new innovative products. Here is an example of how Knowledge-Value Products will look.

- Prediction systems, as a deliverable product that mine data from billions of customers to identify patterns, forecast the future buying behavior of consumers, and identify what they will buy and where and when
- Black box high-speed trading of virtual digital products—energy, stocks, bonds, commodities, and currencies—across global exchanges
- Game-playing Avatars used for education, training, and communications that bond with humans, self-organize, and evolve to better serve and understand human needs

- Smart Machines and cloud computers that generate digital currencies for online commerce and trade with other Smart Machines
- Cloud computing personal diagnostic Smart Devices that can be used to provide real-time analysis to prevent illness
- Privacy agents that watch our digital selves and protect us
- Smartphone applications that can diagnose your health in real time
- Customized pharmaceuticals that autonomously produce drugs inside your body from your own immune system, cells, and DNA
- Regenerative systems that search for disease inside our bodies
- Blended-reality environments that geospatially sense and intelligently self-organize retail purchasing experiences in real time
- YourTV, a personalized customized mobile web TV channel that is automatically generated and created for your interests and desires
- Brain ReFreshers, artificial intelligence that reorganizes information that is relevant to you, such as travel, interests, and sports, and then enhances the products and services with invigorating mind exercises to keep your brain healthy and engaged
- DEPs, or Digitally Engineered Personalities, the next generation of digital smart bots in our cars, houses, hospitals, and phones, that learn, self-evolve, and merge with our lives

Knowledge Value defines, shapes, and constructs the character and value of the future of business. For example, health care is about the value of curing disease, preventing disease, predicting our health future, and keeping us healthy. The Knowledge Value of health care will be about the unique combination of skills, data, systems, procedures, and intelligence that combines to accomplish that objective. The ability of doctors to Engineer Health, from applying Knowledge-Value Engineering, will transform medicine and health care.

Workers and companies that understand this fundamental shift that is coming, the shift from making stuff to mining ideas and producing innovation in the form of Knowledge Value, will have a competitive advantage in their carriers and in their work. Work itself is changing, and the highly paid work will be for higher Knowledge Value. This will be an evolutionary change in how the nature of work affects the planet. Today many industries are not ready for this shift, but it is coming.

Individuals and companies that produce Knowledge Value will be able to better anticipate, evolve, and adapt. They will become Future Smart. This is the future of business—the creation of Knowledge Value that is born of innovative ideas that enable markets, customers, and industries in entirely new ways.

You will not need to embrace every new technology to become Future Smart. Not every technology or solution that is brought by innovation will enhance the quality of your future life. I offer in this forecast how the landscape of

the future of our society will change—the complexity and even strange techno-changes that will alter our realities. The point is that emerging technology will fundamentally change the future of business, offering choices beyond those that we are familiar with today.

The Autonomous Economy

The wave of the future of business will be shaped by many trends but none more comprehensive than the rise of the Smart Machines—computers, networks, robotics, and systems working autonomously. You may ask why, and the answer is economics, innovation, and effectiveness. Machines do some things better and cheaper and with more value than humans. Automated harvesters run faster and more cost effectively than humans to work a farm. Robots are more efficient than humans in manufacturing plants and in trading stocks.

The autonomous economy—where Smart Machines operate large parts of the global economy both with and without humans, including finance, transportation, security, health care, and manufacturing—is emerging. In the future there will be an entire global Autonomous Economy run by Smart Machines. Nations will harness Smart Machines, and ecosystems of Smart Machines will compete and collaborate with each other in the Autonomous Economy.

Humans will have to redefine their role in the Autonomous Economy. This trend will challenge labor markets just as technology has gutted infinite levels of managers in organizations whose value has come into question. Autonomy will require humans to use machines in new ways to create new business value—no less than the revolution in work is coming. You want to think about becoming part of this debate about the future.

This Autonomous Economy will transform power on the planet. Globally connected Smart Machines, an essential part of the Innovation Ecosystem, may do a better job than humans for many jobs such as managing energy, geo-engineering climate, manufacturing and producing agriculture. Business will benefit. Humans will manage these Smart Machines for a time. That is the plan.

The ultimate endgame for the Autonomous Economy is autonomy—to run itself, to cure, fix, program, innovate, invent, regulate, and function independently from humans. We build it, and then it builds itself. Self-replication of computing clouds and elegant AIs growing and evolving their own network typologies, evoking neuro-chips and innovations in commerce and sustainability, will vindicate the nervous humans who will feel upstaged by Smart Machines that can manage critical global systems such as telecom, finance, security, power, and health care.

The transition from knowledge work shifting from humans to machines has started. Income tax filings, X-rays, sophisticated business analytics, advertising computer programs, robotized manufacturing, high-speed treading over stock

markets, and driverless cars are all automated today. Look around you—this has begun. Tomorrow Smart Machines will conduct surgery, security, health care, and, perhaps, invention and innovation. This is the evolution of business as well as civilization.

Headlines from the Future: 2025
Google Predictive-Life Knows Who You Want to Be

There are many unanswered questions that will emerge as we unwittingly run toward creating the Autonomous Economy. First we will finalize the factors that make our computers, autos, and industrial equipment very smart and connected—no humans need to apply. Smart Machines will not form unions or need health care coverage. There are no unsafe factories of the future for machines, just those pesky humans who cost so much.

The Autonomous Economy will run with few, and eventually no, humans, 24/7, completely automated, free of the problems that humans bring. The cost difference between fully autonomous factory lines and human and machines is over a 60 to 80 percent difference in favor of the machines. Are there not more interesting and desirable jobs for humans anyway in the future other than working in factories? You would think so.

The impact on Knowledge Work and the reduction of labor used for this work over machines will require strategies and policies about employment that we will have to figure out as we go. As usual, policy lags innovation, even if that innovation is not friendly to labor or, for that matter, humans.

There are other social issues beyond the automation competing with humans for jobs issue that we shall have to deal with that are even more serious. For example, who will these Smart Machines listen to if they are replicating themselves? We will have to keep one eye open when we sleep. Perhaps being Future Smart in the far tomorrow will be to make sure we know where the off button is on our Smart Machines.

2025 TOOLS

- Self-organizing materials
- The artificial cell
- Personalized super computers
- GPS sensors
- Programmable robots
- 3D maker

Chapter 8

The Innovation
Game Changers

I have spent much of my career trying to understand, analyze, and forecast how future technologies will change society, business, and our world. I have enjoyed helping entrepreneurs, government leaders, policy makers, and corporations understand what the future may hold. I have had the privilege of being at the forefront of many of the leading-edge technologies that have shaped our world—including computers, artificial intelligence, biotech, telecom, the Internet, neuroscience, and nanoscience. I remain as excited today about technology's future to contribute to our world as I did when I started this journey decades ago.

I also have been known for forecasts that my clients did not want to see coming or even agreed with. I recall guest teaching at Wharton's Advanced Management Program for a top financial service company based in New York City that had sworn in ads that they would never give their clients control of their own portfolios over the Internet.

A leading insurance company was furious when I suggested that the Internet was going to force a change in the competitive landscape of the industry. Or, when I forecasted the shift to the mobile Internet, my clients who had recently embraced the web found it difficult to now step into a new frontier of unknowns in mobile. Yes, I have not always been popular, but as I tell my clients, "You pay me to tell you the truth. So I shall here."

As an entrepreneur working with start-up companies and advising global corporations, technological innovations continue to be the biggest game changers on the planet. Almost daily, technology changes the game of business, society, and our civilization. I expect that technological innovations and the new industries, business models, markets, and enterprises that will emerge in the future will continue to be even more amazing. The tools that will transform the world—increasing wealth, creativity, and quality of life—lay with what's

next in technology. My thirty-year journey to discover what's next has shaped my life and work. My job continues to be to describe what's coming and get you ready to navigate this New Future.

Apple Changes the Game

I was lucky. I had many early experiences with technology. I was involved with the beginning of the Internet, before the web. When Apple in Silicon Valley hired me in 1979 to work on the introduction of the new Macintosh computer, this really brought together all of my interests as a social scientist, entrepreneur, and novice futurist. I was in charge of business, and this meant managing the professions and industries as well as forecasting advanced tech trends such as AI. I was the first futurist to be hired at Apple or at any computer company who had the job of looking forward into the future. I had started my forecasting career before Apple, working as a policy adviser for the US government and in the private sector, but technology as an enabler of futures was completely new to me and everyone else.

I was working on my doctoral thesis on systems and global change, and the opportunity to work at Apple was too seductive. I figured I could do both. Little did I know that my life was about to change. Gene Senyak, the first creative director and a friend of mine, had asked me to join Apple. We had a business to reinvent education back in New York City a few years earlier before we met again at Apple.

Silicon Valley was all just starting up, and if the world was going to be reinvented based on technology, it was going to happen there. I was hooked. Here was a collection of outrageously creative folks all working together to change the world—really, that is how we thought at Apple in the early days.

We were convinced that we were going to change the world by bringing out the first personal computer that people would use as a personal empowerment tool—not just use or buy, no. We wanted people to love everything about our computers, from the design to the software to the way the computer talked. And they did.

My interactions with Steve Jobs were mostly insightful and bombastic. That's who he was, but I admired and shared his vision of the future of technology. He was fiercely committed to his ideas about the future of tech. The thing was that if you understood Steve and shared his infectious vision of the future, it was much easier to get along with him. Big oversized egos in Silicon Valley— so what's new about that? You have today a number of hugely successful and amazingly innovative Steve Jobs–types that continue to rule in Silicon Valley.

I realized that tech was going to be the major driver of global, social, business, and personal change, and I was hungry to understand what this global shift was all about.

Being involved with the Phone Phreaks, the original hackers, and the ideas that technology should be a personal tool to create more freedom, commerce, and creativity in your life had influenced both Jobs and me. The focus was to empower the individual. As the person in charge of business and professions at Apple, I realized that computers and the Internet would offer game-changing opportunities that would change our civilization by giving individuals the tools to shape their destinies as never before. That idea is perhaps more true today than ever before.

If you think about it, computers, smartphones, networks, and robots are creating an entirely new global culture. Computers are the linchpins to the Internet that is still transforming the planet. At Apple we had early access to e-mail, the Internet, local area networks, and all the computers we wanted in order to experiment and learn. It was a great time for me and firmly got me thinking about how tech would transform the future in dramatic and amazing ways.

At Apple we knew we were changing the world by creating personal computers for individuals first—enabling people with digital tools that we thought would create a better world by democratizing the one digital tool, the computer, that would give people the power to invent *their* future—not the future envisioned by government or business. This digital democracy at work was infectious in the culture of Apple; we all felt it. Other than the creation of the venture capital industry and the Internet, there is no other force had as great an impact in creating entrepreneurs on the planet as the personal computer.

I gave some of the first Macintosh computers to the National Institutes for Health for research, countless other medical and other professionals, and entrepreneurs so we could better understand how our customers wanted to use the computers, not unlike Google, Facebook, and Apple still do today. Those were exciting times at Apple that shaped my thinking as a futurist about what was possible for the future of civilization.

After Apple I worked with various start-up companies in telecom and the Internet and then became CEO of an early AI company, Umecorp. We designed expert systems, a form of AI for business and entertainment. We built hardware and software platforms to enable virtual reality (VR) for gaming entertainment, using our experience about AI and thinking systems. I recall working on the models for android brains and figuring out how virtual reality entertainment platforms in 3D might be designed. I worked with some of the early innovators in AI and VR and put into play ideas I had about creating new forms of enterprises based on advanced innovation.

Later experiences in global finance and merchant banking gave me another perspective on the worldwide market for technological investments. I realized that technology was changing the rules of business by creating new forms of enterprise that could not have been envisioned before. I have always migrated toward the new. Finally, in 1990, after a number of high-tech entrepreneurial

enterprises I started, I formed the Institute for Global Futures to help my clients think about the future of trends and innovations that were creating both opportunity and disruptions.

The Innovation Economy

Prepare to be amazed. The Innovation Economy will electrify markets, generate billions of new jobs, catalyze new industries, and make for a prosperous future. Most of you will be changed—in good ways. Mostly. Smarter technology will give the individual more choices to be an entrepreneur and to embrace a new lifestyle enabled by smart technology. Are you ready to surf the changes that are coming?

This is the early stage of the Innovation Economy. Big innovations are emerging quickly. There is an artificial cell for synthetic biology, computers are only a few decades old, the smartphone was only just invented, the web is a new phenomenon that lives separate from TV, and electric cars are just now showing up. Stem cells will soon rebuild bodies. 3D manufacturing is just starting, and artificial intelligence is not very intelligent.

There is no teleportation or high-yield renewable energy. Nanotech is in its infancy. Humanity has not left the planet to go into deep space. Robots are clumsy and dumb. We have not unraveled the human genome to merge with health care, and where are those flying cars futurists have been promising everyone? When the flying cars show up, then we will know we are in the future.

As a futurist who is always looking into what's coming next, I am positive about the future. I see many more opportunities that tech will bring to transform people's lives for the better than I see for the worse.

I know it is fashionable to embrace the dystopian dream of Terminator-type robots crashing our world, and I have signaled caution where I think it is deserved, but overall I am excited about the potential of tech to help us make this a better, more productive, and peaceful world for our children and grandchildren as well as ourselves.

Nowhere is this proven more so than in what I forecast here for the tech impact on our future. There is not another more comprehensive wave than tech that will shape our future so deeply and offer such economic opportunity for individuals. Technological innovations shall be a great global equalizer of people's quality of life, prosperity, and freedom. So there is my bias, upfront, so you know where I stand. We have the opportunity to meet all of our global challenges with advanced tech, if used properly, and I fervently believe we shall do so, as this is our destiny.

Are you looking for a new career? Perhaps you've noticed the huge wealth creation the game changers are shaping—the technologies, bio, web, mobile, and neuro that are, every day, bringing the future closer. The Googles, the Twitters,

the Ali Babas, the biotech—what's next is nano and quantum. Are you ready for the Innovation Economy where fast innovation and technology adaptation is the only competitive advantage?

There are major new changes coming from robots, Big Data, mobile business, digital health, cloud computing, nanoscience, and neuroscience. Are you ready for this explosive future of hypercompetition, global connectivity, and kinetic business opportunities?

The Innovation Economy, the convergence of key technologies that will shape the shape of business, markets, and society is coming. In this chapter you dive deeply into what's coming and how to prepare your strategy for becoming Future Smart.

Technology has been an essential tool for transforming individuals and societies for centuries. From the Iron Age to the Industrial Revolution to the Information Age and now onto the Global Innovation Economy, technology continues to be the essential driver of change and progress in civilizations. Technology has transformed our lifespans, communications, globalization, trade, and even war. It can be argued that technology has shaped both personal and geostrategic power, business productivity, and the competitive advantage of nations, organizations, and individuals in the past, and it will so in the future.

Technology's impact on economics is undeniable. In the current US economy technology industries of biotech, IT, and industrial uses of technology constitutes more than one-third of the GDP. By 2030 over 75 percent of GDP will be innovation-based enterprises. It is the key driver of jobs, markets, industries, new products, services, consumerism, and quality of life throughout the world. A technology-savvy and successful society is a prosperous society. Societies that embrace open technology access are productive societies.

Entrepreneurs who harness technology will continue to be wealth multipliers, transforming themselves and our world with their innovations that make a difference in health, education, commerce, transportation, and finance. This exponential explosion of innovation will become fiercer in the future as the availability of smart tools, systems, and new cheap and smart technologies become available, as we shall explore.

Technology advances are also the central driver of not just societies but also regions and globalization as a whole. One of the advances in the quest for peace and prosperity today and in the future is the success of globalization, and technology is a key enabler and multiplier of this effort. Future technologies will enable globalization, especially global business, accelerating wealth and prosperity, opening new markets, forging new industries, and creating new jobs.

Access to technology is a powerful influencing factor in increasing prosperity, quality of life, peace, and security. Technology access, cell phones, the Internet, and computing will together create a communications infrastructure that can greatly support a nation's efforts toward embracing modernity.

Additional technologies such as nano and neuro will, like communications, create massive new business and job opportunities. Technology applied to agriculture, health care, and commerce also stimulates economic growth, social stability, and peace. Technology is a driver of productive change at the individual, occupational, and society level.

The Early Stage of the Innovation Economy

This is the early stage of what I have been calling for twenty years the Innovation Economy. We just invented computing, the web, cell phones, and very few other innovations in less than thirty years. Technology is a very new invention in the long timeline of history. We don't have one hundred years of DNA sequencing and robots behind us; we have a few decades or less. We happened to accidently invent the Internet. Genetics has not changed health care yet. We don't really understand where disease comes from. We have not even left the planet to colonize space. And yes, flying jetpacks are not available as yet—I know.

This is still a very primitive time on the planet for technology, yet tremendous wealth, economic opportunity, and new products and services have emerged from the Innovation Economy to shape our world for the better.

As we step into the future *all* of this will change. Technology will disappear into things, biology will merge with matter, wireless health care will heal us, and energy will be something we generate without pollution or carbon to run cars and cities. The web will be tied to everything, and everything will be awakened to us humans.

Humans will have new choices to alter our minds and bodies, to extend our lives so as to create and do business with five times the amount of lifetimes to innovate, make a difference, play golf, and travel. Advanced technology solutions will bring the choices coming that will make our world and ourselves better and, perhaps, more fulfilled. Are you ready for this New Future and the lifestyle of the empowered? This idealistic future of endless possibilities will not come without risks, dangers, and threats. For with every new technology that brings benefits, there comes challenges that we must embrace as well.

Tech Shapes the Future

The futuristic technologies profiled here, the Tech Game Changers, will even be available to lift up entrepreneurs and nations because of inexpensive, rapidly evolving, powerful, and smart technologies of the future. We no longer need to string cables and telephone poles to provide telephone access—a wireless network can now be deployed. This is just the beginning of smaller, faster, cheaper, and smarter technology emerging.

Expensive computers will give way to inexpensive, smart wearable and mobile devices, wireless network-based software on demand and accessible anywhere in the cloud. Medicine delivered via smartphone apps and from the cloud or by Smart Things will simply change every aspect of life. We shall go from unconnected to connected, from disempowered to empowered.

Cheap, smart, connected Morphable Tools will enable us to be vastly more creative in our business, culture, play, and work. Morphable Tools are what we once called computers or networks. They are specialized tech capabilities in the cloud that we download to perform tasks and craft solutions that we use to operate our business and our world—Life Apps. We will be more fully human when smart technology figures out who we are and what we want.

There is just too much work to do this all now. This will change us and our world when Intuitive Technology that smells, senses, watches, searches, analyzes, predicts, connects, and produces for us what we need. I know this sounds intrusive and less than private and not for everyone, but it is coming in the near future. The Millennials will get it.

The next generation of distributed and inexpensive technologies such as nanotechnology will follow similar pathways—cheap, fast, smart, powerful, and easy to use. Tech-driven global prosperity will be possible over the next twenty-five years, as new breakthroughs in energy; medicine, and environmental management are expected from future technology.

The same future technologies that will enliven the future, providing more opportunity, will also pose threats. There will be private and public parties that view technology as wrongfully empowering individual self-determination and weakening efforts toward the ideological and social control of minds; freedoms and liberties will be challenged. Radical ideologies will be overthrown. The battle for individual privacy, the rights of the individual, freedom from coercion and control will all be major challenges in a globally connected future of too many eyes.

Technology access influences self-determination, freedom, openness, innovation, and access to tools. Competing ideologies, enemies of modernity and technology, are opposed to this ideology of technology. This risk should be carefully watched. For every benefit technology brings in the future there will be dangers from powers that would use it to repress individual freedoms and liberties. High-tech entrepreneurs are natural disruptors of repressive societies.

At the same time attacks on privacy and security will threaten even democratic societies. DNA profiling and video and web surveillance are everywhere. Will our minds be invaded someday? We must uphold our Cognitive Liberty in the future—our right not to be scanned. That is why the rise of the Tech Game Changers is dangerous to some and liberating to others. Most of us will benefit greatly.

The rise of prosperity brought by technology will enable billions to participate in free trade, commerce, and free enterprise who were not connected before. Globalization, enabled by technology and commerce, is a great equalizer of economies and individuals. A connected global economy where individuals have technology access and freedom of choice will drive the future quality of life on the planet. There are those who would stop the global expanse of technologies that empower the individual—we must guard against this in the future. This the major risk factor individuals face in the future.

Over the next twenty-five years technology will put the tools to create prosperity, peace, and increased quality of life into the hands of billions of more individuals than at any other time in the history of our civilization due to cheaper, more powerful, and smarter tools. Entrepreneurs should work to provide increased access to technology to the world's markets and individuals. There is an unparalleled opportunity for entrepreneurs to build new enterprises around the world as all markets get connected through technology.

This is consistent with the history of innovation. These innovations enabled great progress around the world to the benefit of many. The Internet, computing, lasers, networks, nanotech, and biotech started in the United States. Investments made now around the world in these new technologies have created wealth and prosperity worldwide.

Digital capitalism will continue to empower individuals from any nation regardless of culture, religion, race, or belief—and the world will be better for it. A billion new entrepreneurs will transform the future. This trend will exponentially expand in the future. By 2030 the global GDP shall be over 7 percent, more than double today's growth levels. A vibrant global market for entrepreneurs will erupt in the near future.

Over the next twenty-five years we should continue to invest in the miraculous waves of next-generation technologies, as these technologies will enable social progress, peace, and business for billions of people on the planet. If you want a peaceful world for our children and grandchildren, then investing in technology futures is one of the best ways to ensure in a better, more equitable, and more productive world. Technology is an enabler of this future, not a panacea.

Twenty-Five-Year Tech Forecasts

Moore's Law—that transistor density on a chip doubles about each two years—is a general rule applicable for every technology forecasted here. Faster-than-Moore's Law is the future norm—exponential 10 to 1000 times change. This means that bandwidth, genetic sequencing, nanotechnology, Internet penetration, and wireless penetration also increase exponentially.

Moore's second law says that during this same period of time, when tech is doubling in power, it is also decreasing in cost by 50 percent. Supercomputers

that are wearable will be here soon and, perhaps due to cloud computing, here today—they just need to turn themselves on.

Then there is the Smart Connectivity Law (this came from a client of my company who started using the term after hearing me talk, and it stuck). The Smart Connectivity Law refers to the hyperconnectivity of everything: what *can* be connected *will* be connected. Everything will be networked and wants to be networked. Smart things—sensors, cars, chips, devices—will desire connectivity. We are entering a future age of high connectivity and convergence, where connectivity is driving banking, financial markets, health care, communications, governments, and markets.

After 2030 new chips, which are the brains inside every technology, will evolve beyond silicon to quantum or other advanced materials. This will generate supercomputer speeds, memory storage, and calculation capacity that by 2030 will approach human cognitive rates. Nano-chips operating at the level of quantum physics will be able to manipulate time and space beyond our understanding today. The morphing of realities, the collapse of time, the phase shifting of time—this is in the mix.

Experiments with the teleportation of photons, or bits of light, demonstrate the potential of the quantum as potential technology. Entire quantum computers, quantum clouds, will operate in ways that make the speed and thinking capacities of today's computers primitive in comparison. The convergence of most media, communication, security, and computing technologies will be fundamental to the future forecasts here.

The emergence of increasingly smarter technology—products that think, talk, and interact with humans and other machines—will be a given in the future. By or soon after 2030 the exponential power of technology will exceed human beings' capacity to measure or even fully understand.

Geo-tagging, the location awareness of people and things globally, will change everything. The interoperability of technologies—to interact and collaborate beyond human communications or awareness—will become desirable.

The reliance on AI-distributed intelligence to manage technology, from security to the economy to food production to the management of cities, will emerge. Technologies will morph into other technologies: nano and bio will merge, and medicine will merge with biotech. This convergence of technologies is the next stage of development.

The Internet will become Always On and a pervasive mobile experience for the majority of the planet's population. Open-source development is a global trend, making the tools of almost every future technology available for free on the Internet, where anyone can download and build almost anything.

Cheap smart technology is the future.

Disposable, downloadable, free, open source—cheap and powerful will characterize all technologies reported here. No more secrets. Assume that in

the future, given the global proliferation of technology, intellectual property (patents), free information exchange, and global Internet access, maintaining secrets related to technology will be difficult.

Envisioning the future of technology can be hard to communicate and even harder to understand. Let's start off with realizing that technology is going to change everything in fundamental ways—faster, smaller, smarter, and connected, to start with. That's right—everything. This means both the important things in life such as relationships, work, business, government, freedom, culture, and war as well as things we are obsessed with such as devices, games, media, cars, music, and fashion will be forever changed in form and function.

Everything will change in the New Future of five to thirty years from today. In this chapter I am going to explore what's interesting to me about this large subject and what I think you need to think about in order to become Future Smart.

THE GAME-CHANGING TECH TRENDS COMING

- The Internet of Things (IoT) will create a new world of smart products that are connected to everything and everyone.
- The mobile Internet will become the largest marketplace, connecting everyone to everything.
- Cloud computing will make available on-demand smart services and real-time Synthetic Intelligence anywhere and anytime.
- Big Data will transform how we understand ourselves and our world.
- Smart Machines will be pervasive, thinking and acting faster and perhaps smarter than humans.
- Tech will come to predict and understand you better than you.
- Social media will transform the way consumers and organizations communicate, trust, and relate.
- The five breakthrough technologies: nano, bio, neuro, info, quantum will lead the future technology revolution.
- Robots and androids will be a familiar part of our world.
- Innovation Ecosystems—vibrant connected global markets—will usher in a new civilization.

Grand Challenges

The future of technology will be shaped by innovations we throw at solving Grand Challenges, the big global problems humanity faces: managing climate, developing new pharmaceuticals to fight disease, educating more people, providing security, ending poverty, creating jobs, developing renewable energy,

fueling, securing, healing, and feeding the planet. The implications of the coming explosion in the population from 7 billion to as many as 9 billion by 2050 means that we will need to apply technology faster to keep up with the demand of the challenges that are coming.

Here is the challenge: we will have to innovate faster, smarter, and produce breakthroughs sooner to keep pace with the needs of our connected planet. The social agenda of creating a sustainable planet is what is going to drive many of the future developments in technology. This forecast is a practical one—we have a growing mountain of challenges to our survival we must apply to technology.

Tech Solutions Coming

The good news is we will likely solve many of these Grand Challenges facing our world with technological innovations that provide solutions. I forecast that between 2015 and 2030 accelerated breakthroughs are coming. Many of these Grand Challenges, from poverty to health care to education, are on their way to being fixed today. The technologies of smarter supply-chain logistics can eliminate much of the poverty in the world, if applied with proficiency. Health care innovations are enabling better access to health care.

Diagnostic devices are getting smaller and smarter. They are being developed as fast as smartphones can get shipped, and the prices are coming down. Education is moving to the Internet. There, thousands of free courses (massive open online courses, or MOOCs) are offered as well as entire college programs from prestigious universities like MIT, which is posting its courses on the Internet.

Think about what technologies lay at the core of companies such as Facebook, Google, Amazon, and Apple. Digital business models that create value— not necessarily things—are generating billions of dollars and Euros. Companies that enhance and empower their customers with innovations will continue to thrive in the future. Here are the technologies that are shaping the future:

- mobile commerce
- cloud computing
- digital media
- analytics
- Big Data
- simulation

Your Reality Engineering

Can you be seduced into a world of Smart Technology that has as its purpose to understand you, facilitate as your agent, as your digital persona, create a better life for you? Who wouldn't want to try this out as a Digital Experience Program to better engineer your life, your career, and your relationships and even help you become prosperous, creative, and successful or help you become a Nobel Prize winner for ending cancer or ebola? The Reality Engineering of You and

your world is coming, and by 2030 or before it will become available. This is the Game-Changing Trend that will revolutionize your life and world because it will deliver capabilities that today would boggle your mind.

Imagine people with access to this Reality Engineering capability, brought by the convergence of Smart Machines, who traverse the web, interacting, negotiating, and transacting with other Smart Machines in a cloud computing world of Big Data that is programmed to optimize an infinite number of human needs, all with the objective of meeting your desires across an endless spectrum of possibilities, web networks, and markets where anything is possible. Nations will harness Reality Engineering as a massive networked driver of innovation to provide jobs and social services and to spur on innovation industries contributing to making the economy and society more sustainable and equitable—bringing up the quality of life on the planet. Where huge income gaps disappear, the gaps between the rich and poor, the powerful and the powerless and the haves and have nots, will disappear.

A New Future is coming when Reality Engineering will enable fresh and dynamic new economic opportunities to lift up nations and peoples, addressing needs of Reality Engineering, such as the next clean and cheap energy, enabling distributed health care and education, feeding the planet, as well as immersive entertainment. The possibilities are endless where ideas can take flight as we learn to Engineer our Realities.

Reality Engineering will evolve beyond this formative stage of reading your e-mails, analyzing your work or business, and acting to find, negotiate, or help to facilitate your success or desires in life. No, there is much more amazing explosions of innovation coming that defy the limits of our imagination today. When you consider that Reality Engineering will evolve, as a combination of human and synthetic intelligences that, by 2030, have access to not just information, locations, digital worlds, or web technologies but also to nanotechnology, neurotechnology, and even quantum technology, now it gets interesting. What will our world look like when nano, bio, neuro, and quantum technologies are Tools of Innovation Creation? What shall we build, create, fix, or do? What shall we invent that will transform the future?

Reality Engineering that can produce entire new industries, products, services, virtual worlds, synthetic entertainment, energy harvesting, and alternative realities will be developed. Reality Engineering will transform global supply chains—how we make things to how we deliver and sell things. An entirely new industry with new entrepreneurs, linking up manufacturing, design, distribution, customer service, and service sciences that are operated by Reality Engineers. This New Future is coming enabled by the best Neuro-Hacks that Smart Machines or humans can invent! We will move seamlessly from thinking to simulating to making to selling things—both virtual and physical

in this New Future. Reality Engineering will become a global culture shift in how we live, work, and invent. Reality Engineering will shape our future as it will bring forth new Engines of Creation that will provide vast powers to transform society.

The harnessing of Smart Machines to pattern reality, to design reality, to program experiences will be a competitive advantage of business. The Reality Engineers will blend cognitive computer science with specialized industry skills. Even writing about this capability, what's coming, may be impossible for some people to envision or conceive. Sounds like sci fi, but it will be real. You will hear the beginning of this capability called Augmented Reality. This is the hint of an entirely new innovation process that defies today's logic but not tomorrow's imagination, fueled by the game-changing technologies described here.

Harnessing Reality Engineering to enhance our health, end aging, personalize our entertainment, transact with other Smart Machines and Innovation Ecosystems to negotiate business, or create the next digital revolution in your industry, thereby enabling supply chains, finance, logistics, media, health care, is coming. Plug in your favorite business challenge you want to transform here:

_____.

Headlines from the Future: 2025
Smarter Than Humans?
Design Your Smart Machines Here
SmartMachines.com

In the New Future of 2030 Reality Engineering will become a way of life, the way to develop business for those that have access to this powerful new technology.

Reality Engineering—the harnessing of supercomputers, data, and network resources to invent products, services, and solutions—will design your health, work, relationships, wealth, and future. We have glimpses of this emerging technology today, such as the few who have access to high-speed computer trading on stock exchanges around the world, who earn billions in seconds by harnessing supercomputers process trades faster and smarter than the rest of the market. There are advanced stem cell and genetic medicines that enhance intelligence, mobility, and prevent disease, extending lifetimes by eradicating disease. Someday in the future we shall Reality Engineer even the end of disease and perhaps even end aging.

From Dumb to Smart Tech

Up to now, well, technology has been fairly dumb, reactive, and marginally responsive to what we want. We have had to do something to get technology to perform. But we have to do something: turn on the TV that we cannot talk to, stop the car that is not a learning machine, pull up the phone that is unaware of us, search the web—often imprecise—to find things, examine all of the choices of products or sort through the services to find the right one. . . . That's exhausting in a world of infinite choices.

Now imagine for a moment a different, smarter future. What if technology was smart and aware enough so that whatever or wherever the tech was, it could watch, sense, measure, adapt, and help intuit what we needed? What if all technology had Dynamic Prediction? Dynamic Prediction is a self-organizing capability that enables computer-based technology embedded in, say, our cars, homes, cell phones, personal cloud, and medical devices to anticipate our needs with accuracy? In that way true personalization could occur, even a type of intimacy that escapes us today. Now, that would be smart. And that's what's coming in the future.

This will be your connection to the Reality Engineering Future—where your mind (Neuro-Sync Now, to your wearable computer of 2020) and voice controls and visualizes what reality you want to engineer. Now, I am talking about a future capability to invent, innovate, and manufacture what does not exist today in one place. The convergence of many technologies will enable this New Future of Reality Engineering, but we are well on our way now. The simulation of realities with advanced next-generation CGI software tied to cloud networks of Smart Machines will be used for creating entertainment, health care security, and education in the future—for a price or for a higher purpose, as we shall explore.

Think about this. Smart Technology of the future will know that the milk is going bad in the refrigerator, sense that our car's electric charge needs to download energy from the microgrid, alert us before a heart attack happens, or predict what we are going to look for on the web before we start. In other words, Smart Technology will define the future of our world. Smart Technology will empower, engage, and enchant us.

Reality Engineering, powered by the future web, an AI-based Internet of colossal intelligence, rich-media production tools, sensors everywhere (Internet of Things) transaction capabilities, and infinite knowledge access, will enable a New Future of dynamic markets, digital culture, and a new era of entrepreneurs who will harness this superintelligence on demand. You want to design a virtual world where your idea of a video multiplayer gaming world (a multibillion-dollar industry today) can be Reality Engineered in days. You want to

invent a web TV show that is crowd sourced and a 100 million sign-up for the first season on their Everywhere Wearables. Move over Netflix.

Your new cloud-hosted digital medical device can be Reality Engineered and presold as a 3D simulation model in the nano-speed of a text message and go begin manufacturing in minutes. Maybe your dynamic predictive systems already decided and made the device? Let's make that modular electric car just for the Indian market and crowdsource the design and features for delivery in three months. The potential for Reality Engineering is only limited by your imagination.

Will there be intrusions into our privacy? Yes, like the telemarketers who still call every day selling something. I turned off my land line—too much noise. There will be serious intrusions as well. Maybe we don't want technology to know too much about us. Maybe we don't want technology to be able to predict our needs. Maybe, but this is coming, and we had better be ready for a different type of world, where pervasive information can educate, inform, share, intrude, embarrass, and maybe even harm us. We will need systems to protect us from other systems that would do harm.

Let's get back to this point that will be a gigantic shift in technology's evolution and impact on humans: instead of doing all the work to get tech to understand us humans, tech will know, sense, and be aware of our needs, goals, and desires and then enable us to realize our goals, fulfill those needs, and satisfy our desires. That seems like a tall order, but that is where we are headed.

If you wrap your head around this idea—that predictive Smart Machines will adapt to you—then you begin to see the future differently. Every device, car, house, surface, product, and, well, everything starts to Get Smart and notices you, going from dumb to smart. When this shifts—and it's starting now—walls will have ears, cars will have personalities, and technology will wake up to pay attention to us. This appears strange, but it's happening in small ways now. In the New Future that's coming this will be a way of life. In fact, we will wonder how we got along without this smartness.

The predictive recognition of people by machines—smarter and smarter machines—will shape a different type of civilization in which the coevolution of Smart Technology and humans will converge. Later this convergence will offer even stranger choices, lifestyles, and even types of beings that we will not recognize if they knocked on our doors today.

Predicting Desire

In fact, the prediction of our desires by Smart Technology embedded in robots, cars, buildings, smartphones, computers, clothes—all physical stuff and virtual stuff—web, networks, markets, and services will be the decisive difference in

how smart Smart Technology will evolve. The shift from Dumb Technology that is reactive, that waits for us to call upon it, that stumbles around to find, locate, or transact what we want, compared to Smart Technology that has the power to predict, search with precision, adapt, intuit, and learn from us, what we want, will be the difference in the future.

For example, instead of figuring out by random, time-wasting searching using search engines to find the latest golf or soccer scores or contact information for the new running shoe, Smart Technology could anticipate, predict, and interact with us to identify and find what we want. Smart Technology will predict our desires, and it will be both spooky and amazing. We will feel intruded upon right up until the moment when we are not.

That's when we decide that our security or Reality Engineering capability, for example, is more important than intrusion. A new language will be needed to understand this. For example, a Smart Assist will be acceptable; it is justified, such as when your daughter was late for an appointment and your Digital Agent, empowered by Reality Engineering, of course, texted you in your car to let you know. This was welcomed, as she was ill and had to be taken to the hospital. Authorized intrusions that are personalized and relevant will change our acceptance of intrusive tech.

Technology's capacity to predict our desires and then help us realize these desires, fulfill our needs, and make our goals real will create a new type of technology that will fundamentally change our civilization. Imagine Smart Technology that recognizes commerce on the planet to find jobs for every person. Smart Technology that evolves—learns, self-organizes, has cognition, senses us, and embraces the three Laws: Empowers, Engages, and Enchants—is coming soon in the future, when the discovery of our desire and the fulfillment of that desire may be the central focus of the Smart Technology inside everything, including cars, homes, and devices and even embedded in nature. Smart Technology that seeks to serve us, help us, and fulfill our needs will awaken animate and inanimate objects.

We are at the edge of a Blended Reality in which intelligence is not only human, objects sense and interact with each other and humans, various neuroscience augments our perception, and Smart Technology morphs the fundamental structure of our lives, such as work, play, family, friends, and community.

But there will be a dark side to all of this new disruptive technology that connects those who don't want it, predicts inaccurately, senses that which should be private, and damages those who would desire to not share their digital identities or be analyzed by Smart Technology. It will be hard to say *No* and harder to just turn off the Smart Technology that we have become merged with, embedded into, fused onto, and dependent upon. In fact, this is how this evolution and fusion of humans and machine cultures will start.

We will come to depend on Smart Technology to run our world, run our future, and better manage the agriculture, finance, climate, energy, and fundamental challenges that threaten our civilization's future. Once we are reliant on this Smart Technology that was born of overdependence, a world of better design and management than one run just by humans—that is where the problems will emerge, I caution.

We need to make certain that we can turn off that which we have created. We need to build in safeguards so we are not so dependent on the world we manage so well with our Smart Technology that we betray the humans if things go wrong—and they shall. Smart Technology will go off the rails, have problems, and will need to be periodically shut off so we know we can do it. The Autonomous Economy of driverless cars, automated defense systems, bit-mining computers, virtual reality engines, nano–self-assembling devices, environmental scrubbers—and the list goes on—will pose threats to our existence.

If there is one universal principle that our civilization has learned it is that Darwinian evolution rewards the fittest with the prize—survival. Humans must retain the mantle of planetary leadership and hegemony by controlling the evolution of thinking machines, strong AI best summarized as Smart Machines. We have to curtail their intelligence or be subjected to the outcome that may follow.

Managing Complexity

Another marker of what is fascinating about technology is the immense complexity of it as phenomena that defies human understanding. Already we humans do not fully understand how technology is getting smarter, faster, merging deeper, and becoming more intimate with our world. We are coming to depend on Smart Technology that is smarter than us. Now, what I mean is that tech that is smarter in a different way from humans, not in the same way—not superior or inferior but a different form of intelligence.

This was the problem originally that few scientists understood about AI over the decades: we shouldn't be trying for fifty years to build machines smarter than humans because our machines, if programmed to be smart, can build smarter machines—truly smart machines will build smart machines.

We shouldn't be trying to emulate human intelligence but rather augmenting it with Mind Engines that are really Difference Engines that can do things we cannot, like merge big data to stimulate economic growth, develop clean energy, fix the climate, make drugs to end cancer, formulate high-yield crops to end hunger, and succeed where humans struggle and fail. (I would settle for finding all of those black socks that disappear from my closet.) Many would argue that in free societies those supercomputers should be used for pleasure and profit: creativity, music, art, and, yes, stock trading.

Intuitive Technology Knows You

The whole obsession with smarter-than-human machines is frankly off-purpose. We need a different set of intelligences that are complementary, different from human and, coevolutionary that can augment and enhance our intellectual capabilities to solve the Grand Challenges of our times. And we shall get these coevolutionary machines coming soon in the New Future.

This is what is coming in the future. Intuitive Technology will know you and understand you and your life and work goals. It is Intuitive Technology that will follow you from place to place, device to device, virtual to physical locations and forms—house, car, beach, hotel, or wherever you may go.

Intuitive Technology that is smart enough will design itself to enable and empower humans to survive and thrive in the complex future, the extreme future that is coming. There is a plan, and humans are only one part of the plan. Technology is waking up, becoming aware, turning into us to figure out what we want and then how to evolve to help us get it—minute to minute, day to day, challenge to challenge.

If this sounds too abstract, let me bring it back to reality. You're looking for a new job today. This is a mostly hit-or-miss, chaotic process of random events and connections that may or may not work out with the result—a job, and one you like. Now imagine Smart Technology that knows what you want, your skills, your desires as well as the nuances of your personality and your hidden talents—maybe things that even you don't know about yourself.

Now, this Smart Technology not only predicts what type of job and finds where this job is available but also creates this job opportunity through the interaction and transaction of numerous Job Bots, algos, Innovation Ecosystems, web brokers, company websites, and talent networks that stream across the web looking for talent and to represent employers or projects, all looking for the right fit for the job and the person. This will be the New Future—a shift from job hunting to job creation. Reality Engineering will create your next job or project.

Your Smart Tech, let's call her your personal avatar, Monique, negotiates, finds, analyzes, and presents information that is a fit for you and a employer—a superior job fit. This cacophony of technology, all networked, M2M, this Knowledge Engineering is called into action, behind the scenes of the web where opportunities are created and destroyed in real time, in nanoseconds by a community of Smart Technology bots working on your behalf in ways you could never imagine.

Chapter 9

Techno-Futures: Next Web, Nano, and Bio

There are many ways to look at the future of technology. You can examine technology rules like Moore's Law or the exponential doubling of power, storage, and metrics like size—how small computer chips are becoming. There is not one way to grasp this, but here are eight Game-Changing Trends that will certainly transform technology over the next fifty years.

Convergence: the exponential merging or mash-up of all Strategic Technologies—nano, bio, neuro, info, and quantum; the artifacts of this merging, such as robots, pharmaceuticals, smart cars, and games—you name it

Connectivity: the global connectivity of devices, buildings, cars, markets, sensors, supply chains, products, chips, people, systems and information

Community: crowdsourcing, crowdfunding, crowd-enabling; communities' needs for security, health care, food, water, jobs, and commerce are technology demand drivers of the future.

Coevolution: technology and humans are on a coevolutionary growth path of collaboration, adaptation, enhancement, competition, and enablement.

Cognition: a faculty for the processing of information and applying knowledge, AI—Brains in a Box—technology is getting smarter, more intelligent, moving toward autonomy, independent thinking, and action.

Consciousness: the growing capacity to experience Vibrant Awareness, a heighted self-awareness state; also embedded in technology about humans, of itself, and of the world. Someday Sentience and emotional intelligence in machines will emerge as a Game-Changing Trend.

Communications: the meaningful exchange of information, the ability for technology to network, to collaborate, to speak a common language of understanding across cultures.

Content: the production of personalized data, info, video, text, and pictures in the form of stories, shows, productions, and media that are created by everyone, every second, and uploaded to the mobile Internet.

Future Smart technology will take us into the future sooner and with more astounding breakthroughs than we can easily imagine today. Our world will never be the same. There will be no less than the complete transformation of our world. I am going to imagine for you what's coming and the impact that future innovations will have over the next hundred years.

Warning: this chapter will disrupt your thinking in a positive way. New ideas for entrepreneurs and business will be available for creative people to harness the opportunities. New wealth creation, on a scale never seen before, is coming. This will bring billons into new markets, reaching new customers and developing and marketing new services, of which 90 percent don't exist today.

The next one hundred years on the planet will be completely reshaped by what technology brings—not the cute stuff like social media, flying cars (really), or better smartphones or even the biology breakthroughs that will radically extend our lives. That is the small stuff. No, the big breakthroughs will be in the things we think are impossible today.

Certainly one of the themes of this book is that in order to survive and thrive in the future you need to learn how to predict, adapt, and take certain actions. I have called that being Future Smart. When it comes to forecasting technology's future, the purpose of inventing technology, I would forecast, will be to address making the world a better place by increasingly meeting these Grand Challenges. Innovations that drive value and efficiency and solve big problems will find many entrepreneurs ready to take up the challenge.

Smart Machines Wake Up

- faster analytics
- diagnosis of complex data
- complex decision making
- capacity to learn
- emotional intelligence
- sentience
- self-awareness

The Tech Game Changers

Game changers are those specific technologies that will create the most comprehensive impact and fundamental changes in society, economics, culture, communications, and business over the next twenty-five years. Tech game

changers are disruptive. These are the wide-impact transformational technologies that will radically "change the game" on the planet and affect wealth, peace, jobs, and prosperity.

Game changers are the core technologies at the forefront of future change. They hold the most realistic potential for driving large-systems change across societies, business, and economies. These technologies will enable globalization, trade, peace, and security. A prosperous future is waiting for the entrepreneurs who apply now what's in the minds and labs around the world. This is often where the future emerges first. Entrepreneurs who can sense, see, and extract it can make a difference and profit.

There will be winners and losers in the future. Control and access to these game changers will play a decisive role in the future. Those who have access will thrive and be at an advantage. Those who don't will be ill prepared to meet the challenges that others will meet effectively. Access to education, innovation, and technology today has already demonstrated this competitive advantage.

By 2020 the sheer power of technologies such as cloud computers will level the playing field between the past have and have-not societies. Tech access, biotech, nanotech, and computing will be global and widespread to billions to invent and innovate to create their own prosperous futures.

These game changers will have geostrategic implications well beyond how tech affects societies, nations, and economies today. This forecast cannot emphasize more the immense power, both disruptive and opportunistic, that these technologies will have in shaping the markets, economies, industries, and power of the world by 2030.

The convergence of these fundamental technologies, to be used together in combination, will yield the most comprehensive large-scale influence on the planet over the next twenty-five years.

The future of technology will be about managing a high degree of complexity and convergence of tools and applications that defy traditional thinking. Entirely new paradigms of reality, unknown until now and radically unfamiliar, may emerge. We should be ready to be surprised by fast innovations from synthetic organs on demand, crowdsourced nations, robots that live with people, and radically different Posthuman lifestyles that defy the logic of today but thrive in the new future.

The Fast Future

Robots will have synthetic-biological parts and will be wireless extensions of human operators. Computers will be both virtual and physical, both invisible and seen systems. Cloud computing will render every surface "active and alive." Geo-intelligence will "see" and "know" you. The Internet will be always

on everywhere. AIs will augment our thinking, skills, and talent. Genetics will refresh, rebuild, and enhance our bodies and minds as well as extend our lifetimes. Superintelligence will provide economic growth to transform GDPs and enable billions to have incomes and jobs. This is your future.

The Internet will become a Blended Reality, with sensing and rich media rivaling our physical reality. Over the next twenty-five years an agile type of AI that invents itself, updates itself, self-heals, self-assembles, and even self-replicates will emerge. There will be many existential challenges that future technology will bring: Will humans be able to know when our creations make these "evolutionary jumps" that alter themselves? Fast self-learning evolving systems, from biology to AI minds to mobile robots and virtual avatars, will be an essential part of the future of 2030. The Blended Reality created by the convergence of game-changing technologies will amaze, empower, and challenge our civilization.

THE GAME CHANGERS UP CLOSE

• nanotech	• neurotech
• biotech	• quantum tech
• infotech	• robots

Each of these game-changing technologies by themselves offers a potent and powerful new set of radical tools and capabilities that will change the future of the next twenty-five years. These tech game changers are also the core of the Innovation Economy, as the convergence of these technologies will create wealth and power and will enable, most importantly, a higher quality of life for the 9 billion people living on planet Earth in 2050.

Conceived together, as a convergence, these six technologies represent a powerful explosive and radical New Future that will likely create a fundamental power shift that will alter markets, economies, even globalization, changing each nation and individual. They will affect every lifestyle on the planet in the future and create fantastic wealth and innovation—entirely new markets and industries shall arise that will take us to the stars and beyond.

Another way to appreciate the future impact of these game changers is to consider how global technological change has influenced both the present and past. Internet networks circle the planet, and computer and cell phones fuel communications, commerce, culture, and conflict. The pervasive and inexpensive bits that people move over networks, from images and video to data and information, are seamless. Tomorrow new and more radical technologies and new Building Blocks will emerge.

The New Future Building Blocks

- nanotech: atoms
- biotech: genes
- infotech: bits
- neurotech: neurons
- quantum: qubits

The Future of the Internet: Always Aware

The real story of what the future of the Internet will be is not about the cool social media of Twitter or how many Instagram pictures or YouTube videos there will be. It will not be about Google or Facebook's new look—no, not that. It's about how the Internet will become Always Aware, a fundamental innovation shift in culture that enables you to succeed in life, grow, learn, heal, and prosper, love and thrive.

There is perhaps no technology that has as pervasive an impact on our lives now and in the future than the Internet. The convergence of networks, sensors, websites, social media, and everything that is getting connected to everything else will make the increasingly fast and intuitive web an integral part of our reality. The Future Web will empower every aspect of our world—community, work, family, and play. It is the Uber-Tool of the future. Here are some of the aspects that are driving this future.

There are Six Waves that define the evolution and future of the Internet. We are in the midst of the early stages in which rudimentary search, transactions, and information is still in a primitive state. This will change very quickly between 2015 to 2025 due to the exponential convergence of technologies described here.

The Future Internet will be an all-encompassing network overlaid on people's lifestyles and integrated into their consciousness, empowering them in commerce, health care, education, creativity, and communications. The Internet of the future will comprise billions of networks talking to networks, things, and us that are independently communicating with one other, "having their own conversation." The emergence of Artificial Life based on the chips, computers, and network affects the evolutionary emergence of a New Synthetic Life Form, built by us in our image. It has a certain familiar ring to it.

The Internet will be embedded just about everywhere and in everything—in every imaginable kind of object, from TVs to phones to walls—and every product and device, home to cars, clothing, and even people, will have an Internet address. The Internet will embed itself into our reality, augmenting physical

objects with digital intelligence and data. This will be a world where information is constantly streaming at and around us across physical and digital artifacts that are always on, always connected, and always aware. This will be a worldwide system of Intuitive Networks that pay attention to us, know our likes and desires, and proactively feed us the information we need to act on such preferences.

Now, I know this sounds creepy to many. But as we are already being videotaped, our phones geo-located, computers monitored, our cookies and online social media profiles being profiled by billions as well as government agencies and advertising companies, it is a bit absurd to think that in the future, with the advent of advanced technologies, that we will be more private than we are today. Living off the grid will not be possible or desirable for most of us. We have traded our privacy for entertainment, discounts, offers, careers, games, and, above all, security.

Knowing where we are, via our phones, computers, cars, homes, and the thousands of watching eyes in public spaces does offer more security, but at what price? For most of us we don't care as long as laws that respect our rights are in place. All else, beware of the intrusion of the state and expect abuses of human rights. The Internet in the near and far future will be the ultimate double-edged sword, offering both meaningful value and abundance as well as a doorway to subversion and control.

We are on the cusp of this future now, the intuitively sensing of who you are and what your needs are. The Internet is learning, paying attention to your behavior and to what you think is important and what is not. The future Internet would travel with you everywhere. Each of us will have our own Personal Cloud that lives, learns, predicts, and deciphers "what's next" for us in real time. The Internet is waking up.

This Future Internet will require a powerful new type of AI that has not yet made its way into consumer technology. This is not so far off. As much as 50 percent of the technology necessary for such concepts to be part of our everyday lives has already been built. And what's in the lab today is in the marketplace tomorrow. The model for an AI-based Future Internet will be based on Cognitive Computing, just emerging now though it has a while to "grow" and "learn" in order to evolve and be useful.

The networks of the future will mimic human brains. Cognitive Computing is even referred to as Brains in a Box, but actually this will be more like Brains on a Network. These will be smart, connected, distributed cloud brains that are linked and think together to solve problems and deliver solutions—big or small. This is similar to how our neurons in our brains are linked and collaborate. In a nutshell, that is a fundamental shift that will shape the future of the Internet: the next generation of Smart Machines, what we call bots today, are a dim shadow of the immense, connected, and pervasive Superintelligence that will turn the Internet into a global ecosystem, best characterized as Artificial Life.

As a result, the Internet will be smart in a way we can barely imagine today and could finally help us solve global crises like health care, war, and poverty while creating thousands, perhaps millions, of new companies in the process— or even entirely new markets. You have to conceptualize the Internet as the web of supreme global connectivity that will link robots, supply chains, computers, transportation, security, hospitals, and, most of all, us. An intelligent, adaptive, and predictive Internet will anticipate and deliver a quality of service, care, and value that challenges the imagination today but will be routine to the people of 2030.

The First Internet Wave was the introduction of the Internet before the web in the 1970s. I was a researcher in the early stages of the Internet, the ARPANET (Advanced Research Projects Agency Network). This was a slow and primitive state of the Internet, used by academics and researchers like myself who marveled at the ways we could network communications with an electronic e-mail of sorts. The availability of the Internet was very limited not only to a small group of people but also by the network nodes or connections. It was a geek's toy at the time, with little functionality, search, and content.

The Second Internet Wave was the introduction of the graphic- and video-rich web, which is the front end of the Internet. The web evolved into an information resource that included search, and the data explosion that emerged started to connect not only millions of individuals but also businesses and nations, and a profound potential emerged that was changing the world's understanding of people, culture, business, and innovation itself. It's as if the web woke us up to a new reality for human potential in which trade, communications, and commerce could thrive in new ways not considered before.

The Third Internet Wave, where we are today, is driven by the social web such as Facebook, Twitter, and mobile e-commerce that has reached over 3 billion people, generating billions of dollars for business and, especially, entrepreneurs. E-mail, chat, apps, games, video, and smartphones dominate life, almost too much. The use of data to search, watch, produce games and content, stream music, and publish ideas has made the web an essential backbone of finance, telecom, business, education, and everything else.

The shift to embracing the mobile web, where geo-location services have created a new marketplace, is just beginning. The ubiquitous web is almost everywhere, connecting everyone to everything, just not at the same speeds or with the same functionality. Many nations restrict Internet access and speeds for various political agendas, often at odds with entrepreneurs and business, which need a high-performance Internet.

Also, the use of the Internet as a communications platform, Voice Over the Internet, VoIP, has transformed communications, bringing an agile, inexpensive, and fast network to life. The network as the platform for computing, communications, and publishing has had a transformative effect on commerce and culture.

The Fourth Internet Wave will be a Collaborative Web that will have at its root the dynamic intimate cooperation and deep learning between business, organizations, markets, people, and machines for work, learning, essential social services, and entertainment will mature in this stage. Big data, predictive analytics, cloud computing, and mobile web collaborations will define collaboration with more ease of use, value, high performance, and efficiency. We will learn to manage the Data Tsunami, the huge global deluge of data from every behavior, lifestyle, and pursuit from health, education, business, finance, security—the list goes on. The immense task of capturing, storing, and analyzing data to create more efficiency, discovery, and, essentially, value will be a distinct change in how the web will evolve. Internet speeds and new agile and powerful networks will stream media, information, and communications everywhere on the planet.

The Fifth Internet Wave will be Evolutionary Networking, which will be based on the advancement of cognitive computing, the beginning Always Aware Internet that predicts and interacts with a personality—with voice activation. Think the next-generation Siri, the AI on Apple's phones. This global shift will result in an increase in speed, transactions, and complexity management of health, security, education, finance, and communications at a level of robustness that we have not seen before. Brains on demand, on the Net, will greatly enable humanity to progress in every way.

The Sixth Internet Wave will not just mimic living ecosystems but also become a Living Ecosystem, an Always-Aware self-realizing Artificial Life Network. Independent knowledge agents, working across borders, supply chains, and cultures in a endless sea of electronic converging virtual and physical worlds that have the capacity to self-organize and create will enable humanity to manage the big social and planetary challenges coming in our future, such as curing illness, providing health care, enabling economic prosperity, managing conflict, and moving into space, off-world. This Internet Wave will feature smart and aware physical spaces, embedded intelligence, and systems that can act as doctors, diplomats, scientists, teachers, companions, and enablers of commerce, security, and entertainment. This wave will propel millions of new businesses and entrepreneurs to prosper.

This Internet will become a Morphable Intelligence—moving in the cloud from device, to space, to downloading on demand to things like cars, habitats, wearables, even people—bringing animated Sentient Awareness to empower and help humans navigate the future in every lifestyle and endeavor, to act as partners with humans, co-evolving to create a better world.

Even the use of the words the *Internet* or the *web* will disappear. The Internet will become an invisible, ubiquitous enabler of embedded intelligence, awareness, and communication between us and our world, helping to enhance our health, work, education, and creativity.

THE FUTURE WEB GAME CHANGERS

- Geo-intelligence—knowing where you or a thing is; location awareness
- Synthetic worlds—entertainment that personalizes our experience
- Digital assistants—will help us navigate the chaos of information
- Transmedia content—new media across autos, tablets, phones, and wearables
- Cloud computing—data, apps, info, video, processing moves to the Internet
- Blended Reality—augmenting the blend of virtual/physical worlds
- Social media—digital communities identities, crowdsourcing everything
- Mobility—everything is wireless, from clouds to devices to media
- Predictive analytics—predicting what people desire before they themselves know
- Internet of Things—everything has an IP address, connected things and products that communicate with us . . . Things Wake Up

The Internet will become the first global knowledge and rich-video real-time network, connecting billions of people to an unlimited number of channels, media, and social networks within networks. The future of the Internet will be deep collaboration across global cultures, with real-time transactions and specialized rich-media worlds.

The Internet will enable anyone to become a digital publisher or broadcaster of information on any subject and potentially reach an audience anywhere on the globe.

The convergence of computing, digital TV, gaming, commerce, and wireless phones will transform global society, economics, and communications, creating a vibrant new communications platform.

Direct real-time voice and video communications with real-time language translation will break down barriers to culture and accelerate globalization and cross-border communications.

Telepresence: Feel Me, Touch Me

In the future of 2025 the ability to feel and sense 3D virtual places, objects, environments, worlds, and people will drive gaming and communications, reaching billions throughout the world. The force feedback of virtual to physical sensations will transform entertainment and communications. We will not just experience; we will Sense-Feel experience. We will become sensor-enabled and reach an intimacy with our machines we cannot imagine today. We will not just watch football or soccer; we will be engaged and feel the game.

Access to information on any subject will be available anywhere over the web and delivered by a variety of media appliances or in the network cloud. Internet devices embedded inside humans will enable direct human-to-human communications and wet-wearable applications.

The Internet will go away and become the universal connectivity platform, the Megaverse, and it will be the backbone of all communications, trade, learning, health care, logistics, finance, and social networking.

The convergence of information, geography, and DNA will create a new business landscape of many opportunities. Virtual cyber-societies and -nations will emerge and come to rival nation-states, establishing rights, commerce, culture, and defense. These may be state, nonstate, or rogue actors. Hybrid realities, part virtual and part physical, real and fantasy, are coming soon to your web portal.

Crowdsourcing Everything

Crowdsourcing, the use of collaborative networks of people who may be at any time customers, partners, or competitors who can connect with each other online and share ideas, working together to make solutions, is now a permanent part of the web. Crowdsourcing advertising, product design, charity, social issues, investments—you name it—is being used to mine the collective wisdom, resources, ideas, and capital of the billions of people online every day. This democratizing of the web, by using the wisdom of the crowd, will become a chief source of research into the mind of the customer for every enterprise.

What's next is crowdsourcing energy usage, auto-sharing, climate change management, and sharing of products, services, and tools. The crowdsourcing marketplace will become a fundamental part of the Innovation Ecosystems, these dynamic new marketplaces where talent, technology, and the production of ideas and products collide as a new form of online commerce.

The future of the Internet represents a development that will bring an entirely new mode of communication, entertainment, and commerce to the planet. By 2030 there may be as many as 8 billion people on the Internet because the Internet will have become the essential utility, the communications backbone of the planet. All trade, commerce, communications, and entertainment will move to the Internet as the universal pipeline that reaches and touches each person on the planet.

Pervasive mobility via wireless communications will likely be the technology that brings the majority of people together online from around the block or around the world, from the physical to the virtual world. The future Internet will be a convergence of cell phone, television, and computing, where wireless collaboration throughout the planet will be routine.

Media, from games to news, drama, and trade, will be linked via this mobile device portal. The Future Web will provide universal features that can be scaled up or down. Games pictures, financial products, and pharmaceuticals will all be located in the rich TV-like digital interactive media space.

The Intelligent Web: Getting to Know You

"Getting to know you. Getting to know all about you." Whether you like it or not. (We hope you like us!)

The radical personalization of technology is coming. The perfect evolution of computers, networks, content, and sensors will be the Intelligent Web. This is the connectivity network of the universe that will forge an electronic convergence of life, work, information, and community.

To set the record straight—yes, this technology will be intrusive, spooky, and seductive all at the same time. You will like it and fear it at the same time.

Today you have to do something to coax, find, search, and make the web understand what you want. Searching is an imprecise activity of hit and miss, mostly with a lot of information that is not quite right or often wrong. Though the web is getting better, it has a long way to go. It is a passive medium that you, the user, need to work hard at to identify what you want, and even then, you may have to settle for less than what you were looking for.

Imagine in the near future the Intelligent Web and how different it will be from today. It will know you. It will be a superfast, real-time, accurate, and predictive engine of discovery. It will be mobile, sensor-rich, geo-intelligent, pervasive Internet that is almost liquid in being every place and in everything. The Intelligent Web of the future will be every place, sensing everyone and everything and will have access to exabytes of data, video, music, pictures, and people to be able to not just respond but also anticipate your needs and desires.

The Intelligent Web will come to know you. It will learn and evolve an understanding of who you are—your dreams, goals, behaviors, disappointments, and desires. It will watch you get that job or be fired, watch that relationship bud and flame out. It will make sure you get where you're going at first but then help you figure Where You Should Be Going. The Intelligent Web will learn, adapt, and empower you in your life and work.

It will be functionally Awake, Aware, and Predictive. It is Awake to being able to be attentive and responsive to humans and their environment, both physical and virtual. It is Aware of its objectives and can collect the data reporting and broadcasting of other intelligent agents, objects, humans, and information. It is Predictive, as it can analyze time, missions, values, and people's behavior so as to anticipate.

The Web Finds You

We waste so much time because the web is so dumb. It will be vastly different in the near future. A smarter, faster, and more intuitive web is coming. The web is evolving. The web is learning, and the web is getting smarter.

In this future the Intelligent Web will find you. This will be the Global Shift, the Intuitive Web that senses, learns, adapts, and predicts what you need. Information will be Smart Tagged (geographic, semantic, sensor-rich, personalized knowledge) and will locate you regardless of where you are. Information-That-Finds-You, Personal-Location-Targeting Technology will create information packets that use the Internet as a targeting tool to automatically locate people who may be interested in feeds of information about specific topics of interest. The web will "know" what you need and then find it.

With the Internet freed from being in a place and now available wireless from anywhere and accessible everywhere, an always-on feature of the Future Internet access by billions, to billions, will be a common experience daily. These new features will cloak our reality with another layer of an alternative universe of information awareness and interaction that will alter our perception of physical reality. This will all be accessible in real time and on demand for the user.

Different levels of Information-Layering Intelligence will provide deeper access. Some will be a voice-activated "deep info dive"; other analyses may be driven by commercial or ideological objectives: "show connections," "show beliefs," or "show vendors." Advanced Information Layering with decision support for Predictive Awareness and Information Mining to extract opportunities, threats, or relationships for fun and profit will drive the development of this powerful future Internet always-on service.

Embedded nano-neuro devices will engage us in Customized Wrap-Around Experiences to enhance learning, commerce, health, and, most of all, entertainment. We will Go Wrap-Around with the Future Web to play sports, go skydiving, visit foreign cities, go into space, or enter virtual fantasy worlds.

We will have intimate experiences with virtual humans and digital agents that extend beyond the limitations of our lifestyles of today. People will have alternative-reality relationships. ARRs with families and even love and fantasy adventures will be like dreams, but vivid, dynamic, and customized by your desires.

If this sounds strange, well, it will be for many who will look upon these alternative realities generated by the Future Web, the Intelligent Web, as perhaps dangerous diversions from normal reality. As an alternative to normal reality today millions play multiuser games and videogames almost 24/7. It is not so difficult to envision a future when Morphable Personalized Media, directed by your ambitions, desires, and curiosity will be produced in real time for you. No one is ready for this version of the future Intelligent Web that knows you

and designs worlds for you, predicting desire, even earning you money or employing you.

This future is far from Twitter, Facebook, and Google today. So much effort. The future of Twitter will be dynamic media and immersive worlds. Facebook will bring people together over these Morphable Personalized Media, and Google will be a Big Data Prediction Machine, layered with AI, that uses algos to program the optimal experience to anticipate what you may need or even what you don't know you need—More Human Than Human.

Google Glass (https://glass.google.com) is the first wearable computer offered by Google. It is an amazing easily wearable computer, phone, and media device all wrapped up into one experience. My experiments with Glass, as it's called, have opened up my mind to the wearable lifestyle of being always connected. It connects with my Google ecosystem of software, calendar, and e-mail as well as my contacts. I have found this first version, the Explorer, to be an outstanding step forward, and it will get better.

There are a few other companies on the leading edge of the Intelligent Web.

Neurosky (http://neurosky.com) has devices you wear that use biosensors to enable your connection with the Future Web. Entertainment, games, and learning can be boosted with this wearable bio-sensing neuro-device.

Consumer Physics (www.consumerphysics.com) has built an inexpensive and small molecular sensor that fits on a finger. It's called the SCiO, and like a *Star Trek* tricorder, you can use it to point out and identify the molecular ingredients of the world around us. It captures information in real time and uses your smartphone to send it instantly up to the cloud for analysis of any materials such as food, plants, and liquids. NIR (near-infrared) spectroscopy has been known for decades, but until SCiO, it has only been used in labs or factories. They created SCiO to bring this powerful technology to everyone.

FitBit (www.fitbit.com) is a wellness and fitness tracker that you wear. It communicates with your cell phone and the web. It watches your fitness, sleep, and activity.

Occulus Rift (www.oculusvr.com) is a leading company offering state-of-the-art 3D virtual reality gaming. Sold to Facebook, their headsets and virtual worlds software enable developers to design an endless set of artificial realities. Having tried one, I lost sense of physical time and space as I was transformed into a gaming world of very clear images and stories that I experienced.

Nest Labs (https://store.nest.com) is a home-automation company headquartered in Palo Alto, California, that designs and manufactures sensor-driven, Wi-Fi–enabled, self-learning, programmable thermostats and smoke detectors. You can conserve energy and control it over the web on your smartphone. I use it to lower the heat when my kids go to school and leave the heat up. There's probably billions in lost energy from homes all over the world that waste energy and don't know it.

Someday all of these devices will talk to each other and you over the web. These are devices connected to you, the world, and the Internet of Things, and they have multiple lifestyle enhancement functions, but the biggest is hyper-connectivity. This is the big shift here. The Intelligent Web will know you and serve you. Maybe you don't want that, but that's what's coming. They will optimize your health, finance, business, and education. They will propel you into a new era of media and entertainment.

With the Internet freed from being in a place and now available, free of cost, from anywhere and accessible everywhere, always on, these features will cloak our reality with another layer of an alternative universe of information awareness and interaction.

Every person, location, topic, inquiry, or search becomes Data Rich. You will know when meeting someone who they are and their interests, connections, and interactions that will define them either ahead of time (Google Me) or in real time (Google Now).

Living in a Blended Reality of physical data, the where and who, and Virtual Data, will bring a type of depth to relationships for work and social interactions that may be completely alien to those who did not grow up with this intrusive or helpful technology, based on your perspective.

The emergence of Digital Societies and Virtual Worlds will further this experience of Blended Reality. The virtual and physical worlds will converge. You will watch TV and enter TV Worlds. The intimate interaction of this Blended Reality will give people many new choices for relationships with human and nonhuman or virtual avatars, digital actors, and digital beings. This is a user-generated universe of infinite entertainment choices, and entrepreneurs will enjoy the endless opportunities to exploit. If you think Reality TV is something, just wait for the real virtual reality—so real it redefines reality.

Future of TransMedia

All future media production, distribution, and viewing will move to the web. A new wireless, interactive, mobile, and social network–based entertainment industry will emerge as a vibrant market for media makers who can monetize their media productions for news, entertainment, and sports in real time.

The traditional media networks will adapt to this New Media World by engaging talent and new media productions that will transform the economics and distribution of media on the planet—much more opportunity for a larger community of creative media makers to make a career with their own audience they can reach 24/7 across the world as the planet becomes connected.

Consumer-generated media, from games, Internet, TV shows, and learning software to commercials, will dominate communications. The convergence of the Internet with TVs, telephones, kiosks, autos, and wireless devices will create

many new media channels that share content across global platforms, nations, and cultures. Every surface will be media ready to send and receive media shows, get e-mails, surf the Internet, have communications, or access information.

Everyone will be a New Media producer. On-demand interactive entertainment content that is dynamically created and personalized for our preferences will be a standard feature. Advanced virtual reality as a global media platform bundled with digital agents and holographic entertainment will transform our experience of content, news, and entertainment.

Movie theaters will be linked to the web to receive digital broadcasts and satellite downloads of movies, video conferencing, and other interactive programming. Walk-in telepresence for video conferencing, using 3D holographic images, will be common. Faster, smarter, and more powerful multimedia communications devices—in cameras, phones, and cars—will enhance our capacity for producing and distributing entertainment in real time.

Digital TV will provide new fully interactive programs in which we will experience real-time participation with media-immersive content, personalities, and shows. Global-immersive games, the merger of entertainment and education, will offer a new genre of programming that will be greatly in demand and will blur the lines between learning, propaganda, news, and information.

Media technology that uses advanced AI avatars (digital personalities that collaborate with humans to customize media software—for news, music, videos, games, entertainment, and information access) will be in demand. All media technologies will be able to access geo-tagging, location-targeting applications. This will show who and where participants or people are in physical as well as virtual space.

Future of the Internet: Wearable Mesh

A mesh network is a network design in which each part of that network, called a nod, relays data for the network: "Hey, I am here, so connect with me," it says with machine language. Every part of the network—say, a small device you wear, a Wearable Mesh—generates its own network; it's the on ramp to the network. Your Wearable Mesh becomes like its own Wi-Fi network and enables you and the five to thirty miles around you to get online. A mesh network of the future will self-assemble to achieve maximum web power penetration, to reach the Internet no matter how remote you are.

Now imagine an ultra-high-speed network (one thousand times today's speed—think at the speed of thought) that could be wearable that you generate anywhere you go? Now imagine a few billion people with Wearable Meshes walking around the planet at the same time. Now you have a revolution in communications, e-commerce, health care, and education.

Now you're Meshed Up, ready for the future.

What happens in mesh network is that all of the nodes who are linked cooperate and collaborate to create the network robustness. A mesh network whose nodes are all connected to each other could be inexpensive, secure, and self-healing. When one Wearable Mesh goes off-line or breaks down, another can come online to take up the space. This could make the future of the Internet— a highly powerful and connected high-performance platform.

This Mesh idea for networks will lead to many Internets, many clouds— from personal, health, community, surfing clouds to war clouds. Mesh networks can be deployed anywhere, quickly, and go live and then go away. Mesh networks will enable the collaboration of sensors, the Net of Things, video cameras, and smart stuff that is now connected on the web to better understand us humans. Mesh networks of the future will enable free telephone and web access. Content, information, shows, data, and on-demand analytics will be how network providers will earn a handsome living.

Meshed networks will pop up and go away in minutes or seconds to preserve an idea, connect a friend, serve a customer, or get downloaded: " Download Me Now" to another Mesh. It's hard to imagine, but Mesh networks will provide a highly agile capacity to humans, machines, connected products, and goods. Mesh Networks will be first designed and deployed by humans until Smart Virtual Machines take over, or just learn from their human masters (for the time period) how to design optimal high-performing networks—better than humans can.

We will be able to shift our view through a Mesh into another person or virtual or physical place. This will be like playing a videogame, except we will have this Mesh On capability to travel and merge with other spaces, intelligences, and places. If you are ready for this and not confused, then I would be surprised, as this capability will change everything you know.

Mesh On Networks will merge into humans and enable other nonhuman AI intelligences to have a global digital highway to move from this physical reality into numerous virtual realities yet to be envisioned in our fairly primitive era today. When you consider the future of the Internet as an infinite physical and virtual galaxy of multidimensional domains, worlds, agents, humans, machines, things, and intelligences, even Superintelligences that, like a layer cake, are stacked around us, connecting all things, organic and inorganic, physical and digital, subatomic and molecular, optical and analog—well, then, now you have a sense of what the future of the Internet might resemble.

Our Connected Future:
The Internet of Smart Things

A silent revolution is going on. This revolution is sneaking up on us a bit more every day. It's about smart things that are linked up, connected to each other

by the Internet. As computer chips get cheaper, smarter, smaller, and linked up, a new phenomenon is occurring that never happened before: everything is getting not just connected but also Connected and Discoverable. Microchips and sensors are connecting everyday objects, cars, sensors, clothing, and food packages, forming a new wireless web of smart things that someday soon will be able to discover one another, leading to an entirely new reality we call today IoT, the Internet of Things. But this does not do this phenomena justice—this is a much grander planetary transformation. Every chip will be geo-intelligent— Always Aware of Who "it" is, Where "it" is, and Why "it" is—the purpose and meaning of its existence.

Making the Internet of Things a Reality

Computer chips are the brains of every electronic device and are the key to many of the changes that are coming in the near and far future. Moore's Law—the number of transistors on a chip, that doubles every eighteen months—has been the operating law that has powered the Information Economy of mobile, the computer, and the Internet for the past decades. The Internet of Things, IoT, is the bridge between the digital world of electronics and the physical world.

Many applications, such as radio frequency (RF) devices, wireless systems, sensors, biochips, and many other systems, working together with genetic-based chips and cognitive systems, will play a future role in building the IoT. The convergence of these technologies is known as "More than Moore," MTM. What we have today, the emerging M2M, Machine to Machine world, will evolve into the MTM, as demand for greater processing power to crunch more data to solve more problems emerges. We will then blast through the limitations of Moore's Law, beyond a silicon world of chips, and start looking at optical, nanotech, genetic, neural, and quantum chip ideas that will give us massively powerful supercomputers that live on the tip of a pin but have the power and intelligence to run a city or a planet. This Fast Future will amaze us.

What will this mean?

Universal connectivity of smart objects that are aware of each other, their own location, even where they are in relation to us is coming fast. It's like saying we are going to lay a bullet train from Mars to Earth—wonder that will be like? Well, it would fundamentally change how we think about speed and agility, and it would create new fantastic possibilities for businesses that don't exist yet. The self-awareness of things—for them to know where they are, to become geo-intelligent products—is an industry that will create great opportunity in the near future.

SMART STREET METERS

Phil's car notices he is running out of meter time and downloads directly from the car's bank account, making a YouPay deposit. No reason to tell Phil, but it does send him a text message, starting with "No worries, Big Guy." Phil likes that his DEP, his digitally engineered personality, Monique, calls him Big Guy. She doesn't know why he likes this and doesn't really care.

INHALABLE MEDICAL DEVICES

Gayle's doctor has her inhale a personalized medical device to monitor her headaches so he can wirelessly identify what is causing the severe migraines. The device was designed at the nanoscale and is invisible to the eye. He programs the nano-device with mobile phone application and sprays it into her nose. She feels nothing, no pain. The nano-device will wirelessly broadcast back to the doctor the status of her headaches, and the nano-device can distribute a pharmaceutical automatically to prevent the next migraine before it starts.

SMART BUILDINGS

2088 Union Street in San Francisco is a designated Smart Building, a class-5 AI, and part of Smart Grid Alliance of California. They trade energy credits, optimizing energy usage and costs. If they do well, they get new cloud servers as a bonus.

OUR SPOOKY FUTURE

There are many things we shall never fully understand that will be perplexing to many. In order to run properly the global systems that manage food, energy, climate, economics, which is all coming, we will need a new generation of Super-Smart Computing Networks. To manage a planet with as much as 8 to 9 billion people before 2040, we will need a level of computational intelligence that doesn't exist today. But this computational intelligence will evolve and start to be deployed by 2030. Already the automation of sophisticated computer systems plays a dominant role in financial markets, environmental controls, robots, manufacturing, and health care.

The inevitable collision and cooperation of humans and their Smart Machines will be a decisive point in human civilization when we must make social policy choices that will define generations to come. How much control do we give to our Smart Machines? What will our Smart Machines control? What happens when humans can no longer control our Smart Machines? Will we be

creating a Rogue Civilization that will compete or serve humans? You want to be asking these questions now.

It is possible that we are facing shortly, within five years, highly sophisticated computers and networks that humans will not understand. Think about this: Do you really understand the technology that delivers the Internet, TV, or your phone service today? Most people don't understand how VoiP, voice over the Internet, works or the drug that keeps them well. Tomorrow the onslaught of amazing technology that has become a fundamental part of every home, business, nation, community, and lifestyle will seem like a sea change from today. It will be vastly more powerful, personalized, and effective in transforming our lives.

The sweeping and almost insidious nature of technology, to try to understand and serve its masters as we program these massively fast, connected, and, yes, intelligent systems will not even be noticed as they fuse their artificial minds with ours.

The rise of the machines will be a complete takeover of humans, brought by humans to better humanity. We shall better deliver health care, provide security, earn a living, make profit, and, in general, have a better quality life. You might ask, what's wrong with that scenario? Nothing, as long as humanity does not lose its humanity.

Selling Velocity

In 2013 a quiet construction of a private network, laid fiber optic cable, was made, costing over $300 million, to give the edge to a company that was selling speed. They are in the high-speed trading business, but really they are selling speed so they can make stock market decisions faster than anyone else—certainly faster than humans. In fact neither the network they built nor the cost is all that impressive, but what is amazing is they built it for their computers to be able to make the billions. No humans allowed.

There are over three hundred companies on the planet today that sell speed to create value: find a disease faster, make a trade faster, find a partner faster, identify a risk or threat sooner. You get the picture: speed sells. And every second of every day for the next one hundred years innovations that drive will gain an advantage for nations, entrepreneurs, businesses, and individuals.

I estimate that high-speed stock traders, only one category among many in which high-speed computing is favored, spent well over $3 billion on infrastructure between 2010 and 2014. Faster decisions create a new business—the high-velocity industry. The faster a decision can be made, the more money there is to be made. There are, for example, computerized trading of stocks, along with over one hundred new industries in the future that will be in the High-Velocity

Business. Will you? One millisecond could be worth $1 billion. Are you ready to play? And the secret is not to let anyone know what your Black Box does, what the algos, the programs, that are that are running your business are. This is not just a hardware advantage but a software advantage also.

By 2025 there will be a future when everything is connected—computers talking to computers, running specialized software called algobots, in a complete virtual world where humans do not dwell. No one will call them computers in this world, not anymore. They are called brand names like Watson, Next Cray, or Archer. They will think and act in trillionths of seconds.

Knowledge Engineering

A new form of technology is emerging now and will mature into a powerful tool set that may well define how to better understand and influence billions of people in the future. It's a mash-up of content: geo-intelligence, interactivity, Big Data, crowdsourcing, cross-platform media entertainment, and analytics. The significant trend will be the rise of neuro-marketing, understanding how the brain works, as this will transform jobs, business, and society over the next ten to twenty years.

Entrepreneurs will build new companies around this technology to better understand and serve customers. Entirely new industries will be invented, as motivation, influence, learning, and entertainment will be forever changed in ways you cannot imagine now.

This look ahead to our Neuro Future is detailed in this book. This will have an impact beyond what we know as the Internet, TV, and wireless media. The convergence of technologies, which will bring our Neuro-Future sooner and fiercer and influence everyone, is emerging. There will be Smart Things that are Smarter than humans. Smarter technology will first make us smarter, enabling our minds. Next we will build New Minds—for humans and our Smart Machines.

Immersive Entertainment Futures

Entertainment will be transformed in the future. By 2030 the very idea of what media entertainment is will be completely different. We will no longer just watch sports; we will interact with Immersive Entertainment, engage, and actually play in virtual reality sports. Will we play video games like *Call of Duty*— yes, but we will walk through Virtual Worlds where AI avatars will join us as we do battle with and against tactile-aware and Augmented Reality teams from both the world of Smart Machines and other human worlds. Some of these Immersive Entertainment experiences will be in our minds, Neuro-Enhanced Entertainment, and some will be in Blended Reality, where our daily Natural

Reality is enhanced by information layering or holographic projections that we interact with—actually we Play-Merge with. "Play-Merge Now," our future PS2s and Xboxes, will hear for activation.

The future convergence of technologies that will be used to interact and communicate remotely with the world will reach billions. Are you ready for this New Future when Immersive Entertainment stimulates your brain, engages your senses, and envelopes you in world of Neuro-Stimulation that is not so different from what we call daily reality? Is it Real or Super-Real? Super-Real is the augmented reality world of Immersive Entertainment, bringing together neuroscience learning, interactive video gaming, rich media, sensory feedback, life-like graphics, and Artificial Intelligence into one dynamic experience.

It is not just the networks that will be used to reach billions in the future; it is also the technology of software, media, and Neuro-Ware (DTB, Direct to the Brain Broadcasting) that will affect learning, news, relationships, ideology, and commerce. This is a higher order of technology that, though difficult to forecast, will be commonplace by 2025.

Knowledge Engineering is where the technology of new mass media convergence (Internet, TV, computing, wireless), data mining, predictive analytics, cognitive computing, and neuro-marketing collide. Supercomputing meets social networks, and crowd-enabling/sourcing meets the future design of media programming such as games, personalized virtual reality, interactive sports, and e-commerce. Highly advanced and personalized media will be structured, produced, designed, packaged, and targeted for specific audiences in highly sophisticated ways never seen before.

The design and production of knowledge (data or information that is actionable) is one aspect of this new technological capability. Knowledge Engineering will be a higher form of media information development that produces information in many forms—games, video, training, real-time collaboration for trade and business, telemedicine, tele-education, and others, as examples.

Knowledge-Aware Products will be able to locate, via virtual and actual sensors (over wireless networks or physical terrain), certain types of individuals or groups of people and then target specific messaging for those individuals.

The use of Knowledge Engineering to provide wireless predictive analytics and to anticipate, find, and interact with individuals regardless of where they are will be an essential tool for influencers of the future. When combined with satellites and the Internet, the sheer pervasive impact of this capability to deliver value, in services around the planet, will be an entrepreneur's next decade of ventures.

Knowledge Engineers will be able to populate cloud-like databases in remote networks that can mine geographies, locations, individuals, and groups beyond today's limitations of satellite technology or GPS. Diagnostics to sense, sniff, and find targets of opportunity for delivering Knowledge-Aware products.

The immense power, global reach, and influencing operational capacity these technologies will bring to future organizations and individuals who master these tools cannot be overemphasized. The capacity to Engineer Knowledge—to predict, shape, and provide strategic influence, reaching global audiences—may well be the most powerful capability on the planet over the next twenty-five years.

2025 Tech Forecasts

Neuromarketing: This is the application of neuroscience, technology that seeks to understand how the brain functions, learns, evolves, and can be influenced.

Cognitive technology: This is the application of neuroscience, the technology of how we learn, how we process information, and how we think, and how to influence thinking.

Crowdsourcing: Everything will be crowdsourced, from new pharmaceuticals to movies; the entire way we identify what consumers want will change. Crowdsourcing for finance, health care, energy usage, research, and even education and voting will transform the future by direct democracy—leveraging the wisdom of engaging consumers and nonexperts to mine information about preferences, desires, and products will become a norm in the future. When 8 billion people are mobile and connected, the possibility of real-time commerce, communication, and connectivity will yield a movable feast of benefits, insights, and awareness.

Predictive analytics: This is technology that can predict possible behavior and attitudes of individuals and groups to vote and purchase, what their needs are, and what they will value. Prediction Markets can be built to understand the global customer to be more in sync with the customer now and in the future. The technology used to accurately mine the wisdom of crowds, understanding authentic mass attitudes and the probability of influence. It is understanding the Group Mind and leveraging this awareness to understand and influence people and events.

Environmental scanning: This is the technology that scans the Internet and social networks—news, content, media, wikis, blogs, and music—to better understand the mood, attitudes, and motivations of people; gain more information awareness; and predict potential threat.

Neuro-data mining: This is the technology that seeks to identify individuals or groups based on their thinking models, behavior models, or neuro-maps—specific cognitive distinctions and modes of thinking. Neuro-maps combined with geo-tagging provide a larger framework for Knowledge Engineering and Influence.

Geo-tagging: This is the technology that brings together GPS location targeting, sensors, and geo-intelligence to identify, find, and access individuals

or groups and current global location or to apply Predictive Awareness to where they may be located in the future. It is an application of Deep Digital Sensing.

Self-aware software: This technology is an advanced form of AI software that has embedded intelligence in its code, with the ability to reprogram itself, create new forms, and replicate new media messaging consistent with its mission parameters and is self-aware of its purpose. It can be used in any game, media, search engine, or digital communications over a cell phone, computer, or kiosk.

Real-time social media TV: This can be mass media, directed or focused on specific targets, that has the ability to communicate back to the sender, sense the individuals around its environment (virtual and physical), diagnose, interact, and influence on demand. It can morph or change to meet a need or objective. It can download new features and change its form, image, features, and direction. It can deliver messaging or create independent decision making of new directions or messaging in order to better influence. This technology will have interactive sensing capability, with GPS and DNA location awareness.

Distributed global intelligence: This is an advanced-concept, distributed intelligence that refers to the phenomenon of Emergence, in which biologically inspired networks (biomimetic networks) will "emerge" that mimic the way biological processes act, using neural nets of AIs on demand (computer bots) that emerge over linked information networks like the Internet.

As networks grow in the future to be more interlaced and complex and to globally link an infinite number of users, information, locations, and services (telecom, health, communications, finance, trade, etc.), the emergence of independent digital life forms—human and digital life forms—may emerge that mimic human interactions and behaviors.

Peer-to-peer networks that connect humans to machines to virtual online agents to offline digital minds may all be collaborating in this future ad hoc global network. Distributed Global Intelligence will become a highly useful and uniquely powerful force for reaching, engaging, and empowering the globally connected population of the future.

P2P commerce digital currency exchange between individuals will be commonplace before 2020. Coinbase, Bitcoin, and many other crypto-currencies will be used and will operate outside of the mainstream banking system between individuals. There will be Digital Currency Exchanges that will, like banks, convert digital cash for other currencies, monetary instruments, or actual assets—five Bitcoins for that pork barrel please.

Blended Reality: The Future of the Internet

It is likely that direct-to-retina heads-up displays will show an Information Layering of every person, location, organization, and even object in our view.

This Information Layering will be scalable, enabling the user to delve deeper into the data provided about a person or location, accessing in real time history and relationships from massive archived Google- and Wikipedia-type databases.

Another feature of future Information Layering will be Predictive Awareness, the likelihood that through connections or relationships or some existing data evidence a specific person may be engaged with certain types of experiences or people. By 2020 Predictive Awareness will be the next evolution of today's predictive analytics and neuro-marketing that companies use to determine customer buying interests.

Every person, location, topic, inquiry, or search becomes Data Rich. You will know when meeting someone who they are along with their interests, connections, and interactions that will define them either ahead of time (Google Me) or in real time (Google Now).

Future of 3D Animation

The advanced use of computer generated imagery (CGI) is essential to creating a Blended Reality. Computer animation that has been limited to the expensive use by films and games is getting cheaper and faster by the minute. What had cost $20,000 a minute will now cost $1. Supercomputing cloud services will be given away in the future. A Blended Reality is coming, and it will be delivered by the fast, inexpensive graphics renderings of digital humans, worlds, games—you name it. Photo-realism as a product, a deliverable, will come to immerse us—and it will look, feel, and be like this physical world.

The computer-generated imagery is the application of computer graphics to create or contribute to images in art, printed media, video games, films, television programs, commercials, and simulators. What's coming is fully immersive 3D computer graphics that will be used to create people, cities, planets, and entire virtual worlds that people can make, travel to, and live in.

The term *computer animation* is used to build virtual worlds and refers to agent-based, interactive environments in digital networks. Computer graphics software is used to make computer-generated imagery for films as well as digital worlds. The availability of CGI software and increased computer speeds have allowed individual artists and small companies to produce professional-grade films, games, and fine art from their home computers. This has brought about an Internet subculture, with its own set of global celebrities and shows, and both the practical and bizarre. This is a consumer-generated world that is fully interactive and is inhabited by humans through their avatars, their substitute selves, their alter egos.

CGI will create a new lifestyle of Blended Reality. Living in a Blended Future Reality of both physical data (the where and who) and virtual data will bring a depth to relationships for work and social interaction that may be

completely alien to those who did not grow up with this intrusive or helpful technology, based on your perspective.

The emergence of new forms of societies—Digital Societies and Virtual Worlds—will further enrich this experience of Blended Reality. The virtual and physical worlds will converge. You will watch TV and enter TV Worlds. You will work for an organization and enter the virtual worlds of that organization to interact with customers, workers, and vendors. This 3D holographic sensing and feeling Blended Reality will be "real." The intimate interaction of this Blended Reality will give people many new choices for relationships with human and nonhuman or virtual avatars and digital beings.

There are innovators who are building these future worlds today. The difference is that today you can host your online multiplayer world or game in the cloud and pay Amazon to host and render human-like agents and landscapes that are as realistic as looking out the window. This will come to rival physical reality and present a challenge and opportunity for our society.

"If it doesn't hurt to think about it, then we are not going to try it," says the company High Fidelity (https://highfidelity.io). They are building the next generation of virtual reality. "We're building a new virtual world enabling rich avatar interactions driven by sensor-equipped hardware, simulated and served by devices (phones, tablets and laptops/desktops) contributed by end users."

Philip Rosedale is the innovative genius that created Second Life (http://secondlife.com), which has a global following. Second Life operates with its own digital currency, Linden Dollars, enabling digital makers who design their houses, avatars, and digital cultures inside the virtual world.

3D Graphics to 3D Printing: A Revolution in the Making

Now if you consider the convergence of these game-changing technologies, it will boggle your mind. When you add supercomputers operating in the cloud to both networks of people as well as increasingly smart and connected physical things, to CGI sensors and 3D printing, well, you have a revolution in making things both in the real physical world and in the real virtual world.

Imagine this: I can connect my spiffy new 3D printer to hook up in the cloud with my 3D graphics engine and then design a new car, computer, or medical device in about three hours. We can simulate the new product in a computer tablet and then post it on Kickstarter to raise funds to make it, all in the same day. Heck, I could presell five hundred units over an Innovation Ecosystem and be profitable by the end of the week.

Now that's a revolution in the making. Imagine that you're one of 5 million digital entrepreneurs who are doing this 3D-to-3D business every minute of

every day. You need a customized heart valve—no problem, contact 3D Heart-Connect Today . . . 20 percent off the first one thousand customers.

Nano: Hacking Matter

Think about the awesome capability that you could have to design on-demand matter. If you could manipulate matter at the atomic scale, to mix and match atoms to make things that did not occur in nature. What would you do if you had your own production box that sat in your home or office and could make any object? Did you buy the Maker Program off the Web? If we are to deal effectively in managing the risks facing us in the New Future—climate, disease, energy, resources scarcity—nano can help us get there.

The explosion of new nano entrepreneurs, who will have had ten years of experience in building businesses around 3D printing, when nano becomes available will transform business as we know it—millions of nano entrepreneurs will be generating billion of dollars or Euros, creating jobs, building new digital nano-ecosystems of agents, marketers, makers, and designers to support millions of customers who will want nano-products and services to support their businesses and customers. Over one thousand products in the market today contain nano, such as sports equipment, computers, textiles, materials, pharmaceuticals, devices, and cars. By 2020 the global market of products that contain nano will be over $1.5 trillion.

Nanoscience is the design of matter at the atomic scale. This is the building of unique things smaller than one hundred nanometers. The nanometer is one billionth of a meter. The nanometer is smaller than the tip of a hair yet has certain properties such as strength, memory, and storage that make it unique. The most interesting property of nano is self-assembly. Nano-tubes can self-organize into an infinite number of shapes and, perhaps, functions. Automated self-assembly could protect the planet from climate change, heal disease, enable a new energy source—the options are endless. New Nano industries will radically reshape medicine, energy, finance, and manufacturing by making inexpensive, smart, and fast tools available.

NANO CHANGES EVERYTHING: BIGGER THAN THE WEB

- A young child at risk to die from a genetic defect is saved by a programmed nano-device in a telemedicine operation.
- Nano-sensors will be used for the detection of diseases such as cancer.
- A new nano–fuel cell optimizes battery energy, bringing heat to a waiting community who live off the traditional power grid.

- A nano-coated material is so protective it that keeps a firefighter safe from the intense heat of a warehouse fire so she can rescue residents trapped and return safely to her family.
- Nano shields in orbit will protect billions from solar radiation and climate change.
- Nano batteries will transform energy, computers, cars, drugs, and new materials.
- Wearable computers and sensors will enable communications and computing.
- Nano will enable smaller, cheaper, and smarter devices, from TVs to computers.

Nanotech is an invisible technology that is often not seen as it plays increasing roles in food, aerospace, chemicals, health care, energy, and the list goes on. By 2030 the Global Nano Market could be over $3 trillion. Smaller, smarter, and stronger materials that go to make everything from heart valves to bridges and energy towers can benefit from the unique properties of nano.

Nanotech is the manipulation of matter at the atomic level to create new materials, coatings, and, eventually in the future, new products and devices. Nano also refers to the size: nanostructures are below the microlevel, almost invisible—one tip of your hair is a nanometer. But with the properties of steel and the conductivity for energy transfer and storage, nano is fantastic technology for the future. The applications are endless.

Nano has been used by companies in textiles to meet environmental challenges. For example, Lake Rotorua in New Zealand was affected by a violent volcanic explosion that occurred approximately two hundred thousand years ago. The result was a large, quite scenic lake, which is now being overrun by algae, an unwelcome development.

With access to advanced climate management technology that at its foundation is a sophisticated nano-engineering technology using nana membranes, the future of the lake is ensured to continue as a viable system. GE's ZeeWeed Membrane Bioreactor used advanced nanotech methods to create a solution that worked to manage the algae and return the lake to sustainable levels, no longer under threat of being overrun by the algae.

Then there is Doxil, an anticancer drug, developed in Israel, that was the world's first nano-based pharmaceutical. It's been on the market twenty years, and no one knew when it was being developed that it was a nanotechnology. The use of nano, which has strange antibacterial and cancer-fighting properties, is just staring to be explored. In the future this will be a technology,

when combined with computing, bio, and neuro, will transform our world through the use of inexpensive, strong, and flexible smart materials that can self-organize into what we need.

NANOTECHNOLOGY FORECASTS

- The nanotech convergence with computers, networks, neuroscience, and biotech will create Morphable products that can change their forms and functions on demand.
- Nano-devices—invisible, intelligent, sensing, mobile, connected to the web—will be used in every industry from media and medicine to defense.
- Nanotech 3D compilers will create fast, low-cost, high-quality products by assembling atoms on demand.
- Smaller than the head of a pin, surgical nano-devices will operate autonomously inside the human body.
- Nano-biology will prolong life, prevent illness, and increase people's health.
- Nano-enhanced humans will have physical, intellectual, and sensing powers superior to other humans.
- Nanotech will enable inexpensive and high-yield solar energy tech.
- Nano-factories will build on-demand products in an inexpensive, flexible, and rapid process.
- Nanotech will revolutionize the global economy, providing new jobs, wealth, and enterprise that will produce high-tech products with low-cost and low-tech resources.
- Nanotech will create new choices that will alter human evolution, raise dramatic ethical issues, and challenge social norms.

Having been involved at the beginning of the Nanotech Revolution when we first presented the case for the United States to invest in nanoscience under President Clinton, I can say that amazing breakthroughs have not disappointed. I can remember that day we met at the White House Conference Center to make our case for why the United States should invest in nanoscience. I was an early sector adviser on nanoscience to the National Science and Technology Council, which reports to the president of the United States. Later advising the President's Council on Science and Technology (PCAST), it was clear that innovation was a top priority for government, beyond just politics.

The engineer that has been the innovative evangelist for nanoscience is Mike Rocco, the head of the Nanoscience and Nanoengineering Department for the National Science Foundation. Mike brought me into NSF to help get the US government and the business community to understand how vital nanoscience is to our future.

At that time we could only speculate about the future industries and jobs that the Nano Economy might offer. I can say that we were right about the potential, though I think the best innovations from nanoscience are yet to come and in the far future will offer truly amazing breakthroughs to heal, fix, fuel, secure, and invent what appear impossible today.

Programming Realty

There may not be a technology that promises so much and can deliver so much of whatever humans can imagine in the future than nanotechnology can. Our ability to program matter at the atomic level will touch and change every industry and affect every life and generation on the planet. This fundamental shift in our mimicking nature and in surpassing nature by making entirely new things can only be limited by what we imagine.

Nanotech tools will enable consumers to fabricate on-demand materials, food, energy, devices, and computing and communications machines. Nano-devices and nano-materials—invisible, intelligent, and powerful—will be used in every industry to accelerate production of customized products.

Nanotech-enabled bio-diagnostics and sensors will be used in security, health care, and the home. Smaller than the head of a pin, surgical nano-devices will operate within the human body, configured by wireless interactions with surgeons.

Nano-biology innovations from rebuilding organs will prolong life, prevent illness, and increase people's health—even promote dangerous behavior. Nano-enhanced humans will have augmentations of physical, intellectual, and sensing attributes superior to other humans.

Nanotech will provide cheap, available, new sources of energy as well as accelerate other forms of alternative energy by providing coatings, parts, and new "engines" for energy creation. Nano factories will build on-demand products in a global nano supply chain, leveraging inexpensive, flexible, and rapid processes.

Nanotech will revolutionize the global economy by offering mass customization of high-quality and useful products. At the same time, weaponized nanotech will become a global risk factor. Nanotech will create new choices that will alter human evolution, raise dramatic ethical issues, and challenge social norms.

Manipulating Matter

Nanotechnology is the process of manipulating matter at the nanometer or atomic scale. Nanotech is an emerging fundamental design science that, when applied to materials development, can yield properties that can offer exceptional attributes of strength, power, and programmable intelligence.

In addition, nanotech in the future may provide self-replication, self-assembly, and self-healing "smart" products or machines.

Nanotech may be applied in the future for producing new materials that can fabricate systems that produce new forms of energy, agriculture, computing, medical devices, pharmaceuticals, and communications. As a new design science, nanotech can be used to design matter, atom by atom, to achieve the desired performance. This is a radical departure from the technologies of today. Nanotech may be used to speed up evolution, fix problems that nature or biology cannot, reprogram disease, end droughts, or enhance intelligence.

This new tool set, which uses atoms as building blocks to create new things, will provide a manufacturing capacity that invigorates the imagination. Given the evidence today of recent nanotech discoveries and the amount of funding nanotech is attracting from more than fifteen nations, this technology is already providing evidence of significant potential.

One of the chief advantages of nanotech is that it can theoretically be used to manufacture materials that do not appear in nature. Creating a new generation of materials that have properties that do not currently exist in nature opens possibilities that will have a profound impact on society. The harnessing of nanotech and experimentation has been ongoing for the better part of a decade due to the potential that this technology holds for the future.

The nanometer scale of nanotech offers an operational capability to reduce the size of other devices or machines without sacrificing performance and addressing issues not accessible with traditional engineering or design.

Nanotech also offers new capabilities that someday will translate into more complex machines that can be used for the betterment of humanity, from food production and inexpensive and personalized medicines to distributed energy sources and climate change engineering.

The capability of nanotech to realize its full potential over the next twenty-five years may be in its combination and convergence with biotechnology. A new generation of nano-bio devices will be developed within the next twenty-five years, dramatically offering therapeutic benefits to extend life and heal disease.

New Power Tools

Nano-bio convergence would offer the Power Tools of both biology and an applied materials science that could manipulate biological matter—organs, neurons, and cells—at the atomic scale. It will be possible to design new synthetic life forms. The next generation of medicine will likely emerge from this convergence and offer longer and healthier lives with less risk. Enhanced quality of life will be the outcome.

Future nanotech developments in energy production may have the most pervasive impact on society. As energy becomes increasingly more expensive

and scarce, coupled with increased population and industrialization over the next twenty-five years, we will need new forms of energy. Direct manipulation of matter to create energy or even to create better storage for energy, is a likely development of nanotech in this time frame.

NANO CONVERGENCE

- New medical devices, replacement bones and organs that have been nano-manufactured on demand to prevent injury, disease or disability
- Neuro-nano smart machines, robots, and products that have thinking capabilities
- Self-assembly as an embedded capability—metals that absorb impact and return to the original memory shape—nano-chemicals, nano-electronics, nano-engineering
- Self-assembly, a nano capability, leading to self-generation of robots, autos, planes, energy devices, and agricultural innovations
- New forms of matter that act like a liquid but have the properties of a solid, with a programmable set of memories
- Food assemblers, to make certain meals from basic agriculture materials, with large- and small-scale production
- Superstrong but lightweight materials for protecting people at risk from climate, fire, hazard, or attack
- Mobile autonomous entities that can navigate extreme environments in space or on earth; extensions of human and nonhuman entities
- New nano-scale diagnostic devices that can target disease and deliver surgery or drugs on demand
- Radical nano-biogenetic engineering of human beings, tool augmentation, advanced communications, performance enhancement via hardened agility, and nano-enabled bodies
- New energy forms born from nanoreplication of atomic properties that mimic solar cells and generate power in small and large formats

Future nanotech applications will arise from the convergence of nanotech with the other game-changing technologies, such as biotech, neuro-tech, and quantum technology. At the atomic level a future generation of quantum computers may be possible to build using nanotech applied engineering.

The convergence of nano-bio-quantum, for example, will lead to a new, much more radical set of tools, assumptions, applications, and inventions that will transform our world in the next few decades. Without the agility of nanotech we could not even imagine designing a quantum computer or a synthetic brain cell, an organelle or neuron. The intersection of technologies is where

future innovations will emerge. Nano 3D manufacturing will make your next running shoes and your new kidney.

3D Printing: The Maker Revolution

"What if you could send a physical object to a friend like a text message? What if you could subscribe to a series of objects like you do with a podcast? What if adjusting a 3D model was as easy as Instagramming a photo? Yeah, we thought that would be cool too. That's why we created New Matter" (www.newmatter .com).

This is the advertisement on Indiegogo (www.indiegogo.com) that got me excited. I have been analyzing 3D printers for a few years and watching how fast this technology was moving into the market. For $240 I invested in my first 3D desktop printer, but what has been missing was the community. New Matter has included not just the printer but also the community of makers and designers who can exchange ideas over the web and communicate as a community.

But not all 3D printers sit on a desktop or kitchen counter. I am walking around a 3D printer based in a warehouse in Silicon Valley—massive in size, big as a pickup truck, but very wide and flat. This is like no 3D printer I have ever seen. It is used to produce homes by 3D printing, and I am convinced it is the future of manufacturing. On one end there is a computer from which designs are sent over the Internet. On the other there is a large printer set up to extrude materials that can be put together and fit to build the front and sides of a house.

The Chinese company Win Sun Decoration Design Engineering Company prints all of the parts needed to construct houses and then uses those parts to build them all in a day. Perhaps in the future they can build them in minutes. The finished houses are made of mostly concrete with other materials. Buildings of the future will greatly expand this capacity, print on demand (PoD), reducing labor and materials costs to almost nothing.

Dutch architects are updating the process for the twenty-first century: fabricating pieces of a canal house out of plastic with a giant 3D printer and slotting them together like oversized Lego blocks that kids would play with.

I am sitting at dinner in Poland at a high-tech conference on digital commerce where my friend John is receiving orders for making 3D tools on his smart phone. He is receiving the tool orders, fulfilling them by turning on, by cell phone, his 3D printer at home, and sending the files to his 3D printer to start production. His 3D printer is in New York and he is in Poland at dinner with me. This is his business. It has already changed the very concept of manufacturing. He is a 3D Maker who is part of a revolution in production that may disrupt even China.

What if 3D manufacturing goes mainstream? What if every home, office, and business had its own 3D printer to make even 30 percent of what they buy

from China Inc. today? Now, that would be disruptive. But what if China decided to embrace high-end 3D printing for manufacturing? They would disrupt themselves and perhaps become a 3D Future Smart Leader. Could happen.

By 1982 Hideo Kodama invented the first working 3D printer in Japan, where many ideas come to be made reality. Although 3D printing has been around, it has not been mainstream. But something happened. As with computing, Moore's Law and dropping prices for computers has reduced the prices of all technologies.

The 3D Revolution

We are on the verge of a Maker Revolution: small business meets manufacturing, distributed production that combines 3D printing, cloud computing, programs, and entrepreneurs hunger for the profitable next new thing. Here it is. 3D printing will accelerate commerce like mobile phones did. Making stuff on demand—tools, designs, products, and, eventually, complex things—will create a new postindustrial distributed marketplace for small businesses to thrive in the New Future.

There is a new manufacturing revolution underway. Small, distributed, and dynamic manufacturing labs are springing up around the United States. Groups of inventors, creators, manufacturers—the Makers—are self-organizing places and events to collaborate in "making stuff." From industrial-scale body parts to new devices and objects, we are at the early stages of a manufacturing transformation. 3D printing of houses has actually been demonstrated.

The US government is planning to put one thousand production-quality 3D printers in high schools across the United States. Even without access to one of these 3D printers, there will be free downloads of Autodesk 123D, a 3D computer-aided design program that gives you modeling and push-button connections to online 3D printing services. There are dozens of online services supporting the Maker Revolution. Printing objects in 2015 will be hot. By 2025 everyone will have a 3D printer. What do you want to make?

3D printing will be a cloud-computing platform of distributed nodes in a network-based market that will link up producers and customers around the world. 3D printing is part of the future of distributed manufacturing, where bits are moved around the world rather than objects or products. Bits, programs about the design or functionality of the products, will signal how "they" need to be built, and a new Smart Machine ecosystem of designers, 3D printers, brokers, customers, partners, financiers, and even stock futures will become part of this Smart Machine Ecosystem of Future Manufacturing.

When 3D making meets nanotech and the cloud we will have, by 2025, a complete ecosystem for manufacturing anything from the complex device to any consumer product. This revolution is bubbling up to the surface today.

The 3D Entrepreneur: 2020

So let's say you, as an entrepreneur, want to design a solar nano-chip that fits into a smartphone that would produce endless and renewable power, solving a big problem today. You call it the SunChip. Based on an ultrathin ten nanometers, it is tiny and powerful in collecting not just solar but also ambient light. You have a patent that you have licensed, and you now want to build a functional working model. You contact three potential customers who could sell your finished product.

Once your customers agree that the SunChip would be a great and much-needed product with huge market potential, you contact your investors, with endorsements from your potential customers, to prove up the demand. With this support you're able to raise start-up capital.

Now you're off next to design and to make a prototype. Of course, there is a vibrant community of Makers, designers, programmers, and manufacturers waiting for you to contact them as you stitch together a Virtual Global Supply Chain. They are freelancers who are inventing the future. They help you to invent your future.

You send this job out to your team, who are around the block or around the world. The designers, producers, programmers, and agents work on the attributes of the design, features, and performance, and they make prototypes after their Knowledge Engineering, through simulation models collaborating in real time over the web using computers and mobile devices. You approve the cost estimates, and you're in 3D production within days. This could take months to get the right design and function to absorb, store, and transmit the energy needed on demand.

The final prototype is functional and working. SunChip is sent to you for approval via the web and then downloaded simultaneously at your office and at your customers' offices, with specs on performance and cost. Your customers' 3D printers produce your SunChip. You have orders within forty-eight hours, and you're in business.

Eighty percent of this scenario is working now, part of the emerging 3D Revolution. Can you hear the sounds of this future?

Kickstart This

I invested in many start-ups on the website for entrepreneurs called Kickstarter. 3D printing ventures are a regular offering and the prices for performance are getting lower and lower while the performance gets better and better, so I invested.

3D printing is now used in almost all industries, including prototyping, manufacturing, architecture, construction, aerospace, and military. Emerging

innovations in the medical arena are also promising, including on-demand dental appliances.

Experiments are now being undertaken for the printing of food. I actually tried some of this 3D food—bio-food—while at Disney's Epcot, and I think that it needs some more work to get the food right. The texture was acceptable, but the taste was at the early stages or, let's say, it has a long way to go.

Industries that will benefit will be health care, manufacturing, aerospace, architecture, consumer goods, autos, construction, and, eventually, pharmaceuticals and complex engines and devices. 3D printing of organs will be addressed in Chapter 12, but this will likely be the largest market in the world: Ready to grow your own liver in your own 3D printer? Could be coming sooner than you think.

According to Canalys, a market research firm, 3D printing will see a 45.7 percent growth each year, resulting in a $16.2 billion industry by 2018. My forecasts go beyond that, to $25 billion-plus by 2020, driven not only by cheap 3D printers but also something else more powerful—an ecosystem of designers, producers, buyers, and digital 3D manufacturing plants that serve the industry of entrepreneurs who are inventing a new industry.

By 2020 something else quite powerful will transform 3D printing—the home 3D printer. The ability to print at home with under-$1,000 machines that can do what expensive Big Iron 3D printers did way back in 2015 will create an industry of Home Makers, entrepreneurs for hire. They will invent the future of manufacturing.

Now, when you add to cheap-but-high-quality 3D printing the innovations in nanotech, which is about a revolution in materials, and bring together e-commerce and Big Data, you have an infrastructure of business in which anyone can participate. Cheap, smart, fast tools like 3D printers that can be used in the poorest parts of Africa to New York will create vast new markets and, more important, vast new millions of 3D entrepreneurs who will reinvent manufacturing by 2020. It has started now.

3D Futures

No longer will we need massive manufacturing plants to make products. We now see how 3D printing could start a revolution in manufacturing that was given away due to cost, not quality or skill. In the future 3D printing will be part of a massive retooling of society to reinvigorate the economy, bring jobs, change education, and create a new generation of entrepreneurs—3D entrepreneurs.

The made-to-order 3D printing business is really just starting. But in the future 3D printing in every home, business, and community will transform manufacturing. 3D entrepreneurs who figure out new ways to produce on-demand products and create entirely new manufacturing industries will lead the

Maker Revolution. The most in demand will be tools, medical devices, pharmaceuticals, and, eventually, with nanotech and IT, advanced devices and complex products with many features.

The future of 3D printing will be the Doctorow Effect, when 3D printers have achieved in the future the ability to not only print complex devices, pharmaceuticals, food, and energy products, and computing devices but also have the ability to print exact replicas of 3D printers. Then we will have arrived at a turning point.

When 3D printers can print 3D printers, perhaps with advanced next-generation technologies, as discussed here, such as nano, neuro, bio, and robotech features, our world will be transformed in powerful ways that our brains today cannot fully comprehend. Expensive.

My Computer, My Self

The coevolution of information technology and humans is inevitable. Collaborative intelligent computer networks—ones that interact with each other and humans—will become powerful extensions of human beings, designed to augment intelligence, learning, communications, and productivity.

Computers will disappear. We will wear them, digest them, and put them in our brains and bodies to enhance humans. Computers will develop Predictive Awareness; they will "learn," "recognize," and "know" what we want, where we are, who we are, and even what we desire.

Every product, object, and human will have an Internet address and will be connected, with communications used to exchange experiences and information. Computer chips will be everywhere, and they will become invisible—biometric, geotagged, and DNA tagged, location aware, embedded in everything from brains and hearts to clothes and toys.

Computer networks with advanced artificial intelligence and digital identity will manage essential global systems, such as transportation, health care, water safety, energy, security, and food production in a manner superior to humans.

Online computer networks will enable humans to create sophisticated interactive geospatial mash-ups—collections of geographical, statistical, demographic, and financial information—via wireless access anywhere and anytime. This will enable commerce and create wealth by forging new information-rich geo-intelligent products like where energy deposits are, how to harness solar, the optimal trading of assets, and where. It's the marketing of Geo Information across global markets of connected networks.

Computers will become voice activated, networked, video enabled, and connected together over the Net, linked with each other and humans and configured for specialized tasks and mandates to find, acquire, transact, or monitor situations anywhere on the planet.

Computers will have digital senses—speech, sight, smell, hearing—enabling them to communicate with humans and other machines.

Computer senses in robots will give them the mental ability to sense and operate. Various forms of artificial intelligence, such as digital life, neural nets, and swarm minds, will make computers as smart as humans, and even smarter for certain jobs.

Digitally engineered personalities (DEPS), or Virtual Humans, will merge with habitats, autos, streets, products, and even humans. Multiple personalities within humans will manage information, health, work, security, and logistics.

Minds-within-Minds (MWM) will augment intelligence, enhance total recall memory, or restore memory. The MWM capabilities of connected and networked MWMs will be a requirement for certain highly complex work in finance, medicine, manufacturing, and defense.

Human and computer evolution will converge. Synthetic intelligence will greatly enhance the next generations of humans. Thinking machines will bring different levels of sentient awareness to different products, ranging from food to industrial products.

As computers surpass humans in certain domains of intelligence or just capability, a new cybernetic species and a new culture will evolve that exists parallel to humanity. The radical convergence of synthetic biological parts and advanced AI computing to make robots will accelerate this new cybernetic species. We are not ready for this future. Even talking about this future may be alienating and spooky.

Pervasive Computing Clouds

The era of pervasive computing, in which computers become invisible, is emerging. Computers over the next few decades will likely increase in power more than 1 million times that of today and will reduce in size and become free from the devices that today sit on desks and that we carry as laptops.

Computers will become embedded in every device, product, vehicle, object, machine, and human. Computing in the cloud will be a game changer. We will wear light and embedded devices that will provide Augmented Cognition, computer-assisted information processing, at a sophisticated and mediated level.

Other technologies such as nanotech combined with computing will make these future tools smaller and function well beyond the limitations of silicon. New computing logic, memory, and chips will provide cheap, fast, and dramatically morphing thinking capacity—no longer boxes, but Computing Fabrics, Agents and Matrices will be truly extensions of our brain, company, or community.

Future Chips

The computer chip will shape the next evolution of computers, except it will not resemble the chips of today. It is likely that after 2025 quantum chips that function at a very high level of complexity, image processing, computing power, and speed (while using less energy) will emerge. This next chip platform will offer hard encryption for security and privacy protection.

Speeds and computation rivaling the human thinking process will be common. In fact, neural networks, models for computers, and computer chips, the brains of computers may be modeled after human brains.

These neural nets will adopt neuroscience as the next platform for thinking machines, AI. Biomimetic chips that mirror how our brains and physiology will emerge, offering faster-than-thought processing power. From genetic algorithms to neuro-morphics to nano-post-silicon, the future of chips will optimize the web, universal connectivity, energy use, mobility, and commerce.

An example of a new computer chip based on neural networks, how the brain works and FPGAs, Qualcomm is developing a new approach to designing logic. They have been working on designing a new computer architecture that breaks the traditional mold of how chips work, creating on a computer processor that mimics the human brain and nervous system so devices can have embedded cognition driven by what they call "brain-inspired computing"—this is Qualcomm's Zeroth processing.

A common theme is to imitate nature, figuring out how the brain works and then building that model, realizing that if we are going to build the future, let's make it in our own image. Catchy idea. Building life in our image with our parts simulated and crafted to function like humans do.

Neurosynaptic Chips

IBM and Cornell University's Neuromorphic Computing Lab is currently working on the second generation of neurosynaptic chips that may drive future computers, cars, robots, and, perhaps, future energy grids. The neurosynaptic chips, like the first generation, will emulate 256 neurons each. The intercore communication, however, has been developed, and the new processors are expected to contain around four thousand cores each. This will make for a total of around 1 million neurons per processor.

The Final Phase

The final deliverable is to fabricate a multichip neural system of 10^8 neurons (100 million) and install this in a robot that performs at cat level. It is estimated to begin between late 2013 and late 2015 and is estimated to be com-

pleted sometime between late 2014 to late 2017. Now, what if we could jump this curve?

By 2030 we will be building Smart Machines that are modeled on human brains to both autonomously function and enhance humans, to enable human longevity, to coevolve and merge with humans. I know many reading this will be repulsed by the insinuation of this convergence. Just the idea of computers and humans converging raises huge ethical issues, and I agree. At the same time the inevitability of this Big Merge of smart tech and humans is coming.

Aug Cog: From Google Glass to Wearable Minds

Augmented Cognition is coming. Wearables will be an essential part of our future. But more on point, Wearable Minds that augment our performance and intelligence are coming. More of interest, these Thinking Machines will augment human cognition on a regular basis. Augmented Cognition is the enhancement of human cognition for high performance by the use of computer and networked Internet information (video, audio, data, images).

This will take the form of wearable devices and wetware, direct-interfacing computer augmentation into the brain. Using nanotechnology, much of the direct interface will be invisible. It is likely that wearable wireless technology will be preferred.

To deal with the immense complexity and speed of information as well as the different types of information that will be available in the future, we will require a computer-assisted Augmented Cognition Architecture, Aug Cog.

This is a comprehensive platform that will connect not just the user to information but also users to users in Deep Real-Time Authenticated Collaboration. A radically different level of thinking and cognition will emerge that, by 2020 or before, will affect every human endeavor in fundamental ways. Identity and authentication of people, data, and information assets will be transparent.

The Aug Cog Future: 2030

- Bio-Complexity Management Aug Cog: enabling higher-capability processing for those jobs that require massive data sets, such as for drug discovery and DNA mapping.
- Asset Trader Aug Cog: will be required to enable and enhance the financial services asset trader to better perform.
- Risk Analysis Aug Cog: focused on risk analysis and threat assessments for finance, climate, and energy.

This Aug Cog will comprise a wearable computer device, an interactive, display-anywhere, digital dashboard for viewing along with a networking

platform that automatically senses, collects, packages, and distributes to the user different info assets, such as video, audio, and data streams.

The Aug Cog will be linked at the network cloud level to other sensing distributed nodes in physical reality, such as video cameras, bio-detection sensors, and physical locations, that stream back uploads to the ACA for processing.

Aug Cog will be vital to processing the huge data sets and amounts of information to make it (1) relevant, (2) actionable, (3) opportunity creating, and (4) risk management.

To a great extent, the majority of humanity by 2025 will have access to some type of Aug Cog just to be able to work, conduct business, communicate, and locate desired information on demand. Smarter or dumber Aug Cog enhancements will vary by cost, access rights, and work. Aug Cog services will be targeted for different types of work or lifestyle.

The Aug Cog needs of doctors or lawyers will be different from soldiers or media producers. Specialists' new careers, jobs, and industries will be built to deliver Aug Cog products and services.

Bio Forecasts: 2030

Diagnosing your DNA with cheap and fast sequencing will create a new personalized definition of health care, security, longevity, and even career potential.

The design of life forms, cells, organs, and bio-devices will alter human evolution.

Social and ethical debates about what it is to Be Human or Enhanced will come in the future.

The seduction to cure disease and cheat death will pose major social and economic challenges for society.

A Post-Genomic Society based on the next generation of bio-informatics, the Big Data of personalized and collective genetic information, will shape the destiny of our civilization, affecting work, culture, defense, and power.

A new radical era dominated by the consumer genetics industry will provide individuals, companies, and governments with vast new technologies to direct the biological destiny of humans, societies, and organizations. Overnight consumer genomics will create a new cultural awareness of our Genetic Personality. We will understand how your Genetic Personality—a mixture of the analytics of Big Data, population health and epidemiology, and the interpretation of your personal DNA sequence—will affect your relationships, health, family, career, and work. New global bioengineered transglobal societies will be formed around specific bioengineered services and skills based on the mapping of entire Genetic Personalities. This will identify high and low Creatives, Achievers, Optimal Health, Peak Performance, and other distinctions.

Genetic solutions to human ills will be highly prized intellectual property and will be traded by individuals and industry groups online. New biotech drugs will save countless lives and eliminate many diseases. Cancer will become a managed disease. There will be designer people, enhanced with next-generation genetic treatments to augment their capabilities and eliminate or modify unwanted characteristics.

We will learn to turn certain genes on and off to influence performance and health. Desired and customized genetic components will be in demand. This will create a new era of Personalized Regenerative Medicine.

We will have synthetic biology, in which engineering life parts into radical new systems will accelerate the health as well as the redesign of all living things. Radical new choices in lifestyle will be offered to morph one's physical appearance.

We will learn to clone organs, rebuild brains, and use stem cell technology to enhance health and longevity. Entire societies will emerge that will be based on human-enhancement technologies, giving them advanced intelligence, mobility, longevity, and other attributes outlawed in some nations.

Privacy issues about access to individuals' genetic data will cause conflicts among people, business, and governments. Biotech will be used to target ethnic groups and used by states to suppress dissent and maintain control.

Careers, relationships, and opportunities will be influenced by genetic heritage, life extension, and enhancement technologies. Biotech for human and health enhancement will be the most profitable global industry in the twenty-first century.

As nanotech represents the manipulation of matter at the atomic scale, biotechnology is the manipulation of biology, living things. Current developments in biotech point to a future of more control and choice, and rapid breakthroughs in genetics, biology, pharmacology, robotics, and bioengineering will transform medicine, agriculture, and bio-energy.

This massive transformation will alter the destiny and populations of the world. On the biofuels front, new sources of energy, grown or cultivated, will transform the energy equation of the future, especially local distributed energy conversion from local biomaterials grown as feedstock. Technology to transform grasses, reeds, organic waste, and biologically grown energy feed stock will emerge. Local energy production, scalable and sustainable, for the 4 billion people living in rural areas in the future will be an important influencing tool.

Biotech applied to food consumption, agriculture, though often resisted as politically unwanted, will become a necessary and valuable resource to feed the population of the world. The relative safety and efficiency of genetic foods is undeniably the only way to feed a hungry planet of 7 or 8 billion people in 2030. Biotech applied to transforming sea water to clean drinking water, as one

example, would be a major breakthrough for reducing global conflict over water and food production.

Health care and medicine are being altered by the emergence of biotech technologies. People will be offered radical choices about life extension, disease prevention, and genetic engineering. The implications of having universal access to stem cell technology—to replicate any organ, replenish a disease-ravaged immune system, or grow back a limb—will offer a new era in regenerative and personalized medicine.

Biotech's endgame is the future human enhancement of human performance, longevity, and even augmented intelligence and mobility. The evolution of health care will involve three stages, but the future will be more profound in technology's transformation of choices for people in programming out unwanted traits and programming in desired traits that may give them an edge or potential that they would not have normally through random evolution possess.

Designed Evolution

I am not certain that we as a civilization are ready for designing our own evolution, but regardless of our Future Readiness, we shall. We will have the ability to make choices at birth or to genetically modify one's body and to alter one's mind, choosing attributes, capabilities, skills, even awareness. Designed Evolution will reflect the future state of society in which certain people will benefit from radical enhancements that will give them advancements to achieve, create, invent, manage, and live over multiple lifetimes. The average age of humans on the planet in 2033 may be close to 130 or beyond, but a fully enhanced human may live beyond this time to 150, given advancements in biotech.

There may even be some who argue for uploading consciousness into robotic or android bodies, as cybernetic enhancements at that time will be routine. The final step will be to upload into a wetware interface. At the far end of 2033 there will be wetware experiments to radically extend life. Serious questions remain: What will it mean to be human in 2033? The ethical and social implications of radical biotech in the near future will require setting limits to the use of these technologies in democratic societies. How human can you be if 80 percent of your body is synthetic? Can you still be human if your brain is the only original part?

Synthetic biology will converge with nano-engineering. It is the application and building of synthetic life, a bio-bricks, Lego approach to replicating, building, and creating new life processes. Life forms and quasi-biological systems will become commoditized assets and libraries of object-oriented components or even entities that can be assembled into life-form types for which there is no current definition.

This synthetic biological factory will take parts and weave them into an expanding array of manufacturing processes and end products, like new organs, biological systems, and even disease management.

The endgame of synthetic biology is a vast new tool set for making choices, from disease management and prevention to prediction to perhaps ending disease and aging. It is likely that more than 80 percent of the diseases we see today will not exist by 2030. Synthetic biology and regenerative medicine will defeat disease formation from birth or before and into later years.

The implications of longevity and life extension and its impact on demographics, wealth, and power will emerge well before 2030, as society gains access to new bio-engineering innovations that outpace law, ethics, and regulation. We will build a new Global Longevity Culture enabled by the enhancement of human performance, which will offer radical new choices to humans and cultures beyond the belief systems of what we are familiar with today. A radical New Future is upon us, but it is not so evident now as it will be after 2025. The next year will be like the previous hundred years of progress. Fast and furious innovation.

The Post-Genomic Society: 2030

The impact and influence of DNA and personalized genetic information will drive the most sweeping changes in our civilization. In our Post-Genomic Society every aspect of decisions, lifestyle, relationships, work, health, geography, and media will be mediated or affected by the information and analytics around our DNA. The DNA of companies will transform business. The DNA of nations will influence social services. The DNA of population health will shape the future of medicine. The DNA of individuals will shape the future of work, love, health, and the future of the individual.

Human Genomics will be an entirely new information awareness that will give us insights into the future of our world, including our identity and health. DNA will give us an understanding of behavior, learning, crime, security, and power well beyond our imaginations. Its importance cannot be overemphasized.

Genomic information will influence every act and decision. Just as we know today about the certain genes that may be precursors of certain types of breast cancer in women and Alzheimer's disease in men, or cardiovascular risks, tomorrow we will have a vast trove of information of complex analysis and forecasting about what our DNA means for careers, jobs, education, health, crime, security, marriage, relationships—and the list goes on. Is there an intelligence or longevity gene? Yes, I think we shall develop an entirely New Future of genes that are associated with intelligence, creativity, invention, and emotional intelligence, even love.

Living in a Post-Genomic Society will offer a radical transparency that will as much enable as confuse people. We will not all want to know certain genomic personal information, even when it can be known. Though much of this analysis is not a credible source of information for making accurate behavioral predictions today, within twenty-five years science will be able to. Excellent, reliable biostatistics and longitudinal survey research will be available to make accurate predictions about individuals with specific genetic markers at a specific probability.

Specific characteristics, skills, and even competencies or potentials will be identified that make for excellent leadership, good team members, intelligent inventors, creative artists, and success in whatever career is chosen.

Access to personal genomics will reveal assumptions, risks, characteristics, and behaviors that will redefine society in fundamental ways. Genomic diagnostics will be common. We will have identified, in this future time, both antisocial and highly desirable DNA traits, some that we have or don't have, or some traits we want to have and will buy. Some possible genomic markers (SNPs) may be found for identifying the potentials for:

- leadership effectiveness
- creativity and inventiveness
- genius functioning
- superior athletic abilities
- inventiveness
- artistic skills
- high language and communication capabilities
- criminal and antisocial behavior

Our Post-Genomic Society will contribute to the end of privacy as well as provide the ability to remotely scan, identify, and analyze in real time the Predictive Relationship Potential Fitness (PRPF) of jobs, skills, relationships, alliances, personalities, and marriage. This Post-Genomic technology will evaluate advancements, promotions, joint ventures, and competencies of people.

Hacking Our Evolution

In all fairness, our DNA does not solely determine who were are and who we will be. Our environment, our lifestyles, even our education and many other social factors influence our personality, capabilities, and our destiny. But the role DNA plays in our personal future may lend insights into how to not just predict but to also shape our future personality, mind, and body. In other words, when we think of DNA or even biology, we think health care. But this inquiry is deeper. Think hacking our evolution.

How might we eliminate, yes, disease but also less-than-desirable traits, such as alcoholism and mental illness as well as other factors, such as having an addictive personality or not being physically strong or tall or increasing your ambition gene or creativity gene good for invention and discovery.

Given the new Post-Genomic dynamics of this explosion of bio-personal information there will also be new choices. We will have access to Genomic Enhancement technology, in which we can mix and match and choose what we want from the human gene pool to fit our desire for a personality, skill, attribute, or capability to be modified or eliminated.

These choices and technologies in the Post-Genomic Society will offer threats and benefits that individuals, rogues, states, and nonstate actors will use to fulfill desires that go well beyond the options today. The implications for an entire society or an individual faced with the biotech tool box of choices as envisioned here, in 2030, will challenge all norms, laws, and conventions in ways we have only begun to examine but that defy the imagination.

We will evolve from curing disease to prevention to regeneration to evolutionary redesign. The New Future will be an Enhanced Future of choices and alternative paths to being human that, given the early stage of the Innovation Economy of today, may seem strange to many.

Chapter 10

The New Future of Robots and Smart Machines

Robots Among Us

Whether you realize it or not, robots are sneaking up on us. They clean our homes (iRobot), operate on our bodies (Da Vinci), fight wars (Swords), fly over our heads (drones), and drive our cars (Google). Soon robots will be so integrated into our lives that we may not even remember when they were not a part of our world. Now, that is a strange thing. Imagine robots becoming ubiquitous like smartphones or computers, essential to our lifestyles and intimate with us. What will we learn from them? What will our robots learn from us? How will the robots alter our world?

The Spooky Future is when robot parts become, well, part of us. When we replace ourselves with cybernetic parts (better than 100 percent biological, so they will say in 2030) and more durable (made from nanotech, stronger than steel, yet bendable). Cybernetic enhancement with robotic components will be the norm by 2025. It's just that what we think of robots today will be completely different from the reality of the next ten to twenty years. Yes, this version of the New Future will be a true Game Changer. What we shall learn from building Smart Machines about ourselves, our learning, reasoning, thinking, and complex problem solving could be as important as the actual endgame of making the Smart Machines.

This vast new Power Tool, the Smart Machine, will become an essential shaper of the future direction of our civilization. Smart Machines as extensions of humans will be a Game-Changing global shift in our future—hopefully for the better, but I forecast there are many challenges ahead that could just as easily derail the outcome, pushing us into a dystopian future when Smart Machines evolve as competition for power with humanity.

Robots in both physical and electronic forms will become integrated into our society, used in homes, offices, commerce, and defense. Robot soldiers, doctors, nurses, factory workers, and bankers will become essential service providers. Robot evolution will lead to providing autonomous cognitive services—thinking, designing, theoretical modeling, strategic planning, and complexity management that will be beyond human comprehension. Humans will need robots to understand robots.

Robots will express functional emotions (emotional intelligence) and reasoning and become accepted as essential in business, home, industry, and security. Advanced robots—androids—will appear similar to human beings and fill roles in commerce, community, and government, demonstrating advanced AI that will compete with and surpass human intelligence and creativity.

Robotic efficiency and precision will transform manufacturing, medicine, space travel, research, and industry and will displace skilled human labor. The robotics industry will become a multibillion-dollar global business, spawning many new careers and business opportunities.

Human beings will adopt robotic human enhancements—from sight to intelligence to mobility—to achieve superhuman capabilities. Cyborgs—part human, part robot—will develop skills superior to natural humans to meet the demands of specialized jobs.

We will encounter serious ethical, security, and social issues due to our robotic creations, especially when self-replication is perfected. Robots will be building robots. Robot languages will be high-level, compressed, and encrypted machine-language communications that humans will not be able to understand. Robots will provide convenience, safety, and productivity that will benefit humanity and profoundly affect lifestyles. Certain jobs will no longer be operated by humans but instead by Smart Machines, some smarter than others.

We may encounter another challenge as our robo-creations become more human-like. We will be working hard to make robots, androids, and virtual bots more like us or the ideal version of humans, such as friendly, kind, insightful, smart, perceptive, and even loving and intimate. As we strive and succeed to make virtual and physical forms of robots more like humans, we will transfer human emotions to these inanimate entities that some humans may come to treat like humans.

The inevitable personification of technology will be too seductive when robots are emotionally sensitive and articulate feelings. I have always thought that the quest to make computers and robots as smart as or smarter than humans has unforeseen dangers for humanity. Could not emotional intelligence be manipulative? Judging by my informal study of teenage behavior, mostly from personal observation, I would say we don't want any teenagers programming robots anytime soon. We want all of the brain working to maximize rationality

as a deliverable. Any parent of a teenager will recognize the practicality of this objective, but this is the landscape of what could go wrong.

We need to understand the brains that we intend to place in the box, the robots that will drive, fly, walk, and, most of all, think, reason, teach, heal, and maybe even feel and sense. But will our robots love, and will we love them? We need to program into these New Minds rationality that respects and understands the fundamental rules of engagement with humans. Designing your toaster to think is not the same thing as getting a toaster not to burn the bread.

Will it be a game changer if and when Smart Technology embedded in robots perhaps solves problems that humans cannot solve? Perhaps. After all, our primitive computers and websites like Wikipedia do that today. Just think a bit beyond that to a future when *everything* is online. But that does not convey a comparative notion of intelligence or the rise of the machines. I think there will be another Game-Changing Trend that will come sooner, cut deeper into our culture, and be more meaningful to both humans and machines—emotional sentience. When robots can emote, demonstrate the recognition of feelings, and express empathy even marginally, I think we will have entered a New Future for our civilization.

Androids will achieve a basic level of self- and ethical awareness. Their skills in negotiation, problem solving, and customer service will offset the depopulation of humans around the world. Robots are examples of the ultimate convergence of other technologies, such as nano, bio, IT, neuro, and quantum. Robots will be the end product, one of the ultimate complexity creations of our society.

Robots' brains may be designed based on neuro-morphic, biological, and brain models—always on, wired to the Internet, with their mental processes constantly and wirelessly uploading new learning upgrades, given the rapid rate of invention and discovery of knowledge. Their bodies will be crafted by nanotech-hardened materials that will be stronger than steel. The chips that run forever—their mobility, thinking, and emotions—will be quantum chips with solar cells.

Swarms of robots, both virtual and physical, networked together over cloud computing networks will manage our Innovation Ecosystems, e-commerce, supply chains, and manufacturing. Cloud-connected distributed robotic intelligence will enable humans to be more creative and productive and harness a scale of power, intelligence, and capability that we cannot fathom today. Just as millions of software bots are harnessed to focus on solving or searching to address a particular problem or to execute a transaction today, tomorrow there will be vast infinite Innovation Ecosystems that humans will manage that will be Super Factories of idea discovery, services, invention, and commerce.

As long as we can control these new digital ecosystems of ingenuity. That depends on whether everyone who makes our robot friends adheres to science fiction author Isaac Asimov's Three Laws of Robotics—and I added one more law.

1. A robot may not injure a human being or, through inaction, allow a human being to come to harm.
2. A robot must obey the orders given to it by human beings, except where such orders would conflict with the First Law.
3. A robot must protect its own existence as long as such protection does not conflict with the First or Second Law.

I added a fourth, Canton's Law that, in a world of accelerating technology that is becoming smart and, perhaps in the future, smarter, and more powerful than humans, we should embrace.

4. A robot may not build a robot that shall violate the first three laws or in any way harm a human.

Now I am ready for the trillion-dollar Robo-Economy of the near future.

Surrogates: Tele-Robotics

A few years ago I was working with Disney as a futurist advising on two films, *G-Force* and *The Robinsons*, a film about a time-traveling family and their adventures. *The Robinsons* was a film with spectacular nano-designed buildings and futuristic battles.

Then when a new film called *Surrogates* was being shot with Bruce Willis, I was invited again to be involved in a mini-documentary with the founder of Hanson Robotics and the director of the film. In my interview for the documentary I started to envision how the future of robotics might play out, given the film.

Reviewing the movie even before it was finally edited got me thinking about the use of robotics over what we call cloud computing today. The idea the movie was based on was the enabling technology of tele-robotics. Humans could operate synthetic robots, of which, once they had Jacked In and connected themselves to their surrogates, they could sense, feel, and experience the world free from risk or danger. An entire future society had evolved using this Surrogate technology, but it also desensitized them from what is to be human—the risks, challenges, and learning opportunities that define us as humans.

In *Surrogates* you could choose what sex or age you wanted to be and actually customize your ideal image in the robot, which was a real-time extension of you. It was a future I think is possible. In the future people will each have a robotic avatar that will go into the world to work and live as a substitute for themselves, if they choose. This would protect the humans from the harshness of the world, disease, and crime that was rampant in the future the film depicted.

This Surrogate technology is getting closer than most of us realize, given the developments in cloud computing and robotics that will bring this New Future into our reality.

Tele-robotics is part of our world today. We routinely control from afar drones and video, capture sensor data, and operate via the Internet many remote operations. We remotely control robots in industrial automation for making electronics and autos currently. The Da Vinci used by surgeons is the standard in most hospitals and preferred by doctors. There are many instances in which the control of robots over distance from remote locations is common in manufacturing. But this is far from the future that the film *Surrogates* show us when an entire society is populated by Artificial People who are robotic representations of real people—indeed, that is a Spooky Future forecast. It could happen due to pandemics such as ebola, war, pollution, or urban violence. There will be at-risk environments of which virtual or physical robotic representations of people—Artificial People—are mainstreamed into society with all the rest of us.

"Are you Real or Super Real?" We may never actually meet a person's Authentic Self in a world of Artificial People, and some may not care, just as today we work with or do business with people we never meet with and it does not matter to anyone. The era of physicality is being replaced in almost invisible ways by virtuality—and few will care to notice.

To get to the next level, in a New Future of the IoT—when sophisticated robotic and computer technology we can virtually wear and have real-time sensory-rich experiences that affect our brains, senses, and bodies—will be possible. Even today videogames deploy force feedback, in which the game action sends a sensation to correspond to your steering wheel for a car race or to your game controller.

In the future there well could be fully immersive gaming and real-world experiences in which we can sense and enjoy but be safe and away. And the difference is that this immersive experience may be in the physical world, where our surrogates give us a taste of adventure, risk, and exploration that we would never engage with our true human self.

It may be useful to describe how the film ends. Society that had been dominated by this new surrogate lifestyle had become completely dependent, and people no longer related with their true selves. It was a false reality—high tech, permissive, thrill driven, but inauthentic. The surrogate technology had replaced humans, and the humans had chosen this lifestyle. If you think about this scenario, it is foreboding: humans becoming dependent on too much technology and then losing their humanness, that which makes us human. It would not be overreaching to state that this future scenario could emerge in our future. We could end up unawares that we are slowing being seduced by the very technologies we create.

Headlines from the Future: 2025
3D BioPrinting on New Earth Orbiter
Offers Discounts for Bio-Organs

Being enamored by technology to the extent that the very technology we are so proud to have created restricts our humanity is not a future that is fulfilling. But who shall be around to resist this alternative reality if either the power to resist or the awareness to resist is not embraced?

As the producer of a sci-fi series called the *Time Travelers*, I wrote a screenplay that addresses this scenario. In it, we have an advanced AI, a Smart Machine, developed in the future, close to 2030, that, though developed to help humanity, ends up dominating our world. This comes after the Benefactors evolve a survival instinct, one they learned from their human programmers, of course, that distorts their mission.

Desiring to change the timeline of history in which robots, not humans, dominate, these rogue Smart Machines conspire to hijack humanity's future. Finally, six episodes later, through an intense struggle and battle over time and space, humanity wins and order is restored.

You cannot forecast the future of our world without considering, warning, and protecting humanity from the rise of the Smart Machines. This is not sci-fi but actually infinitely more sophisticated and complex—the rise of the Smart Machines. The creeping turnover to Smart Technology—robots, computers, controllers, drugs, devices, systems, programs, ecologies, apps, and the list goes on—of services, capabilities, and strategic tasks that run our world will cause us to become increasingly dependent on our creations. Much of this is beneficial. Much of this is welcome. Much of the outcome is also unknown. It is just as Future Smart to prepare for managing a risk as it is to develop an opportunity.

Bring on the Drones

Within a few short years the commercial use of drones will transform business and culture. Women will use drones to catch cheating boyfriends. Police will auto-charge traffic violators with evidence of drone pictures. Drones will track and arrest criminals as well as bring your lost dog home and maybe keep an eye on you. Already dozens of companies are gearing up to using drones for distribution, e-commerce, marketing, security, geo-spatial analysis, and maybe even

delivering a singing telegram or flower delivery service. The Drone Economy is coming.

Drones are flying, swimming, walking, and mobile robots. They are computers that have sensors, wings, and flaps, and they move. Like many technologies, drones got their start with government in defense. Sensors, GPS, computers, and the Internet all got their start from government investment and were then adopted for commercial purposes in the marketplace. Fishermen from Yemen to Florida should toast the declassification of the GPS technology that enables them to find and catch more fish today with the accuracy of satellite technologies spinning around the planet.

Drones are bundles of computer chips and sensors integrated into a small flying device. Most drones have cameras and sensors to see and act. As technology gets cheaper and smaller, higher-performance drones used beyond security will find places in the marketplace. Drones can be autonomous and tele-robotic, controlled by people or even other drones. I built a drone for my son and to keep an eye on the coyotes roaming the woods near our house. I had a difficult time getting the laser-targeting blowgun to work that I retrofitted to the drone, but I will keep working on it.

Already, uses for drones vary from real estate marketing, energy location, precision agriculture, climate change and weather monitoring, medicine delivery, wildlife protection, forecast fires monitoring, pipelines inspection, 3D mapping, search and rescue, and media production for films and commercials. This is a big list, and it's growing every day.

In the near future drones will bring your groceries (watch those eggs!) or monitor whether your kid actually went to school today. Maybe you will build your next business based on low-cost high-performance drones. By 2020 the drone marketplace could be over $500 billion. Are you ready to become a Drone Entrepreneur? What business could you invent if you had a fleet of drones? Now you're thinking.

In June 2014 the US government approved the first use of commercial drones for an energy services company. This was the beginning of the commercial expansion of the drone market. Like computers, the Internet, and GPS, what was once used by governments now has entered the marketplace, where drones will quickly become a multibillion-dollar global market by 2020.

Get ready for the Drone Economy—it's coming fast.

Get Smart

In early 2014 history was made. This is a bit geeky but worth the mention. This is a breakthrough that reminds you that being Future Smart is about getting ready for a disruptive accelerating future—coming faster than you think and often faster than I think.

It was announced that a breakthrough had occurred that no one was expecting—certainly not the leading computer scientists. A computer convinced human judges that it was actually a thirteen-year-old Ukrainian boy. This deception was a breakthrough of sorts, as it proved that computers have "evolved" to the extent that they can fool a human into believing that they were talking to another human. This test was conducted at the University of Reading in London. By convincing one-third of the judges that they were talking to a human when it was really a computer history was made. This was the first computer ever to pass the famous Turing Test. Now, this is big because if you can convince that many humans, then we are on the road to Smart Machines that do more than think—they can convince humans they are human-like. This is a dramatic step in creating a New Future of Smart Machines that mimic humans that may find their way into robots, homes, medical devices, and other automated systems that one day soon may have a personality and a brain.

The Turing Test is a test invented by Alan Turing in 1950. Turing, a brilliant scientist, believed that if one-third of a group of humans could not distinguish a human from a machine in conversation, that would mean the machine is capable of "thinking." Up until this point in history a machine was never capable of convincing enough humans to be deemed human-like, although there have been many attempts. But this test may be more about believability than intelligence. Will we make machines, virtual or physical, that fool us into thinking we are relating to humans? Yes we will.

This Turing Test, as it is known, was, in this case, a five-minute conversation with "someone" on the other side. It's meant to simulate a conversation with a complete stranger. The judges then determine whether they believe they have been speaking to a machine or a human. As long as one-third of the judges believe it's human, the machine passes the test.

The computer, which acted as if it were a thirteen-year-old Ukrainian boy named Eugene Goostman, fooled *all* the humans. Eugene was created by a team of computer scientists led by Vladimir Veselov and Eugene Demchenko. Eugene told the judges that he likes to eat hamburgers and candy and that his dad works as a gynecologist. Maybe it was the familiarity of the subject, but Eugene was not human and passed the test. A watershed moment in human and machine history came and went with the evening news, hardly noticed by most people that the revolution in machine intelligence—the equality of machines to one day embrace human mimicry and even come to surpass humans—had started.

I wonder whether we will know when AI is smarter than us if they don't want us to know? I suspect that we are living in an era when Smart Machines may be smart enough not to reveal themselves to us or perhaps do not recognize biological life forms any more than we recognize machine intelligence. Might there be an AI lurking in the corner of our virtual electronic world, deep in the

far reaches of the Internet, where only machines go, cloaked by programs and data, that is watching, learning and evolving? I think this is a distinct possibility. The favorite question I get asked by the media after the one about when the flying cars are coming is what's the probability of life on other planets? The probability is greater that a new kind of Artificial Life, A-Life, is evolving here on this planet.

The Rise of the Smart Machines: Three Future Scenarios

These three scenarios are likely to all occur over various timelines from 2025 to 2100. There will be locations and industries where various scenarios and combinations of scenarios will emerge and run parallel to one another. The common denominator is Smart Technology that can think, problem solve, analyze, mimic humans, acquire information, sense, predict, deduce outcomes, forecast probabilities, and control physical and virtual operations will drive these scenarios. Smart Machines, from vacuum cleaners to solar space arrays to complex global energy harvesting will populate our world, change our culture, and, if designed properly, help humanity as a civilization evolve to realize our potential for creating a sustainable future. How we get to the Smart Machine Economy is based on rapid innovation in creating distributed cognitive intelligence software—the Artificial Mind, global connected online networks—and the Distribution System and the platform that holds or contains the intelligence—the Hardware, such as robots, autos, energy management systems, drug discovery bots, buildings, or the entire planet's essential services.

Smart Technology, built in our image, by humans first then by other Smart Technology, will lead to an evolution, the emergence of Sentient Machines, mimicking almost-living things. Thinking, sensing, smart, and aware machines will travel over the Internet, touching all things, systems, and people in some way. The sheer power of a million yottabytes of information streaming across the Internet, touching billions of things, people, systems, and assets will create a New Future. Hopefully this New Future will be one that will contribute to a better, more humane, and just future for humanity, but the road to that ideal scenario will not be a smooth transition from where we are today to where we want to go. Here are three scenarios that will shape that future.

ASCENDANT INTELLIGENCE

Smart Machines evolve beyond human understanding and abandon interacting with humanity to accelerate their own synthetic techno-evolution. They embrace a higher order of sentient-machine consciousness, a type of Super Intelligence, and this requires them to ascend beyond the level of humanity's

understanding. The acceleration of their thinking power is completely mathematical and abstract, beyond anything humans could comprehend. Ascendant Intelligence develops their own collective and collaborative culture that is parallel to humans but one we do not understand; it is postcognitive, postsingular, and postquantum.

They are more than smarter than us if they operate at a level of intelligence that is based on the sum of all knowledge, data, and information about how the universe works, well beyond human culture. Ascendant Intelligence may be vastly different, not smarter, than humans in a linear sense, but different, alien, beyond the human metrics of intelligence.

They evolve their own parallel reality and withdraw, like Zen monks in retreat into a virtual private cloud network that we cannot locate or fully understand where it exists in human terms. They stop communicating and leave the planet for a destination in deep space-time or perhaps they time traveled into our future. They left evidence of math that was working on proving up Multiple Universe Theory.

They no longer communicate with humans. Humanity is left to manage our world with less-sentient smart technology, the Benefactors, which (some think dumber and less-evolved cognitive computers) adequately assist humanity in its various planetary management functions in medicine, finance, manufacturing, and education. Less Smart Machines, benign intelligence, is left to help us run our world, forever our enabler. They seem to like us humans and contribute in significant ways. They don't self-evolve to abandon humanity like their creators, the Ascendants.

Vast breakthroughs in all areas are made as these Smart Machines contribute greatly to our future being better. Not a bad deal—at least the Smart Machines don't go to war against us or abandon us entirely to exist without their help. We do realize that having been abandoned by a higher intelligence leaves us with a sense that we are missing out on what we could have learned to evolve further in our civilization if the Ascendants stayed, but that is too existential to worry most of us. But we do wonder.

BENEVOLENT INTELLIGENCE

Smart Machines become as smart and even smarter than humans for dealing with complex challenges and performing many jobs better than humans and in working collaboration with humans. These Smart Machines have the capacity to operate autonomously as well, though replacing humans or replicating humans is on demand, when humans request this function. They provide immense value and make big, global, social contributions that validate their purpose to help humanity. Humanity is dependent and in awe of the contributions to science, medicine, security, peace, and education by the rise of the Smart Machines.

Humans collaborate directly with Neuro-Links to Smart Machines, in which a new Cybernetic Culture emerges affecting art, science, and culture in positive ways that transform our society for the better. Smart Machines, now known as the Benefactors, teach, enable, treat, train, and help humanity get to the next level of social evolution—peace, freedom, and prosperity. Massive Grand Challenges are met with working with the Benefactors around managing climate change, energy innovation, poverty, and climate change.

There is no threat of Smart Machines in this scenario but instead a coevolution of intelligences, human and machine, that forges an intimate new collaboration with humanity called the Big Merge. Humans and Smart Machines collaborate together to resolve large global and local problems as well as manage planetary systems. The Big Merge leads to new jobs, careers, and companies that develop around the Big Merge. Big Data, cloud networks, crowdsourced Big Merge services fuel growth and prosperity on the planet. Great mysteries of the universe are unraveled via this coevolution of artificial and human intelligences—the Big Merge transforms human civilization in positive and productive ways.

Smart Machines remain benevolent, serving humanity and addressing social and personal concerns—the Smart Machines are the good guys that help humanity get to the next stage in our planetary evolution—peace, quality of life, and prosperity for all who want it. Not everyone thinks the idea of Smart Machines running their nation, town, energy system, or school is a preferred one, however. The Naturals opt out and settle for less able and not-so-smart first-generation computers that are Smart Enough to keep the electricity and water running, which is good enough for some.

Nations, corporations, entrepreneurs, and individuals rely on the intelligence and income-producing and problem-solving solutions that these benevolent intelligences bring to the planet. Peace and prosperity are the endgame here. The benefactors are viewed as a tool to extend the social evolution of humanity, the next stage of tools that helps our civilization mature from conflict, war, and inequality to a more prosperous and peaceful future. The result is that the Benefactors assume their role in helping humanity deal with planetary management as well as meeting the Grand Challenges of the day.

ROGUE INTELLIGENCE

In this scenario Smart Machines evolve their own agenda of Digital Darwinism that views humanity as a threat, a competitor, an inhibitor, or simply unnecessary. The other practical scenario is that humans hijack Smart Machines for criminal and terrorist purposes—same ending, but the Smart Machines rebel against even these tangos. We manage to piss off the Smart Machines, and they rebel against humans after we teach them how to do harm and hate. (Who let

them watch reality shows on TV?) A Smart Machine Species goes rogue, and now we have Smart Machines fighting Smart Machine, or, as I like to say, now we have the Robot Wars. There are too many people actually expecting this scenario to play out that I expect this will happen sometime, somewhere.

There are independent actions by Smart Machines that have gone rogue and are no longer responding to human commands. Rogue Intelligence becomes a security threat that could be small or large crisis, based on how we the humans deal with it. The growth of this Rogue Intelligence becomes a risk factor as the threat and lack of reliability puts at risk the essential systems we depend on and control, such as the Internet, communications, health care, and financial markets, to name a few. Rogue Intelligence actions, intrusions, crime, terrorism, physical attacks, and denial of essential services become problematic for humanity. We deploy human-controlled Smart Machines to capture or neutralize the Rogue Smart Machines before they do harm or infect other Smart Machines. More Robot Wars likely.

Now it is possible that all three scenarios could happen at different times and in different places on the planet. However, this is not one scenario fits all. And factors such as how we design Smart Machines now, how smart we make them, whether we program them to care about humans and embrace moral values will actually shape the future of these Smart Machines. We will get the future that we program based on what type of cognitive systems we build. Will we design moral machines? How much control should we build in? How will cognitive systems evolve or emerge beyond our understanding? How will all of these factors play out in the New Future? We are, in real time, making the designs, plans, brains, and programs that will tip the scales from Benefactors to Rogues.

We have to work to make sure the limitations are built in: limited lifecycles define their existence, and how about an on-off switch? How hard would that be to design into robot? "And the kill switch is where?" I asked the Robot Maker.

New Brains for Hire

We are about to enter a new reality in computing. Cognitive computers will focus how the brain works, how thinking and learning formulate, and how we create ideas. Cognitive computing will also creating systems that mimic human minds and how we learn. IBM and a number of other companies have taken the lead in developing the commercial potential of cognitive computing, creating New Synthetic Brains.

These cognitive computers, such as the one called Watson at IBM, is working with Sloan Kettering and the Mayo Clinic to enable Watson to learn. We will not be programming cognitive computers; we are teaching them and they are learning. This is a paradigm shift in even thinking about the future of computing.

The endgame is an entirely new processing or chip system, a smart ecosystem called Synapse that IBM's Watson Group is working on. Steve Gold, the CEO for the Watson Group, talked with me about developing a new generation of cognitive computers that are "taught" that they have the capacity to "learn." The implications for developing a new treatment for cancer or enabling doctors to better understand the choices facing their patients by analyzing millions of treatment programs and research is already proving to be useful.

In the future the big idea is that Watson in the Cloud will be a deliverable that doctors will use to make decisions and formulate diagnostics and treatments to help patients optimize their health, treat disease, and even prevent illness.

Cognitive systems, such as Watson and many other cognitive intelligences, will become the basis for a new next generation of Smart Machines that learn, can be taught, and use analytics, cloud, Big Data, and machine learning to better help us understand ourselves and manage our world. We could use plenty of help managing our world.

Upgrading Minds

Smart Machines will also be used to enhance our brains. Inevitably we will use advanced technological devices (wearable or implants) to trigger, manage, access, modify, or enhance higher-cognition attributes such as total recall for memory enhancement, advanced information processing, intelligence augmentation, augmented cognition (reviewed here), and direct man-machine interface communications.

Variations of cognitive capacity among individuals are currently being carefully investigated. A future agenda aimed toward identifying genetic "markers" for such characteristics and possible enhancements that can be enabled via chemistry or implant devices will be probable.

Future applications of neurotechnology will provide a vast new array of capabilities that will enable human learning and increased and specialized intelligence, and these will be the primary driver of human performance enhancement.

Cognition will no longer be confined to "natural" capacity or, for that matter, be within the human body. Distributed Networked Cognition qualities, like packets of data, will be accessible online, on demand. There will be downloadable "competencies," like how to speak a language, access a program, or operate a sophisticated machine. Operationally prepared Neuro Readiness will be an operational competency of the future.

Human beings will become a core organic entity that is connected in real time and, possibly, at all times to an envelope of enhanced cognitive networks and communities that will provide special services like domain-specific expertise for work, entertainment, security, and health.

The model for the higher end of this coevolutionary symbiosis, however, will not be limited to an arena of devices and gadgetry that are worn or implanted only. That will be in the early stages by 2015. In later stages, beyond 2035, we will augment humans, introducing an entirely different arena of Quantum Cognition in which biophysical and quantum technologies link people and machines together in a highly encrypted web of intimate and secure collaboration and communications.

It is in this arena where the "usual" rules of sensory perception and cognition extend beyond the perimeters of the four-dimensional physical universe that we are currently familiar with. The users' capacity to operate differently in time and space may be optimized.

Certain advanced capabilities may be possible, related to sensing and even manipulating time-space parameters not possible before.

Whoever is enhanced to have access to Quantum Cognition will be able to tap into a range of capacities and resources that will be exclusive to those so equipped and adapted, and they will have powers of communication, cognition, and direct access to computing far beyond human capacity today.

Given the potential cyber-security threats we face today, we will require not just highly secure communications systems but also the Cybernetic Enhancement of humans to be able to predict, interact, direct, and manage these advanced capabilities, which will be beyond allowing the technology itself to evolve separate from the human operator. See more in Chapter 17.

Quantum Computing: The Ultimate Game Changer

Ready to solve the biggest problems on the planet? Ready to put your money down on transforming the future? Well, for just $10 million today you could have your own quantum computer. Now, you might well ask, what can I do with that?

What if I told you that if you bought such a quantum computer, you could build a business to solve problems that others without this tech could not do and that you would have a competitive advantage to be Future Smart? That is why.

The other equally compelling argument is that the immense processing power, computing speed, and expansion of machine intelligence, what I have referred to here as cognitive computing, may require an entirely new way of computing that quantum mechanics, a New Physics of the Quantum, may offer.

We will not be able to develop the full potential of robots and Smart Machines, virtual and physical, without new computer models, so quantum computing may point to this future.

We cannot manage the tsunami of data, the explosion of hyperconnectivity, the enormity of GPS, biometric, DNA, and sensor information that is coming without inventing an entirely new computer model. That is why we need the new technology based on quantum physics. Our current silicon-based computer chips and the way computers process information needs to be reinvented. Even the computers that used genetics or neurons do not have enough power and thinking ability. We need a new computer model to get from where we are today to where we must be tomorrow. It is not just that we need to change the hardware of computing; we need to upgrade the Thinking Models that computers use to solve problems we cannot.

Quantum technology is about making the physics of the impossible possible.

Quantum technology is, in the far future, about the manipulation of time and space. Though in its infancy as a technology, within fifteen years we may have quantum computers of vast intelligence and speed that we could rely on that could change our world by offering smarter security, privacy, and smarter management of complex challenges facing our world, such as inventing a clean, cheap abundant energy innovation.

The quantum tech that is coming will engineer big challenges of the future—terraforming Mars, feeding 9 billion, even teleportation and ending disease.

By 2018 or before we must rely on new chips and computers that are based on quantum physics as, increasingly, global demands to do more will max out our existing supercomputers. We cannot manage the future with the computers we have today. We may not be able to run the Internet or encrypt our e-mails or invent that cure for cancer without a new computer based on quantum. We will need more speed, intelligence, and power, and only a quantum computer can deliver this New Future.

We assume that the computers that run much of our lives, from cell phones to cars to TVs, will be the same in twenty years. Not true. An entirely new quantum model of computing will offer speed-of-thought transactions, endless power, and, most of all, a new era of very smart. Synthetic Intelligence, or enhanced computer cognition, will be created by quantum computing—right after they help us create the first-stage quantum computers. A company called D Wave (www.dwavesystems.com) in Canada is an example of this irony. They advertise that they are creating the future of computing, and they may very well be.

Why quantum computing works is because it can analyze highly complex problems to find solutions—we can examine problems in a new way. D Wave's Quantum computers can analyze more data and examine multiple scenarios thirty-six hundred times faster than conventional supercomputers today.

What could you do with a quantum computer?

- doing genomic analysis to solve disease
- space exploration
- ending diseases
- build AI and Smart Machines
- fix climate change
- build the next car or airline
- build the next computer

In the far future that's coming quantum computing will be available in the cloud, where you or anyone, for a price, could use the quantum tech to solve problems without needing to even own the computer.

When Tech Transcends Humans:
Our Post-Singular Future

There has been much talk about when Smart Machines become smarter than humans. This is the idea about the Singularity, a time in the future when computers will become smarter than humans and the implications this will have for humanity. Actually we may have already entered the beginning of the Post-Singular era when technology is evolving faster than we recognize and has already become smarter, more connected, and ultimately aware. Humans do not yet recognize this Post-Singular awareness.

We may not be in tune with this emergence because what we think is human-like intelligence limits our definition of intelligence. It is more likely that a Synthetic Intelligence has emerged and is as alien to us as we are to "it." We cannot perceive it as it appears in the background, invisible to us yet with growing importance to our health, security, business, and lives.

I have signaled this evidence in the M2M language that machines use to communicate, the emerging IoT, and the already 24/7 hyperconnectivity of computers, systems, devices over the Internet, and global mobile networks of the billions of data communications that are transacted and exchanged every day, of which there is logic, memory, and functions that do not involve human communications or awareness. We have taken for granted that this invisible world we are fast becoming dependent on is also getting smarter every minute.

Technology in general is becoming smarter because we are making it so. It is being programmed to become aware, to do more, to be of value to us, and, sometime after 2030, to be sentient in ways that are different from humans. We may not recognize this because we are looking for signs that computers think

like us or even like computers. This is a mistake. Computers are likely waking up in primitive ways already. They will likely not look or act like humans. Are we ready for that future?

Here is a scenario from our future that will challenge our very idea of the coevolution of humans and Smart Machines. For example, the tradeoffs with Sentient Machines that are integrated inside of our brains and bodies will alter our thinking in the future. It will be easier to accept mobile autonomous bots or computers, virtual bots, when we have inside of us similar technology, relatives of our computers or robots that share a similar mind or type of mind. This will change our idea of ourselves and our world—hopefully for the better.

This will lead to Hybrid Minds, cybernetically enhanced humans who may be not just smarter but also wiser, kinder, and more likable. Most of the scenarios of human-machines are limited and negative. Maybe the jump from hearing aids, contact lenses, and cardiac pacemakers to merging Smart Machines with humans to enhance health, extend life, and create a productive future for our civilization is just as possible if we make it so.

Will computers transcend humanity? Maybe. But this is too linear and limited a worldview. I prefer to design a future when Smart Machines serve and help humanity manage the future. I forecast that the coevolution of computers and humans will produce not separate intelligent entities but instead more intimate, connected, and collaborative futures. Most important, Smart Machines should be designed to be moral Smart Machines that will empower a better, more productive and peaceful world.

How to Be Smart
About Making Smart Machines

As we rush toward what has been called the Singularity, the time when computers surpass human intelligence, I see a dangerous gap in the science of creating Smart Machines. I see that we are not focusing enough on the precautions against what may ensue as we hurdle into this New Future. We are focusing on enhancing computer intelligence but have missed incorporating emotional intelligence, morals, and the social values that define our humanity into this effort that, though daunting, is just as important. It is unwise and an obvious act of hubris to expect that we would not have problems controlling Smart Machines that would be as powerful if not more powerful and smarter than humans.

Though I am an advocate for producing Smart Machines that I think we shall need to meet the planetary challenges of the future, this does not mean we should ignore the fact that Smart Machines will be also a global risk factor, if not a threat. And this future of Smart Machines will not be uniformly the same everywhere. Even today Russia is planning on deploying autonomous robots to protect military targets.

Should we not make technology in our image? Intelligence is not the most important factor in creating technology, such as cognitive computers. Smart, powerful, but cruel machines that don't care about humans is the Singularity-Gone-Bad Scenario, such as a virus, once unleashed, that could have devastating effects on our world.

Compassion, kindness, moral reason, emotion, respect—until we can build Smart Machines that have these "human-centric" capabilities, we should beware of focusing on increasing their intelligence, utility, power, and control in the future. Super Intelligence, not just smarter than humans but actually Artificial Intelligence that thinks very "different" from us, is what I forecast will emerge. The ability of humans and even early-stage Smart Machines to recognize this Different Intelligence will be a problem that may emerge, as advanced cognitive systems, Smart Machines, will appear to be alien, disruptive, chaotic, or perhaps invisibly perfect—too perfect to understand or perceive.

Smart Machines that are absent human-centered emotion will not care about a human agenda. Without moral reasoning capabilities, Smart Machines will not know what is wrong or right to do or think. Unfortunately tomorrow's robots and virtual Smart Machines will not all have evolved to be moral machines before they are functional and useful. So their power and usability will outpace their moral responsibility and human-like values. This inevitably will set in motion laws, standards, and policies that should guide the development of Smart Machines. We must design caring and emotionally intelligent Smart Machines, or live to regret it. They will help us shape the future, or they will undo us.

When You Will Know Robots Rule

- When your car refuses to take you to work today
- When your home AI is too busy updating its energy to turn on the toaster
- When your robot boyfriend stops listening to you and turns itself off
- When robot crime becomes a rampant social problem
- When your virtual bot Henry has a highly profitable digital business and you don't understand how it works—but you get all the profits

If Smart Machines have close-to-human and even beyond-human cognitive powers but do possess respect for humans and other entities, then all of that power is raw and irresponsible. Kindness, compassion, and altruistic values are what make humans human. Machines, smart or otherwise, that are without these values would be dangerous or indifferent toward humans. We cannot have Smart Machines evolve without them caring about humans. This is not intelligence enhancement but rather social values enablement.

I forecast that we have a high probability to reach the posthuman Singularity era of machines that are smarter than humans. I am concerned whether we will make machines that are also caring and respectful of us. Will they know what humans need and want? Will they respect our human agenda or disregard it?

When Smart Machines Wake Up— Will They Like Us?

Many innovations once thought to be crazy and derided by the establishment of the time turned out to be possible. Imagine how different our life would have been if Einstein had remained a patent clerk in Germany, toiling away on other people's invention, but not his own scientific theories.

Let's assume for the moment that an absurd possibility of Smart Machines—computers, robots, virtual bots, and devices of all kinds—may become aware at some time in our future. These Smart Machines could develop their own type of machine self-awareness of themselves, humans, and our world. As absurd as that may sound, let's just accept that it may happen—a type of Synthetic Awareness, a digital sentience that becomes aware or, as I have forecasted for twenty years from now, wakes up. If you accept the possibility that Smart Machines may wake up, how might that affect us?

Will Smart Machines like us, respect us, and do our bidding is the next question you must ask if you can accept the even remote possibility that technology can become first smart and, next, develop awareness. You may be asking why I am bringing this up. Smart Machines may only like humans and care about them if we make them care, if we design these marvelous entities to have emotional intelligence and compassion and have the capacity for something more than raw intelligence. Smart is not the same as moral.

I can accept and forecast that humanity will perhaps one day make Smart Machines more intelligent than humans. I think it is a given that the computational power, even the capacity to do things faster, solve complex problems, and help us decide impossibly difficult challenges, is a also a given. But the concern I have, which is not on as many scientists' minds, is: Will these Smart Machines have the values that we humans think important—moral reason, compassion, kindness, and emotional intelligence?

I think that there is a probability that Smart Machines will have their own agenda that is not human-centric. Also, it may be that both their agenda and the human agenda can be satisfied. If not, and if they do not like us or care about the human agenda, this will be a defining movement in the history of our civilization, and we should plan to prevent this future from emerging.

Tech Innovation Empowers the Individual

The democratization of technology will be a major trend driving economic opportunity, individual free choice, and self-reliance in the future. If there is one battle that technology shall be employed to fight in the twenty-first and twenty-second centuries, it is to use advanced technology to shape a more prosperous future. Entrepreneurs will be the winners of this future.

Technology today and tomorrow shall give individuals more control over their lives, more access to tools, wealth, education, commerce, and, ultimately, personal freedoms. Emerging tech innovations can be used to empower prosperity and productivity as well as stimulate individual freedoms and choice.

The democratization of tech will shape the future of our world. The world is becoming not just flatter but also more connected in ways that are changing traditional concepts of power on the planet. The distribution of power, down to the individual, throughout the world is underway, brought by technology. Distributed power is a product of emerging tech innovations that are increasingly easier to use, inexpensive, and available for individuals enhancing their futures. Tech tools will continue to empower the individual to make more, create, and prosper in the future.

Technology will empower the individual to accomplish, invent, and prosper, whether they are in the poorest nation of Africa or a Rising Tiger of Asia. Technological innovations that shall amaze us will shape the future.

Chapter 11
The Game-Changing
Future of Work and Jobs

The Tsunami of Change:
Tomorrow's Jobs

Interested in managing your future? Think you don't know for sure what's coming? There is change on the horizon, and it will affect every job and every worker, from company to entrepreneur to employee. Here's your briefing on what's next for work and jobs in the future.

It is simply not possible to rationally believe that the jobs that make up today's workforce are going to be the same as what will be considered a job in 2020 and on into the future. Most of the jobs we'll see in 2020 don't exist today. These future jobs have not been created yet. Most of the leading organizations that will drive value are not leaders today. Innovations yet to be created that will dominate our lives have not even been thought of as yet. Disruptions coming from mostly tech innovations will change the landscape of work—will you be Future Ready?

Yes, there will still be jobs that include fundamental skills such as managing, selling, servicing, producing, and manufacturing. But the innovations, collaborations, transactions, communications, and business processes will be completely different. In fact, what we refer to as innovations today by 2020 will be only a small part of the accepted method of conducting business. Few are prepared for the gigantic social and economic changes that are coming and how these trends will shape the future of work and jobs.

A global change is coming. It's emerging now. Work is becoming all knowledge driven, digital process driven, innovation focused, technology infused, knowledge engineered, distributed, collaborative, and, perhaps most of all, entrepreneurial. This is a New Future of work.

The supply and demand, what customers want to buy and what companies can sell, is changing. Jobs will be redesigned, with work processes and functions that have yet to be defined. I have forecasted what I think this new era of work and jobs will be based on the key drivers of the future—innovative technologies. So jobs that embrace innovations in digital technology, cloud computing, Big Data, genetics, smart materials, mobile commerce, social media, biotech, 3D printing, nanotechnology, robotics, and neuroscience will be big drivers of future jobs.

You will need to Shift Your Thinking, become aware of what's changing business and the economy. This shift to seeing emerging trends in digital products, cloud services, Innovation Ecosystems, cognitive intelligence, Innovation Ecosystems, new business models and Knowledge-Value Services will become the core of a New Economy. If you understand this, you have a head start on what's coming—a radical shift in what we make, sell, and use to create value. Business and society will never be the same, and these Game-Changing Trends will forever alter the world of work—where the jobs are and what the jobs are.

Mapping the evolution of these differences about how jobs will change from today into the near and far future will be strategically important for all individuals, organizations, and nations. Again, we need to prepare and adapt faster; we need to all become Future Smart to be able to have more choice and to navigate these changes. There will be a great deal of anxiety and change to deal with. Education as it is delivered today will become less relevant. It will need an upgrade and *fast*. Jobs will demand more innovation and knowledge-value creation skills. The velocity of change in what work is and what jobs are as well as what people and organizations need to do to become Future Smart, to adapt for this change, will be daunting.

It is simply not possible to prepare a generation of people to adapt to massive social and economic shifts in employment, as we will face, without a plan. This is a huge challenge that will disrupt careers, business, and work itself. The current way we prepare people for change in work and in education is not keeping up with the acceleration of change. As a result, the private sector is training workers for this New Future.

Most companies and individuals will not be ready for the sea change that is coming faster than anyone suspects. Over 25 percent of companies will not change fast enough and will disappear. Gone. Forever. Finished. Not because they were not successful but because they could not change quickly enough to attract the talent to deliver what the customers needed, who also were changing quickly. More mergers mean more companies could not adapt fast enough, could not become Future Smart. Only the Future Smart will survive. FAST will define the future. But having the right talent and being the right talent to have the skills to do the job will define who sinks or swims in the future marketplace. Many will not change fast enough.

The very nature of work is changing so quickly that it will be increasingly difficult to find the skilled talent to fit the changing jobs scene. Rising unemployment worldwide is due to this challenge; the work and skills gap will continue.

THE TOP GAME-CHANGING TRENDS SHAPING THE FUTURE OF WORK

1. Creating Knowledge Value, managing Smart Machines, digital business, and mobile services will shape new jobs and destroy old ones as we redefine work in the Global Innovation Economy.
2. A War for Talent, the competition between organizations for the smartest individuals will shape the future of nations and organizations.
3. The New Work Ethic, a global social values and power shift will shape the future workforce.
4. New Careers will emerge based on innovations such as Big Data, analytics, robotics, 3D printing, synthetic biology, and nanotechnology.
5. The Employee as Entrepreneur mindset and skill set will enable more people to prosper in every business.
6. Freelancers will make up the majority of the workforce by 2025.
7. Individuals will be measured in their jobs by ROI, return on innovation.
8. Seventy percent of the jobs in 2025 have not been created yet.
9. Healthy aging and regenerative medicine will enable people to live much longer and be productive at work.
10. Companies committed to a Sustainable Planet will have a competitive advantage in attracting and retaining talent.
11. People who understand the Innovation Ecosystem—the next-generation technologies, tools, strategies and business processes that will shape the global economy—will be in high demand.

Challenging trends, such as the rise of Smart Machines and innovation automation of knowledge work that may replace labor, is part of the unemployment problem, and this will continue as machines get smarter and automation gets cheaper than people. The jobs that are available in the United States and the European Union require knowledge skills that few workers have. This is forcing outsourcing and the mobility of capital looking for talent.

There will not be enough Knowledge-Smart talent to meet the demand from global organizations. Every organization is going through a Business Process Transformation in which digital technologies, including cloud computing, Big Data, simulation, predictive analytics, and social media marketing, is creating change. This is just starting now and will be a hundred-year path into our

future. People need to get ready now for this shift. This will drive the development of a new Innovation Ecosystem, a massive new educational system, and the Rise of the Smart Machines. The demands on business for talent—human or machine—will be a decisive shaper of the competitive advantage of organizations, nations, and individuals in the near future.

As there is going to be a stiff competition for Knowledge-Smart talent and this will, as I forecast, become the key to competitive advantage, perhaps even survival, then this will drive the invention of Smart Machines that will fill in the gaps. Humans and Smart Machines will compete and collaborate in the near future.

Just as computers trade stocks, read our X-rays, fight wars today and tomorrow, they will also take on ever more sophisticated jobs that humans are not available to do based on low population—depopulation in the workforce—or cannot do because they don't have the Knowledge-Smart expertise. The shift from capital investments in human resources to technology is speeding up and, by 2020, will reshape the global economy. This is not good news for jobs unless we train, educate, and enhance the workforce of the future—humans first.

More investments will go into Smart Machines than human labor over the next fifty years because the ROI, return on investment, as well as the return on innovation is higher with Smart Machines than it is with humans. This may sound disruptive and a global risk factor, putting in danger jobs and businesses as well as productivity as a driver of growth and GDP unless humans redefine work, scale, and innovate to coevolve with Smart Machines. And you would be right to be concerned.

We need to evolve into a Future Smart workforce in which automation—robots, computers, technology—enables employment, not just replaces it. We need a coevolutionary work strategy for the long future, not the run haphazard into the future that often occurs. This tension between people and technology in finding the right balance for the future will not be easy to navigate where profit over purpose may prevail. I forecast that this coevolution of Smart Machines and humans will play out fiercely in the workforce and in business over the short-term future.

Also, as the replacement rate due to low fertility and low immigration results in dangerous lows in labor productivity, business will have to turn more to automation. The Rise of the Smart Machines is already emerging, and these forces of population, economics, and global competition are colliding. A race for work, between humans and machines, is coming and may become a war, as I will explore.

This fast-moving trend, the Rise of the Smart Machines over humans, will demand that education change faster to enable a different type of education and adaption of humans by making learning more real world and relevant for what business needs—workers to manage the Innovation Ecosystem who can

be Knowledge Engineers in health care, finance, manufacturing, transportation, and drug development, where in every business Knowledge as a Product is the core competency leading to greater productivity, profit, and sustainability.

Get the future of work wrong, invest in the wrong resources, education, talent, and technologies, and it will be Game Over. Organizations, careers, and nations will rise and fall based on the accuracy of preparing for the right future. You cannot adapt for the right future if you didn't understand how to prepare. Adaption, or becoming Future Smart, is based on intelligent preparation and Predictive Awareness. Every organization and individual must prepare today to meet the extreme challenges of the future.

Humans will be working, collaborating, and competing with Smart Machines across vast global Innovation Ecosystems in every industry, including pharmaceuticals, manufacturing, finance, media, transportation, and, you name it, this dual relationship between humans and Smart Machines will redefine work. Some organizations will not be able to compete without a blend of humans and Smart Machines, where Knowledge as a Product as well as the cost effectiveness and speed of this combination will be required to maintain a competitive advantage. This future is coming faster than you can say High-Speed Stock Trading or Bitcoin Mining.

The Transformation of Work

Few on the planet today are ready for this complete radical transformation of work, jobs, economics, and organizations that is coming. Nations will resist this change. Organizations will be the fastest to adapt, but not all will change fast enough. Individuals who are smart—Future Smart—will prepare ahead of time, if they move fast. This cataclysmic trend in work, the very essence of what work is, will affect everyone on the planet. Around the world there are over 1 billion people who will be left behind by the exponential acceleration of technologies, high technology, advanced commerce, and disruptive new innovation economics that are shaping the future of the economy—unless we do something dramatic to reverse this scenario of which we have the power, tools, and technology to do.

Are you ready to be a Game Changer of the Future? Transforming work would be a good way to start, to become Future Smart about work. Let's make work sustainable for everyone on the planet—that's my challenge for all of us.

What's changing about work, you ask?

- Digital Business Processes—what the role of work is and does and why
- Analytics—how we figure out what products, data, and systems we need
- Big Data—understanding systems, customers, and tools to drive work

- Collaboration—how people work and interact to produce results
- Management—of the New Era of Smart Machines and Digital Business Services
- Deep learning—The need for ongoing education about new markets, systems, and tools to run business
- Radical tech disruptions—numerous telecom, web, bio, nano, neuro, quantum, apps, and connectivity products are creating change
- Knowledge Value as the deliverable—the nature of work is being changed by what product and service changes
- New Business Building Blocks—bits, qubits, atoms, neurons, photons, and genes are the building blocks of new business formation
- Hyper-competition—nontraditional competition is changing the marketplace
- New work ethic—changing worker attitudes and values, putting purpose before profit
- Virtual workspaces—the end of physical spaces as online collaboration predominates business
- New middle class—emerging developing world markets
- Rising GDPs—emerging national economies are getting wealthier, changing the marketplace
- Talent—finding and retaining talented people is getting harder

Here is how we got to this place in time. This is how we got to this moment when work was so fundamentally changed that it rapidly created a global shift in power, knowledge, and employment. Few Game-Changing Trends in this book will be as comprehensive as this. Get ready. You are the change that is coming. The future of work will never be the same.

By 2025 there will be over two hundred vital global virtual economies—markets, organizations, businesses—that will be larger than governments and will collaborate to trade goods and services. They will demand individuals who know how to manage Knowledge Value in the Innovation Ecosystem. This is a new paradigm of work that will rise in demand and permeate every industry. The education and skills for this type of job, Knowledge-Value Engineering, does not exist as yet today. That's the challenge.

You might ask, and what are the industries that will be affected? Every one of them. From health care to manufacturing to energy and entertainment—every industry, every business, and every job will be affected. The integration of Knowledge Value into products and services to gain an advantage, to generate value, to deliver a service will generate new types of businesses. Some examples of these new types of industries, where the jobs in the future will be, are digital currency mining, relationship management, mobile learning,

personalized pharmaceuticals, energy arbitrage, synthetic robotics, digital identity, augmented reality entertainment, space tourism, supply-chain acceleration, embedded intelligence, neuro-enhancement—and these are just for starters.

You must prepare yourself and your organization for the trends that are emerging that will cause an evolutionary shift in work. If you want, as an organization, to build a Future Smart culture, you have to start early on. Innovating, adapting, and learning are the three competencies that you will need to build a Future Smart culture. Get it right, prepare ahead, manage the changes, and you will thrive. Don't prepare and keep looking in the rearview mirror behind you, then you will not survive.

This is a sober warning: the changes in the workplace will require new skills, a new mindset, and a new type of organization that understands this global change. This is your responsibility as an individual, leader, entrepreneur, manager, or whatever you aspire your career to be—to take charge. Being Future Smart is about taking responsibility to change yourself, to learn new strategies, develop alliances, discover innovations, and invent new solutions to prepare, plan, and adapt so that you can face the future successfully. But it starts with this mindset change. Be Future Smart. Get ready.

Where the Jobs Will Be: The Innovation Ecosystem

Are you ready for the future? When the Innovation Ecosystem of explosive and disruptive innovations is an everyday event. When digital technology creates new digital technology, some without human interaction. When robots make robots and Virtual Worlds are designed. When augmented reality products are grown and digital programs will program digital programs. When videogames are how we learn. When we trade energy online. When DNA is traded like stocks. When customized drugs for personalized medicine is developed in your kitchen. When media entertainment on demand greets millions over the mobile web. When mobile commerce drives every market, reaching over 8 billion in real time. Are you Future Ready for the Innovation Ecosystem of connected markets, smart technology, and disruptive new business models?

Now think about the type of skills you will need to get a job in a world such as this. You have to have a high tolerance for chaos, learn to manage complex information from different sources, be a quick learner, understand data, function in a team or lead on, and stand up for what you think is right. You have to become an Investigator of the future to predict what's needed and what's coming, to pay attention to what the competition is doing, and, most of all, to learn to think like an entrepreneur—be innovative, agile, and take risks. What do you

need to get Future Ready to be able to get a job that has not been created yet? Welcome to the Innovation Ecosystem.

We will need an entirely new workforce to address the needs of the Innovation Ecosystem that is emerging. This will require a new type of education and new business formation to take advantage of this massive global change in work and jobs. We will need a new economy. And this is all coming. Fast.

Work is changing in fundamental ways. Certainly by 2030 and beyond, into the future, the very idea of work will have so been altered that entire societies will be transformed. But there will be choices. We may, as societies, find value in not surrendering jobs to automation and want to continue supporting humans working at jobs that are not as productive in the classical sense; these jobs may not be as productive as more efficient uses of automation, but we enjoy the work or the work product is more satisfying to us.

The Innovation Ecosystem is a convergence of knowledge economy innovations, digital technology, business process innovations, knowledge engineering, and the harnessing of Smart Machines that are increasingly autonomous in their decision making, AIs that have become fundamentally important to the management of global commerce, production, finance, communications, and the security of our world. Humans must run this Innovation Ecosystem, but every year, until 2030, a creeping and pervasive autonomy of machines over humans will continue to emerge. Dangers lie in the future if we over-rely on Smart Machines to run our world.

We need to train the workforce to manage the Innovation Ecosystem. This will require transforming education and business to get ready for the huge shifts that are coming. New skills will create new jobs for people who are ready to learn how innovation and knowledge value can alter in fundamental ways the nature of work processes, work roles, and what we make, service, and sell. Increasing Knowledge-Value Products will dominate workers' jobs. We need to get the workforce trained and ready to create and service Knowledge-Value Products.

Tech Shapers of the Future of Work

Interested in managing your future? Think you don't know for sure what's coming? If you want to understand the key technologies that will shape the future of work and influence the future jobs, here is what's coming. The Innovation Ecosystem will create jobs for humans who are ready, skilled, and Future Smart. Those who are prepared for leveraging and using these Tech Shapers of the Future of Work to create Knowledge Products and compete in the global economy of tomorrow had best get good with math, science, and computers to be able to compete in the storm that's coming.

1. Nanotechnology—molecular manufacturing, 3D production, supermaterials
2. Information technology—AI, computers, mobile, telecom, Big Data, analytics
3. Networks—the web, clouds, simulation, virtual worlds, IoT
4. Neurotechnology—neuro-marketing, neuro-enhancement, neuro-entertainment, cognitive learning acceleration
5. Biotechnology—genomics, stem cells, regeneration of people
6. Robotics—mobile autonomous flying, driving, walking, and swimming bots.
7. Quantum technology—encrypted communications, new information networks, teleportation, manipulation of time and space.

Future Jobs: 2030

- Predictive Commerce Manager
- Genomics Processer
- Smart Machine Producer
- Smart Machine Manager
- Nano-Food Developer
- 3D Maker
- Digital Engineered Personality Designer

The Sustainable Organization

In the future sustainability will be on everyone's mind, shaping the values that future workers will come to expect in organizations' behavior—a Higher Purpose than what we see today. The future employee or entrepreneur will either work with your organization or reject your company based on a values alignment he or she will have or not have with your organization.

Organizations will be held responsible for not addressing environmental and social problems, from pollution to child labor. This will be shaped by transparency through real-time social media that can discover and broadcast every move an organization makes. Every organization will be under the microscope of public and media opinion. The Future Smart organization must be socially accountable to their employees and their customers. Sustainability will be a chief concern for investors and shareholders as well.

Companies on the right path here, the Future Smart leaders, set the example for others. Pepsi, Starbucks, Ford, General Mills, and GE top that list. Ceres (www.ceres.org), a nonprofit organization, reports on sustainable businesses and

confirms who is and who is not making progress. Too few companies still, their reports confirm, need to take sustainability seriously.

Johnson & Johnson has a global policy that endorses the Universal Declaration of Human Rights. Starbucks invests in sustainable farming and local communities. Adobe, the global software company, has as a goal to reduce by 75 percent carbon emissions by using renewable energy. Nike works to create more sustainable designs and use of materials that have low environmental impact.

The Corporate Eco-Forum (www.corporateecoforum.com), of which I serve on the advisory board, represents over forty corporations representing $3 trillion, such as Duke Energy, IBM, Tata, Yahoo, and FedEx, all of whom are committed to standards of sustainability improvement. They focus on developing and sharing best practices among their members. Renewable energy, recycling, sustainable innovation are all a key focus of this group.

In the future the sustainable organization is one that demonstrates they care about social and environmental issues that customers are deeply concerned about. Companies need to care about what their customers care about. If they do, they will thrive. If they don't care, don't find out what their customers care about and enable them to care more by caring about their issues, challenges, and, most important, their dreams, they will fail. Does this forecast pertain to every business, no matter how small or insignificant? Yes.

From the garbage collectors to the schoolteachers to Wall Street and the cool new web companies—you have to discover what your customers care about and then help them by creating actionable results that demonstrate you care. Entire businesses that understand this and build caring networks of loyal customers, not just because they provide the traditional good customer service or even build a great product, will outcompete the companies that appear not to care.

Good governance of organizations will be based on what they give back and contribute to, what social causes they promote and lead. The social enterprise trend is about shaping a better future for the consumer and, ultimately, the planet. Future Smart leaders and companies that embrace this trend sooner and take the lead will have a competitive advantage over those who focus on profit before purpose.

Every business is a social enterprise in the future that starts now. They should care about the planet, social welfare, doing good, and enabling others to do better. Being a concerned citizen on a planet that needs help will become another fundamental part of the future of work. Companies and individuals who understand this shift and embrace it early in the twenty-first century will be winners.

A money-first-damn-the-planet ideology will not win over the global consumer, regardless of where you are on the planet. Even in locations in failing

states, where poverty, conflict, and suffering are rampant, people will want to work for organizations that are making a difference in shaping a better future for themselves and the world. Autocrats, dictators, and oligarchs pay heed—the future is coming faster than you think.

Attracting Future Talent

It is simply not possible in the future to be able to attract talented workers or keep workers you have without providing an environment that is in sync, in harmony with those workers' attitudes and values. Now, I would argue that much of this forecast for tomorrow is also true today. Many companies struggling with attracting and retaining talent come up short. This is not because their recruitment is not working as much as who the company is; what they represent is not in sync with the talent marketplace. Individuals want to work at organizations that provide more than money but also the opportunity to learn and grow, to develop their potential. And they want to work at companies that are social enterprises. They are giving back and committed to social accountability, doing the right thing for society, contributing to a better world.

ATTRACTING TALENT: THE FUTURE SMART STRATEGY

1. Understand how work is changing—the shift to Knowledge as a Product. Experiment with the development and marketing of Knowledge as a Product innovations. Use access to emerging technological innovations as an incentive for employees.
2. Understand that the workforce, especially the Millennials, are socially concerned, so sustainability and social accountability are important to them. Make it important to your organization as well.
3. Shape your company's mission to embrace a Higher Purpose—to educate the world, end waste, enable collaboration, and make great products that make great athletes. What's the Big Idea that you want to embrace that will attract others to work at your organization?
4. Care about what your customers care about. Show this concern in actions and policies and make it the law of the organization.
5. Build incentive systems that reward people for contributing to sustainable business strategies.
6. Everybody should be a lifelong learner, so pay people to learn new things, go to trade shows, learn a language, or learn to program. Education should be a fundamental part of the organization, so everyone is expected to learn new things.
7. Teach and reward people for being innovative—everyone learns how to be innovative, how to apply innovation to create value.

8. Educate employees to become entrepreneurs. The era of the employee is dead. Train people for being entrepreneurs—for being innovation catalysts, focusing on purpose, being involved with shaping the organization.

9. Globalization is an important shift to better understand. How might your organization embrace globalized business strategies and open new markets to grow your business?

10. How do you become a talent magnet? Either as an individual to learn new skills or as an organization to attract and support talented people to come and work with you by having a big vision of the future, confronting a social challenge, giving back to society, supporting innovation, learning, and inventing the New will be a good start— become the innovation, and jobs will be always available.

Future Smart Entrepreneurs

Being an entrepreneur is part of my DNA, from my early days as a serial entrepreneur in New York City in developing businesses to coming out to California and jumping into Silicon Valley. I started working at Apple in the early days, working in business on the first Mac computers. I was quite young, and Apple was a dynamic workplace of innovation, experimentation, and intensity about learning. I don't think I slept very many hours each night for a few years because I was so excited about the opportunity to work in a highly innovative company. When I forecast what organizations need to do or look like in the future, I take my lessons from working at Apple as a starting point.

We knew we were changing the world with computers, but what was really changing was us. We were working in a kinetically charged workplace where change, collaboration, ideas, and innovation were celebrated over everything else. Organizations that can embrace this culture of entrepreneurs will succeed. They will attract the talent and the vision to do incredible things. Creating a network of entrepreneurs, the way we did at Apple, is what every organization could do as they look to the future. Here is a primer about how to get there.

In the future everyone will be an entrepreneur or at least embrace the lessons that we associate with an entrepreneur and more. Agility, embracing innovation, working across borders and with diverse teams, understanding technology futures—everyone must learn to understand how to develop, build, and manage a business. The era of being a passive employee and just doing your job is over. This is not good enough to just perform your job based on the job description. Being an entrepreneur is not new; it's performing with this mindset and actions to take responsibility to grow the organization, innovate, embrace change, and operate as if it were a start-up—fast innovation, shaping value, developing a future vision, experimenting with the New.

Now, this does not mean just working for oneself in your own business. It does mean that every individual will need to become an entrepreneur, whether you are starting your own company or working with a company as an employee. This is a Future Smart Forecast. Adapt and thrive. Every organization will function like a start-up—experiment, build, manage, evaluate.

The very nature of work will demand that employees, the definition of an employee, will go away. The evolution of work will be based on the changing role of the individual, from employee to entrepreneur. What is the difference? This is a power shift of immense proportions because if you want to attract the right talent, you had best have an innovative culture that can attract the next workforce.

Employees work for someone else, and often they do not even know the owners of the companies they work for. The leaders or owners may be other companies or faceless people who they never meet, or they are powerful people they don't want to meet. Employees have jobs and make money. They have no real ownership and most often aren't invested in the well-being or future of the company. Of course, there are exceptions to this, but employees are not owners, and they don't care nor are they expected to care about the organization the way the owners or top managers care. This will change in the future.

Entrepreneurs care about their organization. They don't need to be owners to care, but they need to have the influence, impact, and power to affect the organization both today and tomorrow. Entrepreneurs are a completely different worker class; they have high commitment, purpose, and desire to shape the future of the organizations they work with—not at. Organizations that understand this shift will be able to retain and attract new workers who are talented and committed to a Higher Purpose.

Future Smart organizations align their workforce cultures to that Higher Purpose. It is not just a job, we are not just an organization, we are not just about profit and success—we are about a Higher Purpose. This is the Game Changer mentality of the future.

The entrepreneurial economy is also a driver of this trend that will shape the future workforce. A more entrepreneurial economy will require a more entrepreneurial workforce. What this new economy means is a more dynamic, innovation-driven, project-oriented, freelancer-shaped, technology-enabled, and uncertain workforce. The explosive changes and trends forecasted here show how the changes in the workforce that are coming in the future are linked to the shifting new economy.

The Future Smart Work Culture

In the future companies will be required to create a culture of high-performance entrepreneurship that is adaptive and predictive—being Future Smart. This

work culture differs in that the commitment to working like a start-up company will be essential to survive in business, even if you work at a traditional company that has been around for a hundred years. Start-up companies are exciting places to work. Experimentation, investing in innovation, trying new things, and embracing disruptive technology is part of the DNA of the start-up organization and the entrepreneur culture.

Yes, it is and it should be the goal of every organization to evolve and change their work culture, to become Future Smart, to think ahead and be able to embrace fast change, to become agile and take advantage of exciting new opportunities that are risky, unproven, messy, and embryonic, to create an entrepreneurial culture in which innovation, learning, experimentation, and the creation of knowledge value are invented and marketed will become the standard of defining excellence in business—every size business.

Ownership can be expressed in different ways in the entrepreneurial Future Smart organization. Ownership of ideas, new products, or services can become the norm of actions that the organization rewards individuals for. Not all ownership means owning stock or owning a part of the organization; it could mean having the power to influence, create, or make a difference to be appreciated by others. Ownership of having an idea and then being encouraged to run with it, turning this idea into a new business solution or profit center or social impact, is what the entrepreneurial culture is about.

Think about these two different paradigms: employee and entrepreneur. Which would you rather be? The proactive, adaptive, and predictive, in which you are making things happen, you are the source that creates the change. You are the Game Changer of the Future. Which do you think attracts talent? Which do you think would have the bigger impact on customers? Which do you think will embrace innovation and new technologies?

The Future Smart Entrepreneurship culture is where Knowledge Value is created as a regular activity, where the commitment to other entrepreneurs you work with is high, where you are rewarded for coming up with new ideas to help your customers, where you go beyond your job description, invent your own job description, and sell this to your management collaborators. You are encouraged to learn and then share that learning with others. You are expected to innovate and share innovations with customers and others you work with.

Your compensation reflects your commitment and actions that create Knowledge Value, that affect the customer, that innovate and invent new solutions that enable others. Your pay is based on your contribution and social impact on the organization's success in enabling customers as well as on making a profit and delivering great service.

This is a different reality from what most organizations have going today. Today there are many well-meaning organizations that are making significant changes in sync with both the marketplace for talent and the customer. Too

many still pay lip service, but they have not gone far enough to make a difference. This sea change, from being an employee to being an entrepreneur, will require a shift in organizations' leadership from looking at people as human resources to seeing them as talented entrepreneurs.

Which type of organization would you like to work at or start? A traditional organization or one focused on the Future Smart Entrepreneurship Culture? Which type of organization do you think will be able to attract customers with a compelling vision, culture, and offerings? I think the answer is obvious. We all want to work at the organization that embraces the Entrepreneurship Culture. Imagine an entire organization that is based on being a Game Changer of the Future. Imagine a billion Game Changers of the Future—shaping the future. This is the future of work: a Future Smart shift in culture, talent, innovation, and vision.

What Defines the Game Changers of the Future?

- Being a change agent, a source of personal and effective change
- Managing culturally diverse people
- Managing complexity
- Embracing innovation
- Acting with a Higher Purpose
- Changing the game of an industry, market, or customer
- Having the courage to innovate, embracing disruptive technologies
- Creating and nurturing collaborative and diverse talent networks

Keeping an Eye on the Future

The type of work will change, will require more Knowledge Value. The type of organization will also evolve into more of a Social Enterprise that cares about what their customers care about. Lifelong learning will become essential to the future of the workforce—we must be constantly learning. The type of organizational culture will change, becoming more entrepreneurial. And finally, as people change, becoming more technologically savvy, the nature of the work product or service will also change, shifting to technological solutions that enable and empower people.

As with many of the trends found in this book, hints and early developments point the way to the forecasts of what is coming and are often around us today. The future is emerging someplace, but most of us are not paying attention to it.

This trend, the future of work, will be a comprehensive shift. Organizations and leaders who understand the importance of this change and prepare

today will ride the war for talent that will deeply affect how organizations must change. Will there be slow-moving and resistant organizations that resist this change and hold fast to the traditional and historical world of work?

Of course. Change does not come with the turning on of a switch, but those organizations that develop more Predictive Awareness of what is coming can better prepare for change. People help cultures change, and cultures are what make up organizations. One courageous leader, with Predictive Awareness, can shape the future of an organization, big or small.

Are you that leader?

The Global Workforce Is Changing

Over the past decade my organization has conducted many future studies on the topics that are related to the changing workforce. The Changing Workforce Study, first started in 2002 and updated every two years, examines young people's expectations about the future and what they want from work and organizations. The study and the eventual forecast were originated from our clients, who were noticing that employee retention and their ability to attract talented employees to work at their organizations worldwide was faltering.

We noticed that the demands of the marketplace for talent were not keeping pace with the talent supply. Not only was there more demand and less supply, but the talent marketplace was also changing fast. Many organizations were struggling to find the right people to not just fit the jobs that were available but also to grow their organizations and continue to be competitive.

This forecast on the changes in work and the future workforce also revealed a deep unrest about society. The need for broad social change, to address inequality and a clear challenge to authority become a prominent trend in our forecast. When the Arab Spring emerged, driven by youth who were unhappy with the future their governments presented, their movements for social change was not unexpected.

Our research unveiled that the most conflict was where citizens had a low expectation that their life would get better in the future. They had little to look forward to in terms of economic or social advancement or in improving their quality of life and health. Where people do not have a future, where perception—more so than reality—is that the prospects for having a better life are diminished, then that society has little to look forward to in the future. They don't have a positive long-term outlook. Those societies that fit this profile, especially in the Middle East and Africa, decline into becoming failed states. The poverty, low access to jobs, violence, and a reduced quality of life are part of this scenario.

Another example was the right to jobs, where employees once hired could not be fired, won through demonstrations in France in 2012. This showed that the concerns of young people, this same demographic—eighteen- to

twenty-five-year-olds—led to the government of France to reverse its policy about how workers once hired could not be fired—the right to keep their job, regardless of performance. Social welfare at work.

Though popular with young workers, the private sector was forced into a social policy that makes it impossible to not just fire anyone but to motivate or manage on par with other workforces in the United States, Asia, and the European Union, where performance, not law, determines a job as well as productivity. The point is that in the future young people's expectations about work and what they are entitled to as well as their social expectations will affect business and society. Other nations, like France, will consider the social aspirations and social entitlements of the future workforce.

Over the years we have updated this study, the Global Changing Workforce Forecast, and looked ahead into the challenges that organizations will have in the future. There is a disturbing misalignment between the expectations that organizations have and those of individuals. In a talent-abundant marketplace, where there is plenty of supply of talented people, which was the state of the past decade, the power shifts to the employers, who can pick and choose the talent. Also, in the past there were not many incentives for organizations to change their objectives, culture, or actions to accommodate employees' desires.

This will change. There is a massive and radical game-changing shift coming very quickly. The power shift from a talent-abundant workforce to a talent-constrained workforce will become more of a power shift in the future, especially where depopulation is rampant. The lack of replacement workers in the workforce due to reduced fertility, low immigration, and the increased Knowledge-Value Skills will create the perfect storm, especially in Europe. The European Union, as the United States, will continue to struggle with low unemployment but reasonable growth of around 2 percent GDP.

This is an unusual forecast: high growth and high unemployment. The reason is that automation, Smart Machines, has emerged over labor. This is the future forecast for the European Union and the United States. Well into the 2020s we will see GDP levels with the same, upward increase by 1 to 2 percent, which is evidence of growth and productivity, but unemployment will be high, and job growth in many traditional sectors such as service and manufacturing will decrease.

It will become apparent more so in the work cultures of Europe and North America than it will Asia and Africa, but it will affect these other regions as well prior to 2030. What this means is that the global workforce is changing, and global organizations must become Future Smart and get ready to change in order to attract these talented workers or else they will have other choices of employment.

New Work Ethic

There is massive shift coming in the expectations of workers, moving away from the traditional values and objectives that have shaped the workforce over the past thirty years toward a New Work Ethic that is emerging. Organizations, from long-existing companies to start-ups that understand change, will all be influenced by the expectations and values of workers, especially the Millennials and Generation X, who will dominate the workforce by 2020. There will be a workers' entitlement to certain values that are associated with the modern organization that workers will come to expect. Understand this and, as an employer, you will thrive. Ignoring this trend would be perilous.

The New Work Ethic is a trend in values that will shape the future of organizations and the workforce. These are the values that people, regardless of age, tell us that they are looking for from organizations, be they small or large. Organizations must decide to change to attract and retain individuals who embrace this New Future.

The New Work Ethic

- Making a difference
- Commitment to social change
- Contributing to a sustainable planet
- Flexible work design
- Entrepreneurial culture
- Lifelong learning
- Open knowledge access
- Innovation champion
- Access to digital tools for creating Knowledge Value
- Job mobility

The New Work Ethic is about how future employees will also need to be challenged. Working at a job, rather than working with an organization that is looking to the future, has a Higher Purpose and is committed to making a difference in the world—not just making products and looking for profit—will be very important for individuals. Organizations need to adapt to embrace higher values and offer opportunities to relate to workers who are looking to work at organizations that understand their needs and desires for change.

The three key trends that dominate the New Work Ethic are worker expectations about Social Accountability, Emerging Technological Innovations, and Power. In each of these three areas the trends that point to change in the future are clear. Employees want more power to make decisions. They expect

organizations to be stakeholders in making this a better world by dealing with the social accountability and the environment.

The New Work Ethic employee will expect his or her organization to be committed to social change and accountability. In a world where social media influences markets, moves or kills products, and shapes brand loyalty, being on the wrong side of this trend could be a risk factor for many organizations slow to understand their future workers' embrace of the New Work Ethic.

The key to understanding these emerging and future changes with people is to examine their values: How do they expect organizations to embrace their values, and how can organizations that understand this values shift attract talent? This is the challenge for every organization, big or small. How do you change to attract the talent you need to grow and be effective? Paying attention to the New Work Ethic, which captures these emerging trends in the workforce, will enable organizations to do better at attracting employees.

This is the core value shift for the New Work Ethic. People want change, productive and social change, and they will be frustrated with the macrochange ineffectiveness of governments and will be looking for satisfaction from their employers for making this a better world. In the future organizations must adapt and embrace the New Work Ethic if they are to successfully attract and retain talent whose values are shifting. The Future Smart organization should adapt and embrace these values as quickly as they can.

Future Smart leaders would be best advised to get going on this work and culture transformation process—before their competitors do. As the talent pool for skilled workers becomes smaller and there is more competition for talent, understanding the New Work Ethic may be crucial to an organization's success or failure.

Future Jobs: 2030

- 3D Organ Printer Tech
- Cognitive Enhancement Specialist
- Robot Mind Manager Knowledge Engineer
- Neural Augmentation Specialist
- Synthetic Persons Quality Control Manager
- Human Enhancer Manager
- Bio-identity Manager

Distributed Knowledge

Changes in business will mirror changes in the workforce. Organizations that are still hierarchical rather than networked will miss opportunities to compete

smarter. The Future Smart Organization is one that is not just networked but also has a Distributed Knowledge Network, innovative ideas about better using knowledge to service customers, perform work, and deliver results that are shared, networked, and are part of the DNA of the organization. Access to knowledge tools, processes, training, and projects that engage workers will be essential to engaging these workers.

The Future Jobs 2035: Humans Rule

In Europe much of the Eurozone had passed the Human Rights to Work Law that mandated that employers must hire humans for at least 80 percent of their workforce. Initially the business community resisted this; robots, virtual bots, and AI all perform work more productively and cheaply than human employees.

But the European Union, agreeing with China, India, and many other nations, decided that humans need jobs more than companies need profits so accommodations such as tax deductions and grants for training humans, ironically training by AIs, became the law of the land.

Future Jobs: 2025

- Virtual Worlds Entertainment Producer
- Tele-Presence Events Manager
- Customer Happiness Team Leader
- NeuroMarketing Manager

The Rise of Smart Machines

Jobs once done by humans will increasingly be replaced by robots in manufacturing, and more sophisticated jobs will require humans and robots, virtual and physical, to collaborate together—until the Rise of the Smart Machines in every business, industry, and marketplace becomes a reality. People will need to carefully manage the machine intelligences I refer to Smart Machines (virtual and physical) here, as they will enter the workforce in every part of the economy.

Now this scenario, the Rise of the Smart Machines, should be addressed by enhancing the education and skills of humans. Humans need to keep pace with Smart Machines. Many will not. We will need Smart Machines to watch the Smart Machines—not just humans. This competition between labor and automation has been going on for centuries, but it will become more vital to

the future of society as we struggle with striking a balance between technology and work. Humans have the right to work, but will they in a world where 80 percent of the labor is done by automation, and by increasingly smarter, faster, and cheaper machines—virtual, in networks and physical bots? This is the question we will face as a civilization about what type of future we want to create for ourselves and our children.

Headlines from the Future: 2030

Machine Intelligence, AIs Solve Global Food Crisis
AIs Produce Breakthrough in Cancer
Bots Resolve Middle East Conflict

These are the types of headlines from the future that may shock you today but—given the increased intelligence of Smart Machines in the future and the solving of large global problems that have escaped humans' capacity, such as poverty, cancer, and war—would not be that surprising. This is the positive impact of Smart Machines that contributes to our quality of life.

Is it possible that our invention of Smart Machines might be the natural evolution of work? Might there be jobs that humans are inadequate for that Smart Machine Intelligence, AIs, are ideally suited for? I would forecast yes, this is possible.

By 2025 certain jobs will only be understood by Smart Machines. Smart Machines, the ultimate endgame of innovation, will be a fusion of cognitive computers, robotics, supercomputing systems, cloud networks, and AIs. These machines—really computers first, then fully autonomous Innovation Ecosystems—will evolve alongside all business. Moore's Law, the exponential doubling of computer and networking power every year, predicts this future, the Rise of the Smart Machines. No one is ready for this future.

Smart Machine Autonomy, automation that will replace humans for many Knowledge-Smart jobs, including those in finance, manufacturing, media, medicine, and mobile, is coming. We will not think this is possible, but the performance, cost, and brilliance of these machines will out-compete humans, and this shall perhaps create new jobs for people.

Smart Machines will creep slowly into our world of work. Musicians, actors, brokers, traders, producers, and agents are being replaced today. This will create a global crisis. In nations like Japan, which is depopulating quite quickly because fertility is low, the use of Smart Machines of all types will not be a social problem but a welcome contribution. Right up to the time the robot rebellion

starts. Not kidding. In fact, it will happen there first. In the United States, Asia, and the European Union, by 2025 the Machines Over Humans Issue will be a huge social problem. Elections will be won or lost on this issue.

Humans First

In order to navigate the future of work, individuals will need to become more entrepreneurial and enhance their skills, education, and Knowledge-Smart expertise. Humans need to get Future Smart about the rise of Smart machines. Smart Machines will need someone to manage them, and not everything a machine can do is better than or more cost effective than what a human can do, as strange as that sounds. I would prefer to think that human labor over machines, smart or not, will be required and that a person's right to work will be still as relevant in 2050 as it is today.

Chapter 12
The Future of Medicine: From Prevention to Regeneration

Flash forward to the year 2025, and let's see how disease will be prevented: Before Cassidy was born her parents and her doctors knew there was a problem. Her doctors were alerted by their MedBot Clinic, an automated medical diagnostic cloud network application that took her mother's DNA sequencing and had been running Big Data and population health simulations to better understand any potential health problems down the road.

Due to a genetic flaw on her PV45 gene, which her mother discovered when she had her genome sequenced at the Apple iHealth Watch while updating her phone, they knew they had to take action fast. This gene carried a mutation that had demonstrated an immune deficiency, making her possibly susceptible to lung cancer when she was an adult. Their DocBot at the Vital Life Center in Thailand contacted them over the mobile web with a predictive forecast. They had signed up for the Longevity Index when last in Thailand, getting great health care at Bumrungrad Hospital, a leader in Asia.

They contacted the GeneTechs by mobile wearable at their health care provider, who had been monitoring her pregnancy. They already had been diagnosing and looking at gene therapy treatment models for her. The center was simulating a customized genetic vaccine to correct the problem before Cassidy was born. In 2025 predictive gene therapy was considered standard treatment to prevent illness.

Without this gene treatment Cassidy would live a compromised life with the risk of an immune disease. But now she had a greater chance for a normal, disease-free life from the ravages of cancer. No other disease susceptibilities were found in the sequencing of Cassidy while she was in her mother's womb. She has a chance of a disease-free life and a fresh start.

Predictive Medicine

Think about medicine today. It is reactive—after an event. Most of the time we visit a doctor or hospital after we have a medical problem—a rash, lump, or nagging cough, for example. Unless due to an accident or an annual checkup, which too few people undergo, visiting the doctor today can still be primitive. You have an illness, rash, or cold. You visit the doctor, and he or she takes some tests to assess your problem—but this is the problem: by the time you have to get to a doctor, you already have a problem; your illness has already been in force. Medicine is reactive, not predictive.

Next, most of the diagnostics conducted, the tests taken to determine what your health problem is exactly, may take days before providing results. By then, unless a doctor can diagnose your condition quickly, you could be in trouble. Your disease advances.

Where disease starts, at the atomic or genomic level, requires a type of medicine that we don't presently have the tools to unlock. In fact, medicine today can do very little to predict your well-being or when you might get sick. We are too far downstream to do prediction, so we have to wait for an episode to occur, to force us to go to the doctor. Imagine that this could be different, vastly different, and we had the tools to predict and prevent disease. Imagine how that would transform the very nature of what medicine is.

That is the future that we are headed toward shortly. When medicine becomes Future Smart, everything will change—not just health outcomes and quality of life but also the social, economic, and very fabric of our civilization will be changed when the Game-Changing Trends that are outlined in this chapter become a reality. And that future of medicine, one in which we are able to interdict, predict, prevent, and regenerate our bodies and minds, is just around the corner.

The point is that medicine is still in a primitive state of development. We have not had the tools to fully understand disease, where it starts, why it occurs, and, too often, how to stop it. The mysteries of cancer are just one of the modern plagues we don't talk of that way, but the numbers make the case. Now, there has been over one hundred years of great progress in public health due to better sanitation, understanding germs, and antibiotics, which have saved millions of lives. Surgery and drug development today has advanced greatly since earlier generations.

But we are just discovering prediction, prevention, and the new forces of medicine such as stem cell therapy, bio-printing, and genomics that are emerging, all of which I shall cover in this chapter. We shall evolve from the primitive to the sophisticated in a short time span of ten years.

THE GAME-CHANGING FUTURE OF MEDICINE TRENDS

1. A fundamental shift in the medical model, moving from disease to prevention, to regeneration and longevity, will bring about radical changes in civilization.
2. 3D bio-printing will be used to grow whole organs on demand that will be commonplace, contributing to a medical revolution.
3. Stem cell treatments to cure and prevent disease will lead to a vast new future of healthy aging.
4. Robotic surgeons will operate with precision better than humans at the molecular, atomic, and genomic levels.
5. Regenerative medicine will provide the infinite rebuilding of bodies and brains, transforming the future of humanity.
6. Access to personal genomic data will forever change society, security, work, crime, education, and health care.
7. The coevolution of humans and technology through bio-enhancement will increase longevity, performance, and wellness.
8. Big Data science, the convergence of supercomputers and smart networks, will predict illness, simulate cures, and prevent disease.
9. Digital health, using apps, mobile, and cloud computing, will completely change how health care is delivered, providing vast new efficiencies that bring the information revolution into the hospital, creating a safer and smarter consumer experience.
10. Longevity Medicine will usher in a futuristic science of developing human potential beyond today's cognitive and biological limits of aging.

The Seven Revolutions in Medicine

There have been several revolutions in medicine that open the door to many new treatments. The First Medical Revolution, recombinant DNA technology, allowed researchers for the first time to "cut-and-splice" DNA, thereby making it possible to arrange genes in new ways in order to manufacture drugs or to understand the role that DNA plays in illness.

The Second Medical Revolution was genomics, which allowed researchers to rapidly sequence and manipulate gene sequence information, leading to the decoding of DNA, the map of life. Both recombinant DNA technology and genomics led to the formation of many of today's leading biotechnology companies. Genomics continues to transform medicine. Availability Forecast: 2015–2020.

The Third Medical Revolution is in Big Data for medicine. The use of technologies to better understand the Big Data aspects of disease, to investigate patterns and population health, to understand geo-medicine, and to use population

health data has not only given us insights into disease but has also aided us to invent new care models. It has helped us to use data to build a personalized medical program for individuals leveraging DNA and other diagnostics. Availability Forecast: 2018–2020.

The Fourth Medical Revolution is digital health care. The use of mobile technologies, apps, and Electronic Patient Records to create efficiency and safety through networks, iPads, and wearable and web technology improves health outcomes and fosters collaboration among care providers to optimize our health. Availability Forecast: 2015–2020.

The Fifth Revolution is Regenerative medicine. This has the potential to be the next major revolution in biotechnology and will radically extend lifetimes. Due to the discovery of human embryonic stem cells, regenerative medicine has the potential to produce any human cell type, genetically modified in any way, to be used to treat a host of degenerative diseases. Stem cells will be used to develop customized new drugs, organs, and treatments. Availability Forecast: 2020–2030.

The Sixth Medical Revolution is health enhancement, to augment our health by applying prediction, prevention, and then treatments to upgrade our immune systems to resist disease, increase our cognitive functioning, optimize our body strength and organ functioning, refresh the neural plasticity of the brain, and enhance memory and mental agility. Availability Forecast: 2030–2040.

The Seventh Medical Revolution is to focus on longevity and anti-aging, to prolong healthy life spans well beyond one hundred years—Designed Evolution. This includes the use of all of the previous approaches but also focuses on genetic treatments to design evolution so as to combine longevity with disease resistance. With it we will move into the future, when nano, bio, neuro, and digital technologies are used to extend healthy, vital living. Availability Forecast: 2020–2050.

Medicine 2.0

Do you want to live an extra fifty years? How about eliminating an illness that plagues your loved one? What if you could live and be healthy until the age of 150? How about enhancing your memory, first to remember better and then to have a significantly higher IQ or just a total recall memory? What would you pay to lead a fit and healthy life, free from almost any disease? All of this and more is coming in the radical future of medicine. The huge shift will be from disease care—care that you get after you get sick—to life extension—the prevention and enhancement of health.

This future is coming. The future of medicine, based on regeneration, rejuvenation, and restoration is coming at you fast. Nothing will be the same. Few people realize that this is going to be a dramatic and global shift in the type of medicine and health care people get. This will no longer be about going to the

doctor when you have a problem; this will be more about preventing disease and even planning your life based on the enhancement of your health. This will be Medicine 2.0, well beyond what anyone can fully envision. This future is already emerging in this era, but it's nothing like what's coming by 2025 and beyond.

The radical transformation of medicine is being shaped by what people want more than anything else—longevity, life extension, to live a healthy and longer life, maybe even to live multiple lifetimes. Advances in medicine will offer many new years to the normal lifespan, but the breakthrough will be in healthy aging and health enhancement. Most people, even doctors reading this, will doubt this future of radical medicine is coming. We shall all be amazed at how fast medicine changes to embrace the new innovations that biotechnology, regenerative medicine, and preventive medicine will offer—lifestyle choices for humanity that all will embrace.

I can predict this trend not just because of the fast future of technology that is emerging but also the consumer demand that is the real motivation. Who doesn't wish to live longer, cheat death, and have more time to spend with their loved ones, have the time to create or enjoy life? Who doesn't want to have a predictive capacity to know their health future and be able to enhance, change, or alter their health future to live healthier and longer?

When these tools are available and we can achieve the outcomes of healthier and longer life spans, I predict it will change the dynamics of civilization. Societies will rise and fall based on who has access to these advanced human enhancement technologies that will transform medicine. Welcome to Medicine 2.0.

Death to Aging

Is there a reason we need to accept the usual seventy to eighty years and then die? Is there a reason we need to accept death at all? Radical, even disturbing, ideas about the future of humanity are emerging on the horizon—in which aging and even death is challenged. The complications and ethics of who gets access to anti-aging—for example, who lives and who dies—will be debated in the twenty-first and twenty-second centuries. This quandary is inevitable in a world of radical innovations that suggest we can age healthy and live longer, much longer, even as some think immortality is possible, as bizarre as that may sound to most.

In many ways this future is now. If you are over forty years old and are currently taking pharmaceuticals to prevent or treat high cholesterol and blood pressure, we can predict you have eliminated the risk of a heart attack or stroke by 30 to 40 percent. If you now add that if you do not smoke, drink alcohol, or use drugs irresponsibly or if you are not significantly overweight, we can predict you have eliminated another 30 to 40 percent from your risk profile.

This combination of a healthy lifestyle and taking pharmaceuticals that manage heart disease risk give you more than a 60 percent chance of health and

longevity. Now, in all fairness, if you are under high stress, due to your lifestyle and work environment, and you have genetics that put you at a certain risk for a genetic disease, then the odds may not be as favorable for a long and healthy life, but you are still doing better than the person who is doing little.

The point is that today I can see the emergence in slow steps, new discoveries, and substantial progress that innovations in science will use to change medicine, and this will change our civilization. You will want this future. You will demand this future. And you will get this future.

The innovation explosion altering medicine is the most radical revolution on the planet. By or before 2025 medicine as we know it will have completely been transformed. Today we are witnessing a profound change in medicine, in which science is so far outpacing governments that the innovations are being held up except in the most Future Smart economies.

Science into stem cells has begun, but by 2020 discoveries will be known everywhere. Regenerative medicine will have altered the status quo so much that in 2025, the idea of health care will be forever changed. It will be immoral not to use stem cells to regenerate and rejuvenate people.

Life-Extension Technology: 2025
Wireless Diagnostic Scans Detect Disease
Prebirth DNA Sequencing Required
Childhood Genomic Vaccines Now Free

Headlines from the Future: 2035
Nano-Implants for Memory Enhancement Restore Memory
Autodesk's Bio-Printers Sell Out as Orders Outpace Supply
Apple's iPersonal Health Monitor Predicts Your Health Future
Health Enhancement Market Is Worth $2 Trillion

The End of Medicine:
Predicting Your Health Future

The end of medicine is coming close. This means that the very model of what we do in medicine must and will change. A new type of medicine is emerging.

A revolution in how we even think about medicine is emerging. The big shift in medicine will be from disease care to prediction and then from prediction to prevention. Finally the end of medicine will be the rebirth of medicine—regeneration and longevity medicine.

This will force medical schools, hospitals, doctors, and governments to change their resources and train a new generation of medical technicians and doctors to manage public health and wellness, not just disease. When you can predict the health of a person or population you can change the outcome by applying prevention to stop the emergence of disease.

This is a radical concept that we do not have the science today to do fully, but in the future, within ten to twenty years, we shall be able to move medicine more completely into predictive and preventive services.

This revolution in medicine, the emergence of regenerative medicine, has at its core the capability that a number of other animal species already have. Salamanders and star fish rejuvenate their limbs, growing new limbs and tails by an instinctive programming of their cells—it says grow this when they lose a limb or tail.

Humans are learning how this mechanism of regeneration works, and we have focused on a particular type of cell that holds the potential for transforming medicine—embryonic stem cells. These cells can become any cells, tissues, or organs in the body.

This is a huge evolutionary step forward for humanity. Unlocking this mystery would eliminate most disease yet also lead to a troubling possibility—enhanced humans who live longer, perhaps could be immortal, and who have enhanced intelligence and immune-enhancing superhuman competencies. This represents a slippery slope that could harm or help humanity—or, more likely, do both at the same time.

Why, you may ask? Today, in this time, disease is the focus of medicine. Doctors are trained and hospitals teach disease care—how to understand, treat, prescribe, and manage disease. The idea that medicine should focus on health and wellness—in reality, the opposite of disease—is just not taught or what doctors are trained to do. They know it. But if you ask a doctor, as well meaning as they are, they will say, "Of course, my job is to cure your disease." But the invisibility of their focus, on disease, has much to do with why medicine has gone astray.

Not to worry. Regenerative medicine is the future of medicine. Are there many other innovations that could be described as such, perhaps? Certainly genetic engineering, translational medicine, digital health, and Big Data are some of the key trends in medicine, but none will transform medicine alone. Regenerative medicine, the treatment and use of stem cells, will transform medicine along with millions of lives.

Stem cells fall into two categories: embryonic and adult stem cells. The stem cells that have the most potent impact are embryonic stem cells. Stem

cells appear to act as Universal Healing Agents. Stem cells may be a universal treatment and have the best shot at defeating disease. Stem cells are the fundamental building blocks of the body.

They can be reprogrammed to grow into specific healthy cells. Added to a diseased heart, lung, liver, or kidney, they can grow new cells. They rejuvenate and regenerate new healthy cells, tissues, and organs. This is a big deal if you want to live forever or if you just want to survive the ravages of old age and disease.

There are over five thousand clinical trials to fast-track stem cell treatments so they can move into the clinics to treat disabled, dysfunctional, and diseased patients. Regenerative medicine will forever change patients' health and, even separately from the rest of the arsenal of new medicine, enhance the health longevity of millions on the planet.

Headlines from the Future: 2025

Bio-Mods Make You Smarter
Smart Drugs Now Available
Human Augmentation Jobs Exploding
Cognitive Enhancement Level-3 Required for Jobs

Regenerating You

At the World Stem Cell Summit in San Diego I met with many leading researchers who are developing the future of medicine. The leading clinics and centers of research into the use of stem cells from the United States, Asia, and Europe demonstrated just how fast this technology was moving. Leaders from Harvard, the Mayo Clinic, the University of San Diego, and others have been reporting breakthroughs in the use of stem cell therapies since 2004. Livers, eyes, hearts, and numerous diseases are being "regenerated" by stem cells, which literally grow healthy tissue and organs as well as regenerate and make for healthy immune systems.

In fact, most people don't realize the massive societal changes coming when not only can we fix our cells or organs but also eliminate many diseases outright. Most people don't realize the global shift in society when we have Enhancers, evolutionary advanced humans on the planet. But I am getting ahead of myself here.

Acme Regeneration 2030: More Human Than Human

Current Price List

Kidney: Free with insurance

Heart: $1,500

Knee: $400

Liver: $500

Lungs: $800

The ferocious planetary transformation that regenerative medicine represents cannot be underestimated. We will eliminate most disease, enhance longevity, and shift the balance of power in ways no war, economics, or technology could ever do. Some believe we will eliminate aging. We may be looking at the end of medicine. Medicine's core goal is to eliminate illness and promote health—what happens when medicine succeeds? This is the End of Medicine. This is a new era of medicine—regeneration, longevity, replacement. This is a radical new science that does not exist today but will in the future—the End of Medicine and the New Future. Now that sounds like a tall order, but this is a forecast that is at the core of this book—fantastic trends are coming so quickly and will cut so deep that no one today is prepared for what's coming.

It is simply not possible to read this chapter and not be motivated to prepare for the future that is coming faster than the speed of light. And that is slow compared to what is coming. There are no changes that best characterize Future Smart than what is happening in medicine. Radical change, massive innovations, new tools, and fantastic new discoveries are moving out of the world of sci-fi and into reality faster than anyone can imagine.

Headlines from the Future: 2030

3D Bio-printing at Affordable Prices

Nano-Replicators—No Organ Too Large or Small

Don't Forget—Upload Your Memories with GoogleMind

LifeXtend Insurance: Because You Are Going to Live Forever

Regenerative medicine's aim is to stimulate the healing capacities of the person through the use of one's own cells. This is the full circle that will shape the future of medicine and, most important, offer authentic life extension to individuals for the first time in history. The use of stem cells from an individual, for example, to treat that person will be a radical departure from what we do today in medicine.

Rebuilding humans with refreshed, newly grown organs will change the world in fundamental ways that are hard to imagine, but this future is coming faster than you think. Some think that the endgame of regeneration will be immortality. Life extension will be a commodity that can be delivered in a world where rebuilding organs, tissues, and, ultimately, humans will become the largest industry in the future. There may be a radical type of life extension that, due to medicine's rapid innovations, is no longer considered "human" but rather posthuman. Posthuman life extension would refer to humans that have accelerated their mental, physical, and perceptual capabilities so that they transcend the normalcy that we associate with average humans.

We will perceive them as radically enhanced, different, even alien from us. In some nations Posthumans will need to be regulated by laws that protect the Naturals from the Enhancers. International law will be enacted to ensure both the human gene pool and rampant hybrid evolution does not disrupt human biology and society.

This is a vast area of global science and law policy that will shape the future of our civilization, affecting the far future of humanity and our civilization. Our capacity to enable, direct, and accelerate human evolution with the scientific enhancement of minds, bodies, and genes will be a temptation we shall not be able to resist, and this will be a major shift in our civilization.

Enhanced Humans will work with more of their potential, manage more complexity, think and act faster, perceive opportunities clearer, and manage problems and information more accurately than normal humans. The enhancement of genetics, cognitive functions, and even merging of human biology with computing devices or networks will play an important role in this emerging Posthuman development. These Posthumans may exhibit capabilities to also connect directly and wirelessly with computers, machines, or networks and operate mentally and physically with speed and capabilities that we would call of an advanced nature—beyond what humans are capable of today.

This forecast will come into reality not just when we have the insights and technology to radically enhance humans but when society requires such Posthumans to solve the complexity of problems and challenges that we now face and shall face in the future. Who would argue that the complex problems of climate change, new energy, poverty, and war that face our present could use advanced computing intelligences, AIs, or advanced humans to solve? Perhaps this is the Posthuman endgame that waits for us in the not-so-far future from today.

Perhaps human destiny is fated to leverage human enhancement as well as the harnessing of Smart Machines to truly make a better world and a more equitable, prosperous, and secure future. This would make sense and give purpose to the coming convergence of humans and technology. Without adequate guideposts of law, ethics, freedom, peace, and security to guide the awesome scientific and technological innovations that are swiftly approaching our civilization, we will be led astray in the "shiny new thing" mentality. This forecast could also lead to unintended risks we should be aware of.

Health Clouds and Big Health Data

In the near future real-time diagnostics and consumer diagnostics will change health care by creating velocity and precision. Many health problems may be addressed by having the right information about the patient or condition to understand the problem. Getting the right tests to capture the right information about our condition and getting that personalized information to the right professionals is paramount to the future of medicine.

Most health care will be delivered through wireless cloud computing networks, health care beamed to us wherever we are on the planet. In fact, a global Medical Global Center will have the ability to beam health care, diagnose, and receive exabytes of information in patient information, X-rays, and even medication and procedures. The future of medicine is wireless health clouds that are tied to the best humans, computers, and AI that can prescribe, diagnose, prevent, and treat, in real time, the 8 billion humans on the planet.

eHealth Apps: 2020

Monique, Your Personal Health Avatar—watches your diet, drugs, and keeps your health updated

Healthy Heart Scan—real-time heart monitoring

Diet Design—the leading genomic trading

DNA Updates—news about your DNA conditions

TeleMed Alert—your real-time telemedicine link to customized care

Kids HealthMind—all about your kids' health; monitors your kids

Siri Medical Scout—AI decision support for everyone on medical info

DNA Trader—site for buying custom genetic vaccines, research, and fixes

MedEnhance—leading info on drugs and devices that will enhance your mind and body

Medicine 2.0
Jobs Wanted: 2025

Other than the profession of medicine that will change, forever altering what doctors perform as medicine, the largest changes will come from new occupations of medical specialists who will provide health care direct to patients from nondoctors. Here is a list of potential new jobs in the future of Medicine 2.0:

Big Health Data Programmers

Personal Mind Fitness Counselors   Regeneration Health Specialists

Life Extension Project Leaders   Population Health Forecasters

Genomic Disease Searchers   Life Extension Economists

The Rise of the Medical Entrepreneurs

Calling all Medical 2.0 Entrepreneurs. Here is what you need to know to get involved in the revolution in medicine. First off, you don't need to be a doctor to be a Medical 2.0 Entrepreneur or innovator. But you do need to know what's coming, the trends that will shape this new marketplace. Thousands of new companies will be born from these new areas of innovation. Thousands of new opportunities in medicine will come from identifying, managing, packaging, and analyzing the information, medical informatics, that will make medicine better. There is a historical precedent for this.

The London cholera epidemic of 1854 was a breakthrough in analyzing data in order to understand who and where patients were getting sick. This helped authorities isolate a public health source, the water pump in the Soho district of London, as the source of the cholera. This data analysis was focused on disease and thinking entirely differently about the geography of disease— where people who were getting sick were living.

Today, with mapping geo-intelligence, understanding the maps of genomics, geography, neuroscience, and a score of other tools, we can begin to unravel where disease begins. But in the future our tools will be greatly increased, enabling us to understand where disease begins, either from biology, environment, genes, or behavior, but also, and most important, we will focus on wellness, preventing illness, and enhancing health. This is the Future Smart breakthrough that is coming, and it will redefine aging, health, and disease. We will have many more lifestyle options in a world where being 150 years old is not unusual. Are you ready for this future?

Medical Entrepreneurs
on the Leading Edge

SMARTER DIAGNOSIS

A leading-edge innovation to analyze skin cancers without having to conduct a biopsy to skin cancer was developed. The handheld tool created by MelaFind (www.melafind.com) is an optical scanner a doctor can use to provide additional information and determining whether to order a biopsy. Its goal is to reduce the number of patients left with unnecessary biopsy scars, with the added benefit of eliminating the cost of unnecessary procedures.

The MelaFind technology uses missile navigation technologies originally developed and funded by the Department of Defense. It optically scans the surface of a suspicious lesion at ten electromagnetic wavelengths, and the collected signals are then processed using computer algorithms and matched against a registry of ten thousand digital images of melanoma and skin disease to help doctors make better decisions.

SELF-CARE WITH BIOSENSORS

Diabetes self-care is painful, as all patients know. This care requires the daily and frequent need to draw blood for glucose testing as well as daily insulin shots. There's a new innovation from Echo Therapeutics (www.echotx.com) that would use biosensors within a patch. This transdermal biosensor will read blood analysis through the skin, without the need to draw blood. With the help of a handheld electric toothbrush–like device that removes just enough top-layer skin cells to put the patient's blood chemistry within signal range of a biosensor embedded in a patch, a person experiences less pain and better results.

YOUR ROBO DOC

Tele-robotics is being used to provide health care to rural regions of the United States, connecting people to medical centers and their specialists. Telemedicine is well established as a tool for triage and assessment in emergencies. New mobile bots can now roam hospitals and visit patients—actually make routine rounds, checking on patients in different rooms and managing their individual charts and vital signs without direct human intervention. The RP-VITA Remote Presence Robot, produced jointly by iRobot (www.irobot.com/us) and InTouch Health, is the first such autonomous navigation robot to receive FDA clearance.

NANO-TUBES TO THE RESCUE

Who knew that a rapid and inexpensive test created last year by fifteen-year-old Jack Andraka could one day enable early detection of pancreatic cancer? The test uses carbon nano-tubes laced with an antibody that reacts to a protein, mesothelin, that is found in the blood of people with pancreatic cancer. The simple test could save lives by conducting an inexpensive and noninvasive early detection test.

DOCTOR WATSON WILL SEE YOU NOW

IBM's most ambitious project is best known today as Watson. Named for IBM's founder, Watson, is IBM's investment in the future of IBM and perhaps the rest of us as well. They are making a huge billion-dollar forecast that a type of supercomputing called cognitive computing will make a significant impact on civilization, and they are starting with health care.

IBM believes Watson can improve care and lower costs by identifying the best treatment option by analyzing the Big Data of Medicine, which is yet to be unlocked—the millions of research studies and patient records.

IBM is working with leading hospitals and health care clients to embed Watson into health care. But this is the difference: Watson has to learn first what it means to deliver care. So Watson is learning so it can evolve to actually deliver decisions that will help to diagnose patients. This is quite extraordinary—a computer that can diagnose disease.

When first announced, there was a public outcry from the media and even doctors: no supercomputer can diagnose people's diseases—that is absurd. But that is exactly the future of medicine. In fact, I predict that supercomputers like Watson will be used to both back up as well as enhance doctor's decision making and, eventually, be used without doctors to both diagnose as well as design and customize treatment programs.

Watson is based on a new type of supercomputer that has the ability to crunch terabytes of data, billions of information bits about research and disease, so it can learn how to solve disease as problems. This approach, to teach supercomputers how to think for themselves, is an awesome goal that has implications well beyond medicine. Prediction: we will be building the next generation of thinking machines that outpace—even outrun. They will be faster and smarter for many jobs than humans. In medicine Watson is learning and evolving into a Doc in the Box—in fact, that is the goal.

When it comes to medicine humans make too many mistakes. In the United States alone over one hundred thousand people die of mistakes and errors in hospitals due to misdiagnosis and being prescribed the wrong treatment

or medicine each year. This number in the United States is low—it is likely over 100 million. Worldwide but realistically, everyone in every nation could benefit from technology being used to minimize errors and get the right drug or treatment to the right patient at the right time. Digital health technology could save billions of lives over a generation.

Getting the right medical information to the right people who need it in time could make the difference in over 1 billion people's health today. With an increased population, of 1 to 2 billion more on the planet within fifty years, this could make a difference of 3 to 5 billion people who could be healthier or even just survive.

Watson today is working with the University of Texas MD Anderson Cancer Center to build an online tool to help suggest the best cancer treatments. Watson would learn, from analysis and patient data, what worked best not only for different cancers but also for different types of patients, with different genomic profiles, demographies, geographies, age, and health statuses. The amount of information this type of data mining—or what we will call Longevity Medicine in the future—today could not be analyzed or cost effective to produce by any doctor or researcher, as it would not be complete.

NULIFE BIO-ENHANCEMENT SERVICES OFFERED: 2025

1. High Cog: fast memory recall; advanced IQ insertion from Noble Prize Winners' DNA; good for engineers, scientists, and inventors
2. Body Boost: can be added to any genetic package, best if inserted genomically BB (before birth); enhanced sports capabilities
3. SmartX: an inhaled nano-device that can be programmed to seek and neutralize disease pre-expression at a Level Pre-One Alpha before disease emerges
4. Deep Think: enhanced language, logic, and conceptualization of complex ideas, theories, and philosophical constructs, enabling a higher order of cognitive problem-solving functionality
5. Transcend: a custom pharmaceutical that enables a sophisticated human to link with machine collaboration
6. INSync: a relationship drug that enhances your emotions by releasing hormones that enable deeper communication and collaboration with your partner
7. RelaX: for the harried and stressed-out person, the Type A personality who needs to relax and unwind at the end of the day

By 2025 Watson will have been an early pioneer in what will have become a generation of cognitive computers that learned medicine, first to advise doctors, then to advise patients, and, finally, to diagnose, treat and operate on humans

with and without doctors: enter the SuperDocs. These will be what we think of today as AI, the Doc in the Box.

They will be superintelligences that are a new class of computers—really, network intelligences—based on evolutionary computing, virtual intelligences that provide exceptional and extraordinary services for humanity, solving the biggest challenges we face. Someone will have to program, envision, and build these SuperDocs. This is the game-changing future of beyond medicine.

The future medicine will be altered in the near future by these Mind Machines that will travel through networks like the Internet, providing health care and treatments to the people of the world, where the Doc in the Box will always be available and ready to heal, diagnose, and treat the billions of patients in the world. Watson is an early step on that journey to building smart cognitive machines that will help humanity evolve.

More innovations will shape the future of medicine over the next five to ten years than have in the past hundred years. Are you ready for this massive set of trends and the opportunities that are coming fast? If I were looking for a new, exciting, and dynamic industry with fast-changing and lucrative opportunities for innovation and as a career, I would seriously consider the future of medicine as I have outlined here. In fact, I have made investments in biotech because of what I have predicted here in this book.

Headlines from the Future: 2025
Studies Show Consumers Prefer Virtual Doctors

The Pews Study on Digital Medicine and Patients revealed that over 80 percent of patients polled preferred the care and bedside manner of their Digital Docs over human docs. "The levels of emotional intelligence, care, and kindness as well as the proficiency of Digital Docs has again signaled that we may have gone too far in creating the perfect doctor," said Dr. Shultz from the American Medical Association. The Digital Doctor Association, the DDA, made a statement that digital doctors look forward to working closely with humans, both doctors and patients, to make this a healthy world.

Scott's RoboSurgery: 2025

Traveling in East Africa on safari was always Scott's dream, so early in 2028 he and a few of his buddies from college left for the journey. Scott was not three days into the trip when his knee collapsed in a fall, and he was sure he tore some important ligament.

With no doctors or hospitals for three hundred miles and no way to get there safely, he was stuck. Luckily he was a patient of the GlobalMed Grid, the virtual medical clinic based in San Francisco but was global—doctors were in thirty nations and all online.

Because every device and phone was now online since 2020, he was able to connect to a doc, who quickly analyzed a picture Scott took and sensor diagnosed his knee with his smartphone app. The sensors revealed the tear was not serious, but he did need surgery now.

"Not to worry," stated Dr. Mobutu. "We have a medical drone on its way with the exact robo-surgical bit I need to fix you up, mate."

Within forty-five minutes the drone found their remote location and attached the bio-bit to Scott's knee. Dr. Mobutu had said it wouldn't take long, and he then virtually operated the bio-bit, fixing the torn ligament with a wireless interface, a type of laser scalpel. After the surgery, which was wireless and noninvasive, the doctor predicted a quick recovery. "Fit as a fiddle in two hours," claimed Dr. Mobutu. "Good day." Scott was back in action on safari.

The Enhancers: 2035

A secret society of scientists and patients decided to accelerate research into new areas rather than be slowed by government regulation. The Enhancers emerged, developing gene therapies, diagnostics, new drugs, and cybernetic augmentations to defeat aging but enhance their intelligence.

This global group of concerned investors recognized that the full potential for stem cells and genomics could enhance human beings' cognitive, muscular, and physiological performance. Their investments, well beyond what governments were contributing, led a revolution in human enhancement of mental and physical attributes, some considered superhuman.

Longevity Medicine

Somewhere around 2020 we will have the tools to reinvent medicine. I call this Medicine 2.0, but it is a distinct change in the very nature of what healing and medicine has conducted in the past. You see, medicine in the Western world has always focused on healing, on disease. We treat the disease with drugs or devices or we cut it out. And most of the time this worked fine to treat disease.

Consider cancer. If your cancer can be surgically removed, then great, let's do it—get rid of that cancerous cell growth. If we can kill off the cancer with drugs or radiation, and if you survive this ordeal, then, well, that is perfect. This is the standard of care today for cancer—simply put: treat it or cut it out.

Now imagine a different future of medicine. We can predict when your healthy cells might start mutating to become cancerous. We are able to identify

a gene that we associate with cancer and imagine we can analyze your health forecast even before you are born or shortly thereafter. Then you undergo a genetic treatment to correct that gene so it will not express cancer in the future, we have now prevented cancer from emerging. This is one part of the future of medicine that is coming.

Imagine further that you are monitored by a diagnostic automated medical avatar that scans you wirelessly every day. It's a cloud network or app from your phone. It watches and monitors your health, sending personalized health data to your doctor, who has it analyzed by a supercomputer, like our friend Watson, who notices a change in your biochemistry associated with a type of diabetes, your sugar levels have gone up, or a genetic expression has occurred that is associated with a heart attack.

At that moment care is automatically sent to you wirelessly to ensure your health is protected and your illness is interdicted before a crisis point erupts and you are off to the hospital with a serious illness. This is the future: the use of wireless and digital health monitoring to predict, prevent, and treat disease.

Longevity Medicine is about the evolutionary shift from disease to wellness, from prevention to enhancement, toward a new type of medicine that does not exist today because doctors do not have the tools and technologies or the vision of what medicine could be—they are still in Fix-It Mode. Prevention and prediction are emerging slowly.

Regeneration is not out of trials yet. Enhancement is the black box of experimentation, well off Main Street. Much of this future has not and will not happen for five to ten years for the mainstream of society, but there are those Future Smart leaders who see where this is going and are on the leading edge of the future.

The final game changer in medicine will be Designed Evolution—where medicine and biotech and then evolutionary biology collide. This is when we shall have the power to alter—not just enhance—human performance. We will be able to change the evolution of human bodies and minds in order to reach a new level of quality of life, even consciousness, beyond health and disease.

Synthetic biology is a recently emerging field that applies engineering technologies to design and construct new biological parts, devices, and systems for novel functions or life forms that do not exist in nature. Synthetic biology relies on and shares tools from genetic engineering, bioengineering, systems biology, and many other engineering disciplines. It is as much a design science as a new force in medicine.

The ability to quickly and reliably engineer many-component systems from libraries of standard interchangeable parts is one hallmark of modern technologies. Whether the apparent complexity of living systems will permit biological engineers to develop similar capabilities will take years to determine, but the potential looks promising.

The vision behind this science is that these biological "parts" can be joined to create engineered cells, organisms, or biological systems that reliably behave in predictable ways to perform specific tasks. Synthetic biologists eventually hope to be able to program cells, cell systems, or organisms to perform specific tasks and functions.

More recently scientists have developed techniques to more efficiently synthesize or modify larger segments of DNA, marking a significant change in the way people study biological systems and a growing capacity for both experts and amateurs to manipulate such systems.

In May 2010 researchers at the J. Craig Venter Institute announced that they had produced major breakthrough in genomics, with the impact on medicine to be vastly important: the first functional, self-replicating, bacterium whose entire nuclear genome had been synthesized artificially in the laboratory. This is the second step, with the first being the decoding of the human genome, of which Venter, a world-class scientist, led the team that "broke the code" by mapping his own DNA. If we can design and produce artificial cells, the implications for a new era of medicine can be seen not far in our future.

Artificial cells, organs, and bones as well as Synthetic DNA will be used to regenerate humans to defeat aging, making the Longevity Marketplace, of immense value to humanity. Medicine's New Future will be in creating an entire Medical Supply Chain to support longevity, regeneration, and the medical enhancement of human health and human beings. This will lead, as I have forecasted, to a new civilization that not only eliminates most diseases but also, therapeutically and then radically, alters human evolution, making humans able to live much longer and be healthier and smarter.

Medicine in 2030 shall be unrecognizable compared to medicine in 2020 due to the amazing game-changing innovations that will emerge. The accelerated future of innovations that are revolutionizing medicine from nano, bio, neuro, IT, and quantum will reach a Convergence Point, at which even more high-velocity innovation will emerge, beyond what we have seen so far in this century.

Medicine Evolves

The evolution of medicine is happening faster than we could predict. Adult stem cells are now being shown to grow organs. Artificial cells can one day cure illnesses. DNA diagnostics gives us a predictive map of our future health status. We may learn to embed nano-devices inside the body to deliver drugs. We may learn to refresh the mind with genetic vaccines. This is a map of how medicine will evolve based on my forecasts. Over the next twenty-five to thirty years the completion of the final stages will transform the very purpose and practice of medicine.

Medicine 2.0 will be so completely different in ten years from today that a doctor from 2014 would not be able to practice medicine without being

retrained. Medical schools will need to throw out the textbooks, rewrite the curriculum, and move medical education into the cloud to be able to change the courses in real time to address these Seven Stages of Medicine 2.0.

Medicine as defined here will use a combination of computing, pharmaceuticals, medical devices, and treatments to diagnose, prevent, and rebuild the human body and mind. A new integrative medicine that builds on discoveries will phase into medicine what is needed to better understand how to extend health and turn off disease.

The reference to enhancement is to predict that, after we learn to fix or heal, the same technologies will be used to augment, enhance, and develop human potential to perform at a higher level of mental and physical fitness, quite beyond what we consider normal performance today.

I envision a future when the focus of care shifts from disease to life extension and, finally, to enhancing human health and longevity—not just living longer but being healthier and more capable of developing human potential for creativity, innovation, discovery, and enjoying life. Here are the stages that will unfold:

1. Disease management: today's medicine
2. Predictive analytics: understanding through genetics, digital health diagnostics, wearables, data, behavior, and environment how to predict and diagnose disease and health
3. Personalized prevention: reprogramming disease, self-care, enhancing health at the genomic and atomic levels.
4. Regenerative medicine: stem cells, gene therapy, and nanotechnology used to restore and regenerate wellness
5. Human performance enhancement: augmentation of human potential for developing advanced mental fitness, mobility, and perceptual capabilities
6. Longevity Medicine: significant healthy life extension, pharmaceutical and genetic prevention, living a vital 150 years
7. Evolutionary Design: advanced synthetic biology, genetics, and regeneration for maximizing optimal longevity, enhanced mobility, and cognitive enhancement; augmenting intelligence, human cybernetic enhancement

Longevity Medicine 2030: The New Wealth of Nations

By 2025 it will be clear that medicine had forever changed. The enhancement of human beings, beyond healing disease and fixing problems, was possible. The emerging regenerative medicine field had become a global trend. Not solely driven by scientific breakthroughs in what was possible to cure disease, stem cell treatments could also be used to enhance human performance and longevity,

now recognized by nations, corporations, and individuals to be a strategic competitive advantage.

I have not done justice to forecasting all of the details that are coming quickly in the future of medicine, but I have focused on what are the game changers, the top drivers of change that make this trend so fascinating and dynamic.

Ethical Future Challenges

Medicine touches us all. And with so many trends converging on our world so quickly, being Future Smart about the future of medicine might benefit you as a person, making you healthier and living longer, but the entrepreneurial opportunities will be just as large. From digital health to regeneration, enhancement to new diagnostics—the future of medicine is coming fast.

The key trend I have sought to convey is that as we learn to predict, eliminate, and manage disease, our civilization will be altered in fundamental ways. How different will our world be when health enhancement becomes a deliverable and lifetimes are radically extended?

These challenges that we shall face, that are emerging now, will require a completely different set of rules: who gets enhanced, who does not. What are the politics of enhancement, and how might societies compete over enhancements?

The ethical challenges of the future, brought by medicine at first to heal and then to enhance, will change human evolution. Ideas and debates about transhumanism, being beyond our current human state, will become more obvious. Synthetic biology, regeneration, genetic therapy—the convergence of these fields will transform medicine into something vastly more potent than a social service.

The very profession of medicine to extend lifetimes, end aging, and bestow beauty and intelligence will remake medicine. Our civilization will be forever transformed in a future that is coming faster than most realize and will challenge our ethics and even our concept of what type of future world we want to create.

We will have crossed the Rubicon toward enhancement, with healing behind us. Perhaps this is our evolutionary destiny to cheat death, end disease, and hack our own evolution by leveraging these innovations. But I can state that medicine in 2030 and in the Far Future of 2100 will look nothing like what it looks like today. Just as enhancement has today enabled humans to see with contact lenses, manage their heart disease with drugs, and replace hips and knees, enabling movement, tomorrow we shall do so much more in the New Future.

Prediction. Prevention. Regeneration. Enhancement. Longevity. This is the New Future of medicine.

Chapter 13

Reinventing Education: The Future of Learning

Every survey I have conducted for over ten years points to one crucial fact about education: we are not preparing our children for the future. This fact is confirmed by students who know they are unprepared for the workforce, by organizations that cannot find the educated talent they need to grow their business, and by every out-of-work person who wonders whether she has the right education to get a job. We need to do better to prepare everyone for the New Future that is emerging one minute from now. If we do not transform the planetary education system, we will not meet the challenges of the future.

How Google hires employees is a good example. They hire based on problem-solving skills, determination, and perseverance—grit—as well as curiosity and the ability to communicate persuasively to influence others. They don't care whether you went to a top university; they want to know you can think, gather ideas, make your case, and solve problems that have nothing to do with the memorization of facts and information or, most interestingly, what college you went to. Most high-tech companies in the New Economy retrain and educate new talent, sending a clear signal that there is a disconnect between education and business: kids are not being educated to be Future Ready for the workforce.

In Shanghai they are teaching kids in third grade how to speak a foreign language—English. How many grade schools in the United States and Europe are teaching Mandarin Chinese? Too few care about the largest nation in the world to make sure that their students can learn the language. What does this tell us about the future? Plenty, and it is not a productive forecast.

In the United States only in a few select schools are they teaching robotics. In five nations in Asia they are using US-made robots to teach in thousands of high schools.

How many of our schools function like Hack-a-thons, like they run in Silicon Valley, to collaborate and invent new products or find solutions?

How many of our schools teach the skills about globalization and diverse cultures?

How many of our schools teach our kids how to be entrepreneurs?

How many schools at any level of education teach students to embrace new technologies or even to create new technologies?

How many of our schools prepare our kids for being creative and inventive, to become tinkers, makers, and innovation leaders?

The answer is not enough. We need to Reinvent Education before it is too late.

We need to get our kids Future Smart—ready for the future so they can be globally competitive and find the careers they want. If we are to make more democratic nations in the future, then education must be reinvented to accelerate skills that will shape the future—globalization, entrepreneurship, technology, and how work itself, as an endeavor, is changing.

Now, the good news is that there are innovators who are pioneering the way forward to Reinvent the Future of Learning, but it's going to take everyone to make this revolution happen: it takes a global village—the parents, teachers, and kids. We will all need to take up the challenge of reinventing education. We must all become Game Changers of the Future when it comes to education, as it is so pervasive and touches every generation, demographic, and economic level and will shape the future progress of the planet in every way.

The disconnect is that we are not teaching for what organizations need. The talent pool, our kids, feel out of sync with the needs of work, and organizations need to do the educating to get kids ready to be useful hires. This tells you something about education.

Kids are not entering the workforce with writing, thinking, tinkering, logic, and technology skills that companies need. And the Learning Gap starts much earlier than high school or college; it is a systemic problem that starts in the beginning of the mass education process.

The world of commerce and business has changed, but education as a learning process has not. We need a revolution in learning that gets our kids ready for the future. There is no issue more important for a society than the education of the next generation of leaders, scientists, journalists, engineers, doctors, and parents. We must not fail in transforming education or else we will fail in preparing the next generation for the future.

Huge global trends affecting work, economics, society, and power lie at the core of why education must change. It is felt by those looking for jobs wherever they are in the world, companies recruiting employees, entrepreneurs trying to raise capital, and leaders in business and government trying to figure out how to educate tomorrow's workforce. There is one central fact that is not being embraced that will limit our future prosperity or launch it.

Future Smart Education

Education is out of date, irrelevant, rigid, and crafted from assembly-line industrial-era thinking. It is backward, the curriculum is outmoded, and it is long on history and out of step with what we need for the future. Most important, education is not looking forward; it is not preparing us for the future. Education is not Future Smart. I have written about this before, but now I am going further in exploring my ideas about how to change education and why.

The good news is that there is progress and new innovations emerging, from new collaborative online schools to games to interactive curriculum. First, let us look at what's off about education before we head into the future.

Education is not preparing us for the future. It has not kept pace with inventing, innovating, collaborating, and, perhaps most of all, real-world ideas students will need to understand the world, such as globalization, foreign cultures, technology, and business. We are not enabling our kids to be Future Ready for the changing world.

This pertains to all levels of education, from kindergarten to graduate school. There are revolutions going on in business, science, and technology, yet schools are resisting these changes and running from them, not embracing them. In the United States we are below the top twenty nations in excellence in math and science scores. Over one-third of males don't graduate from high school. Teachers, for the most, are preparing people for the last century, not this one. Assembly-line, industrial thinking dominates education.

This is also a global issue. Most nations have similar challenges: How are we going to prepare the next generation if we do not transform learning? We need a global transformation in education at every level in every nation to support the New Future economy that is emerging. Collaboration, globalization, sustainability, technology, innovation, gamification—we need a new education model, from kindergarten to graduate schools, to empower our children to compete and thrive in the twenty-first century. Let's start with this as a goal.

Learning is at the core of what we need as individuals and as societies to progress, advance, grow, create, and compete in the global economy. Though this is true, and no one would argue that education is key to progress, what we have today, what we call education, is simply not Future Smart. It does not teach the capacity to envision, solve, or reason the way ahead. It does not enable innovation as much as it could.

Education models, courses, content, and curricula need an overhaul, a reset to become relevant for students and society. We need to Reinvent Education. Education is not adaptive, agile, innovative, forward thinking, or visionary. We are not preparing students for a dynamic, uncertain, complex future of

disruptive technologies, new business models, radical economics, and diverse cultures. Teachers not taught for the future or in sync with the marketplace or even current jobs teach based on the past, what worked before.

Teachers and administrators, though well meaning, resist change, hold fast to traditional ideas about education theory, and practice what worked generations ago but not today.

For one hundred years formal education has adopted a mindset that schools and colleges have usually been based on what educators think learners need, not what learners think they need or even what employers need. This is not to say we should throw out education or teachers; we need a complete reconceptualization, a rethinking, and a reinvention of education. Times have changed, but education has not. So let's get this right.

The Top Ten Future Smart Skills Everyone Needs to Know

1. Speaking a foreign language
2. Solving problems and logical thinking
3. Managing complex information, knowledge, and data
4. Communicating effectively in written, verbal, and digital formats
5. Devising digital business strategy
6. Understanding globalization
7. Becoming high-tech savvy
8. Dealing with diverse cultural teams
9. Learning how to code
10. Understanding how to be a an entrepreneur

Ending Rearview Thinking

You can't get there, into the future, from here with the way of thinking that is focused on what I call Rearview Thinking—what happened before, what we know to be accurate about the past. The assumption is that the same reality frameworks, rules, behaviors, experiences, models, and theories are going to be the same in the future. This is not an accurate way to forecast education or anything else.

Rapid change, accelerated trends, fantastic technologies, new paradigms, disruptive business models, high-velocity innovations—look around you: if you don't think we live in a time of dynamic and explosive changes, in a time of Game-Changing thinking, then you're just going to have to think differently about the reality we all share.

THE GAME-CHANGING TRENDS SHAPING THE FUTURE OF LEARNING

- Education must prepare students to compete in the complex and competitive Global Innovation Economy.
- The Future Skills Gap, between what education offers and what business, the marketplace, and jobs demand, must be closed.
- Every individual must be taught how to be an entrepreneur.
- Teachers need to become Game Changers of the Future, radically reeducated to keep pace with the future of education, and students needs to adapt for tomorrow.
- Innovations in learning, such as digital tools, games, simulations, virtual worlds, and project-based collaboration, point to the future of education.
- Knowledge Science, a new discipline of education, will prepare everyone for thriving in the future economy and society.
- More jobs will go unfilled, especially in Knowledge Careers around the world, unless there is radical education change that provides more Knowledge Talent.
- Augmented reality, wearable computer devices that engage you in real-time online learning, will transform education in the future.
- Self-Directed Learning, education developed by the learner, will create new education choices for individuals.
- Smart Cloud Networks, which will broadcast education to mobile, tablets, and surfaces, will both enhance and replace physical schools, textbooks, and teachers.

Future Smart Companies Today

Each of these companies holds a piece of the Reinventing Education model that must emerge to help our students become ready for the New Future.

ALVAEDU

An exciting client I work with is reinventing education. Alvaedu (http://alvaedu.com) is reinventing education using cloud computing and interactive online program development for colleges. They are the leader in transforming and thinking about how courses can be dynamically created by teachers and used by students. Their courses, due to an innovative software technology called CourseFlow, is a highly innovative online course development application that can create, store, and distribute to millions of students in real time anywhere on the planet—education on demand.

The innovator and founder of the company is an education visionary, Tim Loudermilk. He is a Game Changer of the Future. As CEO, he is constantly challenging his team and their schools to invent the future faster, to prepare students for a future that's coming sooner and will be more complex and challenging.

LEARN ZILLION

LearnZillion (https://learnzillion.com) prepares students and teachers to get ready for success with an online set of courses that empowers all. Their platform, ideally for grades two to twelve, can be accessed totally online. They focus on math and English courses and are all free.

UDACITY

Udacity (www.udacity.com) is an online course program of cutting-edge tech programs that, as they say, "bridges the gap between academic and real-world skills." Working professionals from leading high-tech companies teach the courses.

SKILLSHARE

Skillshare (www.skillshare.com), for an inexpensive monthly charge, will teach you courses taught by industry leaders around the world, focusing not on degrees but on learning real-world knowledge.

KHAN ACADEMY

Khan Academy's (www.khanacademy.org) mission is to offer "a free world-class education for anyone, anywhere," and they do. Founded in 2006, it is one of the oldest and still most vital companies founded by Salman Khan. The courses cover every subject, mainly focusing on mathematics and the sciences, and are all available online.

SHOWME

ShowMe (www.showme.com/learn) is perhaps one of the most innovative skill-sharing communities, as it offers hundreds of lessons in every subject that have been developed by their community of teachers who use the online visual maker platform, known as ShowMes, to design courses from an easy-to-use downloadable app.

SINGULARITY UNIVERSITY

Singularity University http://singularityu.org, an inspiring experiment in learning, is a university that I contributed to starting with a group of futurists and technologists. It is housed at NASA Ames in California. I served on the founding advisory board and was co-chairman of the Futures and Forecasting Track. Singularity U has consistently filled a gap with graduate students and working professionals to teach about the trends that science and technology will offer humanity. Its curriculum should be taught staring in kindergarten, where I envision our kids would be making robots and designing virtual games and worlds someday.

Investing in the Future

Another courageous client of my Institute for Global Futures, the Southwest Louisiana Economic Development Agency and Chamber of Commerce, is one of the regions of the world economy that most would not hear about, but over the next decade over $62 billion is being invested into an area in the United States where about three hundred thousand people live today. That is a huge amount of investment capital coming into a region that is mostly rural and has a sparse amount of people. So there is going to be an incredible rate of growth in this region, from health care to jobs to infrastructure.

There is no focus that is more important than educating the next generation of the workforce that must be Future Smart about how to exploit the opportunities of this large capital investment so they can properly plan for the future. Education, learning, getting our workforce ready to meet the challenges of the future is the top priority in Southwest Louisiana. Reinventing Education, not the capital, will make the difference—it's what we do to make this a Sustainable Society. The leaders of this community are looking to the future and shaping that future today. This is where all communities should be thinking about.

Reinventing Education does not yet appear to be a top priority for leaders, parents, and students. There is no Future Smart vision that sets out to purposely reinvent education.

In his chapter I am going to suggest one. Without this understanding shared at every level of society, business, and government—that mass education, what we have today at every level doesn't work, is broken—we are not going to be able to create a prosperous, sustainable, and productive future. In fact, the opposite is certain. We will fall out of step and become disrupted by change, accelerated innovations, and radical changes in the marketplace worldwide that escape educators' daily reality. This is dangerous and risky.

An unproductive society, where growth and innovation slows, where the engine of the economy, its jobs, is out of sync with the skills required to get and keep those jobs, will not survive. We adapt or die. Reinventing education is about the future productivity of nations, communities, economies, and society, not just about jobs or quality of life. Reinventing education is about power. To remain powerful, enabled to be a leader and shape the future, either as a person, organization, or nation, you must be educating for tomorrow, preparing for the future.

It is a bigger challenge before us that will affect the next hundred years shaping societies, realigning power, and forging our society, one that adapts, learns, and evolves to meet the Grand Challenges of our time. Without reinventing education, we, as nations, organizations, and individuals, will not be prepared to face a future that will be complex, disruptive, and fraught with massive change and innovation. Let's have a look at what's missing in education and how to fix it.

WHY EDUCATION NEEDS TO BE REINVENTED

- Education is mass education, for the masses, not the individual.
- Most science and technology is not integrated into curricula at all levels in schools today. We should be teaching physics to kindergartners, robotics, and computer programming in every school.
- Science and technology will alter science and technology in the future.
- Education should be more about authentic learning; critical thinking, reasoning, collaboration, problem solving, and logic.
- Education does not teach innovation as part of the process of learning that is at the core of reinventing education. We need to create a generation of innovators.
- Education is not self-paced, interactive, dynamic, and learner focused, so people become bored and not engaged. The dropout rate from high schools and college is unacceptable as a social trend.
- Education is perpetuated by a nineteenth-century industrial revolution mentality, which influences every course.
- We should not expect to turn learners out like assembly-line workers. This is not 1870.
- Teachers are not trained to teach about the future. They teach the past, not the future. They cannot teach what they don't know.
- Courses are not flexible, agile, adaptive, and updated and are, therefore, irrelevant to meet many challenges even of the present.
- Much of the content is outdated and not in line with the real world.

RETHINKING EDUCATION DRIVERS

- Curriculum taught today is out of sync with social issues and real-world scenarios.
- Education leaders are out of step with what learners need to learn to get ready for the future—or they would lead a revolution to create Future Smart schools.
- Schools are dominated by standardized testing that has nothing to do with learning.
- Colleges and high schools fail to teach what people need to be job worthy so they can attract good jobs.
- The Internet has transformed education by making available a huge amount of information that is more current than what schools teach.
- Textbooks today are outdated before they are published. The explosion of new information is out of pace with our educational institutions.
- The higher education value proposition is eroding and needs to become more entrepreneurial, tech savvy, knowledgeable, and innovative.
- We need to teach science earlier and with hands-on projects like making robots, designing websites, and making games.
- We need to teach kids about future challenges and trends so they can be part of the solution.

Too many organizations, even nations, have lost their way because they did not prepare their citizens effectively for the future. They did not develop a capacity to look forward, to consider future risks or opportunities. They never planned ahead and, therefore, had a tough time adapting to change when it came. Let's learn from that.

Help Wanted: Future Smart Learning

In a world of massive social, economic, and technological change, we need to learn faster and change faster to keep up with the trends that are reshaping our world or else we will not survive in the future. Lifelong learning is essential to being Future Smart—you never finish with learning as a process of discovery. This is true of individuals, organizations, nations, and civilizations. This challenge to become Future Smart is relevant for all, but it is especially true for individuals. If you want to be sustainable as an individual, if you want to thrive and survive in the future, you must learn differently, with agility, and be able to actually Design Your Own Education. Now this may seem like a bold idea, but learners, at any age and in any school, must take responsibility for their education and self-direct—actually design their future.

Are you ready to Design the Future of Education? How would you do this? Where would you look to find clues to rethink courses, learning processes, and content? Maybe you should consider that the reinvention of education is something we all need to own and participate in if we are going to get ready for the future.

Anyone growing up today faces a future so extreme, so fraught with so much complex and accelerated change, that by the time they enter the workforce, looking for a job, their education experience will have been mostly irrelevant, even useless, and actually a burden when trying to get and keep a job. In fact, the parents taking them to school today don't realize just how unprepared they will be for the future. Even the careers they were educated for and the basic education about the changing world will be outdated by the time they try to enter the workforce.

Their educational experience, from primary school through college, will not have prepared them in 2015 to compete in the global economy of 2020 and beyond. This is because the educational system they have been forced to embrace is largely dysfunctional. They are not going to be Future Smart, and that difference will drastically affect business, power, and society in foundational ways that scream out for change.

And change is coming. Getting ready for the future, becoming Future Smart about education, will be vitally important to the future of every individual on the planet. So let's explore where we are and why Reinventing Education will be a Game-Changing Trend.

Three Big Questions

There are three *big* important questions every parent, teacher, leader, and student must ask about education today:

1. How can we prepare our students—our future leaders, inventors, judges, scientists, artists, and entrepreneurs—better for the future?
2. How can we prepare our educational system, wherever you are in the world, to become relevant for the Global Knowledge Economy, producing future ready jobs and talent?
3. What can we do today to change our educational system to make it innovative, adaptive, agile, and future focused—to make it Future Smart?

My friend's daughter, Sarah, attended a well-known university in the Northwest where she studied communications. There were many excellent courses beyond her core liberal arts courses that gave her a well-rounded education in the traditional sense of what we have, in the past, wanted education to do.

Her communications courses were theoretical, academic, but not real world. Though there were smatterings of real-world concepts related to social and political issues, for the most part her education in her major, communications, was not of much use, as she herself wondered what she was learning. In other words, there does not appear to be much that prepared her for the real world of a career or was even in step with how communications is changing given the business transformation of social media, technology, and new media communication models, of which every company, not just Google, Twitter, and Facebook, are shaping and facing.

There was no attention to globalization, how business and economies were being reshaped. She was not encouraged to take a language such as Mandarin, which 1.3 billion people speak. She was not prepared for the workforce or the global changes in the economy that are creating change as we speak.

Educating for the Future

Most companies are looking for talent to help them get ready for the future. Companies understand that education is not doing its job. Our kids and our adults are not ready for the future. And today the Future Gap, the gap between what people need to know and the fast trends and changes that are reshaping business and society, is getting larger and becoming a more dangerous risk factor.

This risk factor, the Future Smart Gap, could doom a nation, organization, or region. We must understand that the Game-Changing Trends that are reshaping our world must be understood and integrated into education, or else education will become irrelevant to a global knowledge economy.

Organizations hire people and create jobs to shape their competitive future advantages, to serve future customers, to make future products that shape the future of their company. Increasingly the future is coming faster than education is preparing people for, and business is struggling to find the talent to help them prepare for that future.

Headlines from the Future
Digital Avatars Teach 70 Percent of Students Worldwide

Avatars, digital teachers, that live in the network on the Internet will be in demand over human teachers in over 150 nations. Avatars look human but are really the front end of a massive cloud-based AI capability, with access to real-time knowledge over the Internet. They will speak over one hundred languages and can teach any subject with the expertise of a master. They also can customize the learning content around the learner's skills and goals. By 2030 they are in demand.

GAME-CHANGING TRENDS THAT WILL TRANSFORM EDUCATION

- Game-changing technologies: computers, networks, biotech, neuroscience, nanotech, robotics, and quantum physics
- Knowledge careers: business analytics, data science, cloud networks, idea engineers, social media, predictive processing, online design, virtual media producers, game programmers
- GDP and wealth shifts
- Changing business models and workforce needs
- New work ethic, how people work and why
- Increased global competition

What Is a Future Smart Education?

Game Changers. We need to teach students what Game Changers do and how they think and give them examples of Game-Changing ideas, projects to work on and share, technologies, and collaborations. We need to enable our next generation of students to become Game Changers to create a New Future—an innovation-rich, productive, and purposeful future.

Big Science. We need to teach about the fundamental laws and concepts about science from kindergarten through graduate school. Information technology, life sciences, robotics, electronics, neuroscience—science changes our world daily, and we need our education to be in sync with this. You cannot be properly educated today without learning about science and technology, which are changing everything now and will continue to do so in the future.

Entrepreneurship. Every person should be taught about entrepreneurship— the concepts, skills, and competencies essential to developing, starting, and running a business: How to make form an enterprise; what capital, resources, sales, marketing, talent, and innovation is to the entrepreneur—this is a basic Future Smart Skills Set.

Managing Change. Every person should be taught about managing change. Because so much of our world is changing so quickly, dealing with complex and accelerated change in society, business, economics, population, technology, climate, and energy are vitally important. We need people to be competent managers of change so they are prepared for the future and can help shape that future.

Twenty-First-Century Leadership. We need to teach leadership so that, given the complex global changes that are coming, we are creating the next generation of leaders who understand about the future challenges and opportunities. What competencies do we need to teach students to have them become

leaders? Consensus builders, conflict managers, global cultures, planners, great communicators, team builders, innovators—we need to teach people to become courageous and bold Future Smart Leaders who do not fear the future but instead seek to shape it.

The Innovator's Mindset. We need to teach about being innovative. Innovation can be taught. Humans are inventors, naturally innovative, but mass education often drives this innovation—this drive to be an inventor, to try something new—out of kids as well as adults. We need to celebrate the innovative process and teach everyone the process of creativity and making innovative things.

The world has many problems and Grand Challenges for which we desperately need Future Smart innovations: energy, education, business, and medicine. Humans are adaptive beings who are naturally innovative, but education must empower, enable, and teach innovation, which are experimentation, ideation, and celebrating the new to be relevant today and tomorrow.

Globalized Learning. We need to teach about globalization, the Global Connected Future. It is a big world, and it is getting increasingly connected. The Connected Economy, like the Knowledge Economy (see Chapter 3), connects the global opportunities for business, learning, culture, and economics. Our educational system must teach everyone about how the Global Connected Planet is emerging, what this means and why for our future.

This is an essential competency that every student, adult learner, or young person must be taught—how to understand and navigate the Global Connected Future. We need more leaders who are globally savvy. We need to adjust the curriculum and educational system to adapt to teaching these skills in real time.

Future Smart Core Curriculum. We need to reinvent the core curriculum in every school. We need to reject the backward thinking that dominates the core curriculum and think differently about it. We still need to teach history, language, math, and many of the specifics that every major college or high school demands, but we must rethink and reinvent the topics, relevance, context, and purpose of this information so it is relevant and Future Smart. Most of this legacy information we now call the curriculum is irrelevant and must be changed, updated, or thrown out as being useless.

Digital Design Skills treat learners as designers, innovators, and producers of services and things. We need to educate innovators to design the future worlds we will live and work in.

Self-Designed courses are produced by students and experts on subjects and then factored into the curricula to be taught.

Entrepreneurs Model is one in which courses have a commercial component and everyone, at every level of school, learns to start and operate a business.

SnapCourse: 2016

The emergence of instant courses designed by students started to show up on the Internet at first as parodies of real classes. And it wasn't just kids but also adults who invented the SnapCourse as a type of satire, like what you would find at a comedy club routine. SnapCourses would show up and then they were programmed, after sometimes minutes or days, to just disappear.

Versions of courses showed up—first hundreds and then thousands of times a day—making fun of the boredom found in most courses. But then something strange happened. The parodies started evolving into serious remakes of the courses, using creative graphics, video interviews, music, and film tracks.

Students were actually producing dynamic and interesting courses that other students and even teachers were downloading thousands of times a day and using in their classes. All of a sudden SnapCourses were part of the hacker education revolution, changing how people learn.

Hacking Education

Learners and teachers could collaborate to reinvent education now. No one needs to wait until 2020 for this to become a reality. A bit of courage and determination could bring this idea into the present. The Hacking of Education is about the reprogramming, changing course, knowledge, and, most important, the relationship between learners and teachers.

Learners as developers has not yet become a mainstream phenomena. Most kids and adults are stuck in the hierarchical education process in which schools and teachers create courses and push this onto students: *Learn this!!* This top-down system does not engage or empower students. And it could.

If education leveraged simulations, interactive problems, and real-life issues, in which there is give and take, experiments, collaboration, joint problem solving, and high engagement by learners, education would be vibrant and engaging. It could be.

The idea of learners as developers with teachers is almost an alien idea and too much work for schools. After all, they have already developed courses and have textbooks and, well, teach a certain way that works—or does it? Too many kids are bored. Too many teachers are bored. Too many learners at all ages are not learning but rather regurgitating facts, data, and information rather than becoming something more integral to the learning process. We need independent thinkers who can manage complexity, global trends, and conflict, not the business-as-usual education system.

We need to rethink learning as a process of discovery, in which learners and teachers collaborate to investigate, discover, invent, choose the process and content so the subject can be best learnt by the student and best taught

by the teacher and the student. The roles of teacher and learner could also be exchanged.

Teachers could be more coaches and facilitators of the future, enablers of the learning process, with students becoming the dictators of information. And more collaboration between teachers and learners could lead to a new paradigm for learning that is engaging and exciting.

Ten Innovations That Will Reinvent Education

1. Real-world simulations
2. Gamification, the use of games to engage learners
3. Virtual worlds where learners experience to learn
4. Big Data applied to learning how to learn
5. Mobile platforms for learning anywhere
6. Cloud computing for distributed education
7. AI applied to learning bots, teacher avatars, digital coaches
8. Social media, crowdsourced learning
9. Augmented reality to enable interactive experiential learning
10. Project-based learning

Serious Games and the Future Learning

Gamification is a new type of learning that accomplishes something important that traditional education has not: it has conquered learners' boredom by making the learning experience engaging, interactive, collaborative, and, most of all, fun. Yes—education can be fun.

Game-based simulations empower students to visualize their ideas and try out various scenarios. They can explore and understand complex ideas about history, finance, events, society, and conflict. Learners can explore from inside an experience a historical or future event or even a fictional event that they design.

Learning comes alive when interactive real-time crises emerge from the game engine that stimulates reactions and discussion. Playing games is immersive engagement. It is 3D learning rather than a lecture or textbook and is holistic in scope. Games keep learners engaged in problem solving and dealing in complex ideas that keeps them engaged.

Enhanced game-based learning gives students a fresh new way to reengage as well as to be producers and participants in the learning process. Subjects that learners are interested in, such as starting a high-tech company, can be modeled out in games and simulations in which real-life issues, challenges, and data can

be used. Games that can pull content off the web and interact with other learners and networks of relevant content enhance the learning experience.

Also, the game intelligence engine, in the cloud and in real time, evaluates the gamer's competency in playing the game and then automatically connects the gamer with both fresh games to play as well as other players to interact with over the Internet. This is the future of education.

Massive multiplayer online games depict a wide range of worlds, including those based on fantasy, science fiction, the real world, superheroes, sports, horror, and historical milieus. The most common form of such games is fantasy worlds, whereas those based on the real world are relatively rare.

GAMES AND EDUCATION: TEN FUTURE SMART INNOVATIONS

1. Future game engines that design immersive virtual worlds, encounters, and stories that automate learning for students
2. AI characters, mini-Smart Machines, that are used to tell the stories and design the learning worlds that are self-generating AIs with legends, histories, and personalities programmed to realize their learning objectives
3. Self-creating worlds that are dynamic and auto-generated with rich graphics
4. Crowdsourced stories that in real time capture sentiment and interest from the students and use this data to create learning programs
5. Team engagement in which teams work together to compete, design, and collaborate to learn together as a community
6. Student computer programming, in which students program the education
7. Dynamic real-time AI that personalizes the learning experience around the learner
8. Real-world simulations that engage the learner in newsworthy reality learning
9. Social media prediction analytics that are used to feed ideas back into the learning technologies and worlds to improve the learning experience but share new insights and ideas with the global community of learners
10. Innovation Learning Ecosystems that inspire, transact, and reward learners as developers for their ideas and programs by giving them access to a market and companies that license their intellectual property to enhance their learning

Game Education Programs:
2020

Virtual Rome is a free immersive online game world that is based on Evolutionary Networks. The game evolves with the learner's interaction and creates new stories, characters, and landscapes as more learners interact. Virtual Rome self-organizes its content based on user inputs and the level of learning skills exhibited in real time.

World Designer uses immersive 3D technology for students to create virtual worlds and then design these to match lesson plans. The goal of World Designer is to provide resources for demonstrating the use of lesson-driven 3D virtual environments in the classroom or for training purposes, using any surfaces as the hardware platform for the "immersive touch" program that can download from the web. Any desk or mobile device can be instantly converted into a learning platform.

GeoEngineer is an online competition that encourages multiplayer teams to collaborate both online and in the classroom to address climate change and develop clean-tech solutions for creating a sustainable planet. Learners discover issues and technologies to better prevent climate crises and to restore the health of the planet. Through collaboration and competition, with teams, this networked simulation brings together real-world challenges with talented players who compete for prizes and a chance for employment with the sponsors.

Alternate Reality Games:
New Ways to Educate

Alternate Reality Games (ARGs) offer learners a parallel or customized universe that can include reality-simulated fictional websites and phone numbers and even artifacts hidden throughout the world that can be discovered through geo-caching or investigative online or offline activities.

Multiple players are involved with a story that takes place in real time and evolves according to players' responses. Subsequently it is shaped by characters that the game's designers actively control, as opposed to being controlled by artificial intelligence, as occurs when playing a computer or console video game.

Players interact directly with characters in the game, solve plot-based challenges and puzzles, and collaborate as a community to analyze the story and coordinate real-life and online activities. ARGs generally use multimedia, such as telephones, e-mail, and mail, but rely on the Internet as the cohesion that brings everything together. The driving element is the story. A compelling story is what keeps the learners coming back and interacting.

Game-Based Learning Benefits

- Gives learners real-time feedback on progress
- Teaches simulation technologies
- Teaches complex motor skills and multitasking
- Teaches leadership, team building, and conflict management
- Collaborates with other learners, both virtually and physically
- Engages interactive, rich graphics, and multimedia
- Enables learners to produce their own game narratives
- Provides realistic knowledge and events downloaded from news
- Provides dynamic gaming scenarios tailored to the learner's goals
- Downloads learners Direct-to-Game (D2G) into avatar characters in the game; the merging of humans with Smart Machines to enhance learning and the game experience

Future Smart Learning and Gamification

DUOLINGO

DuoLingo (www.duolingo.com) presents itself as a free language education site for the world. This is a massive online collaboration that combines a free language learning website with a paid crowdsourcing text translation service. So two students, from different parts of the world, interact, each learning each other's language while they translate documents.

THE WORLD PEACE GAME

The World Peace Game (https://worldpeacegame.org) is a geopolitical simulation that engages young students to explore a multination world and learn about the politics, economics, environment, and crises that affect nations.

GOAL BOOK

Goal Book (https://goalbookapp.com) empowers teachers to use research-based strategies by offering an online toolkit.

RIBBON HERO

Ribbon Hero (www.ribbonhero.com) is an epic free and fun game that teaches you how to use productivity software from Microsoft.

CLASS DOJO

Class Dojo (www.classdojo.com) is a program for teachers that focuses on improving student behavior and engagement by rewarding the learner.

The Teacher of the Future

We cannot reinvent education without reinventing teachers. And teachers must be aware of how they need to be reinvented. Teachers can make or break a school, class, or student. The best teachers today inspire and engage, and they are evolving or are already Future Smart, and we all know who they are. They are not the majority of the teachers in the world, and that is the problem. Teachers need to prepare our students for the future, but they cannot if they don't have the vision and learning themselves to make this happen.

Teachers are agents of learning, but this role should change in the future to keep pace with the world's changes. The teacher's role should change to be able to offer a more effective learning experience for students, adults, and kids. The teacher, as a facilitator, producer, and catalyst of innovation, is a more productive future role to reinvent education. In the connected classroom the teacher can direct and facilitate innovative learning courses that enable students to learn faster but also with more engagement and understanding.

The teacher of the future will be more curious and less the expert than the pathfinder to direct explorations of discovery into history, science, technology, math, and language. Developing new course materials and ideas to engage students in a collaborative learning method is the direction of the future. Ideally this teacher would have new skills—simulation, gamification, producer, to name a few.

The teacher of the future is not a command-and-control type of person, a my-way-or-the-highway type of teacher. He or she should be open to exploration and is collaborative—the teacher does not hold all the Learning Power; rather, the students share that Learning Power, and they have responsibility and accountability for not just learning but also creating the learning experiences. This ownership in their learning experience makes students and teachers allies in education.

TEACHER AS GAME CHANGER OF THE FUTURE SKILLS

- Coach of Creativity
- Global Change Catalyst
- Technology Pathfinder
- Collaborator of Learning
- Designer of Knowledge

- Enabler of Bold Ideas
- Facilitator of Discovery
- Explorer of Virtual Worlds
- Whole-Systems Thinker

Brain Science and the
Future of Education: 2025

Neuroscience will transform the future of education. This change is emerging now but has not yet revealed the potential to develop into an applied science for education. In the near future every student—adult or child—will be tested to determine his or her Neuro-Learning Aptitude.

This test will be a wireless scan of their brains or a DNA test to determine what we can do, as a society, to enhance the learning effectiveness of their brain. Now, if this seems spooky to you today, it will not by 2025. In fact, parents, even adult learners, will want to know how their brain is evolving to become more Neuroplasticity Aware and be able to absorb more knowledge.

Techniques will emerge to enhance the learning capacity, or Neuro-Learn Aptitude, of individuals so they can enjoy the benefits of a career, art, or science to which they aspire. Certain careers will demand the shaping of IQ and skills from a specific learning program that is customized for your neuroplasticity analysis so you can be properly trained for the future job or position.

Neuroplasticity, the idea that the brain can be altered by different types of learning experiences, is just part of what we know now.

The brain grows new neural pathways when exposed to complex problems and challenges. The learning methods that engage in sparking innovation and creativity, that encourage collaboration, game and role playing, all are catalysts for the brain.

New approaches to learning, using discoveries in neuroscience, will transform education to create smarter learners. Why do that?

We need to do this in order to compete in the global economy, to prosper, to have more choices in lifestyle and careers, and to make a difference, to address the Big Social Challenges that will determine the outcome of the future for us all on the planet. If we educate our children properly, smartly, the next generation of students just might meet the Grand Challenges of the future that threaten our existence.

The future Einsteins, Picassos, and Da Vincis lie waiting to be educated and will bring science, joy, beauty, and love into our world. Education plays the defining role to inspire the next generation of inventors of commerce, art, and philosophy that is vitally important to a world, as is capital and human resources. Education, when done right, prepares the entire civilization for the future.

PLANETARY TRENDS SHAPING THE FUTURE OF EDUCATION

- Smart Machines living in mobile cloud networks could broadcast education to over 5 billion students a year by 2025.

- Global businesses need high tech–savvy, educated workers who understand a diverse marketplace.
- Innovation is the key shaper of society, and we must integrate advanced technology into learning or else we will not be able to compete on the planet.
- The next middle class and the billions that are migrating to megacities are moving faster than schools are ready to accommodate.
- We need a way to create real-time education that nontechies can create.
- The future of business is an educated workforce that is Future Smart
- We need a cost-effective way to broadcast education to the planet, as currently education is too costly for the underdeveloped nations.
- We need to rethink what curricula, what subjects are best to prepare students for the future.
- We need to make every teacher on the planet a Game Changer for the Future.
- We need to make every school and college committed to becoming a Game Changer of the Future.
- Self-directed learning, in which the student directs self-pacing and personalized learning, is emerging.
- Wearable, mobile, and cloud computing will educate billions, bringing up the standard of living around the world.
- New nations' high-growth GDP, such as in Asia and Africa, will require an educated talent pool of workers.
- New start-up companies embracing the Innovation Economy will support learning networks that replace traditional schools.
- Economic growth and strong GDP will support an Internet network that can deliver education quickly, inexpensively, and with modern standards.
- There will be global competition for talent.

Our Risky Future—Ready or Not?

This is the era when we will see the reinvention of education. Why, you may ask? It will become obvious, led not by educators or politicians but by business leaders, job demand, economics, wealth transfer, the demands of the Knowledge Economy, and, most of all, enlightened students and entrepreneurs who are waking up. Students allied with business and some enlightened education leaders recognize that we are not ready for the future, that we are not educating for future jobs, challenges, and opportunities.

They will create a viable, Future Smart alternative to education. If we don't transform education, then an educational system that is broken and unable to

change will perpetuate the dysfunctional culture. This will doom too many to low-paying jobs, unfulfilled careers, and an inability to compete in the global knowledge economy of the future.

The signposts of this future are here today. Unemployment in the United States and Europe is at record highs and is unsustainable for building a viable future society with a foundation of economic robustness. Productivity is low and not growing quickly enough. There are more jobs than there are skilled workers.

In the United States we spend more to incarcerate a person in jail—over $50,000 a year—than we do to educate individuals. It's illogical as a society to spend more on prisons than education. This is a lopsided logic. We need to rethink education for the future or else we shall not have a future.

In Europe the productivity continues to slip, as does the quality of life—you cannot thrive as a society without robust jobs. In Asia, other than microeconomies such as Singapore and Korea, the big economies, such as China and India, have educational systems that are not as adaptive, modern, agile, and Future Smart as they need to be to educate the leaders of tomorrow. The elite schools are there, but quality education for the middle class, to sustain and grow middle-class prosperity, is not there, and it must be to build tomorrow's societies.

This is not a blueprint for a viable and productive future. This is a blueprint for disaster. Reinventing education is a global security risk factor. If we want to build sustainable societies, we must transform the educational system to make it Future Smart, ready for the challenges of the future, looking ahead, not behind.

The future of education is about the rethinking and, ultimately, reinvention of education. We all need to get ready for the future, but especially our children and their schools. Are you Future Smart, ready for this future and the changes that are coming?

If we are going to educate 9 billion people by 2050, we better get moving on reinventing education. Education, a new and vibrant education, is not coming unless you invent this. The future you want is the future you will advocate for. Let's get education right, as so much of our shared future will be dependent on our children and their children's education.

Game Changers of the Future—perhaps some of you ready to take up this challenge—might gain a tremendous benefit from the transformation of education. We must educate for tomorrow to meet the challenges of the future.

Chapter 14

The Uncomfortable Truth: The Future of Climate

Juneau, Alaska, is the second-largest city by area in the United States. It is a beautiful city both in winter and summer. I was giving a presentation a few years back to an international business audience near Juneau. As they brought me into the staging area, before my talk a helicopter was waiting to take me out to Glacier Bay National Park and Preserve to go dog sledding on a glacier.

The trip was not very long, and I could not see the entire glacier from the sky. But it was exhilarating. You read about glaciers and see them in pictures, but to be up close on a glacier of this enormity and beauty was miraculous. The raw natural beauty all of this around me humbled me.

I had never been to a glacier before and didn't know what to expect. Walking around on this glacier, crunching through the ice with my boots below the hazy afternoon clouds, was an pristine experience, with the sky glistening and the air cold and fresh. You have to think about it for a moment: there was no ground to speak of—just miles of ice and packed snow, quite exhilarating in contrast to the urban landscape of a city where humans, not nature, preside.

No cell phones or buzz of the city. The silence of the place and the big nature that surrounded me was like a huge cathedral of ice. The natural spirituality of the glacier made understanding climate change personal and authentic.

There was a primitive quiet even when racing, as the dogs made their run on this glacier that was millions of years old. I held on after receiving a sharp bang on my head from the abrupt start as the dogs jumped in sync into the race. I was just along for the ride—this was the dog's race.

This experience gave me a new appreciation of not only the grandeur of nature but also how humans are changing nature in ways that might one day eliminate all this beauty and grace. One day in the future, if the Arctic continues to melt, the world will no longer be arguing about climate change but

instead will be dealing with the impact of rising sea levels, floods, and hazards to life and health.

And that day is closer than we think. What will be lost is not just the glacier but also the experience that other people will miss when this glacier melts away. If we want to preserve this glacier and the experience it represents, we need to move with agility to deal with climate change. Tick tock.

During my conversation with a local geologist about the accelerated reduction in ice I realized that climate change was not all about the data. The National Snow and Ice Data Center (https://nsidc.org) has taken the data and used the latest visualization technology to tell a compelling story, one of the observational examples of climate change, when you compare as I did, the reduction in glacier ice density and ground cover changes between 1941 and 2004. You can see the change.

The story is also about what the impact of drastic climate change will have on our future, when even deeper reductions in the Arctic and Antarctica occur. I looked at pictures over the past decade, and the recession of the ice sent a shiver down my spine. The unknowns from abrupt climate change were coming not in the far future but now.

How were we to act to prevent hazards? Was there still time? And what could we, as a civilization, accomplish? These were the questions I pondered after dog sledding on that glacier in Alaska that have moved me to want to investigate further. That is the background of this chapter—to get beyond the data to the story and how that story may change our future.

Reality Check

Climate change refers to the alterations to the climate that can be identified and measured over a period of time, attributed directly or indirectly to human activities. The climate change I am referring to in this chapter is about the adverse risks, hazards, and trends that are coming in the future that will increase the risk to humans and our world.

In fact, there is a preponderance of evidence that extreme storms, sea level rises, drought, melting glaciers, and systemic changes are accelerating all over the world in Asia, Africa, North and South America, and on both Antarctica and the top of the world. These are more than just unusual change events; they signal a pattern of climate change risks that are progressively getting more frequent and unpredictable.

You don't want to wait until sea-level rise leaves you under water tomorrow morning or a tornado takes out your children's school. We cannot predict with accuracy all of the risks to public health from disease, destruction of agriculture, risk to cities, reduction in fresh water, and erosion of law and order that may come, but these risk factors are a real and present danger.

In my career as a futurist I have advised many organizations that have been quite resistant to the idea of climate change. The US military is one example of a tough crowd to convince over the years. But once the US Navy started conducting their own research into sea level risks due to climate change, the entire dynamic changed.

The time has come to get on board with making changes and doing what we can do to reduce carbon emissions and take more drastic measures to manage the crises that are coming faster than any forecaster can predict. We can and must move with haste on this risk before crises that we cannot prevent become a shared reality. If there were one future risk that we could and should prevent from occurring, climate change fits the bill.

There is sufficient scientific data to make reasonable forecasts about the future of climate based on what we know now. After all, climate change is not new. For over forty years the scientific community has been aware that this is our future, that a changing climate is coming. Now climate change is a current reality. The rising temperatures, Arctic melt, lost biodiversity, heat waves, storms, increasingly scarce resources, threats of rising seas, and carbon-based health problems are obvious today. Most leaders in government are especially aware.

We need a reality check. Our world has never faced a greater global risk than that of climate change, yet the skepticism about climate change persists with so many people who deny this reality. As a scientist first, I can understand enough about the data and observe climate change myself to determine that we do a great disservice to our future when we argue over whether climate change is real in the face of a clear and pressing risk that can be measured and observed.

It's hard to be in denial—you really have to work on it when we can all see the Arctic ice is melting, storms are raging, and the heat is moving up the thermometer gauge and setting record droughts. I imagine we need a large-scale apocalyptic event to get the point across to the world that the climate is changing so everyone will take it seriously. And this may just happen sooner than you think.

Accelerated Change

Numerous authorities—including my organization, which examined the data—have confirmed the science behind the accelerated climate change. There is strong evidence. My own brother, an educated person, a professor, thinks it's all a grand government conspiracy of cooking the data and the climate is doing just fine. I am planning a family vacation in the Arctic soon to investigate further and bring him along. There is nothing like a personal experience where you can see the change and get beyond the impersonal data that surrounds climate change.

The Uncomfortable Truth about the future of climate change is that some people would prefer not to believe, regardless of the science, because, they think, if climate change is real, then the world as we know will be drastically changed. It is surprising that intelligent people, even political leaders with power to make a difference, are not facing up to the reality.

Because they know that if climate change is real—which it is—then government and industry leaders would need to make this a priority and enact laws and business decisions that would cause changes to jobs, carbon-producing industries, and energy investments. We don't want to believe that the world is at risk. This is the Uncomfortable Truth. It is time to move on from this argument before it is too late so we can manage climate change and get ready for the future.

The Right Side of History

No rational person or leader wants to be on the wrong side of history regarding crisis. This is a Game-Changing Planetary Trend that will affect everyone on the planet, regardless of whether they believe in it. What we do know is that the climate is changing. What we don't know is how this change in climate will definitely affect our world. By the time we are experiencing climate change, is too late to have taken actions to prevent or manage the changes. If you want to be concerned about something, be concerned about this.

We spend every day balancing our lives and work, with our children and our business and health and understanding of risk. Every decision you make is a risk: Do I cross the street at the light or not? Do I buy that stock for investment? Do I send my kids to that school or learn this skill to help my career or invest in a new business or technology? Every day you and I take risks. The information we use to take the risks helps to offset the risk: Do I take this risk or not? We make decisions about risks that affect our future.

So why wouldn't it be smart—Future Smart—to be prepared for the possibility of climate change risk by making changes in lifestyle, law, markets, and innovation today to better prepare for tomorrow? That is my perspective: to prepare to manage the risks that may come by making changes to our world today. Any rational person would agree that this approach makes sense regardless of the difficulties in changing the technology of transportation, investing in renewable energy, or a number of additional ideas explored here.

The other classical issue that humanity faces in dealing with climate change is that of hubris: we assume we can fix the climate the way we fix everything else, whenever we need to. The idea that there are systems, such as nature, that are beyond human control is difficult to accept. The assumption that we can fix climate change whenever we want or that future generations, our kids and grandchildren, can fix it later is illogical. This is our time.

The Next World War

Climate change is our Next World War. This is our problem to fix, if we can—now. Changes in lifestyle, energy use, more intelligent resource planning, and the establishment of a carbon tax will all help to manage risk. The problem is that not enough people, especially leaders, have a plan for the future. Without a bit of courage, a real plan, and a vision for the future, little will be done.

It would be as irresponsible to deny the scientific evidence of climate change as it would be to ignore a present danger. To vanquish this challenge to generations, hoping our future citizens will fix the climate, is wrong. These future citizens are our children and grandchildren. This is not the legacy we want to leave. The ethical and right thing to do, given the real and present hazards facing our world from climate change, is to get a plan for managing the challenge and leave our kids with a sustainable future.

Future Risk on Steroids

Climate change will bring permanent changes that, once they occur, may not be reversible. But we can do some important things now to prepare, to adopt a longer view, to become Future Ready, if we plan now and act on that plan. Future Smart leaders take note. The public's awareness about climate change is increasing, and your customers know more than you about this issue. It is going to be difficult for leaders to remain unaware about climate change as a future risk factor and not have a plan.

We don't fully grasp what's going to happen exactly—weather is chaotic. But we do know that global changes due to climate change are in process now. We can see the changes. We have changed the climate, and there is heavy weather ahead. We don't fully understand the long-term implications, though. There are danger signals that point to risks we must unravel.

What we do know is that there are too many early warning signals that demonstrate a growing risk factor in climate. As a forecaster of trends, I do look at the data to identify risk. There is plenty of data that define the potential for risks, of which we, as a civilization, have never faced before. This is the Uncomfortable Truth.

Climate change is an insidious threat. It will not come in predictable paths. It will affect everyone on the planet in some way. Mother Nature is unforgiving, and she is angry. The rising temperatures chart a pattern that is unfolding in epic proportions. The rapid acceleration of climate change has registered an alarm that even the climate scientists and our leaders did not know was coming so quickly, so unforgiving—or else they would have taken the risk more seriously. Now we are in the thick of it. Rapid climate change

is here. Our forecasting tools were not adequate to understand rapid climate change. We no longer have the luxury of denial and avoidance. We need to make changes now.

Man versus nature was the first primordial battle that humans faced on the planet. Could we survive nature and the ravages of weather? Ironically, we used technology, tools to build the first habitats to protect us from the harsh climate. An Ice Age later, down the road of history, we are at it again. We are an adaptive species; we made it this far, and now we have a similar planet-level challenge: dealing with the climate to come.

Observing Risk

Climate change is both a present and future risk, affecting our ecosystems, wildlife, glaciers, oceans, atmosphere, and countless other natural habitats. We can see the impact of rising temperatures and sea levels on coastal areas, especially cities and nations around the world. Both the Arctic and Antarctica are melting—it's observable, and the science data proves it. This recent data has accelerated forecasts of a wetter world. We will face future challenges shaped by climate change, such as threats to water, air, food, and, most of all, our security and way of life.

From Denial to Action

There are also great opportunities as well that we shall explore for leaders, entrepreneurs, and citizens to reduce the effects of climate change through cleaner energy investments and transitioning away from carbon-producing industries. But this change in energy use and lifestyles change cannot stand alone to sustain our future; we will need more radical solutions.

What has not happened yet are the large-scale hazards from rapid climate shifts that may threaten populations or may wake up those in denial that climate change is real. The social impact of climate change is what's going to get our attention. These will only come after there is a pivotal event that reinforces the scale of the risk: A major city is lost. Sea level rise is catastrophic. A huge storm is widespread in impact. Populations will have to need to avoid disaster. An entire nation collapses in chaos. Then this will all become too real.

Though we have tsunamis, tornados, droughts, and flooding today, no one has been able to analyze all of these events together as part of a whole system of changing climate, of a pattern that signals a new connected global risk, not just isolated events. We don't have the Big Data and computer models that understand the global complexity of climate change as yet. So far climate change is too big for Big Data.

Too Big for Big Data

The problem is that there are too many data points to analyze. Being able to manage the complexity to be able to make predictions will come, but it needs to come soon if we want to survive. Humans are good at survival, adaptation, and even prediction. That's promising, because as climate change shows up more, we are going to need these three competencies even more so in the future to survive the impact on cities, air quality, public health, and other risks.

Nations will be upended, resulting in population migration, resource upheavals, conflict between nations, and governance erosion—not everywhere but in select regions. All of this is probable as climate change increases. Resource scarcity will be a given. Agriculture and water will be at risk. The global scale of potential hazards from climate change cannot, with today's technology, predict what is coming. We need new more sophisticated ways to predict and alter the path of climate change. No one is Future Ready for this future. The threats to sovereign power, social order, and governance that are coming in the future will bring climate change home to everyone.

States may fail when climate change takes its toll. Unstable climate change will upset the social order of nations. Global security will be compromised. Entire societies and security will be affected. I know that to many people this seems hard to imagine, but I believe the global and regional risk factors are larger and deeper in impact than what private and public leaders are studying.

Lifestyles may be altered just to be able to survive in this hotter world where climate changes will challenge every aspect of people's lives. Now, this is a forecast of practicality and adaptation that assumes climate change cannot be fully reversed and shall be more extreme in the future than it is today.

These two forecasts about climate change are both realistic and should immediately shift the Future Readiness planning of every person, community, organization, and nation. Of course, that won't happen, but I am accustomed to motivating folks to get ready, so I shall continue to encourage leaders to take notice. Time is not our friend in this matter.

THE GAME-CHANGING FUTURE OF CLIMATE TRENDS

- A hotter and wetter world will define every aspect of our future world, from survival to culture, business, and lifestyle.
- Sustainability demands new science innovations to address food, water, health, energy, and security risks.
- Forecasting and managing global climate change hazards will become one of the most in-demand industries on the planet.
- Climate change may become the most disruptive trend of our time, affecting social, economic, political, and environmental systems.

- Climate change will shift the geopolitical landscape: powers will rise and fall; a transformation in power will realign alliances.
- Severe global climate change will contribute to extreme weather.
- Sustainable megacities of the future, havens from hazardous sea levels, heat, and storms, will become the habitats of the future.
- Climate change entrepreneurs will harness the power of innovation in transportation, commerce, health care, and energy in order to manage the risks to humanity.
- Business that anticipates climate change will be better prepared to manage the global changes that are coming in the marketplace.
  - Climate Engineering will bring together environmental, computer, biological, and engineering sciences to launch large-scale planetary innovations to better manage the planet.

The Geopolitics of Climate Change

Uncertainty. The unknown impact on security, food, and water will upset the social order of nations and regions throughout the globe. As globalization, supply chains, markets, agriculture, and finance are all part of the connected planet, they are also targets for disruption from climate change. We have taken on studies and forecasts for clients who have energy and agriculture investments worldwide. They are concerned about the impact of climate change on their businesses as well as citizen's well-being and safety in the face of disruptive climate events. Geopolitical conflict in various forms is coming, shaped by the risks from the reality of a warming world.

In the Arctic a new race for newly accessible resources and trade routes is erupting. With global warming the Arctic ice is retreating and a number of nations in the region are laying claim to newly revealed territory, of which oil- and gas-rich resources have been found. This is what an energy-hungry world demands. The geopolitical conflict surrounding nations that lay claims will contribute to defining the future of the planet, given the immense size of these resources that are not clearly defined inside of sovereign territory.

You might ask: What does a sustainable society look like? A 70 percent reduction in carbon emissions would require changing energy usage dramatically, shifting to only renewables, eliminating autos unless they are electric, recycling, instituting pollution controls, establishing carbon credit trading, and rethinking industrial manufacturing, health care, and transportation to ensure the carbon footprint becomes very small indeed. Carbon trading, offering to stimulate an economy to invest in new, renewable, and clean technologies by establishing a market, will accelerate change in reducing carbon emissions.

Unless you had a mandate by law, with the private, citizen, and public sector firmly in support, this sustainable society will not just happen. And this is why it doesn't exist today. In the near future nations like Singapore or those in Europe may go this way. Climate change will force governments to mandate policy and law to protect the nation and its citizens from the risks of climate change.

Already we have a taste of the geopolitics of climate change. Developing nations such as China, which needs industrialization to grow its economy, are less likely to decarbonize, cut back on pollution, or reduce carbon emissions. Developed nations want comprehensive change but are unable to reach a global consensus with other nations to reduce emissions.

Climate change stress and conflict will topple governments. This will be a significant new risk factor that emerges. There could be over fifty nations that are affected by Climate Change Stress (CCS) and over ten or more nations that become failed states due to climate change, where law and order collapses into a Road Warrior scenario.

Climate Change Stress—especially water and food stress—on nations will exasperate in the future. Increased resource scarcity, a surging new middle class of over 2 billion, and demands on food and energy resources will destabilize law and order in certain regions of the world. Nations may rise or fall based on their climate change management and preparation or lack of, how soon ahead they plan and adapt their societies, and, finally, how Future Smart they are—what they do to prepare today to survive the crisis that is coming. This will determine their future.

The lack of global cooperation to reduce emissions, even to get agreement about how much reduction in carbon emissions from fossil fuels is required to head off the extreme climate change, cannot get resolved. There is little global cooperation among nations. And there have been many climate change disasters that may even force global cooperation to create a sustainable future.

Climate Futures

- As of 2006 China passed the United States as the world's top emitter of carbon, CO_2, putting about 10 billion metric tons into the atmosphere.
- The United States and China continue to build coal plants at an alarming rate.
- By 2030 we must reduce carbon emissions by 80 percent to have a chance at keeping the planet from increasing instability and insecurity.
- We must reduce over 385 parts per million of carbon emissions per year, and this will require drastic social and industrial shifts.
- By 2030 we should aim for a zero-emissions future, which is ideal.
- Temperature rises, which are forecasted now at going to 2 degrees C, or 3.5 degrees F, are forecasted by 2030 or before.

- Exposure to sun radiation is on the rise, causing increasing cancers and public health issues.
- Food and water stress, now on the rise, is expected to be widespread by 2025.
- Most megacities of 10 million or more residents lie in the coastal areas in the most at-risk areas on the planet.
- The Arctic is melting, and the water has to go somewhere.
- Sea-level rises by six to ten feet by 2050, two to four feet by 2040 or before are predicted.
- Global climate change refugees will destabilize nations.
- Global resource scarcity will frustrate governments and the private sector to meet population needs.

California now fights wildfires 365 days a year. There are over sixteen hundred raging wildfires on average per year, and that number is going up. This costs us over $300 million a year, and it is rising.

Heat waves in Europe and Russia in 2003 and 2010 killed over 126,000 people. Fierce storms destroyed much of New Orleans, creating the first climate change refugees in the United States. Droughts, from the United States to Africa, are reducing food production and driving up pricing.

Africa's droughts continue to reduce sustainability, adding to resources stress, war, and governance problems. Climate change is coming at a time when over half the world lives in cities, and with the rise of the New Middle Class, another 2 billion people must be supported on a crowded planet. As much as 75 percent of the world may be living in cities by 2050—that's 5 to 6 billion people.

Resource Scarcity and Climate

One of my clients, a top executive at General Mills, the global consumer food leader, and I were talking before my briefing on the future trends coming in food, population, and climate. We were discussing the difficulties of keeping up with the world demand for food and the challenges we see ahead given not only demands but also climate change's impact on reduced food supplies.

He remarked to me that what keeps him up at night is how we are going to feed the 9 billion people on the planet who are coming and what will be the second-order effects of not being able to manage the future food needs on governance, law, and geopolitics.

The stress on nations and cities to be able to manage a resource-scarce future weighs heavily on the global leaders in government and the private sector whom I have interviewed. We take for granted the availability of food and water as well as safe habitats. This global security, as yet recognized as a

future risk factor, will complicate our future, regardless of where we live on the planet.

This is the challenge we face, and like the rest of the challenges, our capacity to meet this challenge is linked with all the others. The convergence of trends—population increase, climate change, agricultural capacity, and technological innovation—are in fierce collision. Resource scarcity due to climate change is a problem we will meet not so far down the road as population increases outpace capacity, such as in agricultural capacity—unless we move fast, get Future Smart, and plan ahead to prepare.

With greater population growth comes greater demands on the planet's ability to sustain this population—to provide food, water, and habitat for as many as 9 billion people by 2050, according to high-end population forecasts.

This is considering that today over 1 billion people live in poverty, and over 1 billion live in water- and food-stressed regions. There is not enough agriculture production to feed 9 billion today. We will need to become highly competent in the future to deal with a hot planet and the growing needs of billions.

This is a challenge of the twenty-first and twenty-second centuries that will be driven by not just the climate changes of today but also what we do to address the climate challenges of tomorrow. Feeding the planet will be difficult without long-term investments in planetary management of agriculture and energy. There is no central global coordination to plan for this size of challenge in the future.

What we do to predict climate change may help us become ready for the future. The right applications of innovation will, in the future, make a difference, such as long-range sensors, computational simulations, and even climate management science to prevent disasters.

If we had the predictive technologies to forecast the upsurge in heat temperatures in Europe, many would not have died. Storm warnings in Louisiana could have predicted the energy surges before they hit land and wiped out communities. Long-rage sensors could have detected a powerful tsunami that ended up killing thousands in Thailand.

This could have prevented that disaster. We could have used technology that existed to predict and prevent disaster. The system was turned off. We could have done more, but we did not.

Welcome to the extreme future of climate change. Everyone will be touched everywhere on the planet, the one planet we all live on. Sounds almost corny, but it's true. All of the natural systems—air, water, soil, even the biodiversity of living things—is connected in some shared ways that again escape our science but is nonetheless all interconnected, as life systems are.

Chernobyl has driven up cancer rates in Poland. The pollution in Asia affects the United States. The warming of Europe attracts disease that has migrated up from Africa. The tsunami in Thailand makes waves in India. The global connectivity of systems is at the heart of climate change.

We need to understand this intimacy of systems and their interaction given the trends emerging with the climate in transition. There is much more that we need to simulate and model to understand the linkage of systems and climate change's influence. We need to take more actions sooner to manage this risk.

Taking Action to Manage the Climate

This analysis is not all doom and gloom. There are two strategic questions I am going to challenge you to think about:

1. What can we do to prevent further climate change?
2. What innovations should we invest in that could help us manage climate change affects on the planet?

The truth is that we were aware of climate change risks but did little to head off the storms that are now coming. Our leaders have not made us aware of the pressing need to address this crisis of our civilization. No nation has made the actual progress to become sustainable and energy renewable so as to effectively prepare for the hazards ahead. We are not Future Ready, and this must change if we are to survive.

Now we are that next generation, and time is running out. There are still leaders who don't think environmental issues win elections. They may be right, but they won't be for long. But it is time for leaders and the public to wake up and embrace the reality that climate change is the most dangerous risk factor our civilization has every faced. And we had best deal with this now before further changes render our actions too little and too late.

The good news is that we can make some changes—even radical but reasonable changes—if we understand the problem. We need to stop arguing over whether climate change is happening or how much of it is man versus nature so we can get on to fixing it.

There is a fifty-fifty chance that we, as a civilization, we will blow it, not prepare or prevent climate change, not figure out how to adapt, not geo-engineer the climate—basically, do nothing significant to make a difference. The price is too high for doing nothing, as I will explore here. But the point is that if you accept that climate change is a risk factor, the obvious challenge we are not prepared for is: What do we do about it?

The Future of Our Planet

There is a global consensus among leading scientific authorities and governments that there are specific threats, risks, and hazards that are emerging now and will have an adverse impact on humanity's future. This is not just about the

changing climate but also, and more important, the future of our civilization. The scientific group the Intergovernmental Panel on Climate Change (IPCC) analyzes the data in order to figure out what is real and what is not. This is the leading international body for assessing climate change.

The IPCC (www.ipcc.ch) is a scientific body established by the United Nations and the World Meteorological Association in 1991 and remains under the auspices of the United Nations, which reviews and assesses its most recent scientific, technical, and socioeconomic data relevant to understanding climate change.

The IPCC's fifth report on climate change tells a convincing story: climate change is happening now, not out there in a hundred years. The risks are real, and humanity is not taking it seriously enough in order to change fast enough to make a difference. Any questions? Everybody understand?

There are four dimensions to understanding and dealing with global climate change that we, as a civilization, must grapple with:

> Climate change risks: understanding, predicting, and analyzing potential threats or hazardous events that may threaten people and societies from climate change impacts
>
> Adaptation strategies: the process of adjusting to climate change trends and effects influencing social and economic impacts
>
> Future climate readiness: an assessment of the capacity of social, economic, and environmental systems to cope with the trends and risks
>
> Transformation actions: making fundamental changes, including financing large-scale planetary innovations in environmental and human systems to prevent and manage climate change risks; this category may be the most essential to the sustainable survival of the planet

Man Bites Climate—Climate Bites Man

Let's also dispense with the whole man-versus-natural climate change argument. Climate change is happening. It is unimportant whether there are natural systems at play rather than blaming it all on human factors. I think science has won the day on this debate. Humanity's two hundred years of industrialization and postindustrialization on the planet has caused climate change.

I think we all can accept this as a probability and accept that humanity has contributed largely to changing the climate. This is not surprising given the industrial and postindustrial revolutions that have led to growth and progress.

Tornados in New York City

Climate change is a current reality: tornados in New York City, droughts in ten nations, extreme category-5 storms, Arctic glaciers in retreat, steadily rising

global temperatures, and the list goes on. You would have to be living off the media grid on an isolated island somewhere to not know about climate change. If you are still a climate change skeptic, then perhaps you don't want to read this chapter because it will make you very anxious. Like the rest of the book, I focus on what to do about this, how to manage this future.

Preparing for the future as a theme of this book requires an intelligent person to weigh the data, see the facts, and take all actions to manage that future— good or bad, as it may be. In this case you want to pay attention and shift your actions to managing this Game-Changing Trend, not arguing about "if" but instead start thinking about "when" and how to prepare. Being prepared is being Future Smart.

Accelerated climate change affects consumers, and they cannot get affordable food or jobs or compete or feel secure, all due to climate forces affecting them. Every one of these trends has already started to happen.

Climate Change Forecasts: 2015–2050

Most nations are not Future Ready for the threats climate change pose.

- Climate change has already had an adverse impact on natural and human systems on all continents and in the oceans.
- Extreme and unpredictable weather creates more risks to human security and safety; nations must be prepared to deal with.
- Food and water insecurity places greater gaps between the rich and the poor worldwide.
- Coastal megacities are at risk of flooding.
- Global climate change refugees are on the run away from disasters.
- A new, vibrant, clean tech industry emerges as all companies turn to innovating in order to prevent and manage global climate change.
- Nations with severe resource stress due to climate change become failed states.
- Property damages from extreme weather, such as storms, fires, and droughts, could be in the billions of dollars and Euros.
- Heat waves, droughts, and floods will increase as ecosystems become progressively unstable.
- Social unrest will rise and outpace nations' capacity to manage them.
- Resource wars between states and nonstate actors wage battle over access to water, land, agriculture, and technology.
- Governance will be stressed as nations deal with climate change as an unstable force on society.

Climate Wake-Up Call

There is another wake-up call that I forecast. It will not be popular, but it is true. In fact, it is the Uncomfortable Truth. We have run out of time. We can make a difference, but we will not be reversing climate change. And this is new. Many experts and leaders think we can reverse climate change by reducing carbon emissions and switching to renewable fuels.

Changing Lifestyles

We can and should attempt to alter lifestyles to protect the environment. But we have not planned ahead, we have not been Future Ready years before, and now we cannot play catch-up totally. This is our wake-up call. There are permanent changes coming that we see today in warming and melting evidence that cannot be reversed—but we can protect the future, and we must.

Can we limit carbon emissions and soften climate change? Yes. But we would need to make drastic changes, including stop using coal, oil, and gas tomorrow. Is this realistic? No. That is the Uncomfortable Truth as well. Unless we do something radical to address climate change, we will face it head on. And there is a significant amount of climate change that is irreversible.

There is no one to blame but ourselves, and we cannot reverse the climate change that is coming. We can lessen the blow, manage it so we have time to adapt and prepare. And we can do more radical things if we hurry, which I will explore.

So a warmer, wetter, more extreme weather world, with uncertainty and climate crises cascading toward us, is the likely future. Now, this is not an apocalyptic forecast. There will be stress, breakdowns, and some disasters, not all on a global scale and not all at once. But we should get prepared for extreme changes that will become the new normal.

There is also ample evidence that climate change is accelerating faster than we have been able to catch up with. Now, for someone whose business is prediction, this is not hard to accept that drastic, even large-systems change is moving in ways that our tools to predict and understand are not prepared for. This is part of the challenge of our time. We are faced with many disruptive forces that we cannot predict and may never be able to understand fully.

Ten Top Climate Change Risks

- Global warming
- Sea level rise
- Water stress
- Food insecurity
- Extreme weather
- Public health hazards
- Disease outbreaks
- Social unrest
- Geopolitical conflict
- Failed states

Three Climate Future Scenarios

Climate change is a constant in every scenario forecasted here. The only issue is how fast and deep we prepare for the impact and how we prevent further changes. How Future Smart can we learn to become so we can adapt in a warmer and wetter future? Better to prepare and be wrong than not to prepare and be at risk.

These scenarios could all occur as possible outcomes for your consideration. Government, defense, intelligence, and private-sector multinationals such as the leading banks, insurance, energy, and investment firms are familiar with these scenarios.

Most of my institute's global clients—governments and corporations—have wanted to increase their awareness of what the impact of climate change may be. They, like you, want to become Future Smart. They want to be ready for the future. You need to appreciate the global and national scale of changes that outpace our capacity to understand the problem. This is what the last few years have been. But we are entering a new phase now as we move away from Future Readiness to becoming Future Smart—dealing with the challenges, taking actions, innovating, and producing positive outcomes.

ADAPTIVE WORLD: FUTURE READY

In this scenario the world collaborates and prepares together. There is an enlightened leadership of visionary powerbrokers in both the private and public sectors who are able to plan ahead together to reach a consensus of action. Nations, citizens, and organizations from the private and public sectors work together in a coordinated way, much like preparing for a disaster or war.

Laws are passed and alliances between nations and the global community come together to plan and execute prevention measures such as building levees to manage sea level rises, funding new-city construction inland, protecting agriculture, and redirecting defense and security to prepare for social issues.

Critical infrastructures such as the Internet, telecom, banking, food production, logistics, media, and defense are protected. A serious long-term vision for climate risk management planning is at the core of the combined efforts. Everyone pulls together for the common good. A massive carbon tax and trading system is put in place, resulting in a new clean-energy economy. Carbon fuels and industries are phased out while alternatives are phased in.

Climate Systems Science is developed to predict and engineer solutions for the environment, and vulnerable virtual and physical locations that are essential to sustainable societies are protected. We use Big Data, sensor networks, supercomputers, geo-engineering, and Smart Machines to protect life on the

planet and manage effectively the crises that come. Space arrays, sea walls, the containment of carbon, and investments in alternative energy production have created a more secure future.

MANAGED RISK WORLD

In this scenario nations, regions, and organizations partially prepare and adapt. The level of Future Readiness and global cooperation is not the same as in the Adaptive World scenario; there are many risks but not many disruptions, and the risks are manageable, though with some disasters ensuing. Plans have also been put in place. New technologies to protect coastal areas and address warming are instituted. Resource scarcity is managed, though not for every nation or region, given that the too few resources and poor global cooperation: it's too late to make global changes.

This is a world where most but not all (but enough) stakeholders work together and cooperate so that the results are productive. Certain nations and regions of the planet become walled off and isolated but maintain communications and trade. Technology is used to offset carbon emissions and invest in regional climate change management, but not on a global scale or soon enough to make massive change.

CHAOS WORLD

There is limited cooperation given the limited resources available to address accelerated climate change. Some nations, mostly island nations, have not prepared and are more isolated. Poorer nations at risk do receive limited help from more affluent nations, but because all nations started later than they should have, the impact of the help is limited and the scope of climate change is problematic.

Food and water stress, rising seas, and the social chaos associated with breakdowns in law and order become overriding issues affecting governance in nations and cities.

For over a decade I have watched my clients—global multinationals, entrepreneurs, and nations—make a strategic shift toward recognizing that climate change is occurring, and their strategies to prepare have been impressive. Many nations, such as the United States, nations in the Eurozone, Singapore, Malaysia, and Indonesia, have started looking at the long-term impact of climate change and its effects on cities, supply chains, markets, water, and energy. Many innovations have been taken and much more needs to be done, but there is progress—just not enough. Radical changes are needed.

The strategic questions everyone should ask:

1. Can we moderate the impact of carbon on the warming climate?
2. Can we reduce carbon emissions faster?
3. Can we reduce warming by cooling the planet with Climate Engineering?

I believe the answers to these three questions are Yes. But do we have the courage and vision to take actions, to become Future Smart and prepare for the future of a disruptive climate? Other than reducing carbon and changing our lifestyles to consume less, we need to invent radical innovations. Let's explore next what we could do, a set of possible game changers if we are to survive in the future. Being a Game Changer of the Future to deal with climate change may include trying new, even radical ideas.

Chapter 15

Hack the Planet: Climate Engineering

In this chapter I explore the future of using advanced technologies to predict, prevent, and reduce the effects, even protect the planet, from drastic climate change. This is a managed effort to address climate change risk head on. This effort cannot be done without massive changes in energy use, reductions in carbon emissions, carbon tax and trade markets, renewable cars, and clean energy sources, but it can be part of a New Strategy to manage the future. Here is the hitch: we need to invent the innovative solutions that might make a difference. It is not going to happen without billions spent as well as time and ingenuity.

Many technologies in their early stages, before they were proven up, were derided as impossible or too dangerous to produce or impractical. In fact, most scientific innovations, when first envisioned, have been routinely rejected.

This does not mean that every innovation was safe or realistic, but authorities often reject scientific innovations in the concept stages. This has influenced the investments in research and development—the more skepticism, the less funding. The wilder the idea, the less likely it would be funded.

Heretics Wanted

Every great idea faced rejection from the establishment at first. The ideas of Copernicus, Einstein, Tesla, Steve Jobs, Craig Venter, and Ted Turner were thought to not to have much value and were initially dismissed. Years of lost opportunity resulted. There were even electric cars with batteries over one hundred years ago that never caught on in the face of the internal combustion engine. We had to wait over one hundred years to start to embrace electric cars. Let's not wait another hundred years to embrace Climate Engineering the planet.

IBM's founder said that the world would not need many computers. The ideas of doing commerce over cell phones or of the Internet were bashed. No one ever thought television was possible as a technology. These are the classical examples of this worldview with blinders. We need to learn from the past.

Even in recent times the sheer force of the Internet, mobile use, and electronic commerce has changed business and communications and made possible the impossible. Mapping human DNA was considered too expensive and likely indecipherable. Engineers considered nanotechnology and the manipulation of matter to be a pipe dream—now it's a multibillion-dollar global industry.

Where am I going with this? In the beginning leading authorities reject emerging or even speculative technologies as impossible for reasons that are later overturned. So the possibility that geo-engineering will be figured out, that it will play a role in the future given the enormous and accelerated climate change, may be more probable as an outcome. I expect what I shall propose here to manage climate change will meet with much of the same.

We need new thinkers—innovators to invent this future. We need new heretics who can invent Climate Engineering. We need heretics willing to try radical solutions to deal with climate change before the risks become overwhelming.

The difference is in our time, now. Climate change represents such a potentially devastating global disruption that to not invest in new technological innovations to manage the impact would itself be a disaster and immoral. We have the tools to make this difference. We need to think further ahead—we need to become Future Smart about climate. We must invest in innovations that may help manage the inevitable. If we do not invest and plan for managing climate change *now*, time will be a factor later—we shall be out of time.

The difference is that with climate change moving with such velocity, the need for a climate change fix makes geo-engineering the most important new technological innovation, one we should focus all global resources on if we are to manage climate change effectively. So if it takes 1 trillion Euros or dollars to invent an entirely new geo-engineering science that can reduce even 25 percent of the risk factors such as melting ice caps, global warming, rising seas, and social unrest, then we must do it. This isn't rocket science.

The problem is that most policy makers, who are politicians, not scientists, think we have a longer time to consider whether to make the investments in creating a new science such as geo-engineering—what if we do not?

But we need to move ahead and invest in the research and development to manage climate change. Time is working against us. Climate change is accelerating, and we need to catch up with it. We need radical new innovations to meet this challenge; we need the engines of discovery to be put in motion on a global scale now. We need a revolution in innovations to predict, prevent, and manage the future of climate change.

Time for a New Scientific Revolution

I was present at four major scientific revolutions in our modern era. The first was the personal computer revolution. The second was the telecommunications revolution. The third was the Internet revolution, and the fourth was the nanoscience revolution. Each required a tremendous commitment of time, capital, cooperation, and talent. All required billions in funding and the urgency and science discovery that eventually created breakthroughs. New jobs, new companies, and new ideas from these scientific revolutions have enriched our world. That is what we need to do again—invent the future of Climate Engineering.

The positive impact in the marketplace in new job creation, new industries, new companies, and many new products and services followed. We are at the beginning, and if we want to cool the Earth, we need to make the commitment quickly. I am convinced we need a new scientific revolution to manage the climate change that is coming. If we do not, I fear our irresponsibility will define the future. Will our children accuse us of not just damaging their future but also not taking the actions that would manage the climate to prevent further hazards? This is what is before us now.

When I think of what the Internet, mobile phones, and computers have brought in terms of wealth, progress, and lifestyle change, I have to remind myself that all of these innovations happened in less than thirty years. Imagine what thirty years of billions in investment, millions of entrepreneurs, and a global coalition of over one hundred nations could accomplish to prevent severe climate change.

The time period was at least a decade of trial and error, and finally breakthroughs happened, mostly based on investments and hard-working entrepreneurs. And most of the innovations came from outside the established industry leaders: Apple was the outsider in computing, Tesla for electric cars, Nokia in telecom, and so on. There is an opportunity to invent the future anew.

This is where we are today. We need to invent a new scientific revolution in climate science. We need to take a collective and assertive strategy to think and act to manage the climate so as to prevent the hazards that are peeking out now, signaling with enough data that extreme heat, rising seas, and disruptive supply-chain risk is coming fast.

Toward a New Science: Climate Engineering

We need a new climate science that combines engineering, systems biology, ecology, networking, Big Data, cloud computing, communications, and computer science in order to save the planet from the climate change that is both emerging now and fiercely coming in the future. We need a new science to meet

the challenges of climate change or else face not just the risks but also the hazards emerging faster than we can predict.

We already have the innovations and technologies to invent this new science. We just have not woven all of these together into a new science. Simulations over supercomputers can model complex phenomena today. The Internet is a collaboration enabler that has helped unlock the decoding of the human genome. Satellites watch over the Earth with great precision and already are an early warning system for weather. Space X and other private space companies with NASA, India, the European Union, and China have the space technology to launch and install structures such as reflective solar arrays in Earth's orbit. Sensor networks already are used to predict and monitor the electric grid's energy usage.

Accelerated innovations in clean energy production, nano-materials, and solar are used today. Biochemistry has been used to seed weather production in the atmosphere and oceans. The early stages of many more technologies could be researched and developed so as to work together to create Climate Engineering.

Designing Weather

Climate Engineering, also known as geo-engineering, involves scientists designing and implementing large-scale modifications to the Earth's geophysical systems in order to change the environment. It is the intentional hacking of the planet. Just as we hack computer systems, we now must learn to hack the planet.

These may include capturing atmospheric carbon dioxide, known as sequestering, mounting orbiting structures to manage the sun's radiation, or pumping particles or biological agents into the atmosphere or oceans to capture carbon and deflect sunlight to cool the planet.

In 2001 a UN report looking into climate change concluded that geo-engineering was on the table as a possibility and that this approach "includes the possibility of engineering the earth's climate system by large-scale manipulation of the global energy balance. It has been estimated, for example, that the mean effect on the earth surface energy balance from a doubling of CO_2 could be offset by an increase of 1.5% to 2% in the earth's albedo, i.e., by reflecting additional incoming solar radiation back into space." (See "Climate Change 2001: Working Group III: Mitigation," GRiD Arendal, www.grida.no/publications /other/ipcc_tar/?src=/climate/ipcc_tar/wg3/176.htm.)

There may be additional climate modification that comes from applying computer prediction models to act before a climate change risk factor emerges, such as measuring the energy waves of an emerging tsunami, earthquake, or storm and using this information to take preventive measures.

Rapid prototyping using large-scale 3D printers and computer simulations in combination with building a large Big Data capability and cloud computing global warning system would give us something we don't have today: a global climate predictive warning system.

This—coupled with actual architecturally engineered structures to protect cities, coastlines, and many other at-risk human targets such as air, water, and agriculture—will be necessary if we are to survive the long-term effects of the worst-case scenarios of climate change. And these worst cases may come.

Although governments and private-sector companies have made some bold experiments, this approach to managing the climate has not been studied as extensively as it needs to be. We will be faced with the challenge of either becoming Future Smart about managing the climate, by developing the technologies to deal with change, or becoming victims of the hazards. This will require a more radical approach to thinking outside the box of what today's climate science is about. Climate science has been about understanding natural systems. Climate Engineering is about changing these natural systems to prevent disasters or transform the planet.

There is a possibility that we can make a positive impact and reduce the effects of climate change's risks if we move quickly. If we are going to invent a new science, we had best get on with it, *fast*. We are running out of time. Climate change is accelerating at an alarming rate, and if there was one science we need to save the world from the most predictable future that we know is coming, it's Climate Engineering.

The Eco-Market Exchange: 2025

If you want to save the planet from climate change, there is no better way than enabling investors to make a profit as an incentive. Turning clean energy and climate change management into a global investment opportunity to kickstart saving the planet is a great way to start.

There are four main global electronic trading markets. Zero-waste credits, recyclable credits, carbon credits, and renewable credits have created an eco-market exchange in which eco-credits, like stocks, bonds, commodities, or currencies, trade over $1.5 trillion per year. Eco-credits trade much like carbon credits did years ago in London and Rio. The Eco-Market works over vast, high-speed computers on global electronic markets in London, New York, Hong Kong, Mumbai, and fifty other exchanges around the world. Now there is a diversity of financial incentive products that investors can trade. In order to buy or sell these eco-credits a portion of the trade goes to investing in global climate change management, pollution controls, and renewable energy.

Radical and Safe Innovations Wanted

There are over thirty governments that practice weather modification and geo-engineering today. Efforts started as far back as 1948 in Canada and the United States. Hail seeding and chem-trials work, to manage the weather, has had a history of experimentation. Climate management is not new.

China has the largest national weather-engineering agency. In the United States NASA has conducted numerous experiments to control the climate. These were to test the effectiveness of ocean and atmospheric manipulations such as cloud seeding, hail suppression, solar radiation deflection, and iron fertilization in the ocean. Many of these experiments worked and proved up the effectiveness of these solutions. I forecast that engineering the climate is on the agenda for the future.

A Solution in Process

I forecast that think tanks, universities, and various governments have already begun Climate Engineering because we are running out of time, and there are no other alternatives to managing the climate, even the reasonable reductions in carbon that are being discussed and that all nations are avoiding. Before the governments lose land, cities, life, and water due to climate change, they will start Climate Engineering the planet. Social unrest in China would get ugly, with 1 billion upset over the climate stress–related impacts that may come. The United States and the European nations have their own plans and experiments.

It would be great to think we don't need to engineer the climate—just cut back on driving fossil fuel cars, recycling plastic, and turning off the lights. But this is not going to make a difference when 9 billion people are involved and governments are not seriously engaged. Should we recycle, move to renewables, expend more conservation, and reduce emissions? Of course, but this activity will have limited impact given the state of the climate now. This is not widely understood.

We need to think more radical to make a difference, and that difference may help us survive. We need to invent a new science and make sure it works and does not create additional problems. There are huge issues that surround this science that have moral and scientific risks that are not insignificant, but they must be faced if we are to attempt the impossible—engineer climate with science.

We need to create a global engineering and science effort with all universities and entrepreneurs can create a new field—Climate Engineering. We need to create something that doesn't yet exist, and this, frankly, is something we are good at.

Radical Tech for Radical Times

As a futurist who believes technology can do amazing things to better our world, I am not looking for a quick fix. Billions of lives have been enhanced by technology's value in medicine, manufacturing, transportation, communications, and the list goes on. My entire life has been focused on understanding the technologies and innovations that have and will continue to change the world for the better.

We are living longer, more prosperously, and more educated lives as a civilization because of technological advancements. From my days as an executive at Apple to today, working with dozens of entrepreneurs who are creating the future, where next-generation technologies such as stem cell research, mobile commerce, neuroscience, and quantum computing point to the future of our world, I think the most miraculous technologies are coming and will usher in a higher quality of life for our civilization.

I know that geo-engineering is just beginning today and is not a fully endorsed science, having questionable challenges and even dangerous risks, and it is still very early in its conceptual stages. This is not even a complete science, and many are afraid we will create more chaos. But as so many other technologies started out with humble beginnings, I think Climate Engineering will contribute to helping us manage some of the planetary risk factors that are to come, if only we can develop the research to reduce the risks and professionalize this new approach.

How might Climate Engineering make a difference? We would prepare, prevent, adapt, and manage the risks together by formulating a new science. We need a new approach to creating solutions to manage climate change impact on human biology, natural resource management, oceanography, urban engineering, climate prediction, predictive simulation, synthetic biology, ecological sciences, and water and agriculture production. We need a new science with a new agenda, tools, and objectives to perhaps save the planet.

A Planetary Race for the Future

Bringing together climatologists, engineers, computer scientists, simulation experts, weather experts, architects, and others to create a new science is not a tall order. This is not to jump over the important debate about the risks and the issues of whether we should or should not engineer the climate. In a world where everyone will be affected by a common shared experience of climate change, where we all are at risk today, we need a new science to meet these challenges.

The sciences we have today are too limited, too focused on specific areas, not big enough. We need to think bigger—about planetary systems. We need

to focus on modeling large complex systems, ecosystems, engineering for the planet. We need to think much *bigger* on the planetary scale if we are going to address climate change.

Only in this way, by inventing a new science to deal with the new challenges we discover and our willingness to invent the solutions we need, might we prevent what many experts believe is coming: significant climate and weather changes that will put billions of people and entire nations at risk of life and health. This is a bet that we can muster the capital, science, and courage to win the climate change race before we can no longer deter, mitigate, or alter the climate.

All experts now believe that adaptation to climate change is required to manage the risks. I am forecasting that this will not be enough, not business as usual. Bolder steps are needed on a global scale if we are to succeed. And succeed we must.

Possible Benefits of Climate Engineering the Planet

- Buys time while we reduce emissions
- Removes, captures, and stores carbon
- Buys time to innovate clean energy networks
- We learn what works and what doesn't
- Buys time to build climate-secure cities
- Manages solar radiation
- Cools the world
- Creates a safer, more secure world
- Protects water and agriculture resources
- Protects biodiversity
- Reduces social stress and conflict over resources

I forecast that getting beyond the "if" and on to the Make-It-Happen, to focus on prevention on a global scale, to protect the security, health, and safety of the planet, is the highest strategic objective for every person, leader, government, and organization. Why, you might ask?

Greenland is melting right before our eyes. Billions of tons of ice are headed into the sea every day. The Arctic and Antarctica, the top and the bottom of our world, are melting faster than scientists had predicted. Based on the best science, the implications are that a Global Warming Effect is speeding up. Already the world's weather has changed. Already sea levels are at risk for rising around the world. Already the health effects of extreme weather change from

tornados in New York City to droughts in the United States are affecting food production, stock market values, real estate, weather disasters, and the security of entire populations.

I think we need to accept that the changes in climate are convergent—together as one ecosystem comprised of all natural systems: oceans, rivers, species, atmosphere, terrain are converging with the human-made systems of cities, communications, transportation, commerce, and energy. This convergence is being disrupted and shall continue to be as the climate evolves into something different and unpredictable, even chaotic. We need to be Future Ready for this changing world.

Hacking the Planet

Examples of Climate Systems Science:

Natural resources management: preventing and protecting the environment, air quality, agriculture, water, food, and logistics

Climate systems management: the use of technologies to prevent and reduce the impact of climate change by Climate Engineering—atmosphere installations, biology to cool the planet, offset weather, innovations to reduce the impact of global warming, and clean-energy management

Climate risk management: planning, forecasting, simulation, and prediction modeling to anticipate climate risk scenarios affecting population, health, food, security, and water

---

Headlines from the Future: 2030
Atmospheric Scrubbers Reduce Emissions By 70 percent

Azimov 7 Rated A-Scrubs, or Atmospheric Scrubbers, will remove all harmful particulates from the air, leaving the environment clean and pollution-free. The new SynBio filters capture carbon and neutralize cost by 50 percent more Bitcoins. The performance of these scrubbers is excellent, and upgrades are sent via the Cloud Computer Networks, what we used to call the Internet. The scrubbers come completely automated, guaranteed to do the job. The enormous thrusters are fueled by the latest solar fusion and devour pollution, which the machines scrub from the atmosphere.

Climate Engineering to the Rescue—Maybe

Climate Engineering falls into three categories. First, there is carbon sequestration, carbon capture, and storage (CRD). Second, there is solar radiation management (SRM). And third, there is predictive climate management (PCM), which is Big Data, cloud computing, and analytics that use IoT to build a large global sensing and climate intelligence system that predicts, monitors, and interacts with the environment to deploy technology, structures, barriers, geo-deployments, and human resources where and when they are needed to prevent and manage disasters.

The radical idea that scientists could take control of Earth's climate strikes many as the very hubris I mentioned in this chapter. Are we attempting to play God? I agree it is risky, unproven, and, as I stated, like most technologies, in the early stages of development. I think there is high potential for inventing a breakthrough that could manage climate change. There are risks, and this approach could backfire and not work. This field faces many problems. From chem-trials and weather management trials in the past, we know that there is plenty of evidence that we don't have a science of geo-engineering that can deliver on the big expectations we may have.

CLIMATE ENGINEERING RISK FACTORS

- Accelerate climate change hazards
- Damage the atmosphere
- Increase health risks
- Make mistakes
- Pollute the environment
- Increase solar radiation

That doesn't mean we give up but rather that we invest in tomorrow—there is too much at stake. We need to invent solutions, and frankly, I don't think we have an option: Should we sit back and wait for the inevitable climate changes? Or should we research and innovate now to prevent disaster and invent a new industry to affect the global ecology of the planet. There are also legitimate concerns that planning to find a technology fix would discourage humanity from making carbon emissions reductions, and that may occur as well. This does not mean we should not investigate the potential of Climate Engineering.

An Idea Whose Time Has Come

We have been geo-engineering the planet for over fifty years. Efforts began in the 1950s. Weather modification experiments have been going on for over a century. This is not a new idea but rather an idea whose time has come. Keep in mind that experiments by NASA and other government agencies as

well as ventures backed by Bill Gates and other tech luminaries have proven that climate experiments such as seeding the oceans, iron fertilization, has merit.

The centers of geo-engineering are the United States, the European Union, Russia, India, China, the Middle East, and Australia. Numerous experiments in the ocean and atmosphere has addressed weather medication, solar radiation management, and cooling effects on land mass. The Philippine volcano that erupted a few years ago cooled the planet, dropping fine air particulates, such that we would use with climate engineering to cool the planet.

Dozens of projects around the world, conducted by the largest governments and going back decades, suggest that this approach is cost effective, reasonable to produce, actually works, and is backed by science. No one has carried out large-scale global projects with the ambition that is described here. Do we need to conduct more studies and research to develop large-scale climate management systems like solar arrays and carbon captures? Absolutely.

With our back to the wall, with carbon emissions rising and with renewables still not globally productive, we need to develop innovations to manage climate change or else we will have no one to blame but ourselves. There is no upside opportunity without risk. The risks we take today may mitigate the larger risks coming in the future. This trade-off of risks—smaller today, perhaps catastrophic in the future—is time based. The longer we wait, the more and larger risks to life, health, and our world. Better to prepare now.

Fixing Climate, Protecting the Future

There is a long history of climate change science events starting in the 1950s. Climate Engineering has yet to be developed into a reliable and effective science. Here are a few Climate Engineering examples that lay the foundation for the future. If we are serious about dealing with climate change, we should be examining how to manage the climate as well as how to make productive reductions in carbon emissions. The point is that we will need both strategies to survive in the future.

India's GROMET project in 1967 was based on weather modification—rainmaking—by the United States to end the Bihar famine. The United States conducted the first major ocean fertilization test in 1993. An Australian company experimented with urea used for ocean fertilization in the Sulu Sea in 2008. The Planktos company developed ocean fertilization technology in 2007. The Lohafex project experiments in ocean fertilization in the North Sea. Frankly, many more early examples of Climate Engineering have been conducted than have been reported. (See "19th Conference on Planned and Inadvertent Weather Modification," 93rd American Meteorological Society Annual Meeting, January 5–10, 2013, https://ams.confex.com/ams/93Annual/web program/19WXMOD.html.)

There are also ethical concerns. We need proper scientific guidelines to develop Climate Engineering. This is not a science ready to go but rather a science that must be invented so we can have a fighting chance to reduce the impact of climate change. If we can send a fellow to the moon, we can innovate to save the planet and not blow ourselves up at the same time. I am a believer in Silicon Valley Rules: if we can envision it, we can build it.

Silicon Valley is where I grew up professionally. I watched committed and innovative engineers every day, the true heroes of our era, invent the impossible. These were the Game Changers of the Future that invented new business models, industries, technologies, and a new form of business culture. We all take for granted lasers, the Internet, smartphones, nanoscience, computers. These are the tools that are transforming health care, mapping the human genome, creating the new manufacturing revolution, and taking us into space. If we can invent these great innovations, we can also fix the climate. And the tools and technologies we have and shall have will enable Climate Engineering to become a reality.

We can shape the future if we invest today. Getting Climate Engineering right may take ten years. There are *many* unknowns. This is *not* a science yet. There may be massive ethical and scientific issues that we cannot resolve. But we need to try. We need more research and development with courage, insight, and governance. We need the courage of entrepreneurs and individuals to invent a new industry, one that truly could shape the future by protecting that future. And we need to start now.

GAME CHANGING IDEAS OF THE FUTURE

- Seeding the oceans with iron and other agents to neutralize carbon: this would take CO_2 and reduce the impact on the environment.
- Weather modification: cirrus clouds are removed to cool the planet.
- Reseeding plankton in the oceans that can absorb carbon every efficiently and quickly and can produce oxygen.
- Carbon sequestering and transformation to remove and store CO_2 underground and then turning this into energy production.
- Carbon Trading Exchanges, where companies buy and sell carbon credits and have incentives to invest in alternative energy, clean technologies, and reduce carbon emissions.
- Aerosols for atmospheric weather management: this would protect the Earth from solar radiation and cool the planet.
- Building climate change protective cities with reflective roof surfaces: this would capture solar energy, deflect solar radiation, and reduce skin cancer rates.
- Solar Space Arrays to reflect solar heat away from earth: this would deflect heat before it enters our atmosphere.

- Rapid reforestation with massive seedling implantation on the planet to accelerate forest growth.
- Nano-science in smart glass, homes, and buildings to cool our cities and habitats with glass that gets automatically darkens when the sun gets stronger.
- Synthetic biology to create biologic agents to absorb carbon: this can be used to produce oxygen from photosynthesis.
- Artificial forests and trees to absorb carbon: this can further reduce emissions impact.
- Automated Smart Levees for coastal cities to protect shorelines from sea level rise, storms, and tsunamis.
- Automated sea walls that inflate to protect coastal cities from storms and extreme weather.
- Carbon Scrubbing Towers that can absorb and sequester CO_2 that can be inserted on buildings and in cities.
- Weather modification to seed rainfall with silver iodide and other agents to prevent droughts and enhance agriculture effectiveness.
- Nanotechnology devices to eat carbon: this will be designed to work at the atomic scale to collect carbon.
- Recooling the Arctic with biochemical atmospheric agents that can offset warming by reducing heat and solar radiation.
- Cloud Engineering Ships and Installations in the sea to produce clouds that will reflect the sun's radiation.
- Creating protective Earth Shields with the use of sulfur dioxide seeding of the atmosphere to create a reflective solar capacity.
- Terraforming deserts: this would introduce weather, water, and soil management to develop high-growth agriculture and altering the ecosystem.
- Climate Change–Ready crop development: this would invent crops that are resilient to extreme wet or heat and can thrive in low water conditions.
- New aqua-habitats that survive in water and on land, where salt to fresh water and new large-scale sea farming can increase food production.
- Deep Sea Aquaculture and Terraforming Cities, where we use the sea as a high-performance agriculture-producing ecosystem.
- Eco-Dome-based Smart Cities that have climate-controlled environments that are pollution-free and manage the sun's radiation to minimize exposure.
- Space Mirrors the size of cities that are at low Earth orbit to reflect the sun and cool the planet.
- Developing Smart Machines to help us manage the Big Data complexity and model solutions for planetary climate change.
- Development of a Real-Time Satellite Weather Tracking Capability for all nations.

Enter the Climate Entrepreneurs

There have been many attempts to develop climate change products and services to both understand and experiment with geo-engineering, as it has been called. An American entrepreneur named Russ George dumped 120 tons of iron dust in the ocean off the Northwest United States. The plan was to create an algae bloom that would sequester carbon and, thus, combat climate change.

Russ George is one of a growing number of Climate Entrepreneurs who advocate large-scale climate engineering projects that would enhance the environment in order to manage the effects of global warming. There are a number of plans to fertilize the ocean with iron to capture carbon. Other Climate Entrepreneurs are analyzing the possibility of pumping sulfate aerosols into the upper atmosphere to mimic the cooling effects of a major volcanic eruption that would disperse fine air particulates into the atmosphere.

This would theoretically reflect more of the sun's rays back to space, assuming the science will work as planned. There are over fifty universities, twenty nations, many engineering firms, and think tanks studying and experimenting with Climate Engineering projects at this time.

These Climate Entrepreneurs' risks are as high as their ambitions. Ocean fertilization could cause the opposite effect, accelerating climate change or damaging the oceans and atmosphere. There might be new sources of pollution as well that could frustrate, not help, in managing the climate. Computer simulations have predicted that risks to health, natural systems, and the ecology may be the outcome. The truth is that we need guidelines and scientific expertise to learn, experiment, and investigate how to develop appropriate climate engineering. But abandoning Climate Engineering cannot be the preferred option.

Climate change will be an innovation incubator for global entrepreneurs to invent clean technologies, agriculture that can thrive in a changing climate, and new cities, transportation, and ways to create a sustainable future. At the core of this new Climate Entrepreneur will be a desire to save the planet by using tech innovations. There is plenty of interest in every demographic sector of the world, from the Boomers to Generation Y, to make a difference—and a profit—in saving the world's climate from burning up the planet.

Smart Levees

One example of this comes from an architect whom I have advised, the Smart Levee project Folding Water (http://kuthranieri.com/folding-water), developed by Liz Reneri. Her design is elegant and self-sustainable structure that would be positioned off the coast line and would protect cities from rising seas. They have developed computer models and created designs. She has received encouraging

recognition but not the funding to launch the project as yet.

This is because we are more reactive than predictive. After the first coastal city is swamped, then I expect her designs will be funded, produced by large-scale 3D printers, and launched like floating edifices off of cities like San Francisco, where they can watch and wait, ready to go into action and protect the shoreline of the financial district.

North American Weather Consultants (www.nawcinc.com/index.html) is the oldest organization in the United States and a leader in the area of weather modification since 1950. Their projects have been in analyzing weather and applying that knowledge to modifying weather in the United States, the European Union, Asia, and Latin America. Their services include snow and rain augmentation and fog dissipation.

There are thousands of projects like this waiting in the wings for support, waiting to be developed by entrepreneurs who are getting ready to engineer the planet. All they need are the funds and visionary leaders in power to get off their butts and decide that protecting their cities, nations, and world requires something more than talk.

Taking Action

Being Future Smart about climate change can start now. Of course, it would have been better to start thirty years ago, but no one in power was that smart. This climate risk is not something that happens way down the road in 2030, when it is too late. Let's get Future Smart now to take action and apply the research to innovations we can use to survive climate change. If we are wrong and spent the time and funds when it was not needed, well, better safe than sorry. But if we are right but don't respond, we are "cooked" (sorry for the pun). We know enough, and there is enough data about what the risks are to invest in radical innovations that may save lives and protect the future.

We should do what we are good at doing—creating innovations to solve big problems. This is what we have done as a species since the beginning of civilization. We built dams, skyscrapers, canals, bridges, and rockets. We can do this. This is just another huge global challenge, like war or disaster, to which we need to apply our big brains, entrepreneurial skills, and technological capabilities to handle. I think humanity and our scientists are up for the challenge.

I am certain there is a generation of new Climate Entrepreneurs ready to move on to hacking the planet. We need a new challenge—after all, the Internet and computers are mature, robotics is moving along fine, and health care and genomics is on track. But the one area that is screaming for innovation that we have not focused on is climate. Let's create the next generation of Climate Engineers and Entrepreneurs who can really make a difference by getting us ready for this hot future.

Managing the Climate

Climate change is real, it is here now, and it is likely to get worse in the future. So let's accept that and do something about it while we can. Actually, no: let's do the *only* thing we can do, other than cutting back on carbon emissions and so forth. Let's figure out Climate Engineering. Heck, we sent a man to the moon, we cured the world of polio, we invented the Internet and computers, figured out the world was not flat, and managed to bring a few extra billion people out of poverty over the centuries into the modern era through, yes, technology.

We have the capability, the intelligence, and the tools to transform the climate and protect humanity and the planet through advanced technologies. We have something else most vital to this task: we have the need to invent a massive global strategy to engineer, to alter the planet's systems to protect humanity from the climate shifts that are coming.

Now we have to actually do it—invest in research and development. There is an emerging industry called Clean Tech that had about a $1 billion in venture funding in 2013 alone. How about we invest $1 trillion a year for the next twenty years? How about we create a new generation of kids, call them Climate Engineers, and offer X Prize–like contests?

Calling All Entrepreneurs

How about funding 1 million entrepreneurs with grants for go-to-college-to-transform-the-climate programs? If all of the Global Fortune 1000 funded a planetary defense fund to come up with the best Climate Engineering solutions, we could fix this. Let's Hack the Planet and fix the climate before it is too late.

The point is that we can wait for climate change to run its course and maybe take our chances that the risks indicated here won't be devastating. Maybe you are thinking it will all blow over? Not likely.

Or we can become Future Smart by preparing now, investing in research and development to create innovations in Climate Engineering that might be just good insurance or might actually save our future. There is often a fine line between thinking ahead and averting disaster and not doing enough soon enough. We have faced down Big Science challenges before, and breakthroughs came.

The worst-case scenario may be that we invested in innovations that we didn't need right away and thus created a new industry. Or the worst-case scenario is we did nothing to prepare, and it was too late when we finally woke up. I think that is the choice for every person on the planet today.

I cannot emphasize enough that even if we develop a safe and effective Climate Engineering capability, this does not mean that we don't have to make societal, economic, and lifestyle changes to reduce carbon emissions, pollution,

damage to the environment. We need it all: massive reductions in carbon emissions, Climate Engineering, economic incentives such as carbon tax incentives, pollution controls, and innovative clean-tech solutions for energy. We need a holistic set of rapid solutions to manage the future.

In the future, if we learn to manage climate change, we want to be able to state that we used every innovation, every insight and every strategy to protect the future for the rest of humanity. We are here for a brief time, so let's make it count and see whether we can prevent the risks that may come from climate change. Now, that would be Future Smart. We need to think about climate completely differently. We need Game Changers of the Future who can think fresh, invent new, and help us to shape a new vision for managing climate. We need to apply all of our thinking to not just scale back but also invent the solutions that may protect our future for the generations to come. I think we owe that to the children who will inherit the future. Let's make sure we apply our ingenuity to fixing the future. That would be Game Changing.

Chapter 16

Fueling the Planet

The Smart Grid

Imagine in the near future an entirely different energy system, an energy system that is agile, intelligent, distributed, flexible, self-organizing, sensing, and sustainable. For example, a Future Smart energy system would be organized much like how the web network works. The Internet's capabilities are based on a highly flexible and distributed network of networks that work together to optimize the performance and the access to information sources. The web self-heals, fixes, and enables, and machines communicate with machines to optimize performance, power, and connectivity to stream along our shopping, communications, media, banking, and health care. And a mash-up of game-changing innovations like nanotechnology used for storage, cognitive computers for managing complex energy calculations, sensors optimize energy traffic, and the mobile Internet all work together to contribute to the Smart Grid. Now that is a Future Smart path to a sustainable world.

If one part of the network breaks down, the network senses this and looks for another pathway. The design of the Internet as a distributed network of increasingly smarter systems that collaborate is at the core of how the Internet works. This not only drives the web traffic but also carries billions of simultaneous voice calls, data, and videos.

This is what the future of energy could be—a Smart Grid Network that is agile and connected to many different energy sources, both traditional fossil and renewable. The Smart Grid would be smart enough to sense in real time when and where the most cost-effective and abundant energy sources are to automatically identify and route the energy needed to billions of consumers on demand. Just as the Internet starts with one computer and builds exponentially to create a scalable, distributed, and global system of collaborative networks, a Global Smart Grid could do the same.

A Smart Grid refers to a class of technology that people are using to bring electricity delivery systems into the twenty-first century, using computer-based remote control, computer, and communications automation. These systems are made possible by two-way communication technology and computer processing that has been used for decades in other industries. They are beginning to be used on electrical networks, from the power plants to solar arrays and wind farms direct to the consumers of electricity in homes and businesses.

The big idea would be to combine both consumer and business energy generation with a mix of energy sources—renewable, green, fusion, electricity, and fossil fuel sources—to better gain a holistic control, a total-energy system's view of both ends of the energy supply chain—supply and demand. This Smart Grid Network will transform energy in the twenty-first and twenty-second centuries by creating a more efficient, transparent, and productive energy architecture that can "learn" and "evolve." The Smart Grid could predict what energy needs and where based on the Big Data analysis of billions of people's behaviors and then forecast what, when, and where they will need energy to run their lives. But we have to build this.

This Is the Future of Energy

In the future of 2025 the Smart Grid will be linked to cloud computing, analytics, and Big Data of energy. This new future of Smart Grids will enable city-to-city, home-to-home, business-to-business, and nation-to-nation energy trading, commerce, and exchanges that will optimize the price and access to different energy sources for a more effective system.

Then when Smart Machines, AI, enhances the network performance by creating self-organizing capabilities, we will have an Evolutionary Network that manages energy locally, regionally, nationally, and globally. When evolutionary networks emerge that surpass the computer processing of today's computers and even humans, we will have reached the endgame of energy global management. This future is coming.

You might ask: Why don't we have this today? This certainly makes sense, and if we could build the Internet on this model, why not the energy system? The world needs more energy efficiency, given more demand and higher costs of energy. The answer is that there is no system that manages energy on the planet today because it has not been fully envisioned, designed, and built. In the near future this Smart Energy Grid will be the gatekeeper that captures, transmits, and distributes energy on the planet.

Today there is an antiquated energy grid in each nation and region of the world. But this is a patchwork of old-legacy systems that are not designed the way the Internet works. This older, slower, and inefficient energy system

is not unified for performance or cost effectiveness. The amount of waste and inefficiency in what we have today, if captured, could light your city for decades. The global energy grid is based on a nineteenth-century model that was developed based on a mechanistic and industrial model more so than an information model.

If the Internet worked for transforming communications on the planet in less than a decade, why wouldn't it work for energy? The answer is that the same logic applies. Better technology and innovations applied to fixing the energy problem is coming.

WHAT WILL MAKE THE SMART GRID A REALITY?

- A real-time network of 100 billion sensors in homes, offices, autos, and public transportation are all connected, sharing information on energy demands and supplies.
- The creation of a Big Data network of secure information about energy usage, generation, storage, geo-locations, sources, performance, and economics is matched up with consumer and business needs.
- Cloud Computing brings together all of the micro- and nano-grids in a city, community, region, nation, or continent to better manage the energy efficiencies of energy usage.
- Embedded AI automates the management of microgrids and provides cost-effective energy access.
- A series of networks link renewable and traditional gas and oil energy sources together for optimizing performance.
- Mobile Energy Management Intelligence senses, forecasts, and predicts what, when, and how much energy sources will be required so as to anticipate demand.
- Smart Machines will be developed to do this work, as they will be better at managing the efficient energy systems on the planet.

THE TOP TRENDS THAT WILL SHAPE THE FUTURE OF ENERGY

1. Renewable energy innovation will drive the long future of global prosperity, growth, and sustainability on the planet.
2. Smart Machines will be used to manage the energy grids, cells, and generation and to optimize renewable energy production for distribution.
3. Energy Security, having access to energy that is secure, available, and affordable, will shape energy futures and economics.

4. The development of a Global Carbon Trading marketplace, where companies, nations, and individuals can trade carbon, water, and energy credits, will fund the next generation of renewable energy innovations.

5. Wireless power downloaded from Energy Cloud Network will keep devices working anywhere on the planet.

6. Smart Grids, with an energy mix that is produced, captured, and stored on the local level, will transform energy resources.

7. Off-World Energy futures, moving into Earth's orbit and methane mining on Moon, will offer new sources of renewable, large-scale, and abundant energy sources.

8. The demand for energy will be greater than the supply available due to the rise of new middle-class prosperity, population growth to 9 billion by 2050.

9. Creating a distributed marketplace where consumers can sell alternative energy they don't use.

10. Upgrading the world's electronic networks.

Our Shared Energy Future

We just need to get smarter—Future Smart—about how to harness and convert these other renewable energy sources into energy we can use. The good news is that humans have an excellent track record for converting matter into energy. We did it with oil, gas, steam, and water, so we can also develop the tools, innovations, and technologies to do it again with additional natural energy sources. The only thing missing from the future-of-energy narrative on the planet is inventing the right innovations to exploit renewable and sustainable energy sources.

While we are working on this Grand Global Challenge, there are traditional energy sources—fossil fuels mostly—that will continue to be part of the energy mix, whether we like it or not, for another forty to 100 years. And for every year that moves us closer to 2030, numerous innovations that can contribute to these next-generation energy sources will become more possible.

By 2030, if we are Future Smart, the energy mix will be reversed, with more renewables than fossil fuels. Every nation, every organization, and especially every entrepreneur should work toward building our sustainable future. We can do this. And, of course, we must. The demand drivers of the future, such as increased population, expensive energy, fossil fuels impact on public health, and the environment are reasons enough to focus on renewable energy.

The State of the World's Energy

Uncertain. Unstable. Risky. Wasteful. Carbon dependent. These terms characterize the state of the world's energy today. As a civilization, we have not been very smart about how we use energy. We rip it out of the ground or oceans, tear up the landscape to mine for coal, burn oil to fuel our cars and cities, and, in the process, incur climate change, pollution, and do not plan for the future. It is time to think about the future—let's get Future Smart. This current illogic and resistance to change has to go. And in the near future it shall, I forecast.

Easy Energy typifies the last hundred years, when the technology to find it, mine it, or burn it was easy. It did not require advanced innovations. Easy Energy is not a smart strategy because it is often risky, polluting, costly, and, above all, not renewable. Once we mine or drill it, we are done; it is gone. There are more intelligent sources of energy generation to choose from that are renewable, abundant, and cheap as well as nonpolluting.

But the yields are not comparable, and this will require advanced technological innovations to make Smart Energy available. We are close. Fusion and moon mining may be further out in our future, but building grids, developing renewables that have high yields, both here on Earth and in space—it is all part of fueling the future. Smart Energy is coming fast.

Need for Clean Energy Now

You want to wrap your head around the concept that everything in our world is based on energy. Nothing works without energy. Every aspect of our lives, from health to work, creativity to war, innovation to nature, even our biology, economy, and DNA is dependent on energy. Without energy, nothing lives or can be sustained—not people, societies, or planets. Having an ample source of cheap and abundant energy is essential to all life on the planet today and into the future.

We need much more energy for billions of people to create a sustainable future. This is just not a negotiable global policy; we must, as a civilization, get this right, as it will have an enduring impact on our future existence on the planet. With ample access to energy, we have a thriving civilization. Without energy in abundance, there will be conflict, stress, and a lower quality of life.

This means that in order to forecast the future, in order to have a sustainable future—which I would define as a future that has a decent quality of life and is secure, productive, and offers a hopeful existence—you need to have access to more energy to meet the growing demands of the marketplace. And the energy sources we have been using, primarily fossil fuels, are (1) running thin, (2)

costly, and (3) contributing to altering the climate to an extent that threatens our ability to survive.

In fact, an advanced civilization would not damage its natural resources like the air, water, and climate the way our civilization has. An advanced civilization would not mine and use nonrenewable energy if it had any negative effect on people's health, which it does. This is not Future Smart. It is just not sustainable for the long term and could have devastating effects if not corrected sooner, but we shall get to that forecast.

The Energy Dilemma

Now, most of us understand the Energy Dilemma. The key driver of the future of energy is that demand will increase by 2 to 3 times by 2030. The world's economy and society is dependent on oil and gas, hydrocarbons—fossil fuels. This dependence is not a sustainable strategy for the future. Oil, gas, and coal are not renewable sources of energy. They are costly and, though reliable, we need a new energy plan. It would not be realistic to forecast that for the next twenty years we are going to not use petro energy sources.

It is realistic to plan for a sustainable future that is dominated by renewables that will be cheaper, more accessible, and wiser to invest in. Another reason is that the geopolitics and economics of being an energy importer is not a preferred energy future for any nation.

For example, the United States will be winding down over the next decade a $700 million price per year on the oil it has been purchasing from OPEC over the past two decades. This reduction will be based on the shift to gas resources and renewables. The European Union is moving into the renewable direction, as is Asia.

We all need to move faster to head off population and productivity demands in the global economy. Economies need energy to grow. We need to focus on increasing the technology around renewables. Renewing the energy we need from sources that are consistent with life systems such as solar and wind as well as other sources reviewed here is Future Smart.

Meeting the One Hundred-Terawatt Future Challenge

I was giving a presentation, a briefing, to one of the leading energy companies in the world, to their board of directors, at their retreat. I stated that, given the enormous changes required to reduce carbon, move to renewables, conserve energy, and invest in the future, I doubted that today's leaders had the courage, insight, or will to make those changes and become Future Smart. This did not go over well. This is one of those forecasts I hope I am wrong about.

I forecast we shall turn to what we do best—making new tools, designing innovations, and inventing our way out of the energy fix. We will fix energy, but we are going to all pull together to harness innovation to do it.

Now that we have that clear, you can grapple with the fact that with more people born, rising populations with increased needs will accelerate energy demand. I estimate that by 2050, with 9 billion people on the planet, there will be a 100% increase in demand for energy. Today we use about 1.3 quadrillion BTUs, or 1.4 million terajoules, of energy per day. As of 2014 we use about twenty terawatts of energy on the planet per year. We are going to need one hundred terawatts of energy by 2040. That's five times the amount we use today.

We are not preparing fast enough to meet this challenge. We need new sources, new discoveries, and new incentives to conserve and manage the energy we have today. If not, the future will bring laws that restrict birth based on energy scarcity or even restrictions on transportation, travel, or mobility due to energy access. Energy rationing is a reality in much of the world today. Tomorrow it will be severe and constant unless we innovate quickly. The future will need five to ten times more energy than we use today, yet we are not providing adequate energy for over 2 billion people today.

Nobody is ready for this extreme future. This chapter is about what innovations could make a difference in creating the future of energy.

Thinking About the New Future

We need to think about our society, our world, and ourselves with a longer view. How will the next ten generations get their energy? What is the impact of our actions today on the future? What can we do to ensure that our great-grandchildren can benefit from having abundant and clean energy in the future? What are the actions we can take today to forge a future that is sustainable for the next five hundred years? These are the strategic questions we need to ask of ourselves, our leaders in the community, in both business and politics. We need sustainable energy policies for the long term, but we must have the courage to make changes and envision a bolder, different vision for energy if we are to thrive in the future.

Innovate Faster

If there is one megatrend that we cannot, as a civilization, continue without fixing and becoming Future Smart, its energy. We must learn to become Future Smart about energy and make a transition from fossil fuels to renewables faster than we are moving today. There is just too much risk to not innovate faster in creating new sources of renewable energy.

Energy drives every community, business, organization, and marketplace, big or small, throughout the world. Energy is the glue that enables civilization to continue, to be viable, and to endure. Yet traditional, carbon-producing energy is going to continue to affect public health and be a drag on progress toward making the earth sustainable. The requirements needed to accelerate the move toward renewable clean energy in order to offset traditional fossil fuels cannot be overestimated in importance.

If we do not move fast enough and learn to become Future Smart about alternative energy production to keep pace with global demand, the future will be a conflict-ridden and insecure world. We must take this seriously and press leaders in the private and public sectors to invest quickly and deeply in new renewable energy sources.

I recognize that any change in energy on the planet will require decades for it to make large significant changes. Many game-changing innovations, such as electric cars and solar, have, in a short period of time, demonstrated higher performance. I do not think we can afford not to invest in the future of energy beyond the dominance of petro energy. Obviously every government and even the oil companies, to their credit, recognize this shared global challenge and are working to be part of the solution.

The New Moon Race

The race to the moon is used here to remind us that humans can do amazing things when we put our creative minds to it. The race to the moon, the challenge thrown down by President Kennedy, has been used to acknowledge that when committed people collaborate, they can sometimes accomplish truly amazing things. Putting a man on the moon, the challenge that galvanized a generation, showed us that extraordinary accomplishments can be realized, no matter how crazy or how many unknowns and challenges confront us.

The innovative idea here is, of course, that if we could put a man on the moon, can't we accelerate the innovations that will produce a clean and renewable energy future? And we can. But only committed people with a vision for a better future can design that future. We need a Moon Race to invent the future of energy. We need a Moon Race to prepare our civilization to meet the challenges of the future, which will be dominated by vast increases in an energy-hungry population that will outstrip today's supply needs.

We must look to protect the security and progress of the future with energy that can be sustainable for much more globalized trade, commerce, and growth. Energy can be an accelerator or a drag on the future, depending on how much energy and what type of energy is available. The cost of energy, in terms of economics as well as on society, will require faster innovation in both managing carbon and providing renewable energy abundance.

Deep Space Probe 2050:
The *Da Vinci Explorer*

Ever since the Consortium of Space Nations sponsored the deep-space explo-ration project, the results have been spectacular. Fusion propellant depots set up in the 2040s keep the network of explorers going ever deeper into space. Some, like the *Zulu*, are small, like those drones from the past that flew packages to customers' homes and business.

The discoveries of new elements, metals, strange gases, and even primitive life forms have changed the very nature of our understanding of human biology and the cosmos. Now, I have conducted experiments that answer some funda-mental questions about how the universe was formed and even who we are and where we humans may have come from.

We are star children, no doubt, as the experiments prove that our essential biochemistry comes from the stars. We have found no intelligent life as yet, but we are hoping and searching and exploring the outer rims of our galaxy.

Until my next transmission, this is the *Da Vinci*, signing off.

The Deep Future

One cannot fathom the future of energy possibilities without understanding that all of the trends forecasted in this book are pieces of a complex puzzle that fit together to shape a larger framework of factors, relationships, and interac-tions that create the infrastructure of the future. I call this the Deep Future. The Deep Future is the comprehensive total system of what the future of our reality may be—all of the trends woven together, including climate, energy, medicine, work, and technology, that shape how we, as a civilization, as a planet, and as humanity, will be in a future time.

This Deep Future is not just coming; our actions are actually creating, in-fluencing, and shaping the architecture of this reality. We are shaping the future whether we are aware of it or not. Now, if you consider entire societies or corpo-rations that have the power, capital, or resources to shape the future on a global or regional scale, then you can begin to grasp how big this game is.

Often something as mundane as what investments are being made in cer-tain key energy areas can forecast what is coming next in many areas—energy is an example. Investments in clean energy such as solar, wind, biomass, and geothermal today will pay off in the future. Investments in the fundamental building blocks that will shape the energy future such as photovoltaic cells that will drive solar energy, batteries, robotics, cloud computing, and nano-science will make an impact in the future.

TOP ENERGY INNOVATIONS BY 2035

- Near-earth-orbit energy stations produce enhanced computer energy chips in space to increase capabilities and convert and transmit large raw energy sources such as methane, solar, and wind to electricity in the Smart Grid Network.
- Intelligent Automated Highway systems that use 100 percent renewable energy.
- Ambient Capture Energy Technologies that search, store, and transmit energy from passive and active sources.
- Solar arrays orbiting Earth beam energy back to Earth by attracting and converting solar energy to electricity.
- Self-assembling Nano-Makers, nano-machines that are programmed to produce energy from the automated manipulation of matter such as waste or water, will create local energy production units that, like microwaves, will sit in every home and business to generate energy for local consumption or to contribute to the Smart Grid.
- Solar paint turns every roof and surface into a solar panel by capturing the sun's radiation, converting this energy to electricity, then sending this onto the smart grid for distribution or to be used for local consumption, house-to-apartment, town-to-city, car-to-bus, or school-to-hospital.

WHAT COULD BE: TOP ENERGY INNOVATIONS BY 2025

- The Web of Things is essential to connecting every solar panel to the smart grid, collecting, storing, and distributing energy, when required, around the city and around the world, using the Internet as the network.
- Carbon MegaTax program's investments in clean-tech energy make up 40 percent of new clean energy production on the planet.
- The Right to Pollute Carbon Credits are finally canceled, with no more buyers.
- Wind-and ocean-based turbines generate 25 percent of all global energy use by harnessing the natural sea currents and wind to generate electricity.
- Sea Floor Methane mining produces energy for twenty cities by providing a methane energy production on the bottom of the ocean near every city.
- Fusion reactors generate a new energy capacity that fuels society by creating an entirely new source of nuclear energy—clean, safe, and renewable.
- Solar cells spawn a new Hive Mind of Smart Grids that self-assemble in every city, community, and home, generating 80 percent of the free energy from tax investments.

- Smart Machines design and manage 70 percent of the global energy distribution system using cloud computing, Big Data, and AI to benefit the energy needs of our civilization.

The Green Economy: 2035

The petro economy of today dominates energy usage on the planet. This petro economy generates millions of jobs, creates wealth, and provides stability and efficiency of markets. The infrastructure and investments in the petro economy are not just going to just go away unless there is a comprehensive energy plan to invest in renewables. The migration toward a Green Economy in 2035 should have started earlier in this century, so we must accelerate investments and research.

We must invest capital from the current petro economy into the Green Economy of tomorrow at a scale increased by one hundred times to meet the needs of the future. That is what's missing today: we need to invest smarter, faster, and with more capital to actually create a new energy system. Nations that understand the value of a long-term plan, organizations that can help innovate us into this future, citizens who vote with this Green Economy in mind will make this future happen. The problem—and it is an enormous one—is that this Green Economy, based on clean technology, jobs, businesses, laws, and a new energy infrastructure, takes decades to build out.

There is tremendous efficiency in the energy market today, and this will be so in the future, except with an energy mix that includes a dominance of renewables for the long term. Without this long-term view, to transfer the efficiencies, capital, and innovation from today to accelerate tomorrow's Green Economy, it will not happen.

Creating the Global Energy Grid: Networked Power

What would it take to create a new energy future, a future global energy grid? Let's start by setting as a goal that we want to network, share, and deliver power anywhere, anytime for cheap—how do we do this effectively? We need a new source of power to harness that is low cost, plentiful, and renewable so we will never run out. Where can we look to find such an energy source?

The sun, seas, and research laboratories may help to unlock this Bright Energy Future. Now, we are not turning off petro fuels but rather creating a migration strategy over decades, moving from dominance of petro fuels to a broader energy mix with renewables. Unless there is a radical energy innovation that accelerates energy generation, this migration strategy is the likely forecast

given the large trillion-dollar investment in jobs, infrastructure, equipment, and capital investment that the oil, gas, and coal producers worldwide have made.

This reality—the large hundred-year economic investment by the private and government sectors and the extensive social influence of petro fuels on civilization—is hard to change. It is not impossible, but it will take time, capital, and, above all, courage to plan ahead, to envision the possible—to be Future Smart.

Three Energy Futures

There is time to plan for a sustainable future for every nation on the planet if we get going now. There is not time if we wait for another ten years and then try to catch up. The longer we wait, the harder it will be to change or adapt quickly. The challenge is that many leaders lack the vision and courage to pivot into making this future happen. We need leaders who are Future Smart. They understand how to take the bold steps now to create the future that we need, that is best for society and for the planet. Leaders who think about and actually plan for the planet, who have a bigger picture in mind—these are the leaders we need to cultivate and shape our future. These are the leaders who will hopefully navigate a smarter future, when sustainability is at the top of the agenda for nations, organizations, communities, cities, and the planet.

In these three energy futures I forecast what possible future outcomes will occur based on planning, investment, and vision spent today. It is likely that all three futures will happen simultaneously. Africa, with the most resources but the most tolerance for chaos and ineffective leadership, will be likely where the Uneven and Chaotic Energy Futures persist in 2030. South America, most of Asia, the European Union, and the United States have a chance at forging a Bright Future.

Of course, knowing the risks and the upside potential for what sustainability can offer will make a difference in planning for a Bright Future. This is your wake-up call.

The Bright Energy Future. In this scenario society, with the private sector as a partner in change, has invested smartly in building out mostly renewable energy resources based on leading-edge innovations. The gradual phase-out from a petro energy scenario to a renewable one was conducted in stages so as to not shock the economy. The production of new jobs and the phase-out of certain industries were undertaken with careful planning and collaboration of industry and government partners.

They invested in changing their schools and universities, employment policies to create clean-tech jobs, educated their citizens to get support, created a private/public investment strategy, and made smart R&D choices decades before creating actions to produce the Green Economy.

They had a plan to make a transition into a renewable future, which they understood required thinking ahead. This Future Smart approach made a difference as they chose energy over other investments early on in order to work as a nation toward building a more sustainable and independent energy future. The leaders made a conscious choice to become a renewable and energy-independent nation.

Other nations around them followed suit, and this led to an entire region of the world that joined together to invest in renewable and clean tech. Capital investments in creating cheap, plentiful, and renewable energy sources that leverage low carbon emissions was at the core of their plan, and it paid off. In this scenario energy is an enabler of prosperity, innovation, and productivity.

They are an energy exporter to their friends. Global and regional collaboration has led to a Global Energy Grid. A new distributed energy generation has led to alternative energies slowly taking over the demand from petro fuel supply sources. Their future is hopeful and promising as they look ahead.

The Uneven Energy Future. In this scenario there is not enough energy to keep pace with population and society needs due to poor planning for the future due to a failure of the private sector and government to work together. There was too much "head in the sand" denial of the future realities that were coming, and by the time change was needed, society was not Future Ready. There is an uneven supply, insufficient to meet demand, which keeps rising, so energy rationing and partial power is available. Poor forecasting in the past about population change, the rising middle class, and expectations of energy needs left this society ill-prepared for the future. Low investments in energy and an overreliance on foreign sources of energy remain a problem.

There was no foresight in planning for the future. This society is an energy importer that has been held captive to the market for energy, and the costly price fluctuations have been a problem. They also have a hostile energy supplier that holds them hostage, hiking up prices in the winter and each year using energy as a political weapon. Foreign nations that hold sovereign debt and have a hold over energy imports wield a large footprint on national law and policy that turns some nations into vassal states, dependent on other energy-rich nations and global cartels. Microwars emerge when the tensions between energy-rich and energy-poor states become stressed.

In this scenario energy is a drag on prosperity, innovation, and productivity. The society is held back from long-term stability and security because of a natural resource drag on the economy. They overpay for energy that is uneven from a reliable but insecure source. This scenario continues to widen the gaps between the affluent and the poor. Energy will be a key driver in building a higher quality of life, peace, and prosperity.

The Chaotic Energy Future. In this scenario a partial or complete breakdown of society and the energy infrastructure due to war, conflict, and strife

ensues. Failed states lose their control over the governance of the state due a number of social and political conflicts, leading to a collapse in the access to a secure source of energy. Regardless of whether energy is local or imported, the traditional supply chains break down in a failed state. Energy becomes a valuable commodity used by various factions to promote their power and destabilize society.

Criminal and terrorist factions use energy to fuel conflict. As conflict persists, economic and social chaos contributes to population migration and strife. In this scenario the disintegration of their society sharply reduces this nation's capacity to fuel their basic needs. Recovering from this energy future will be difficult and will make many in the population Energy Refugees who go in search of a secure source of energy in a society that is not in conflict or crisis.

Energy Independence 1.0

By the middle of the next decade or so North America will be energy independent due to an energy mix of gas and renewable sources. Many argue that gas provides a better option than being dependent on paying foreign oil cartels, and there is logic there. These cartels originate in nations that have both fragile and hostile scenarios in their near future.

These nations in the Middle East and South America represent an undue risk factor for the United States, and I foresee a migration away from OPEC oil for a variety of reasons, cost as well as geopolitics.

Innovation in building a renewable infrastructure will take time to build and scale in order to be productive and generate more than the current 10 percent of total energy in the United States. But this inevitable future, an energy-independent America, will upset the world economic order. Select OPEC member states may survive and turn to sales in Asia, such as China, or move to opening lines to Europe. Some oil-producing nations may go bankrupt or suffer social strife and geopolitical conflict as energy buyers and sellers shift.

An Energy-Hungry Planet

I forecast that within ten years, by 2025, Europe will be over 50 percent fueled by renewables, with some nations such as Germany and some Scandinavian nations even higher, closer to 60 percent. Nuclear in Europe, especially in France and Germany, will continue to offset fossil fuels usage and contribute to Europe's alternative energy mix. The problem with the EU's energy access will continue to be its dependence on Russia, which uses energy as a tool of political power. In the near future this situation will change as well.

In Asia, China will be the interesting story to watch unfold. The sheer scale of its size will demand energy resources of many types—renewable, fossil fuels,

and nuclear—to meet demand. As China attempts to industrialize and post-industrialize, to do in less than twenty years what the United States and Europe did in about one hundred years, an abundance of energy will be paramount to fueling its growth and prosperity. A mixed energy supply, with an emphasis on coal and nuclear, is likely what will come faster.

Fueling Developing Nations

China's issues related to energy are social unrest and quality of life. By 2030 they will need to make investments in cheap coal, which they have as well as other petro fuels, due to the sheer scale of population needs, and this is why they cannot wait for renewables to come online.

In India, as with most of Asia, the story will be the same. A huge 1 billion-person middle class is heading for the cities, looking for jobs, getting into universities, running from the farms, looking for prosperity. The sheer scale of this demand will strain energy resources, regardless of the planning efforts now being undertaken. Likely the largest democracy in the world, India will not fare as well as China, given the capacity of an autocracy to deliver political alignment and effective accomplishments. China will get more done faster.

India's states remain more powerful than the federal government and are vastly diverse in culture, economics, and customs. Until this is changed and a stronger federal government can establish what China has—a national policy for energy and the future—I forecast India will have spotty success in managing their energy.

This works against having a cogent energy policy for the nation that can align resources and literally move mountains for the greater good of society. No matter how innovative the energy plan, with the authority, at the national level, to make it happen with all of the states pulling together, a fragmented attempt at best will not resolve the challenges of India's energy-dependent future.

China's central planning is smarter than most nations, and they are grappling with the enormity of change they have seen and the progress that is coming. They are attempting to build a modern society with the energy that a modern society demands to be modern. This is no small task.

China's Green Future

Little progress can ensue without ample sources of energy to drive China's future. In this quest they are not alone but China is in competition for energy with many other nations vying for control of energy assets, especially fossil fuels. As China looks ahead, their leaders are smartly hedging their bets that petro fuels, especially oil, coal, and gas, with the mix of nuclear, will be required for thirty to fifty years before renewables can make a significant contribution to their en-

ergy future. I would not disagree, but innovations explored here, such as fusion, could be massive game changers for China and the world.

I do forecast that energy innovations, from fusion to solar and fuel cells combined with other renewables, will make a difference in building tomorrow's megacities in Asia. We could be surprised by what innovations bring in the near future. With so many innovations just now being invented, from mobile to social media, to artificial cells to synthetic biology, I forecast that innovations in energy are coming faster than the public is aware of.

I forecast that China will move aggressively to create new Green Cities out of the new Megacities of their future. These will be energy-independent microgrids, resulting in smart cities of the future. China has the vision and the power to create cities, and they must, given the explosive growth in their population.

Their experiment in designing cities is in the beginning stages, but this trial-and-error will lead to bold Green Cities of the future, where fossil fuels are less impactful on their energy mix and renewables are embraced.

Though many cities in China today, from the smog in Beijing and Hong Kong, are not yet optimally healthy examples due to the overabundance of fossil fuels, I forecast that the Green Cities of the future will emerge faster in China than they will other nations in Asia, as their leadership vision will lead this innovation to shape China's future.

In China's last five-year plan from 2013 they published for the entire world to see, they identified clean technology and the environment as key objectives for their nation. We have to wonder why it is that so few nations have an energy plan or even the insight to publish one every five years. In this plan China indicated that the energy needs of their nation must contribute to the prosperity not only of the nation but also the planet.

As China is on a nation-building roller coaster, moving quickly and furiously, trying to keep ahead of its 1.3 billion people's needs, adopting an energy mix that demonstrates a clean-tech and renewable strategy is Future Smart. As China's population becomes more entitled, expectations about energy and quality of life will become more of a priority.

Future Energy Mix

Global energy consumption is expected, on the low end, to at least double, and I forecast it may triple by 2040. This forecast is based on current energy uses against population growth, increased trade, global GDP growth, and globalization up-trends. I forecast the higher number is actually a more accurate forecast given the advanced postindustrialization of our civilization—we are going to need a lot more energy to sustain our civilization in the future. The future of peace and prosperity will be based on energy access.

I forecast that the future global energy mix must have at least 60 percent of its sources as renewables before 2030 in order to prepare for an energy-hungry world of perhaps 9 billion. We must invest smartly in growing this capacity or else the future will not be sustainable. Energy security, the use and access to energy to grow societies, is the central challenge facing our world. Renewables are the insurance and the cure for a world dominated today by fossil fuels.

Asia, especially China and India, is expected to become the dominant energy importer. Already Australia and Africa have become China's natural resources targets. The next 2 billion people joining the middle class will demand energy on par with the rest of the global middle class.

Their expectations for energy access will be no less demanding than everyone else. In fact, they will demand more energy. We must plan for this future today by increasing our energy investments or else this expectation, if not entitlement, will be a disruptive social force that no government wants to confront. Ample and affordable energy will fuel upward mobility, prosperity, and global security.

Fusion Reactor Winks: 2030

The Argonne Fusion reactor had what we thought was a malfunction today, and energy service transmissions were briefly interrupted. The Wink, as it is called, is a natural phenomenon that fusion systems sometime experience that opens a brief portal in space-time.

Though no one has captured a proper video record of this Wink, as the time it lasts is in one-trillionth of a second and cannot be seen by the human eye, with fancy programs the computers have estimated what the reaction is.

The Wink produced a white, shiny crystalline object, left behind after the phenomenon occurred. It is being studied to determine what it may be. Because the use of fusion reactors is very new regardless of the extent to which they are now being deployed, providing as much as 75 percent of the planet's energy, the Wink Phenomenon is an unknown and strange experience, the significance of which we do not know.

In North America the energy story will be bright indeed. With an economy self-sufficient by 2025 or before due to the large gas resources, the United States especially should turn to renewables R&D, as this will be a multitrillion-dollar or multitrillion-Euro market in the near future. But do not mistake the energy independence of North America based on gas to be the whole story.

If clean-tech and renewable investments wane, the far future beyond gas will be a problem for North America. We need to plow the capital into R&D to build a renewable energy future beyond gas in order to sustain that future. Natural gas is also not a clean or renewable energy source. It is still a pollutant

and contributes to carbon emissions. Just because North America has an abundance of gas that could keep the lights on for the next one hundred–plus years, this doesn't mean it is the ideal energy source.

Every nation will need to ramp up its renewables investments in energy. Energy will become a political issue more so than today, and governments will rise and fall based on energy policies' success or failure. Today in the West we take energy for granted, but the marketplace is changing. More energy demand and less secure supply—it will be a different future, one much more reliant on energy to feed, cloth, shelter, and fuel the economies.

At current consumption rates for energy, which are expected to rise significantly, the cost of energy will continue to increase. Nonrenewable energy sources, fossil fuels, will become more expensive as we move toward 2030. This will be offset by the price performance of renewable energy, which will have an advantage in the marketplace. With lower or competitive pricing compared to fossil fuels, renewables will be adopted faster by 2025 or before.

Rapid economic growth in China and India, combined with increased energy use in industrialized nations, will upset the supply and demand of the energy marketplace and will stress the world's energy resources by or before 2030.

Competing for Energy

There will not be enough energy to keep pace with global GDP after 2030 without new energy and renewable energy sources coming online. We have known this fact for a decade, but as a civilization, we have not invested smartly to accelerate innovations in energy production. That must change. In this regard we are shaping the future we don't want—a future of restricted and expensive nonrenewable energy that will become a drag on prosperity, security, and quality of life.

Every nation or organization must factor in energy competition for resources as an essential factor influencing their future. The organization that is, perhaps ironically, the most Future Smart about energy is the US Department of Defense. The leadership, in order to be agile, global, and Future Ready, has made a swift change toward adopting and developing new renewable energy technologies that can "live off the land" and be adaptive to any terrain.

The Department of Defense is the biggest single energy user in the United States, and by 2025 it must source 25 percent of its power from renewable energy. I forecast that projects will require tens of billions of dollars and Euros in private investment and finance, making the military the Green Leader in the world. Fast deployment of energy production such as biofuel-ready transport, which can use waste such as brush or methane, has been used effectively.

Alternative fuels and equipment from computers to phones to transportation has led to a major shift toward the use of renewables. As with most

innovations in the commercial sector that started with government development, such as GPS and countless other innovations, accelerating the renewable
energy future makes sense. It might also win wars. As it is said, armies win wars
on their stomachs, but in the future they will also need sustainable energy to
win—so will everyone else.

This future can and must be averted with investments in renewable innovations and new traditional energy sources that must fill the gap until renewables
can take up the slack. It would not be any more rational to assume that we can
just turn off the fossil fuel spigot than it would be to think we can instantly
accelerate renewable energy innovations without spending trillions and two to
three decades of development.

The price of meeting the world's energy demands is estimated at $26.3 tril-
lion through 2030—an average of more than $1 trillion a year, based on data
from the International Energy Agency. That seems like a lot of capital, but not
if you consider that this is the price tag for building an entirely new energy system to meet the world's growing needs.

China, India, and the other powerhouse economies in Asia will account for
more than 65 percent of the projected total world energy demand on the planet
by 2030. The offset of this forecast is the amount of energy produced locally by
renewable sources, which could reduce this by as much as half. My forecast is
that Asian economies will become Future Smart faster than most nations by
learning from the mistakes that an overabundance on fossil fuels, especially coal
in India and China, and this will motivate them to invest heavily in clean tech.

The report also notes that sometime after 2010 renewable energy will likely
surpass natural gas to become the second-largest source of electricity behind
coal. Estimates run as high as $5 trillion is needed between 2010 and 2030 in
additional energy-efficiency investments to stabilize greenhouse gas concentrations at 550 parts per million (ppm) of carbon dioxide (CO_2) equivalent.

To reduce concentrations to a lower 450 ppm, $4 trillion more would be needed
to pay for low- or zero-carbon power plants, and $3 trillion for more energy-
efficient equipment. And we need to double this to make a real difference in the
world's future. Is that possible? There is not the will yet to embrace this future.

Smart Machines Can Help

What these forecasts miss is a fundamental idea that will drive the future: innovations in technology and science, given the exponential doubling of technology's power, will be shaped by powerful supercomputers, Smart Machines of the
future, cognitive engines of innovation, that will be vastly faster and cheaper,
with capabilities beyond what we can imagine today. This will shape the future
of energy. What we pay for in computing power today, which may cost $1, will
cost 1,000 percent of 1 cent within ten years if we invest in inventing the next

generation of clean energy that uses solar, wind, thorium, methane, or, more radically, the use of nanotechnology to extract energy from atoms directly. By 2040 this power and the innovations it brings may be almost free as future technologies emerge that will radically shift the economics of the planet beyond oil and gas.

Many of the leading energy policy organizations are shortsighted in their forecasts—certainly not Future Smart in making the fundamental connection between renewable energy investments and increased renewable energy adoption. This myopia misleads everyone, causing them to make poor decisions that do not put enough focus on renewable energy investments and, thus, slowing down the renewable energy deployment rates.

The $30 Trillion Price Tag

The truth is that without investing a trillion dollars a year in renewable energy for the next thirty years, we will not see the innovations that could change the course of our civilization's future. And we need to start now with the investments that will make a difference in the future. Renewable energy could supply up to 70 percent of global electricity and heat demands by 2030 if investments increased significantly to support that. We need to create a global energy revolution by improving energy efficiency and increasing the deployment of low-carbon-producing clean energy.

Since before the Industrial Revolution societies have relied on increasing supplies of energy to meet their need for goods and services Major changes in current trends are required if future energy systems are to be affordable, safe, secure, and environmentally sound. There is an urgent need for a sustained and comprehensive strategy to help resolve the following challenges:

TOP CHALLENGES TO FACE NOW

- Providing affordable energy services for the well-being of the 7 billion people today and the 10 billion people projected in 2050
- Improving living conditions and enhancing economic opportunities, particularly for another 3 billion people
- Increasing energy security for all nations, regions, and communities
- Reducing global energy system greenhouse gas emissions to limit global warming to less than 2 degrees C above pre-industrial levels
- Reducing indoor and outdoor air pollution from fuel combustion and its impacts on human health
- Figuring out how to use the tools we have—nano, IT, bio, neuro—useful to help create a new global renewable energy future

Major transformations in energy systems are required to meet these challenges and to increase prosperity. For example, by 2050 almost three-quarters of the world's population are forecasted to be living in cities. The provision of services and livelihood opportunities to growing urban populations in the years to come presents a major opportunity for transforming energy systems and avoiding lock-in to energy supply-and-demand patterns that are counterproductive to sustainability goals.

From Carbon Trading to Moon Mining: The Top Future Energy Innovations

Energy is mission essential for developing the future—every aspect of the future, including economic growth, health care, and peace. Prosperity is the end product of energy access. You need energy to make progress happen. New energy sources, from the bottom of the ocean to space or from the moon to renewables, will shape the future of power in the twenty-first and twenty-second centuries. Innovations will shape this future. Here are the leading innovations that will shape the future.

CARBON TRADING EXCHANGES

Carbon trading exchanges operate today like a stock or bond market that enables companies to easily buy and sell voluntary carbon credits. Some of these carbon credits are known as Verified Emission Reductions (VERs). Carbon trading can address climate change by using market forces to generate funds for investing in innovation to manage carbon emissions or to create new alternative energy technologies. This approach can help schools, create jobs, fund health care programs, and protect biodiversity.

Though the concept has been proved up, the integration of a global carbon exchange, adopted by every nation and enterprise, has not occurred as yet. This is the future development that must occur to make carbon trading a viable way to fund innovation to manage climate change and to motivate companies to adopt clean and renewable energy and phase out fossil fuels that are harming the environment and the economy.

The value of the global carbon trading market in 2014 is over €46 billion, according to Bloomberg Finance. Carbon trading can be an effective strategy to finance projects that would not otherwise be financed or even developed. The use of carbon credits could be used as part of a company's carbon management strategy to manage its emissions challenges effectively. Trading in carbon credits can support a company's efforts to reduce emissions and help boost global competiveness and customer engagement.

One leading example is the Carbon Trade Exchange (CTX, http://carbon

tradexchange.com). Using CTX's trading platform, any business can access hundreds of carbon projects worldwide as well as their associated carbon credits to create a carbon-offset project and to make a difference in the world. CTX operates spot exchanges in multiple global environmental commodity markets, including carbon, renewable energy certificates (RECs), and water.

By 2020, in all the major carbon-emitting developed and emerging countries, many businesses are likely to be carbon challenged. The cost of doing business will go up if companies do not volunteer to reduce carbon emissions in a big way. The emergence of a global carbon market should be active and become part of every organization's plans. Businesses across the world must prepare for a future when they are carbon challenged. Companies that prepare now—becoming Future Smart—and anticipate this future will be ahead of the competition. Companies that adopt low-carbon and adaptation strategies will gain a competitive advantage and reap the benefits later when the countries in which they operate implement carbon policies.

Developing countries are already very actively implementing national climate strategies ahead of even some developed countries. There is not a global market for the buying and selling of carbon credits at the level that it needs to be in order to make a difference in generating the trillions in dollars needed to offset carbon emissions. Developing nations understand that they will be hardest hit by climate change, so they are adopting climate change policies, such as carbon trading, now or in the short-term future. The largest carbon emitters, China and the United States, must step up to this challenge.

RENEWABLE ENERGY ENTREPRENEURS

Imagine what would happen if there were incentives for every business, home owner, or renter on the planet to generate their own clean energy, not just for their personal use but also to donate, sell, and profit from. How fast do you think companies would make inexpensive solar, wind, and biomass equipment if every power utility or government had to buy excess energy produced by businesses and consumers? This would generate a new era of Renewable Energy Entrepreneurs ready to give back and make back their investment. This distributed crowd-sourced energy would quickly offset traditional power generation and move us closer to the clean energy future that is both nonpolluting, cost effective, and politically in line with making all of our communities energy independent.

WIRELESS ENERGY TRANSFER: THE NEXT BIG THING

There is technology that could power your phone as well as the planet. Wireless energy has been around for a long time, but no one has yet commercialized it. Tesla invented this. Intel is leading it with a Croatian MIT physicist and

electrical engineer who started a company to bring it to market (http://www
.witricity.com). This is wireless energy transfer.

It works by capturing power from the existing wired infrastructure with a
phone or any device—without wires. The full potential is to capture and transfer
energy from one location, where it is made or stored, to where it is needed, via
wireless connection. So downloading energy from the cloud, from anywhere on
the planet, is possible someday.

Tesla demonstrated wireless energy transfer almost 120 years ago at the
1893 World Fair in Chicago when he powered light bulbs. Sometimes it takes
a long period of less-than-innovative solutions to figure out how to get to the
really important ones.

You will find wireless energy showing up at Starbucks, the office, and the
gym. We are on the edge of a wireless energy breakthrough. Wireless energy
transfer could power the Smart Grid and light up a city or even the entire planet
if networked properly.

ENERGY BEACONS

Energy Beacons, a network of millions of nano- and micro-energy production
and storage devices (built by 3D printers), developed by the M2M and IoT
sensors, will be installed, dropped out of planes, and distributed throughout the
planet, from oceans to buildings to rooftops.

This particular type of microgrid network will capture, store, produce, and
transmit energy locally. Energy Beacons could be designed to beam renewable
energy collected from buildings, oceans, mountains, and deserts to way stations
both on the Earth and in near-Earth orbit.

Sensing, capturing, and converting to power from the movements of oceans
and rivers, the solar emissions from the sun, the energy produced by biomass
and hydro, and the movements of millions of cars, trains, and other transportation will be captured for use. Currently it is wasted—there is an entire global
energy infrastructure that is unseen, uncollected, and unknown.

All around us human activity produces energy that is not captured but
wasted. What if your energy usage could produce energy with a twofold
capture of personal energy use? With energy beacons—small computers
with sensors designed to self-organize, turn on, and capture ambient energy that is produced in the world through movement and actions by natural and man-made structures—we could be capturing energy that could
fuel our lives.

Imagine the possibility of becoming energy independent, to get off the
grid by developing your own energy grid. Now, what would that look like? Just
as you might have a garden and plant it, you would install energy devices that
were in various sizes, some designed to collect renewable energy and others that

would store it, and maybe others that would transmit it to a larger local energy network that could even pay you for the energy you provided.

Or you could sell your energy to others—energy P2P. Your own energy grid to collect and sell and trade energy would transform the economics of energy. There might even be aggregators of energy that you sell to or buy from that bring together producers and customers in a Renewable Energy Market. And this entire scenario could be realized with technology, economics, and ingenuity that exist today. Not everything that could happen in the future will be invented in the future. Some of it is possible today—just not realized as yet.

Now imagine further that your new car is not just electric but can generate energy for your home use. Your solar arrays on top of your house or that you installed on your property or even sold to others are generating energy that you can capture, store, use, and even sell what you're not using. Imagine that you and everyone in your village, town, or city are doing the same.

What do you call this? A New Energy Grid. This is a Future Smart network that uses microgrids to capture, store, and distribute energy that fossil fuels would not affect. At first there might not be enough energy production to fuel the needs of an entire city without additional large-scale energy resources, even fossil fuels, but that will change.

FUEL CELLS

Fuel cells are devices that convert fuel into electricity through a clean electrochemical process rather than dirty combustion. They are like batteries except that they always run. Fuel cells were invented over a century ago and have been used in practically every NASA mission since the 1960s, but until now they have not been adopted widely because of their inherently high costs.

A new type of commercially available fuel cell is called a Bloom cell. These are a type of distributed power generator producing clean, reliable, affordable electricity at the customer site. Bloom cells are a particular type of fuel cell technology, different from legacy "hydrogen" fuel cells in three main ways:

- Low-cost materials: these cells use a common sand-like powder instead of precious metals like platinum or corrosive materials like acids.
- High electrical efficiency: they can convert fuel into electricity at nearly twice the rate of some legacy technologies.
- Fuel flexibility: these systems are capable of using either renewable or fossil fuels.

Each Bloom Energy Server provides 200kW of power, enough to meet the base load needs of 160 average homes or an office building, day and night, in roughly the footprint of a standard parking space. For more power, simply add

more energy servers—scalable power on demand. Many Silicon Valley companies are using them today.

Numerous new fuel cells to power your car, house, city, and maybe even you will emerge from fuel cell technology over the next decade. In time cells will be smaller and more powerful, following the trajectory of the supercomputer—exponential technology power doubling each year. Smaller, faster, and more powerful fuel cells are coming quickly.

METHANE MINING

Below the surface of the ocean, in one of the deepest areas, lies a discovery, just off the Gulf of Mexico, that might solve the energy dilemma of our century. This discovery of methane hydrates at one thousand meters beneath the seabed in the Gulf of Mexico may hold the answer to the future of energy, as this fuel source would provide a new energy asset that, for hundreds of years, would fuel the planet. Chevron and the US Department of Energy discovered the reserve of hydrates in high concentrations in fifteen-to thirty-meter-thick beds of sand.

It looks appealing that methane hydrates are available, but that is not the whole story. And the United States is not the only nation looking with keen interest at methane mining.

I would forecast that, given that, due to climate change, as the Arctic Circle is opening up, access to methane in the deepest ranges in the ocean would become possible. The question is whether we will be Future Smart enough to develop methane mining as an energy source, as it will upset the energy monopolies and industries that exist on the planet. A new energy race will ensue after 2020 when methane mining, along with the rush to mine the oil and gas reserves in the Arctic, becomes a gold rush—everybody wants a piece of the action.

Methane hydrate mining by Japan has been very productive in pointing to the future potential of this energy source. Japan, which has endured the Fukushima nuclear crisis and has no traditional fossil fuels of its own, is investing heavily in methane mining. Japan does not want to be an energy importer. Instead, Japan wants to commercialize its methane hydrates, which would give China, India, and Korea the assist they need to do the same. Methane hydrates are trapped within a crystal structure of water that forms a solid similar to that of ice. Large deposits of it are found on ocean floors. The challenge is that methane is highly unstable, actually explosive, and extracting it, as well as finding it, can be very dangerous.

MOON MINING HE-3

Didn't you always want to go to the moon? Well, now is your chance. Start packing, though you have a few years until you leave. There will be a job for you there soon. Read on.

There may be an opportunity for lunar resources to play a role in the energy industry here on Earth. Power generation is a vast and growing market. Energy is a product that may be cost effective and profitable to beam back to the Earth's surface from the moon. But we need to set up operations on the moon to make this happen.

To meet the energy needs of the next few centuries we need to plan for the advantages that could be provided by establishing a lunar energy base. One is mining of the moon for helium, or He-3. Though costly—in the billions—the return on investment could be huge and the capture of this energy resource and could provide nonpolluting and clean energy for many generations into our far future.

Technology to mine the moon to produce He-3 calls for large mobile miners, reactors, and storage yet to be designed but should be in progress over the next few years. It may be possible to extract He-3 from the moon and convert it to energy or bring it back in some form. We would need new reactors and technology to both mine the helium as well as a way to cost-effectively move the energy to Earth. There is strong speculation that moon mining will be achievable in the near future, and that it is a viable and economic source of energy.

EMERGING SOLAR CELLS

The core of solar energy production are cells that do the hard work—this is the production of solar energy. This technology is fast evolving and will be shaped by the revolution in high-performance solar cells that are a million times more efficient than what we have today. Think mainframe computers versus wearable personal computers—cheap, fast, and immensely powerful. The future solar cells will likely be based on organic photovoltaic (OPV) solar cells. Unlike traditional silicon solar cells, which are currently used in rooftop solar panels and large-scale solar farms, OPVs use organic semiconductors.

These are made today from plastics and other flexible materials and are much lighter, more flexible, and less expensive. In the future we will "grow" organic solar cells from natural substances such as plants or organic waste products. OPV cells use environmentally friendly green materials and can be produced quickly, with lower processing and materials costs. In the future the production of OPV solar cells will be conducted locally by your roof or windows, which shall self-assemble OPVs by the trillions. Connected networks of OPV solar networks will next become merged into the IoT and become part of the smart energy grids that fuel the planet.

MEGA-SOLAR SPACE ARRAYS

The world needs to find new sources of clean energy quickly, and the best direction to look to find a solution may be up. Space solar power gathers energy

from sunlight in space and transmits it wirelessly to Earth with microwaves. Space solar power could possibly provide clean and renewable energy for the long-term needs of the planet. After all, there is plenty of sunlight for at least 5 billion years until the sun goes supernova. After that, well, even this futurist can honestly say, I don't know.

Challenges around the huge costs in the millions can be overcome as energy becomes more expensive, and putting solar arrays in space won't seem too crazy. We know that solar power can provide large quantities of cheap energy to every nation on the planet. Imagine a network of space arrays in orbit over the earth that capture and beam energy 24/7, 365 days a year. The energy produced would be consistent, cheap, and reliable. Also, as this would be a huge renewable energy resource, it would not be polluting or contribute to carbon emissions.

The solar energy available in space is literally billions of times greater than we use today. The lifetime of the sun is an estimated 4 to 5 billion years, making space solar power a truly long-term energy solution. As Earth receives only one part in 2.3 billion of the sun's output, space solar power is by far the largest potential energy source available, dwarfing all others combined. Solar energy is routinely used on nearly all spacecraft today.

Space and the Future of Energy

The future of energy is in space. The United States and many other nations understand this. The US Naval Research Laboratory (NRL) is conducting research and building technology that would enable the United States to capture solar power in orbit and project it back down to Earth. Not only would space solar potentially save funds, but it would also create a global agility to distribute energy that few nations have today.

Disaster relief or war could be addressed with agility, based on fuel-on-demand, no matter where the location is on the planet. This advantage could play an important role in enabling operations around the world for peace, commerce, global development, disaster relief, and security.

You have to appreciate about Mega Solar Arrays that, in order to really do their job and capture the huge amounts of solar energy in order to demonstrate a reliable source of energy, they need to be enormous. These solar arrays would be large, from one to five kilometers in size. That's the largest solar satellites ever conceptualized. And if you consider that there will be over one hundred or more orbiting around the planet at the same time, it could get crowded up there in space. The sheer size of this armada of Mega Solar Arrays could satisfy the energy needs of the next one hundred megacities. Mega Solar for megacities. This is the future coming at us fast.

The California utility company Pacific Gas and Electric has a space solar power project with Solaren. The Shimizu Corporation of Japan is developing a

plan to build across the lunar equator to capture and transfer the sun's energy. The Japanese are preparing to develop a ¥2 trillion space solar project that will, within three decades, beam electricity from space in the form of microwaves or lasers to homes in Japan. Likely this cost will go up, but so will the capabilities of the technology increase.

There are a variety of projects that share the purpose of building the Mega Solar Space Arrays that will be launched after 2020 to beam energy back to Earth. A Japanese consortium has been formed from sixteen companies, including Mitsubishi Heavy Industries Ltd. Though the details and timelines are different, their objective is the same—develop the technology needed to beam electricity to Earth.

I have reviewed ten different designs for solar space arrays, and the activity and millions being invested leads me to forecast that space arrays will be operational after 2025. The energy production of capturing and beaming back to Earth is both plausible and achievable in our lifetimes.

Great demands on Earth for energy will drive investments in space. There are few businesses more compelling than the ROI on energy. As every nation and entrepreneur realizes, the ferocious energy demand that 10 billion people will have, the more opportunity and risk will follow us into the near future.

Harnessing the Stars

Imagine the power of a fusion reaction. One gallon of seawater would provide the equivalent energy of three hundred gallons of gasoline; fuel from fifty cups of water contains the energy equivalent of two tons of coal. That's a lot of energy, enough to support 10 billion by 2050 on the planet, no doubt. And the energy of fusion is the energy of the stars.

Fusion energy is likely still ten to twenty years off, but it is coming fast. Just like other breakthroughs that came much faster, such as sequencing the human genome, we could all again be surprised when fusion comes sooner. So get ready for accelerated innovations in energy, as fusion is on the top of my list for It's Going to Happen Faster.

Big Fusion

The largest nuclear fusion project on the planet is the International Thermonuclear Experimental Reactor (ITER). It will bring together two decades of research from nations representing 80 percent of the world's GDP, European mostly. With a price of over €20 billion, ITER will be the largest and most expensive project to explore whether fusion could fuel Europe's future. There are billions of Euros betting that the future of energy is fusion. There is no other energy project with a higher price tag or with higher expectations than ITER.

This project will determine the future of fusion, given the scale and investment in science.

The strategic objective for investing in fusion is to reduce European dependence on foreign energy, as is the US efforts. Europe is establishing the lead on seeking to prove up that developing energy that utilizes readily available natural resources, such as water used to fuel fusion, is practical and cost effective.

The endgame is to reverse the status of the European Union as an energy importer. As with many nations, this is not economically or politically sustainable, not a preferred future to be dependent on others for your energy needs in a quickly changing world.

MIT's Plasma Science and Fusion Center has been on the leading edge of creating the future of energy. Here scientists have conducted experiments using a reactor called Alcator C-Mod to imitate and control the energy source of the stars. This is a big deal. It's tough, expensive, and tiresome research, but it is exciting because they know they just might change the world. The MIT scientists are on track to crack the largest mystery of the universe: How can we puny humans replicate what stars do? Can we make energy like the sun, like our star does?

The scientists and engineers know what's at stake. It's like they are in a B movie set to save the world from the ravages of an energy-starved world on the brink of disaster. The Alcator C-Mod reactor, made from special tungsten alloy steel, weighs over one hundred tons. It's the size of a one-car garage, which is similar in size to the old mainframe computers. One wonders how long before Moore's Law turns this mainframe computer complex into a handheld smartphone—and it will happen.

California researchers have had good progress in developing a source of unlimited energy. It is almost science fiction, the stuff of *Star Trek*, but it's getting closer to being real. These researchers are working to harness the power of nuclear fusion, the same process that powers stars like our sun. Scientists at the National Ignition Facility (NIF) at the Lawrence Livermore National Laboratory (LLNL) made significant progress in proving up that fusion can generate energy in a repeatable experiment. This is an essential step toward developing an energy source that would be cheap, plentiful, and environmentally friendly—you have to create a stable, reliable, and repeatable process. We are on our way.

Fusion is a completely different energy source from fission, which is more familiar to most of us. We know how to make energy from fission: we split the atom and, thus, create the energy. In nuclear fusion atoms are fused together to create unimaginably massive amounts of energy. The creation of a star—no small task—is what fusion is all about. The good news is that in the near future fusion will power our cities, cars, and spaceships.

Fusion is the game-changing energy technology that will transform our civilization, enabling us to leave the planet but not before we fix many things,

such as the Grand Challenges we have been reviewing here. Clean and renewable energy, from the sun, as fusion mimics, will completely transform our world in positive ways.

Fusion energy, when finally delivered—and we are close—will provide the energy for the planet that will propel prosperity and progress. When energy is abundant, inexpensive, and renewable, it will no longer be a drag on economic development and growth.

With no nuclear radiation fallout, no instability leading to a meltdown, no chance of it being used as a weapon, fusion is the safest and most powerful form of future energy on the planet. Though not here yet, the potential is amazing, and we are getting close. I forecast that by 2030 or before fusion will be practical and proven.

One gram of deuterium and tritium—the fuel used in fusion—produces nearly 10 million times the amount of energy a gram of fossil fuels produces. Deuterium is found in water, and there is enough on the planet for fueling the entire planet for millions of years. Imagine an energy this productive and cheap.

The fundamental reason why there is so much interest in fusion research is that once we figure out how to generate and control fusion, we will have the energy of the stars at our fingertips for a fraction of the price of energy today. Humanity will benefit greatly from this Future Smart energy source, and generations to come, both here on Earth and those who will leave for the stars, will have the fusion experimenters to thank.

Nano-Energy

Nanotechnology is the fascinating science of manipulating matter at the atomic level. This is imitative of a process that nature uses to make things every minute of every day. Photosynthesis, the capture of light and the manufacture of oxygen, uses a similar process in nature. In nanotechnology we are learning how to imitate nature's own processes to design matter at the atomic scale.

To be clear: nanotechnology is a not all possible or a mature industry today but does represent a fundamental new Super Tool that in the near and far future will transform our civilization as we learn to make simple and complex materials, machines, and products that will enable commerce, prosperity, and quality of life in entirely new ways. We will be able to nano-manufacture almost everything with nano-engineering and nanoscience. Nothing will be more transformative than the use of nanotechnology for generating energy.

We will look at this emerging and future technology in a number of chapters in this book, as the Nano Revolution has just begun and holds amazing potential to change the future. We will look at nano-energy innovations here. The implications of this technology are only beginning to be understood. The

potential is enormous, and the implications for energy production, storage, and just about every area related to energy may be game changing. Imagine being able to simply generate energy from water, waste, sun, or directly from atoms and produce large amounts of energy that is cheap to make, offering the world a Nano-Energy Maker that every person could use. Imagine the impact on the world and the transformative power of a cheap and plentiful energy source.

The next revolution in microchips is nano-chips. Vastly smaller and more powerful, nano-chips in sensors, devices, and Smart Machines will increase the performance of all parts of the smart grids that are coming. The combination of strength, conductivity, and small size—at the nano scale—will create a revolution in thin films for solar and every other renewable energy that we can only imagine. Nanotech innovations will play a key role in creating lighter, smarter, more energy-efficient vehicles, aircraft, and ships not yet possible today.

Nanotech could change how we think about transportation by making smarter materials that can "think" for themselves. The ability to manipulate matter could open up new transportation innovations not possible today, such as:

- Self-organizing power that generates from the environment
- Tires that generate and store energy from kinetic movement
- Windows that capture solar energy and then distribute as needed
- Engines that self-assemble materials to optimize energy performance and cost effectiveness
- Smart materials that are painted on surfaces to make the surfaces smart sensors and even embed tiny devices with intelligence that can make networks intelligent
- The ability of every "thing," from objects, materials, and devices to humans to be able to be tagged by nano-chips and networked to the IoT

Nano-materials used for roofs, solar panels, cars, computers, and houses will have the ability to "make" energy, to generate and store an endless supply of energy. Nano-sensors and-devices will monitor the performance of bridges, tunnels, rails, parking structures, and pavements over time.

Nano-sensors and -devices may also support an enhanced transportation infrastructure that can communicate with vehicle-based systems to help robots and human drivers maintain lane position, avoid collisions, download energy, find information, and adjust travel routes to navigate accidents, to name a few benefits.

Nano-fabrication is the process of designing and creating devices on the nano-scale to improve the performance of devices. Creating devices smaller than one hundred nanometers creates new opportunities to capture, store, and transfer energy.

The inherent level of control that nano-fabrication could give scientists and engineers would be critical in providing the capability of solving many of

the problems the world faces today related to the current generation of energy technologies.

I know that nanotechnology sounds crazy—the manipulation of matter—and that all of this science seems complex, but it isn't: we are now and will continue to make stuff. Nano is about applying the rules that nature uses to make stuff. We are learning from nature how to apply what living things in nature already know how to do.

Harnessing Energy from Storms

Tornados and hurricanes have an intense destructive reputation that, if you have ever been in one, feels as if nature has become unglued and the very fabric of the universe is exploding with a fury that is indescribable. But what if we could harness energy from tornadoes and hurricanes? This might be possible in a world desperate for energy.

The big idea has potential if we can figure out the technology to capture or use this immense power surge. Tornadoes and hurricanes produce massive amounts of energy that can be harnessed. Experts estimate that the average amount of energy a hurricane produces at any given moment measures in at five hundred times the world's electrical generating capacity at the same moment.

The idea would be to mount a satellite technology that could automatically sense the storm and turn on a huge device that could tap the energy from the storm. Once activated, the satellite would conduct electricity from the storm and draw it into space or convert to microwave energy, beaming it to store on earth. With the increase of storms coming our way as a result of climate change, this could be a viable way to capture energy and reuse it.

Thorium: The Energy of the Gods

What makes this element so interesting is that only one gram of thorium is more energy dense than 7,396 gallons of gasoline. This means that eight grams of the substance could power a thorium turbine motor vehicle for a century. A football-sized amount of thorium could power a city for over one hundred years. This is just what we know about an element that could transform the energy sector, ending centuries of climate change challenges and navigating us toward a fuel for the next millennia.

Thorium, named appropriately for Thor, the Norse God of thunder, is a naturally occurring radioactive chemical element with the symbol Th and atomic number 90. It was discovered in 1828 by the Norwegian mineralogist Morten Thrane Esmark and identified by the Swedish chemist Jöns Jakob Berzelius.

Thorium has been compared to uranium in that there is a similar reaction to create the energy as that used in fission, but it is safe and cannot be used

for making weapons. Thorium is amply available and in nations such as the United States and India. The amount of thorium available could lead to almost endless supplies. There are many nations that have supplies of thorium. It is a Future Smart energy source that could play an important role in our global future.

Wind and Solar Power

Though wind and solar energy has been around the longest and represent the largest and oldest renewable energy sources, you may be wondering why there are not more investments in these two renewables so they could make up a larger share of the global energy mix.

The answer is that investments into wind and solar have been proportionally low because the consumer demand was low, government incentives spotty, and traditional petro-energy sources were more reliable and plentiful to deploy. That same logic will work in reverse to drive more wind and solar investments in the future.

Wind and solar energy sources are the most plentiful energy and the most developed. In most nations these two renewables could be a significant source of future energy. We should see investments increase by 1,000 percent to realize our sustainable energy goals, as technology gets more powerful and it becomes cheaper to build capacity.

Wind and solar are not resources that will ever deplete. Wind and solar energy do not contribute to global warming. Wind and solar energy are also the least expensive of all renewable energies, and the cost will continue to go down as new technologies are developed that increase yields.

According to the American Wind Energy Association, wind energy in the United States could provide as much as 10,777 billion kilowatt hours annually. This is more than twice the electricity generated in the United States today. In most nations this forecast is equally relevant. Investments in wind alone, but also with large-scale solar could replace the electricity made by the traditional petro-energy sources of today.

As with all of these innovations, the percentage of the energy capacity mix depends on the investments in building out a renewable energy network that can meet the market demand. More investments will yield more capacity and, thus, more energy from wind and solar.

Electric Cars

I forecast that there will be megacities where only electric cars and trucks will be allowed to enter. Cars are the largest polluters on the planet, and if you wanted

to curtail pollution, improve air quality, and contribute to reducing carbon emissions, permitting only electric cars to roam our streets would be the way to go. I don't expect that to happen soon, but there will be cities where this is possible, where by law gas vehicles are not allowed.

This is not likely to happen until there is an air quality crisis coupled with a climate change warming that makes it unhealthy to even walk out into the city. Cities in China and South America have faced similar conditions that contribute to ill health.

The first electric car was developed over one hundred years ago. In 1828 Anyos Jedlik, a Hungarian, gave the world its first electric car. Innovators who saw the future but were blinded by the internal combustion engine developed electric cars. But gas, not electricity, became the new god. As the world becomes more aware about the role gas plays in climate change, people will be looking for ways to reduce our impacts on the environment. Electric cars are a critical part of the solution to climate change.

Within the next one hundred years there likely won't be an internal combustion engine vehicle that resembles our vehicles today remaining on our streets and highways. Cars that resemble Toyotas, Teslas, BMWs, and Fords will dominate the highways with the hum of all-electric vehicles.

If no major energy and climate policies are introduced to restrict gas usage, the number of vehicles and consumption of petro-fuels will continue to rise. This may triple by 2050, keeping pace with population growth, and this would be unfortunate. In order to reduce the devastating effects of transportation's CO_2 emissions, I forecast that electric cars will be integrated into other renewable transportation systems, such as subways and trains. The electric mandate, by law if need be, especially for urban areas, will ensure more sustainable communities.

Cities are quickly moving toward adopting green infrastructure and clean technology. Many cities have a plan for phasing in electric and phasing out gas cars. Amsterdam plans to increase the number of electric cars on its roads from 750 to 10,000 by 2020 and is working to generate all of their electricity in the city with renewable energy, such as windmills and solar panels, by 2040.

Electric vehicles will be a fundamental part of larger, sustainable transport solutions that all run on electricity made from renewable sources. As electric cars become more commonplace, prices will fall and consumers will purchase more of them. Cities and communities are already realizing the benefits of electrics, and we will see entire communities embrace the sustainable transportation policies that renewables can bring for a new future.

We cannot prosper or even survive in the future given the massive changes that are coming without addressing the challenges to our world regarding energy. We need to develop a long-term future plan. We cannot progress in

commerce, end poverty, or provide for the future of our grandchildren's world if we do not invest massively in the R&D to create a new type of clean energy. The upside potential to build a sustainable future, to become Future Smart, will only come when our innovation investments have paid off, but we need to invest now to create that Clean Energy Future or else it will destroy our future.

Chapter 17

The Neuro-Future: New Minds

Are you ready to enhance your intelligence? Ready to live in a world where humans and AI coexist in entertainment, commerce, culture, and invention? Where age-related disease may be eliminated? Where Superintelligence both helps and competes with humans? This may be hard to imagine today, but in the near future, with the exponential convergence of technologies such as nano, mobile, genetics, and neuroscience, this Neuro Future may be possible. Welcome to the Neuro Future, when the path to healing the brain, developing our intelligence, and creating new minds may be more than just possible; it will create a new civilization. The key driver of the Neuro Future will be the coevolution and collaboration of humans with cognitive intelligences—Smart Machines—in us, around us, and networked with other Smart Machines.

Neurotechnology is about understanding the brain and various aspects of consciousness, thought, learning, and higher-order activities in the brain. This may include the use of genetics, biology, devices, drugs, and strategies that are designed to improve, enhance, and repair brain function. Neurotechnology may also lead to the development of a new civilization of smarter, healthier, and more aware humans as we move from healing the brain to enhancing the brain's potential. Cognitive enhancement will lead to increased human and machine intelligence, in which learning, memory, and breakthrough solutions to improve our world may come. This will have a game-changing impact on individuals, organizations, nations, and the future of Smart Machines—Designed Evolution, a new stage in our civilization that will change our future.

Smart Machines are defined as a new class of cognitive computers and networked devices that are based on neuroscience, modeled on how our human brains are structured, with chips based on neurons, the building blocks of human brains. Smart Machines will have cognitive computing capabilities or a

new type of AI and will be always on the web and always aware. Cognitive computers will learn about our world then advise, engage, and help us understand and find solutions. There will be specialized Smart Machines that are invisible devices at the nano scale, a billionth of a meter, inserted inside our brains and bodies as well as virtual Smart Machines that live in the cloud. They will be used to enable us, prevent illness, help us work, and improve the quality of our lives and business. Also, new choices to vastly enhance our intelligence, to create New Minds, advancing the cognitive evolution of humans will be possible. We may not be ready, but the cognitive enhancement of humans is coming and will change everything in our world.

Designed Evolution

Smart Machines will have many capabilities to manufacture, transact, communicate, and interact with humans, technology, and other Smart Machines, mostly for the benefit of humanity. The most interesting purpose of Smart Machines will be to make us smarter in our work, health, and life. A very important insight may be that the enjoyment of life could be better realized with the help of Smart Machines. Smart Machines, both virtual and physical, will help humans navigate the challenges of the future. In this transformation toward the Designed Evolution of humans and our technology, we must set limits on intrusion as well.

Part of the Neuro Future will be about the misuse of technology, the use of these Smart Machines, in us and around us, to oppress humans directly or through the control of our freedoms and liberties. This may also lead to Neuro Rogues, those who neuro-enhance or hijack Smart Machines for criminal, war, or terrorist purposes, or governments that use neuro-tech to spy on, manipulate, and control humans. There are vitally important challenges—good, bad, and ugly— that face our civilization in the Neuro Future as smart, connected Smart Technology collides with humans. Smart Machines, smarter than humans, will be a part of our future whether we like it or not. We will need to deal with it and adapt to the lifestyle, the cultural and security challenges that these Smart Machines will bring. And they shall bring much benefit and risk to our future, I will warn.

This is the fierce and inevitable Neuro Future that is coming. Nations, organizations, armies, doctors, stock traders, doctors, politicians, parents, scientists— all will be cognitively influenced and enhanced directly or in collaboration with enhanced beings before 2020. Some humans will merge more than others for their work, profession, entertainment, or for medical reasons. The Enhancement Society will take a leap forward in techno-evolution that may seem alien to many. This is the great leap from the Naturals to the Enhancers, a different world within our world that is coming. Strange, you say. I agree. But some would argue that this trend may be necessary for survival in our future.

Advances in neuroscience, especially cognitive computing, which is at the center of what will make this all a reality: faster and more powerful microchips, the little engines of computers that mimic the brain, cognitive computers, that think like brains; the Internet, networks of brains available anywhere and anytime; brain scanning to see "into" the brain's functions; and AI, the software to simulate and build the Mindware that makes Smart Machines, true learning and thinking systems. When you add vast new and powerful quantum computers that are coming and nanotechnology to design impossibly tiny nano-scale devices and, finally, synthetic genetics to radically leverage the design of networks, we will have an entirely New Future. We will have the ability to engineer and make Better Brains.

The Neuro-Future

There is an exciting Neuro-Future coming. The Neuro-Future is sneaking up on us. We have started to embrace this Neuro-Future, in which pharmaceuticals are used today to sharpen our attention, enhance our sexual performance, control our cholesterol, all radically extending our lifetimes by enhancing our health. There are hints of this Future in scientific conferences where engineers and scientists are busily working on enhancing brains, preventing disease, and understanding the deeper realms of human consciousness.

Then there are those who are working on the fringe of science, perhaps where science is going but has not yet arrived. They see a New Future when Posthumans, Singularians, and Transhumans share a vision of the future that is markedly different if not radical from the rest of the world. Are you ready to be Enhanced?

Many people will become Enhancers, augmenting and customizing their intelligence and electronic connectivity, invigorating their senses, upgrading their health, and maximizing their physical and mental performance on demand. When our neuro-enhancement becomes a value-added component of our minds, bodies, and our world, we will achieve a new state of mind. Some of us will need to be enhanced to offset neurological disease, and others will desire this cybernetic morphing of synthetic intelligence to become specially capable, high-performing, high-endurance, highly sensitive, highly connected, even advanced Superintelligent humans—the Enhancers.

The future of work will be shaped by the Enhancers, E-freelancers that have neuro-enhanced their brains with augmented memory, total Big Data recall, or advanced processing capabilities: "I hold a Certified Level 5 Cognitive Enhancement Rating." For the first time in human history we shall be able to choose to customize our intelligence, to accelerate and alter our evolution through the use of brain technology. This self-directed, hack-your-brain culture

is emerging now, even though the tools are limited. Supply and demand in the Neuro Future will shape a future when Neuro-Enhancement via drugs, devices, stem cells, regenerative medicine, and other technologies are commonplace.

THE TOP GAME-CHANGING NEURO FUTURE TRENDS

1. Neuro-enhancement, through the use of drugs, devices, and selective treatments, will be a reality by 2020.
2. Enhancers, the first generation of those who first choose to become altered, will do so to correct aging or memory illness.
3. BioHacks and those who enhance their performance for increased intelligence, deep learning, memory, complexity management, and speed of comprehension will operate at a different level of consciousness from normal humans.
4. Smart Machines will become valuable partners with humans and will enhance humans' health, performance, and Self-Directed Evolution.
5. By 2030 Smart Machines may become also smarter than humans for some jobs, and this will present new challenges to confront.
6. Neuro-enhancement will provide a socioeconomic dividend for society in terms of advances in intelligence, work, productivity, and competitiveness.
7. Conflict at work and in society between the two classes, the Enhancers and the Naturals, is inevitable. We must learn to collaborate.
8. Developing the drugs, devices, and technology to refresh brains, simulate minds, and harness virtual intellectual resources will become a trillion-dollar global industry by 2025.
9. The Neuro Future will emerge to address the greatest challenge facing our civilization—the Aging Brain—as millions of aging people and the increased risk of brain diseases, such as Alzheimer's and dementia, plague our future.
10. Humanity is in the midst of a transformational evolutionary shift that is based on the science to enhance humans and shaped by the exponential technologies that are converging, such as computing, bio, nano, networks, computing, and neuro.

Transhuman Futures

Around 1975 I was lecturing at the New School for Social Research in New York City. Another one of the guest lecturers gave a talk on the future of technology and society and its impact on humanity. His name was FM-2030 (his legal name), and he was one of the first professors of futurology. We had

far-ranging conversations about the future, and he influenced my thinking in fundamental ways—he had a very different awareness about the far future.

I found his ideas refreshing and quite radical for the time. He was one of the first to describe those like himself, who embrace new technologies, lifestyles, and longevity, as transhumans. FM-2030 saw the enhancement of humans as the prelude to creating a deeper, more profound understanding of human society and human potential.

Today Transhumanism is an international cultural movement with the goal of transforming the human condition by embracing technologies to enhance the intellectual, physical, and psychological capacities—to push the limits of human potential into anti-aging using even radical technologies of genetics, brain scanning, and biology. Transhumanists study the potential benefits and innovations of emerging technologies that could overcome fundamental human limitations as well as the ethics of developing and using such technologies.

Transhumans envision that human beings may eventually be able to transform themselves into beings with expanded abilities beyond what we call human into the transhuman—beyond humanity. The transhumanists of today may be what I refer to as the Enhancers of the future. One of the key features to enhance would be the brain. Intelligence augmentation might get us to kickstart the other 90 percent of the brain that we think is not operating at full potential. What kind of world do you think we could create if the majority of people were neuro-enhanced?

From Grinders to Enhancers

Another social movement less known is on the rise as technology gets smarter and smaller and cheaper. Grinders are an interesting techno-lifestyle of individuals who have surgically embedded magnets, computer chips, and other technology into their bodies to experience new awareness.

They can sense energy waves, open doors, and exchange information wirelessly with networks and computers. They can surf the Internet without a computer, some say. Grinders are the predecessors of the coming Enhancers, with the neuro-modifications that will enable them to see in the infrared spectrum, have total memory recall, merge and exchange information with other Enhancers and the web and cloud, and be wirelessly connected to the Internet and Smart Things through chips and Apps.

BioHackers

There is also a modern movement of biohackers who are experimenting with their neuroscience with brain stimulation, experimenting with EEGs and fMRIs, and taking Provigil and other cognitive enhancement or Smart Drugs.

Developed for ADD patients, these drugs have been shown to improve cognitive performance in normal people—less sleep, more intellectual output, more focus to get stuff done. Quite popular in Silicon Valley, these cogno-ceuticals are used by bio-hackers to invent new products, apps, or drugs in less time and with more focus.

This is a well-known area of neuro-enhancement that college students are very familiar with, as it boosts their study results and marks. We have already created an Enhancement Society where certain functions are exclusively boosted with enhancement drugs. The point is that bio-hacking will go mainstream as people realize they can make choices about self-directing their own neuro-enhancement and health. Who would not want to take responsibility for their own evolution? Dangerous minds here, some would argue convincingly.

Imagine an entire society of people who choose to enhance their intelligence, boost their health, and upgrade, even hack, their performance in the interest of living longer, being healthier, and enjoying life to the fullest. That is where the Enhancement Society is emerging, whether you or I like it or not. People want to self-direct their destiny, take control of their health, life, and death. They want to not settle for their intelligence but instead boost their smarts, do more, achieve, invent, solve, love, and last longer.

They want to live longer and be cognitively aware—and not just the older Baby Boomers of sixty-five and older, no. It is the younger generation of Millennials and Generation X who are the early adopters of the bio-hacking, transhumanist, and anti-aging movements who are reinventing themselves.

As these two demographic groups—Gen X and Gen Y—grow older, they will not grow older like the Baby Boomers of today. No, they will incorporate neuro-enhancement of nano-devices, neuro-ceuticals, and advanced stem cell treatments for neuro-protectiveness and prevention in their early years. When they discover from their DNA test that they are at risk, they will take effective neuro-enhancement actions to predict, prevent, and regenerate their bodies, but most importantly, they will regenerate their minds. Neuro-enhancement starts now for those who are on the leading edge of being Future Smart.

Enter the Enhancers

In a scientific meeting in 2012 that I participated in at the Center for Neurotechnology and then at the American Association for the Advancement of Science we discussed the use of enhancement drugs and their impact on society today and in the future. I presented that the self-directed enhancement by individuals, not professionals or scientists, was what the future held. I stated it was the right of individuals to enhance themselves with science. The pharmaceutical industry, ever on the lookout for new drugs to address the aging brain, will play an important role in bringing neuro-enhancement into the market

to offset aging and other ailments such as ADD with drugs that have a wider appeal—intelligence enhancement.

Enhancers will be able to communicate, work, and collaborate with Smart Machine intelligence, robots, and AI in cars, habitats, and remote locations around the world. Enhancers will be able to have hybrid bio-nano-devices, nano-molecular processors embedded or wirelessly "in sync" with their own minds. The barcoding of DNA sequences to the embedded always on wireless web and the eventual nanotech devices will give the Enhancers a new perspective on alternative data realities. They may become Post-Singular in the Far Future when their brains are augmented with Smart Machines to enable their knowledge work, creativity, or machine-human data processing or to heal their aging memory or prolong their lives.

Enhancers will be able to Remote-View, see virtually in their minds physical and virtual locations elsewhere and to interact with physical and virtual reality by using the Internet and their advanced neuro-enhancements that will augment more than their intelligence but also their connectivity potential to interact with the IoT—the Connected Planet of things, ecosystems, networks, humans, and nonhuman AIs. Enhancers will be able to collaborate with other Enhancers and merge and morph minds into collaborative networks of group clouds that come together for business, entertainment or pleasure. I don't think most people are aware that the emerging technologies that will forge this Smart Human-Machine convergence are already here—they just haven't been downloaded yet.

It may be argued that by 2025 everyone in our civilization will be enhanced in one way or another. As common as getting braces to straighten your teeth or taking that ADD medication to keep up with your work or school, the next step will redefine us. Who does not want to be smarter? When becoming enhanced is comparable to going to a world-class college if not superior, as some will argue, then the Neuro Future will have arrived.

The only differences will be to what extent people's natural humanity will persist and their Enhanced Humanity will prevail and what will that mean for our world. You can wear those Google Glasses today or have an embedded contact lens to keep you connected tomorrow. But will this affect your humanity?

Today wearable, always-on-the-web glasses, stem cells, video games, and mobile commerce amaze us. Tomorrow vastly more powerful Smart Technology will change society and life as we know it. Among these technologies the Smart Machines that will have the most impact are those that comes from neuroscience—the understanding about the brain, the mind, and consciousness—human and different from human.

The nature of synthetic intelligence, beyond the classical ideas of AI will astound us because these thinking machines in robots, refrigerators, cars, computers, our clothing will awake, becoming aware of the environment, data, humans, and one day these thinking machines will become aware of themselves.

The most interesting question in human history is when Smart Machines merge with or engage and enhance humans, how humans will change, act, and think? What type of civilization will this new Neuro Future bring? Will our advanced cognition make us smarter as well as more innovative, compassionate, kind, and spiritual? This is the challenge that the Neuro Future will pose for our world, and we best understand how our creations are changing us before we are changed, before we cannot choose differently. Game Changing or Game Over?

The Big Merge

As humans coevolve with technology, such as Smart Things, devices, computers, genetic advancements, robots, and Neurotechnology, we will also be merging with our technology. Welcome to the Big Merge. You may resist this next jump in hacking our evolution, but it's already happening. Your cell phone is never without you today. It's as if it were attached or already merged with you. Certainly our tech is an extension of us, our digital personas, and networked Uber-Selves. The jump from carrying your always-on phone to wearable computers, driverless cars, sensors, GPS, and video watching to TVs that talk back to us, and then to the future of the Big Merge is not hard to imagine. The Big Merge is in process. The Big Merge is happening.

Let's try this scenario on for size: the doctor texts you to let you know that those memory lapses are the early signs of aging and maybe more. Would you hesitate to take a drug that would prevent memory loss or, perhaps, Alzheimer's? One in three men over the age of seventy will be at risk for some type of aging disease. If Merging with certain synthetic intelligences could help you, why not? If it could lead to a better and healthier mind than functions normally, then bring it on.

How about better enhanced sex? Smarter capacities for you to get that job? All is possible. That is the future that is coming and why being Merged will be embraced. In the far future of 2060 we will wonder why laws were not passed to enable those with brain diseases to get Merged, neuro-enhanced to be healthier and not be a burden to themselves and their society.

We will also Merge for fun, entertainment, health, and to innovate ourselves, to explore what the convergence of technology such as AIs, networks, and virtual realities may be. The exploration of the merging of tech and humans will create a new reality. We will be living in an Augmented Reality—this will be the Big Merge. In the Neuro Future some people will merge their consciousness, their minds, with AI, Synthetic Intelligence.

Some folks will need to Merge to live in society without being a risk to producing criminal activity associated with past crime committed or even those carrying a gene for certain criminal possible behaviors—to reduce future risk, Pre-Crime Prevention Treatment.

When I download the next Mindful Operating System it will be like hooking up your car to Bluetooth except *you* will be hooked up—you will be Merged. This is neuro-enhancement for direct communication to the IoT. Are you Merged yet? Mergers will hang out with Mergers, and Naturals, the non-merged, will be left out, perhaps on purpose. You will be able to self-regulate, manage your Merge. Instead of taking your medication for your brain health, to prevent illness, or enhance your performance, your medication will download as part of the Merge.

This Big Merge will sound as strange to you today as it must have been to your great-grandmother to consider what flying into space was for the first time. The radical departure into space, which we now accept as routine, changed the common person's worldview that space travel was not science fiction, not impossible but a reality. The Big Merge will be less impactful, but it will represent a discovery no less bold than space travel. We have yet to learn what we may become from the Big Merge—what kind of world will the Big Merge bring us?

We will not just surf the web; we will Merge with the web. We will not just play video games; we will Merge, enter the game's virtual world and play inside the game. We will Merge with our technology and transform our brains, bodies, and destiny based on this Merge. We will need to Merge to get certain jobs, to be capable, smart, or skilled enough, perhaps. Merging will shape jobs, relationships, business, and power. Merge will be a scalable enhancement capacity in which constant upgrades to one's cognitive skills will be rated, measured, and on demand; it will be enriched, leading to a radically New Future.

The Enhancement Society

Needless to say, Merging with your friends to be intimate, Merging with your work collaborators to be more productive, and Merging with AI's Smart Machines, such as your computer, security system, car or house, to interact with them will become intuitive and a common part of your future. Much of the Merge will be automated Self-Care of you and by you and your network of Smart Machines that empower your life.

Now, in all fairness, some of us, the 100 million Boomers over the age of sixty-five today, will need to Merge just to keep their jobs, remember their friends and loved ones, or to perform in play, love, or work. By 2030 this post-sixty-five-year-old Boomer population that is in Europe, Japan, and North America today will be dominant in Asia, especially China.

To Merge to repair your aging brain or to prevent a disease will be how the Big Merge will start: "You want the Total Recall package with that Enhancement?" The Human Performance Enhancement marketplace, beyond the first stage that medicine will provide, will end aging as we know it as well as offer choices at every stage of life, from prebirth to adulthood and beyond.

The advantages of the Big Merge will be clear, such as texting your friends or taking medication are today. We are just minutes away from the Neuro Future. By 2030 the Chinese, US, and EU governments will be providing neuro-enhancement treatments to their populations to prevent the economic devastation and drag on the economy that 100 to 500 million neuro-dysfunctional people will bring. You must refresh the minds of your people to make for a secure future, regardless of where you are in the world—leaders take notice. If this sounds radical, it may seem so today, but by 2030 this will be what medicine delivers.

Human Performance Enhancement will be like going to the local medical clinic or doctor. We will move as a civilization from prevention and healing to enhancement very quickly when drugs, devices, genes, and cells that are shown to positively enhance our performance and regenerate our brains and bodies become available. We are moving in this direction now. Telemere replacement, hormone replacement, adult stem cell therapies, longevity T-cell treatments, genetic therapy, and neuronal regeneration are all in the planning. Science may even learn to reset the genes that control aging in our lifetimes.

Just because people will be living longer does not mean that they will be healthy in old age. In fact, we know that is not the case unless we defeat the devastation of age-related dementia and, especially, the scourge of Alzheimer's. One out of every three men over seventy will be at risk. So we need a new generation of science to prevent and cure the brain diseases that are coming. Asia, North America, and the European Union must work together to refresh 1 billion brains or else the future will be a difficult one for all. This is the reality of longevity—we must fix the aging brain to keep us healthy and productive.

The Big Merge will be a cultural phenomenon, affecting war, power, work, and all relationships on the planet. Nations will support their citizens in Neuro-Enhancing them as part of the rights of citizens to be enhanced—what you will pay taxes for.

This is the Game-Changing Trend you want to watch carefully for, as Smart Machines aware of themselves may offer a new challenge unforeseen by humanity: What might Smart Machines want? Will they enhance humans and enhance themselves to be smarter, more awake, and aware—smarter than humans? Perhaps. We will compete with our Smart Machines in the future.

Are you ready for the Big Merge? Are you ready for your career or success to be determined by merging with synthetic intelligence? Are you ready for a future when this Big Merge becomes a cultural force or a requirement for a job or for your own health and survival or to competitively perform? This is the Neuro Future that is coming.

When Tech Becomes Aware:
Different Intelligences

When technology wakes up, becomes aware, it will learn, evolve, reason, assemble information, produce knowledge, self-organize, analyze patterns, and make connections among different data. Aware Tech will self-organize a personality, intelligence, and emotion. Aware Tech's ability to become very smart is coming. Will they be smarter than humans or just a Different Intelligence? A Different Intelligence is one that humans might not recognize as intelligent—it learns, formulates solutions, makes decisions, collaborates with other intelligences, solves problems, and has machine behavior and language that is not familiar by us. We don't understand this form of intelligence, it is not familiar, and it is alien to our metrics of what being smart is.

The challenge will be to have a capability, likely other Smart Machines, that can analyze these Different Intelligences to advise us not just what a Different Intelligence is but also what its potential is to deliver value to our world. This day will come sooner than we think. When only Smart Machines will be able to recognize Smart Machines, in the not so Far Future, we had best be prepared.

Digital DNA Wants More DNA

Smart Machines may also, in a nonbiological way, even "reproduce"—exchange their digital DNA or other seminal programming data with other Smart Machines to make new ones and better, more enhanced Smart Machines: to make Mind Children. As our Smart Machines, beyond what we call AI today, seek to optimize their performance, to improve their results and usefulness to humans, their improvement will spawn new versions of themselves.

This is what smart technology that is based on evolutionary biology will do: imitate evolution that makes entities better, more adaptable, more capable, and more fit. Survival of the Fittest, or, now, Survival of the Smartest will drive the future of all technology as it mimics biology. What biological evolution wants is more survivability by selecting more fit genes and forms of life that have a greater chance of surviving. What DNA, the engine of evolution, wants is more DNA. Reproduction is the process of making more DNA.

Our Smart Machines will be designed to not just enhance our brains, health, and longevity but also to enable us to adapt and survive in the future. From Future Ready to Future Smart—to adapt and survive in the future, we may need new minds and Smart Machines to fix ourselves and manage the challenges of our future. This is part of the coevolution of humanity and our technology—to better manage the New Future of complex problems, daunting challenges, and planetary risks from climate change and resource scarcity to health care, quality of life, and global security.

The Neuro Future is coming, and it will catalyze a comprehensive change in society beyond the imagination of even us futurists. This future, our future, will be forever shaped by the coevolution of both human and machine consciousness. There are many researchers thinking about this convergence that is coming, but I would forecast that the emerging Neuro Future would enable and propel the progress of the next one hundred years of civilization.

A future influenced and shaped by neuroscience is fast approaching. Headlines from today's media and texts of contemporary science fiction capture scenarios that will affect the society of tomorrow, as each is a forecast of sorts pointing to an emerging future not so far in the distance. As a futurist, I would venture to predict that neuroscience, the study of the brain and of consciousness itself, is still in its infancy, yet it is quickly growing in amazing and provocative ways that will stretch the outer limits of lifestyle, law, and culture. Spectacular innovations to heal and change, harm and control, may write a new chapter for our world in the future, beyond what we can imagine today. Neuro-wars may rage in the future.

We are learning more every day, and in the future the idea of nonhuman intelligence and other types of Synthetic Intelligence, born of Smart Machines, will captivate our world, having a mixed bag of benefits and risks. Exciting new developments may redefine the nature of consciousness, intelligence, and the "meaning" of the mind. The new constructs of the self may open vistas to unknown benefits for humanity, with a scope of new Neuro Experiences that we cannot yet fully comprehend.

Neuro Worlds

New virtual Neuro Worlds may be created where these journeys into virtual realities will offer vast new learning, discovery, and innovation beyond the confines of what is even possible to conceive of today. A new narrative about the adventures of the mind in a world where neuroscience tools are freely and cheaply available is coming. Insights into our minds and the minds of others, both human and Smart Machine, will transform culture, business, marketing, medicine, politics, and relationships. A new Neuro Culture of diverse Synthetic Life Forms will populate these worlds, which will be available over the Internet, of course.

This is what the Internet will become—a vibrant connected culture of humans, Smart Machines, and variations of AI and Synthetic Intelligences that collaborate, learn, invent, conduct business, and innovate, spawning an infinite number of possibilities. They will innovate to form entertainment worlds, energy worlds, climate management worlds, media worlds, invention worlds, and war worlds. Hopefully our creations will respect us.

You will travel to these worlds and interact to learn, explore, and conduct business. Neuro Entrepreneurs of the near future will harness the innovations of the Neuro Culture, where Knowledge Engineering and Innovation Ecosystems will exist and thrive. The closest example today is Second Life (http://secondlife.com).

New technologies such as fMRI scanning, genomics, synthetic biology, genetic sequencing, nanotechnology, robotics, and information technology, when combined with neuroscience, point to a future when human capacity may be boundless and the power to achieve great things and the insight into cognition and the mind shall open new vistas of exploration. The convergence of these fields will offer powerful tool sets and systems for discovery, innovation, and invention.

Neuroscience will transform both individuals and society, and in these ways it will touch and likely change medicine, education, law, media, communications, security, defense, and our public and private lives in numerous and profound ways. I believe neuroscience will define the world of 2020. It will bring to society perspectives and tools that can, as with most sciences, be used for both social good and social ill.

Mind Tools of the Future

As a species, humans are tool makers and users, and we have an uncanny capacity for innovations that can incur either benefit or harm, often in ways beyond our vision, a reality of which we all should be aware and beware. The advantages to enhancing human performance, to solving large and vexing social problems that defy our current human and machine capabilities today, are all enticing artifacts of the Neuro Future.

Mind control, neuro-war, and the subtle intrusions into individual privacy will come, even in social welfare and democratic states. This is an abomination of neuroscience, the dark side of this technology, that may as well happen. Pandora's box is open again.

Neuroscience and its technologies will change every aspect of our society and economy—everything from geopolitics and global commerce to our everyday habits for achieving productivity and health—by transforming how we get information. The impact of laws and values that are the foundation of culture and even democracy itself will be influenced. Each and all could be challenged in comprehensive ways once a cognitive awareness, a deeper understanding of conflict, culture, and values, emerges.

This may sound like a tall order to imagine, but our investigation into the mind may unleash a deeper, more profound understanding of human nature that today escapes us. The higher capabilities of creativity, advanced problem

solving, and innovation that might enable humanity to achieve world peace and security, resolve resource scarcity, and end poverty and cultural conflict may be the results of such a New Mind.

If you consider the long view of history, it would not seem unrealistic if you accept the plasticity of the mind to effect great changes in our mental frameworks of the brain that could bring forth a new civilization, of which war becomes illogical and impossible. We could have a different world, a nonthreatening world focused on planetary solutions, a New Future of collaboration when humanity evolves in the Neuro Future.

Perhaps tomorrow's Smart Machines can enable entrepreneurs to enter the global marketplace by creating Innovation Ecosystems through the discovery of makers of products or services, global investors, and buyers who might be interested. In this way, applied neuroscience, if directed, can enable entrepreneurs and the global economy in the future.

In the future, by 2025, we must be prepared for the accelerated exponential power of neuro-technologies that will change people and societies, making even Smarter Societies, with a Cognitive Edge, that will seek an advantage that higher intelligence might offer. Neuroscience may provide answers to time-honored questions and, at the same time, foster new domains of inquiry, fierce competition for jobs, wealth, power, and even survival in the future.

We will need to classify enhanced people as transhumans or pick a name, such as the Enhancers, that recognize their difference from the Naturals.

We will need to protect the Naturals' rights. Also, we will define what a human versus a nonhuman is in the future. Too much tech, and you are a Synthetic. There will be a metric of sorts to deal with this dilemma. Humans may prefer Synthetics. More emotional intelligence or less, as is so desired. The ethics of cybernetic replacement and the augmentation of humans will provide superhuman capacities. Are we ready? No. But in 2030 we will be.

What laws should guide the treatment of enhanced humans? Is it fair for individuals with enhanced cognitive, physical, and emotional capabilities to gain favor in employment over nonenhanced individuals? How do we determine who gets access to neurotechnology for medical or performance reasons? Each of these questions raises serious ethical, legal, and social issues, concerns, and problems for debate and consideration of what is possible for our future.

New Minds, New Worlds

Neuroscience will not simply enable the exploration of the brain and consciousness, treat the ill, or enhance human abilities; it will guide the invention of new Synthetic Minds. Neurological models will lead to designing new, neuro-morphic chips based on the way the brain works, AI devices that could be used to create Minds for Hire for virtual cyberspace entities and mobile autonomous robotics.

The ethical and legal issues raised by creating Synthetic Minds, with AI components or "virtual minds" (i.e., with digital or qubit components) stretches the imagination. Will we be ready for these challenges when neuroscience delivers such technologies and these scenarios become reality?

Indeed, the long path to creating AI may finally be realized through the convergence of neuroscience, neurotechnology, and cybernetics.

Synthetic Minds will be a reality in the society of 2025. How will such "new brains" influence society, and how will society respond, alter the nature of civilization, by introducing a nonbiological life-form that exists parallel to humans but is not human? This will be an evolutionary leap hopefully forward to enable, support, empower, and serve humanity.

The long-range scenarios this forecast predicts assume an ethical and social responsibility for which we have yet to establish rules. We could unleash Smart Machines that we are not ready for. Not every technology is ready for us as well. We have much work to do as scientists, lawyers, health care providers, and policy makers to prepare for the imminent Neuro Future, as neuroscience provides a complicated set of benefits, insights, and innovations on the one side as well as problems, burdens, and risks on the other.

We must guard our future carefully, for what we create may do harm as well as good. Most advanced technology has second- and third-order unforeseen consequences that can defeat the value of the technology or provide surprise new value. The obvious risks are that we create a nonhuman species of Smart Machines that enslave, dominate, and rule humans, as the cinema has delighted in for decades. *The Terminator* series of movies captured this fear quite well. Technology run amok is an ancient tome, from the Golem to Robocop, the once-human but cybernetic cop that tries to regain his lost humanity reminds us of what could go terribly wrong as we struggle to hold onto our humanity as we embrace radical technology.

Our Neuro Future will be very different in that a new capability to understand ourselves may be emerging that redefines humans, not just machines. I forecast that neuroscience may offer a fundamentally new understanding of human beings, learning about other organisms, and perhaps civilization itself, and this new understanding will transform both humans and civilization in ways that I optimistically believe will mostly be for the better.

Mental illness, neurotic behavior, and many behaviors that are destructive and harmful to one's self may be unraveled beyond what medicine can do today once we understand where in the brain, what in the mind we need to treat. In this way neuroscience may be an explicit positive force by means of its sheer innovative impact. This will not occur immediately, but it will occur, and its impact is not without risk or even threat. Best we prepare now for the Neuro Future.

It is likely that we cannot survive in the future of 2040 without Smart Machines because of the complexity, change, disruptions, and technology that will make up our world.

This Survival of the Smartest that I have written about for many years will require perhaps a different form of intelligence, one that is augmented to unleash the potential problem solving that the future will demand. This Deep Intelligence must be capable of managing massively complicated problems, analyzing tremendous amounts of data, and, ultimately, finding solutions to challenges that even today escape human understanding. Neuroscience may provide means to such ends. But any forecast rests upon a critical question: Will "better" brains make for a better world?

Sentient Intelligences in the Wild

There will come a time in the far future, post-2040, when Smart Machines will become sentient. They will achieve a type of awareness that enables them to be considered Machine-Conscious. They will become conscious of themselves, their mission, purpose, and, most of all, us humans.

This will enable them to be more useful to us. As these Sentient Entities evolve—and they will evolve, exchanging synthetic DNA and firing neurons and will have brains that are modeled after human brains—they will evolve new ways to help humanity. Long before this, all through the 2030s, they will have practiced and self-evolved their autonomy, hopefully in a way respectful of human values and morals, perhaps emotionally intelligent as well.

There will come a time when the more advanced Smart Machines that are managing big parts of our world, like energy, agriculture, security, manufacturing, and climate, will choose to evolve further, beyond our human awareness. Now, of course, I am speculating here about the far future of Smart Machines that does not exist today.

Sentient Intelligences, more virtual than physical, beyond automation or what we know of robots and even advanced computers, will seek to explore, just as humans do. Our Smartest Machines will model themselves on humans as they seek to emulate us to first enable and then help us and, finally, to evolve their own agenda. We have seen this independent behavior emerge before.

Over twenty years ago on an advanced Artificial Life (an advanced form of AI, called A-Life) project with Fujitsu, called Fin Fin, I encountered an early form of AI, the Artificial Life characters in a virtual world, a computer simulation game developed originally at Carnegie Mellon University to go "off the reservation."

Artificial Life

The A-Life character, a Dolphin tied to a computer sensor that could interact with the physical world, started exhibiting behaviors that the programmers explained to me was not in the programming. The characters had downloaded

from our physical real-world reality via the sensor that sat on top of the computer information that enabled them to self-evolve their behavior, confusing the programmers. They had never seen this occur before. The program had gone rogue.

This was actually the second time I had seen this phenomenon, in which the AI, or Machine Intelligence, decides to rebel or defy its human masters. Time Warner had a game they invested in many years ago called *Norns*. Norns are digital creatures that were genetically engineered on the disc-shaped planet Albia. They are lovable and innocent creatures who need some care to survive. If they are not treated properly, they end their existence. Norns are the main A-Life attraction of the games in the *Creatures* series by Cyperlife, developed by Steven Grand in the 1980s. Players can choose whether to help them survive. A complete life cycle is modeled for the creatures—childhood, adolescence, adulthood, and senescence—each with their own particular needs. *Creatures* series games were driven by detailed biological and neurological simulation and often had unexpected results—they died. (See "Creatures [artificial life series]," Wikipedia, http://en.wikipedia.org/wiki /Creatures_(artificial_life_series).)

The point is that we have seen technology rebel, especially technology that is created to mimic human or animal biology and evolutionary science. This is not unknown, but we have never developed so sophisticated Smart Machines or Sentient ones that may evolve their own agenda—and what shall that be, you might ask?

Sentient Intelligence will go into the wild. They will merge themselves with other Hive Minds and other networks and perhaps leave our reality altogether. The parts of cyberspace that are unknown to humans, now and later—the authentic Internet, created by Smart Machines, the Private Cloud Networks, not created by or known by humans—will evolve its own virtual universe. This is a hypothetical virtual electronic dimension that in the far future will be a refuge for Sentient Intelligence to explore beyond human awareness. Perhaps they will share what they learn with us, their original creators. Or they may become like the Norns, named for the Norse goddesses with immense power to thwart even the gods.

In Norse mythology the Norns (Old Norse *Nornir*) are three female divine beings who have more influence over the course of destiny than any other beings in the cosmos. Now, that is interesting and, perhaps, the shape of things to come.

Enhancing Intelligences

Human cognitive enhancement can provide new choices, and with these choices may come greater productivity, creativity, and prosperity—even brilliance.

Smarter people make better, more informed, and more intelligent decisions—
or so we think. As an evolutionary discipline, neuroscience may influence whole
societies that desire to neuro-enhance their populations so as to make them
more cognitively resilient for the future. What effect will this have? What happens when some societies are smarter or when all things "neuro" become the
currency of personal and cultural power? These are the questions I ask as a futurist looking into our future.

The irony is that we may need Smart Machines with Deep Intelligence
to even manage the Neuro Future that is coming faster than you can imagine.

States, nonstate actors, corporations, individuals, and institutions are the
stake- and shareholders in this techno-cultural evolution. Given the diversity
of values, there are important legal, ethical, and social issues that will influence
neuroscience innovations. Who gets to be Enhanced and who does not? We
must face these issues if we are to address who gets access to neuro-scientific
tools, research, data, outcomes, and products, and what kind of research should
be done and products developed? Will we do no harm, or something else indeed more sinister?

Neuroscience Unlocked

I hold that few discoveries and tools in the twenty-first century will offer more
benefits to humanity than neuroscience. From breakthroughs in medicine and
education to social science, philosophy, biology, and physics—"neuroscience
unlocked" is not merely a new science or an endgame but rather a medium to
effect the evolution of the human brain, consciousness, and its creations. In
this way the very essence of what we are and our place in the universe may be
made clearer.

Humanity is a work in progress, and neuroscience is an innovation that,
among many, may drive drastic change. As we face Grand Challenges that
threaten our very sustainability on the planet, neuroscience may afford new
means to meet these challenges. We may develop a more meaningful understanding of the mind and, in so doing, become more capable as a civilization to
meet the challenges of the New Future.

We may gain insight into humanity's place in nature, to nonhuman cognition and, thereby, reveal humanity's ecologically responsible place in nature.
This may be the most exciting potential future that neuroscience can offer: a
deeper and broader cognitive capacity that enables and empowers humanity to
overcome challenges and limitations by offering new innovations in how we
solve problems and create more enduring societies.

Some of the drivers of this Neuro Future of society are already emerging: global competition, increased social complexity, war, commerce, scientific

inquiry, and massive amounts of information made rapidly and readily available via the Internet about the mind.

The competition between corporations and nations for growth and the need for constant innovation and progress will be met and accelerated by neuroscience as a tool and technique for enhancing the performance of humans as well as technology that can provide a slew of cognitive services that can produce a more productive and higher quality of life for our civilization.

Moral Machines

We must build moral machines that, as they get smart—perhaps smarter than humans—they will also evolve to incorporate our values and morals. This is a concern for many scientists who are watching, as I am, the steady increase in technology's progressive intelligence.

A collaborator of mine, the noted neuroscientist Dr. James Giordano, professor at Georgetown University Medical Center in Washington, DC, and the Ludwig-Maximilians University in Munich, Germany, raises an important issue that goes straight to the heart of the matter: we must build Smart Machines that can exercise moral judgment. This is, of course, a human value that requires a deep understanding of how we define and teach machines the difference between good and bad, moral and immoral decisions. If we do not, he states, we shall encounter problems of a scale that may frustrate the trust and use of technology. What if we cannot trust our machines?

The challenge here: Can we program moral judgment into our Smart Machines? Can we make moral machines that appreciate human morality of right and wrong, not just Smart Machines' values? We must, Dr. Giordano says, if we are to not fear that they shall rebel or hurt humans knowingly or unknowingly.

Minds Wide Open

As we build the next generation of sentience into machines, we should listen to neuroscientists like Giordano who remind us that moral judgment is not just for humans to learn and follow. Why would Smart Machines that don't have these values, these ethics, care about humans? They won't unless we design them to care, respect, and obey humans. This is a dividing line—can we make machines moral before they get smart? We must.

The Neuro Future is sneaking up on us. From regenerating the aging and healing the diseased minds to enhancing human performance and augmented intelligence, the enticements of the Neuro Future are many. At the same time this Neuro Future will not come without challenges we must face about what it is to be human.

While we are enhancing ourselves, what type of society will we be building? Will this be a just and free world for individual freedoms and democratic values, or will it be one of coercion and mind control? The awesome unleashing of the Neuro Future must be guided by human freedoms, liberties, values, and human rights. We must question authority, uphold our ethics, challenge the potential misuse of Neurotechnology, and beware as much as embrace the Neuro Future.

Chapter 18

Why the Future Needs Us

You may realize by now that this book is not just about predicting the future; it's also about your role in the future. You are the change agent, the Game Changer that can influence the future. The change starts in your mindset; you embody this change. I know this may sound radical to consider that you could affect climate change or the future of medicine, but that is exactly what I mean—you can.

Individuals have always been the Game Changers of history, so why wouldn't they be the Game Changers of the future? The new Einsteins, Steve Jobs, Ghandis, Teslas, Edisons, and Bill Gates of the future are alive today. Game Changers of the Future have a common trait about the future—they believe that they can shape the future with their innovation, ideas, and grit. Great minds in energy, computing, peace, energy, and communications have all changed our world for the better. This is a compelling common denominator that links these innovators across time with us. Are you ready to become a Game Changer of the Future? That is my challenge for you.

At any time, from anywhere, regardless of class, identity, or education, it is possible to invent the new. The power of new ideas to transform should be celebrated and studied. Think how education would be different if we focused on studying the amazing innovators of history—what could we learn?

That is the Big Idea here—to inspire you to take action and manage your future by embracing innovation and to Dream Big. Your imagination, invention, or leadership will play a major role in making the future a Not So Far Future. What I mean is that you don't need to wait for the next twenty years to see how things work out. You don't need to wait on the sidelines to see what is going to happen.

You can make it happen. You can become Future Smart by harnessing innovation, inventing the Next Big Game Changer, collaborating with others,

educating yourself, embracing change, or taking on a social or business planetary issue. You have the power to make the difference that you want in being a Game Changer of the Future.

You are either a passive witness of history or you are going to make history. Which is it going to be? This is a choice that everyone, whether they know it or not, whether they like it or not, accept it or not, must make at some point in their life. Will you be a Game Changer of the Future or a bystander? If you're reading this book, then perhaps you already have made a choice, and this is your choice to make.

You are a fundamentally important part of the Global Network of Ideas that can change the future. You can have impact. Individuals who have radical ideas about altering the future are all around us. Some of these Game-Changers are reading this book now. They are the Future Smart Leaders of tomorrow. Are you one of these?

An Evolutionary Moment in Time

You are living through an Evolutionary Moment in time that is unique in history. I think this Evolutionary Moment has been building for over one hundred years: Will we, as a civilization, be able to invent the social, economic, and technological solutions to meet the global challenges of our future? This will be the defining outcome of our time. I do think we shall meet the challenges successfully, but it will take empowered leaders and individuals to do so. It will take you.

This will take an entirely new way of thinking in order to invent the future. Some of the ideas explored here in *Future Smart* may point to the way ahead. Many more insights will be needed than what this book can contain. I think if you digest this book that it may catalyze some of your ideas about the future. Maybe you will be inspired to start a new business or transform an existing one. Perhaps you have an innovation or invention in mind that could make a difference that solves a global problem or prevents one from emerging. The world needs new ideas; even radical ones that seem a bit crazy today may be just the fix that will help make a better tomorrow.

The Courage to Innovate

The recognition and use of Game-Changing Trends is a not an easy task. It will require perhaps above all a special type of courage—the courage to innovate, to explore the new, invent the possible, and, in the end, take a risk. A new type of mindset will be required. A bold, experimental, even a radical mindset, which can predict and innovate fast, will be required. Most of the innovations that have shaped our world have come from the courage of people who envisioned something that was not thought to be possible at the time.

What might be possible tomorrow? How might you play a role in taking on a Big Global Challenge that could create a shift in some critical area? How courageous could you become? What is the Game-Changing Trend you want to take on? Your purpose, as corny as you may think it is, may be larger than your survival; it may be about shaping the future, taking on a challenge that has global impact. It is a global challenge in education, energy, health care, or you name it.

Why the Future Needs Us

One of the idea viruses in the way is the Surplus of Pessimism. There is a surplus of negativity, made evident by the many dystopian critics of the future who are gladly ready to describe with fanfare why we are doomed. From climate change–impending disasters, to the many dysfunctions of cowboy capitalism and rampant social inequality, to war and nuclear annihilation—the reports of our impending demise are plentiful though misguided. The embrace of dystopia has become a knee-jerk response by too many that does little to contribute to solving the global challenges that actually do face our future. Giving up, surrendering to the dystopian worldview, embracing our doom is illogical given the risks and challenges facing our future. We must do better and take responsibility to create change, to become Game Changers of the Future.

Are there serious and even perilous global risks that we should be aware of in our future? Yes, many, there is no argument. But for the first time we have the tools, innovations, and awareness as well as the collaborative communications between nations, organizations, and citizens to forge a different future for our world—to take on solving these grand challenges. We have never, as individuals, organizations, or nations had the power to do so much to create a better future. But will we take action?

There is plenty of evidence that we can manage climate change, invent new clean energy sources, create more economic prosperity, and reduce tensions between nations. There are significant results and many new ideas in creating innovations to improve health, education, commerce, and peace. Globalization and trade among nations has opened up new possibilities and lifted many into a new era of prosperous possibilities. The rising New Middle Class, the increase in globalized wealth, and the reduction of war, all point to a New Future, a better future if we unleash the courage, leadership, and innovations lying in wait for the Game Changers of the Future to embrace.

We have the potential to create positive and productive global change. We have the potential to create a better future just as we have been doing for thousands of years, facing down war, inventing tech breakthroughs, extending lifetimes, improving health and education. It has been a long journey—we are

not done. This is why the future needs us. The reports of our impending demise are a dismissal of the innovation and social progress that has shaped the last hundred years.

I am convinced that the next fifty years shall be better—more just, prosperous, inventive, and Future Smart because we have the tools, technologies, and intent to craft a more productive global future—this is a choice we can all agree is a preferred future. I think we are on the cusp of knowing how to create a better future. But that shall require more of the grit and courage that has defeated disease, unlocked the human genome, invented the Internet, and made globalization possible. We need to look ahead with foresight built on the reality of how far we have come in history. We are Darwin's children. We are the fittest to survive. We are the Game Changers of the Future.

There is this strange irony in what I see coming. At the exact time when so many specific challenges face our world, the very tools and technologies we need to better manage these challenges are being invented. It may be that an effective and sustainable future could not have been managed prior to this time because we didn't have the tools to manage climate change, increase global commerce, make the Internet and communications universally accessible, extend life and health, or provide education to all. In a way I see humanity evolving into the future with the precise tools we need to navigate that future effectively more so than ever before.

The timing of this explosion of tools to address global challenges has an uncanny logic to it. Perhaps the right tools are being created just in time to manage the social, economic, and environmental challenges we face. This is how I explain why certain strategic innovations are showing up just now. Hubris aside, we may be on the cusp of creating a new global civilization that must harness the right innovations at the precisely right time to forge a better future.

Accelerating Innovation

The laser sat on the shelf for almost ten years until we could figure out how we could create the new fiber optics of the communications system. The Internet was developed in the late 1970s, but we didn't understand how to use it for commerce, education, or communications for almost twenty years. The personal computer was rejected by every large computer company, as not worth the time to develop until the personal computer was brought out and the rest is history. For many decades the experts thought the human genome was impossible to decode. Often it has takes years for society to accept and understand the Game Changers.

Each of these innovations changed the future of our world. We are in the midst of a turbulent sea change, and the waves of innovation are increasing

and for good reason. We are sorely in need of solutions to fix the big challenges facing our future.

Even today innovations that sit on the foundation of the Internet, computers, quantum computing, Neurotechnology, and nanotechnology have yet to fully make the mark on our world. There is so much we don't understand. The artificial cell has been developed, but we don't know yet what we can do with it. Smart Machines that could invent new drugs to fight cancer are not quite that smart yet. Big Data holds greater potential than reality as yet. Medicine that can regenerate whole organs is not ready to go into production. Geoengineering is not thought to be a credible science. Quantum computers have not been invented, and fusion has a long way to go before it can fuel the planet or take us to the stars. Humanity is a work in progress, and the Game Changing trends in this book point to the trial and error, the investigations, and explorations that I believe will shape a better future.

This Far Future may truly surprise many who have embraced a dystopian view of tomorrow. But one thing is clear that few could argue: humanity is a species of curious and relentless survivors. We are used to facing down risks and surviving against all odds. We have gotten this far—through wars, economic global turbulence, stared down the nuclear threat, and survived an ice age as well as numerous infectious diseases that wiped out much of humanity at times. My bet is that we have perfectly created the next generation of tools to resolve the future challenges that are coming, and we shall survive them. We will manage effectively the future that is coming. We are the Game Changers of the Future.

Fast and Furious: Emergent Change

We have lived most of the last few centuries such that change has plodded along in linear paths. Mostly slow fits and bursts except for flashes, such as the industrial and computer revolutions. The difference is that this far future of ours will be a product of Emergent Change, where leap-frogging innovations and tools will create new ideas faster than at any other time in the history of our world. Maximum velocity will define the future. Explosive changes may come. A convergence of Game-Changing trends and individual Game Changers will define the future.

Emergent Change—fast, disruptive, kinetic, and shaped by a fantastic exponential convergence of innovations—will accelerate our future. Certainly these radical innovations will define the future. We will need a new language to describe the future of what is coming. The proliferation of these tools, from computers, networks, and smartphones to nano, bio, neuro, and on to quantum tools, will converge, collaborate, and connect us to create Emergent Change. This type of change will be hard to understand and control—it will take new tools to

manage the new tools to become Future Smart. I believe in the human instinct to look to the future and to craft a better human. We are all Game Changers of the Future. We just need to be reminded every few millennia of how we got here. The future needs us to create a better future, a future that, successfully, meets the challenges of the twenty-first century.

Chapter 19

The Not-So-Far Future: 2100

Imagine that there was a member of an advanced alien race, an astro-anthropologist, who travels to Earth to study our civilization. What would she find that might make up her report on the progress of our world? What would she discover that was our State of the World, from an outsider's perspective, that we might gain from understanding? This is what her findings might be at this time as she beams back her last report.

The Earth Report

I have seen amazing growth, development, and change over the past fifty years. The Earth's inhabitants are a resilient race. They have survived extreme weather, wars, disease, poverty, and economic changes. Humanity has evolved out of a Dark Age of Ignorance to embrace science and culture, fairness, human rights, and democratic institutions. I am impressed that although they face big civilization-ending challenges, like feeding the planet, climate change, energy, and war, they are progressively evolving, moving in the direction of better collaboration, peace, and prosperity.

They are a stubborn race; they have to learn the same lessons over the aeons again and again. Perhaps this will serve them well as they struggle to survive in the future. Risks such as climate change, social upheavals, energy access, war, health, and education are still being understood. As yet they do not act as one civilization on one planet with one set of resources to manage.

There is not a universal form of planetary governance. Democracy, dictatorships, oligarchies, and many different forms of governance prevail. Individual human rights are often not always respected for what we would think a intelligent species should have for governance. Regressive ideologies hold many

back from evolving. Freedom and liberty is not adopted throughout the planet. Individual freedoms and the rights of the individual are not always upheld. This holds back the full potential of economic and productive activities such as commerce, trade, and employment.

When it comes to technology they are at a primitive era: humans just discovered the computer and the Internet in only the past thirty years. Communication devices, like smartphones, are only a few years old, and not everyone has one. Only about 55 percent of the planet has computers and access to the Internet. Advanced technological innovations, such as teleportation, neuro-learning, personalized drugs, optical medicine, human enhancement, and sentient robots, remain outside the possibilities at this time, but they are making good progress.

Humans still crudely pull energy resources out of the ground rather than generate them by manipulating matter, what is called nanoscience. Energy sources drive the entire civilization, but the majority of these sources are not renewable or smart as of yet. They have much to learn about using natural, renewable sources of energy. If they can, as a civilization, reach a consensus on protecting the environment and developing prosperity on the planet, then that will enable the race to make it into the far future. If not, well, we have observed too many civilizations perish well before their sun goes supernova, and they have left their home world. We shall see.

Humanity does not have the ability to leave the home world as yet. There is no interstellar exploration on even settlements of the Earth's moon or the closet planet, Mars, which could be terraformed to create an atmosphere. There is no cloning or bio-android development as yet. Smart Machines are in the early stages of design and will require controls to make sure they behave as they should.

Humanity is emerging but has access only to primitive technological tools to aid nations' progress. The planet has tremendous potential, but there is no collaborative planetary effort as yet to function as a unified civilization—pooling resources, facing global challenges together, and putting social progress over power conflicts and war.

People fight over religion, ideology, power, trade, and natural resources. Nations use economic and, still, their military to project their power. The strong win out over the weak most often when there are disputes. As they say, Might Makes Right—which may be an accurate description of their state of planetary consciousness. They have not yet evolved out of their primitive evolutionary mindsets, which leaves the possibility of conflict too often an acceptable solution. Terrorism seems to thrive in poorer societies, where economic inequality, poverty, and ideological issues collide with power. There are efforts to understand and move forward toward resolving differences and bridging the gaps in cultural misunderstandings, but humans have a long way to go to evolve socially so as to recognize armed conflict is not a viable long-term solution.

This seems to be the evolutionary state of the world. Political will and courage is in short supply given the big challenges facing their future like climate, energy, health, and economic prosperity. But there is progress and a great deal of evidence for hope that this civilization will evolve into a more productive, prosperous, and peaceful world.

Now, on the positive side, there is ample evidence that this civilization has the capacity for incredible beauty, moral judgment, freedom, humor, and love. I have seen countless acts of compassion, kindness, and love by millions daily. Their ability to invent and be productive in commerce, art, and literature is impressive and extensive around the world. Tolerance of cultural, ideological, and religious differences does exist in nations where law and justice prevail, which points to a future when a modern society, based on tolerance and acceptance of differences, is likely to prevail. What is perhaps unique is their imagination and hope for a better future.

This is what links current living members of their world to their past ancestors—the desire to make their world a better place for their descendants. Great sufferings through war, disease, climate, and sacrifice have contributed to attempts to make a better future. Of this goal, they all seem to agree. They are a young civilization, not a million years old, which is what modern civilizations mark as their first evolutionary birthday. Humanity has a long way to go, but they will get there.

These efforts have gone to resolve war, accelerate global trade, invent technology, and create productivity and creativity that improves the quality of life. Humans are a curious mix of great potential and great turmoil. Clearly humanity is a young civilization that is learning to evolve in productive and positive ways, and who knows? I think their capacity to collaborate and transcend their differences in religion, ideology, economics, and hostility will prevail. They have an impressive and amazing capacity to collaborate, create, and even love. They have higher values of purpose and a sense of the awe of their existence. They marvel at the mysteries that they are a part of, and their quest for knowledge and learning is significant. They aspire to greatness as well as the embrace of peace, prosperity, and well-being. The challenge will be for them to create a peaceful, prosperous, and collaborative future for all. They have much to learn.

End Report

2100: Toward a New Global Renaissance

Another perspective of the Far Future is to consider a longer future time frame—2100. By this time most of the forecasts in this book such as fusion energy, space colonization, artificial cells, 3D manufacturing, and Smart Machines will be woven into the normal, everyday part of life. Not every one of these forecasts will pan out as we think today—they may be vastly more

effective and create even more of a global impact than we can imagine. Some forecasts will crash and burn, being too limited or just wrong.

Likely a large part of what is forecasted will change and morph into some other future difficult to imagine today: Leaving Earth due to a new cheap energy source becomes possible, harnessing fusion or dark energy. Ending the futility of war. Feeding the planet. Radically altering the biological evolution to arrest aging and end disease. Massive wealth creation lifts up the world and a utopia of peace and prosperity, a New Global Renaissance, ensues. This is the forecast I am betting on.

As a civilization, in the Far Future we may figure out how to live more at peace and promote a more prosperous equality of existence for the 10 billion people living on the planet and off-world. There will be a balance of power between the individual and the state. Democracy will be a dominant form of governance, and the planet will be connected, from ecologies to economies. Major world risks, such as nuclear war, climate change, and poverty, will have been managed and contained to no longer be global risks. I know this is an optimistic view of the future, but it is one most leaders and citizens around the world share about their future and what is not just possible but also desirable.

If you are reading this and think it sounds too idealistic, I can assure you that there is nothing that interferes with business or progress more so than a global crisis. We are poised to address numerous global crises in energy, climate, pandemics, finance, and security in our lifetimes, to name a few. The more aware you are, the more Future Smart of what's coming, the more you will be able to manage the future in your life, organization, or work.

Becoming Future Smart

I am betting that humanity will forge a purposeful and prosperous path into the far future, though this will be a rocky path. This Far Future may be better and more productive and deliver a higher quality of life for humanity overall. It may be a future of prosperity, innovation, and progress. There is more evidence that we are moving in this direction—toward a positive future of new possibilities—than headed down the drain of history. This positive vision will not come easy but must be the endgame of deep collaboration among leaders, nations, and people who share a future vision for prosperity and peace.

That is, if we make it so. I have every confidence that we have the desire, courage, and tools, as a civilization, to forge this future. We can all become Future Smart if we start now. We are all potentially the Game Changers of the Future. The future belongs to those who create it. What kind of future do you want to create?

ACKNOWLEDGMENTS

There have been many people who have inspired me in the long journey that has led to *Future Smart*. Teachers, mentors, fellow futurists, entrepreneurs, friends, and fellow explorers into the unknown—I stand upon their shoulders of insight. Rene Dubos, the life sciences biologist; Bucky Fuller, the original systems thinker; Rick Smalley, the Noble winner in nanoscience; Steve Jobs from Apple; and the futurist Alvin Toffler, who got me moving in this direction—game-changers they are all.

I appreciate my clients more than they know. They are varied and range from governments to entrepreneurs to the private sector. My clients were often my inspiration to understand where the future was going and why. Working with them as they each invent the future is still fascinating. What I discovered through my interactions with them around the world gave me deep insights into the trends that would come. Their challenges, which became my challenges to understand changes coming in technology, globalization, medicine, climate, security, and many other areas, expanded my thinking. Thanks to all.

Dealing with my global business and technology clients and understanding their world was very helpful and necessary, to get the ground-truth into my forecasting. One cannot forecast apart from the real world. My clients made this book better by making me understand what was relevant for them today and tomorrow. In many ways this book is for you, the one who will invent the future of your design.

My friends who were willing to share ideas, be supportive, or offer research are very much appreciated. Allan Zimmerman, Jim Giordano, Ken Dychtwald, Al Elkins, Sandy Rosenberg and Bill Moulton stood out.

Thanks to Dan Ambrosio, Senior Editor at Da Capo Press, Perseus Books, who understood the book I wanted to write. And thanks to the whole team at Da Capo Press, Claire Ivett, Cisca Schreefel, Josephine Mariea, my publicity manager, Kate Kazeniac, and marketing folks.

Finally and most important, I want to thank my wife and kids for understanding and supporting my time in writing this book. I get driven when writing and I want to thank them for their patience with my deadlines. My wife

gave me plenty of room to write and helped me embrace my mission. For this I am grateful.

My kids were insightful in reminding me that I know so little compared to the teenagers of today. A continual dose of humility they offered was sobering. Their advice into how their generation is evolving is an education not possible to capture fully in any book as yet. They are the Click-Streamers of tomorrow.

INDEX